W9-AHQ-009

Irish Opinion and the American Revolution, 1760–1783

This ground-breaking study traces the impact of the American revolution and of the international war it precipitated on the political outlook of each section of Irish society. Morley uses a dazzling array of sources – newspapers, pamphlets, sermons and political songs, including Irish-language documents unknown to other scholars and previously unpublished – to trace the evolving attitudes of the Anglican, Catholic and Presbyterian communities from the beginning of colonial unrest in the early 1760s until the end of hostilities in 1783. He also reassesses the influence of the American revolutionary war on such developments as Catholic relief, the removal of restrictions on Irish trade, and Britain's recognition of Irish legislative independence. Morley sheds new light on the nature of Anglo-Irish patriotism and Catholic political consciousness, and reveals the extent to which the polarities of the 1790s had already emerged by the end of the American war.

VINCENT MORLEY has worked as a researcher with the Royal Irish Academy's *Dictionary of Irish Biography* and lectured in eighteenth-century Irish history at the National University of Ireland, Galway. He is the author of *An Crann os Coill*, a study of the Jacobite poet Aodh Buí Mac Cruitín (1995).

Irish Opinion and the American Revolution, 1760–1783

Vincent Morley

CAMBRIDGE
UNIVERSITY PRESS

PUBLISHED BY THE PRESS SYNDICATE OF THE UNIVERSITY OF CAMBRIDGE
The Pitt Building, Trumpington Street, Cambridge, United Kingdom

CAMBRIDGE UNIVERSITY PRESS
The Edinburgh Building, Cambridge CB2 2RU, UK
40 West 20th Street, New York, NY 10011-4211, USA
477 Williamstown Road, Port Melbourne, VIC 3207, Australia
Ruiz de Alarcón 13, 28014 Madrid, Spain
Dock House, The Waterfront, Cape Town 8001, South Africa

http://www.cambridge.org

First published 2002

Printed in the United Kingdom at the University Press, Cambridge

Typeface Plantin 10/12 pt   *System* LATEX 2$_\varepsilon$ [TB]

A catalogue record for this book is available from the British Library

ISBN 0 521 81386 7 hardback

Contents

Preface

In a still useful article about the impact of the American revolution on Ireland which was written two generations ago, Michael Kraus (1971) observed that the revolution and its effects 'so faded into the more momentous French revolution that the general student often overlooked the particular influence of America'. If the American bicentennial prompted some further investigation of the subject in Ireland, the bicentenaries of the French revolution and the 1798 rising have more than restored the original imbalance and Kraus's observation is at least as true today as it was when first made in 1939. This study is an attempt to isolate the 'particular influence' of the American revolution. Its aim is to trace the influence of the revolution and the international war that it precipitated on the political consciousness of the various sections of Irish society during the period from the beginning of colonial unrest in the early 1760s until the end of hostilities in 1783.

I have not attempted to present a detailed narrative of events – a task performed in considerable detail for the latter part of the period in question by Maurice O'Connell (1965), and for the entire period in a less detailed manner by R.B. McDowell (1979). Instead, my concern has been to chart the evolution of attitudes in Ireland at each stage of the revolution and to identify changes that can reasonably be considered to have resulted from the revolutionary process – whether produced directly through the operation of American example on Irish opinion or indirectly as a result of altered circumstances arising from the war. This aim has obliged me to adopt a chronological structure as a thematic approach would have obscured both transient changes in opinion and the relationship between such fluctuations and contemporary events.

As this study is concerned with the political outlook of sections of Irish society rather than with the stances adopted by individual actors on the political stage, priority has been given to sources that were in the public domain and which may have either reflected or influenced the views of the populace. Newspapers, pamphlets, vernacular song and published sermons have been used extensively while less attention has been paid to confidential sources such as state papers and private correspondence. I have also been conscious of the adage that 'actions speak louder than words' – that is, of the principle that the behaviour of a social group is likely to be a more accurate indicator of its political sympathies than the declarations of those who pretended to speak on its behalf. I have therefore looked for evidence of popular activity that might shed light on the views of those who were excluded from the political nation. Conversely, I have noted the rhetoric of parliamentary orators only when it appears to reflect the attitudes of a constituency 'out of doors'.

Acknowledgements

I would like to acknowledge the courtesy and assistance I received from the staffs of the following libraries and archives: National Library of Ireland; Royal Irish Academy; Public Record Office, Kew; British Library; University of Liverpool; University College Dublin; Russell Library, St Patrick's College, Maynooth; Trinity College Dublin; National Archives, Dublin.

I am grateful to Frank Keoghan, Ian McBride, James McGuire, Breandán Ó Buachalla, Éamonn Ó Ciardha and Pádraig Ó Snodaigh, who read and commented on drafts of this book or of the thesis on which it is based. It need hardly be said that they do not necessarily agree with the views expressed below and that the responsibility for all errors of fact or interpretation is mine alone. I also wish to acknowledge the generosity of the University of Liverpool in awarding me a studentship, as well as an additional grant for research visits to the British Library and the Public Record Office, without which the doctoral thesis on which this book is based would not have been written.

My greatest debt is to Marianne Elliott, the supervisor of my thesis, who was always available as a ready source of advice, encouragement and constructive criticism despite her heavy administrative workload and the demands of her own work in progress.

Textual note

The spelling and capitalisation of all quotations, whether from primary or secondary sources, have been normalised in the interests of readability and consistency. I have also silently corrected obvious spelling errors, expanded abbreviations, and ignored the use of italics except when used for emphasis. Words in square brackets have been interpolated by me; words in parentheses occur in the original.

In the case of Irish-language verse, deviations from the standard spelling have been accepted when necessary to preserve the metre; punctuation and line breaks have been adjusted as I considered appropriate. All quotations in Irish have been translated except for the initial lines given in footnotes for the purpose of facilitating reference to the manuscripts. Where I am aware that a poem or song has been published I have provided the relevant details, but such editions may differ from the version quoted.

Unqualified references to organs or officers of state ('the Privy Council', 'the speaker', etc.) refer to bodies or persons in Ireland; whenever the British equivalents are referred to, this is stated.

In the interests of clarity, references to the Williamite Revolution of 1688–91 are distinguished by use of a capital 'R'; a lower-case 'r' is used when referring to other revolutions.

Newspapers are cited by their date of publication: a reference to the issue of *Finn's Leinster Journal* dated 3–6 February 1779 will thus appear as *Finn's Leinster Journal*, 6 February 1779.

Abbreviations

Anal. Hib.	*Analecta Hibernica*
Archiv. Hib.	*Archivium Hibernicum*
BL	British Library
BNL	*Belfast News-Letter*
DEP	*Dublin Evening Post*
FDJ	*Faulkner's Dublin Journal*
FJ	*Freeman's Journal*
FLJ	*Finn's Leinster Journal*
Hist. Jn.	*The Historical Journal*
HJ	*Hibernian Journal*
HM	*Hibernian Magazine*
HMC	Historical Manuscripts Commission
IHS	*Irish Historical Studies*
LJ	*Londonderry Journal*
NLI	National Library of Ireland
PRO	Public Record Office, Kew
Proc. RIA	*Proceedings of the Royal Irish Academy*
QUB	Queen's University of Belfast
RIA	Royal Irish Academy
SNL	*Saunders' News-Letter*
Studia Hib.	*Studia Hibernica*
TCD	Trinity College, Dublin
UCD	University College, Dublin

Introduction

An understanding of the evolution of Irish opinion in the early eighteenth century is a prerequisite for any attempt to assess the impact of the American revolution on the outlook of the various sections of the population. The purpose of this introduction is to furnish the necessary benchmark by briefly tracing the evolution of political attitudes during the two generations from the Williamite Revolution to the accession of George III. Although the following account is not based on original research, it offers a view of popular consciousness which differs in important respects from those provided by existing surveys of the period.

Throughout the eighteenth century Irish society was deeply divided along largely coincident lines of ethnic origin, religious belief and political opinion: 'Our people, are so heterogeneously classed', wrote one member of parliament in 1775, 'we are no nation.'[1] The task of characterising the political outlook of the three principal denominations on the eve of George III's accession could scarcely have been avoided in any event but it is made all the more necessary by the prevalence of representations in the historical literature that distort the true state of opinion in eighteenth-century Ireland. I refer in particular to the general portrayal of the Catholic majority as politically apathetic, the widespread attribution of a tradition of 'colonial nationalism' to the dominant Anglican community, and the common tendency to associate Presbyterianism with republicanism.

Catholic opinion

The outlook of Irish Catholics in the first half of the eighteenth century has received remarkably little attention from historians. This neglect can be partly explained by the exclusion of Catholics from the political nation after 1691. State papers for the period provide little first-hand information about their attitudes and there were few contemporary publications

---

[1] Charles O'Hara to Edmund Burke, 28 August 1775, in R.J.S. Hoffman, *Edmund Burke, New York Agent* (Philadelphia, 1956), p. 597.

1

on political subjects by Catholic authors. Faced with the silence of the sources on which they normally rely, historians have tended to view the Catholic community of the early eighteenth century as a historiographic black hole from which no light can emerge – an attitude encapsulated in the intellectually indolent and unscholarly concept of a 'hidden Ireland'. Some writers, equating failure to publish with political indifference, have represented the Catholic population as an inchoate mass, normally passive and apathetic, occasionally provoked to acts of agrarian violence by transient and localised factors, but always lacking a coherent ideology or a national perspective. Writing in the 1890s about the period of the American revolution W.E.H. Lecky, the father of modern Irish historiography, asserted rather than demonstrated the political passivity of the rural masses: 'The mass of the population remained torpid, degraded, and ignorant; but, although crimes of violence and turbulence were common among them, those crimes were wholly unconnected with politics.'[2] This view has remained largely unchallenged by historians during the intervening century. In the 1940s, R.B. McDowell justified the omission of any investigation of Catholic opinion from his groundbreaking study of Irish public opinion in the eighteenth century in terms that differed little from those employed by Lecky in the heyday of empire.[3] Maurice O'Connell still reflected mainstream historical thinking when he argued in the 1960s, on the basis of reductionist reasoning rather than an examination of the primary sources, that the Catholic masses are unlikely to have been interested in the American revolution and that their views are, ultimately, unknowable.[4] More recently still, S.J. Connolly has written that the Catholic populace of the 1740s was cut off from the world of politics by barriers of language and poverty.[5] But the Catholics of the eighteenth century were not an undifferentiated peasantry sunk in squalor and ignorance. Their community embraced a middle stratum of comfortable tenant farmers, craftsmen, schoolteachers, publicans, shopkeepers and priests, a stratum which was increasingly literate in English and which maintained a vigorous oral and manuscript-based literature in Irish.

The documentary record left by eighteenth-century Catholics is far from blank. In two regions – the province of Munster and an area straddling the Ulster–Leinster border – the compilation of manuscript anthologies of vernacular poetry and song was common. Much of this verse

[2] W.E.H. Lecky, *A History of Ireland in the Eighteenth Century*, II (London, 1892), pp. 202–3.
[3] R.B. McDowell, *Irish Public Opinion 1750–1800* (London, 1944), pp. 5–6.
[4] Maurice R. O'Connell, *Irish Politics and Social Conflict in the Age of the American Revolution* (Philadelphia, 1965), p. 32.
[5] S.J. Connolly, 'Varieties of Britishness: Ireland, Scotland and Wales in the Hanoverian state' in Alexander Grant and Keith Stringer (eds.), *'Uniting the Kingdom?': The Making of British History* (London and New York, 1995), p. 194.

was inspired by contemporary events, both at home and abroad, and it furnishes a unique insight into the political sentiments of the rural population. The importance of this source for students of popular opinion can hardly be exaggerated but it has been largely ignored by those who have previously investigated the impact of the American revolution.[6] This neglect must be principally attributed to the common inability of historians of eighteenth-century Ireland to read the language that was spoken throughout most of the country and by the greater part of the population in their period. The failure of historians to comprehend the political culture of the majority of the Irish population, as reflected in the attributions of ignorance and apathy noted above, is a predictable consequence of their inability either to utilise the vernacular sources or to assimilate the findings of scholars who publish in Irish.[7]

As might reasonably be expected, the popular political verse of the early eighteenth century indicates continuing support for the principles espoused by the Catholic community during the seventeenth century – that is, for the 'god, king and country' ideology of the Confederate Catholics. The vernacular literature expressed the hope – at times, the expectation – that the Revolution settlement would be overthrown, thereby freeing the Catholic church from Penal restraints, restoring the legitimate dynasty to the throne, and securing Ireland's position as one of three equal kingdoms linked by a personal union of their crowns. Catholicism, Jacobitism and Irish nationalism are intimately associated in the political literature of the period.[8] A poem composed around 1715 by the County Armagh poet

---

[6] For two brief but perceptive exceptions, see David Doyle, *Ireland, Irishmen and Revolutionary America, 1760–1820* (Dublin, 1981), pp. 168–78 and Liam de Paor's foreword to Diarmuid Ó Muirithe (ed.), *Tomás Ó Míocháin: Filíocht* (Dublin, 1988). For relevant work by Irish-language scholars see Diarmuid Ó Muirithe, 'Amhráin i dtaobh Cogadh Saoirse Mheiriceá' in Seosamh Watson (ed.), *Féilscríbhinn Thomáis de Bhaldraithe* (Dublin, 1986) and C.G. Buttimer, *'Cogadh Sagsana Nuadh sonn*: reporting the American revolution', *Studia Hib.* 28 (1994).

[7] A substantial secondary literature on the political outlook of the Catholic community in the early eighteenth century has been produced in recent years, but this is due more to the efforts of Irish-language scholars than historians. See Breandán Ó Buachalla, 'An mheisiasacht agus an aisling' in P. de Brún, S. Ó Coileáin and P. Ó Riain (eds.) *Folia Gadelica* (Cork, 1983); Ó Buachalla, 'Seacaibíteachas Thaidhg Uí Neachtain', *Studia Hib.* 26 (1992); Ó Buachalla, 'Irish Jacobite poetry', *Irish Review* 12 (1992); Mícheál Mac Craith, 'Filíocht Sheacaibíteach na Gaeilge: ionar gan uaim?', *Eighteenth-Century Ireland* 9 (1994); Vincent Morley, *An Crann os Coill: Aodh Buí Mac Cruitín, c. 1680–1755* (Dublin, 1995); and Éamonn Ó Ciardha, 'A fatal attachment: Ireland and the house of Stuart, 1685–1766' (PhD thesis, Cambridge, 1998). Breandán Ó Buachalla, *Aisling Ghéar: Na Stíobhartaigh agus an tAos Léinn 1603–1788* (Dublin, 1996) is now the pre-eminent work.

[8] It would be tendentious to describe a demand for political autonomy grounded on a sense of ethnic identity by any term other than 'nationalism'. Those who object that its use in

Raghnall Dall Mac Domhnaill illustrates the fusion of religious, dynastic and national sentiment in a potent ideology which retained the loyalty of the Catholic masses throughout most of the eighteenth century. The poet engaged a pre-reformation churchyard in conversation:

> **The poet:**
> *Féach ár bpian le sé chéad bliain aige Gaill in éigean,*
> *gan rí dár rialadh de Ghaeil, mo chian, i ríoghacht Éireann.*
> **Creggan churchyard:**
> *Le ceithre chaogad atá treibh Gael ina ríoraí tréana,*
> *ins na trí ríochta, nach mór an t-ionadh a ndéan tú de bhréaga!*
> **The poet:**
> *Ar ghrá do ghaoltaí a theampaill aolta an dearbh an scéal so?*
> *an de threibh Mhíle an aicme chéana tá tú d'fhéighliú?*
> **Creggan churchyard:**
> *A dhuine ba rí agus sinsir fíor den ardthreibh chéanna,*
> *seisear díobh, idir fhear agus mhnaoi, dar gabhadh géilleadh.*[9]

('Consider our torment for six hundred years by violent foreigners, with no king of the Gaels ruling us, my grief, in the kingdom of Ireland.' 'For four fifties [i.e. 200 years] a lineage of Gaels have been mighty dynasts in the three kingdoms, isn't it a great wonder all the lies you tell!' 'For the love of your relatives, O lime-white church, is this story correct? Are they of the Milesian race, the same group you are watching over?' 'Sir, there have been kings and true ancestors of the same noble lineage, six of them, counting men and women, for whom allegiance was won.')

Here can be seen, in close association, expressions of religious loyalty to the pre-Reformation faith represented by Creggan churchyard; dynastic loyalty to the house of Stuart; and national loyalty to '*ríocht Éireann*', 'the kingdom of Ireland'. Clearly, the ideology of *iris agus athartha* (faith and fatherland) which had facilitated the fusion of previously antagonistic Old Irish and Old English communities in the early seventeenth century survived the social and political upheavals which took place later in the century. Given its primarily oral nature, the ideas and expressions employed in vernacular literature could be much more outspoken than was possible in the case of printed material, and they varied little from region to region or from generation to generation. One may note, for

an eighteenth-century context is anachronistic should note that the earliest citation of 'royalism' in the *Oxford English Dictionary* dates from only 1793; those who find the very concept of eighteenth-century nationalism problematic are referred to Adrian Hastings, *The Construction of Nationhood: Ethnicity, Religion and Nationalism* (Cambridge, 1997) for a cogent critique of marxisant theories that represent nationalism as a product of the French revolution, democratisation, capitalism and mass literacy.

[9] '*A Chreagáin uaibhrigh, fána mbíodh sluaite d'uaisle ríoraí*' in Énrí Ó Muirgheasa (ed.), *Dhá Chéad de Cheoltaibh Uladh* (Dublin, 1934), p. 29.

example, the similarity between the sentiments expressed by the accomplished County Kerry poet Aogán Ó Rathaille in a poem composed before 1715 and those of an anonymous west Ulster folk song from around the middle of the century:

> Beidh an Bíobla sin Liútair is a dhubhtheagasc éithigh,
> is an bhuíon so tá ciontach ná humhlaíonn don gcléir chirt,
> á ndíbirt tar triúchaibh go Newland ó Éirinn;
> an Laoiseach is an prionsa beidh cúirt acu is aonach![10]

(That Bible of Luther's and his evil lying doctrine, and this guilty gang who don't submit to the true clergy, will be expelled across countries to *Newland* from Ireland, and Louis [XIV] and the prince [James III] will hold court and assembly!)

> Tá Séarlas Óg ag triall thar sáile,
> beidh siad leis-sean cúpla garda,
> beidh siad leis-sean Francaigh is Spáinnigh
> agus bainfidh siad rince as éircigh.[11]

(Young Charles [Edward Stuart] is voyaging over the sea, there'll be a few guards with him, there'll be Frenchmen and Spaniards with him, and they'll make the heretics dance.)

The prevalence of popular Jacobitism is confirmed by sources other than vernacular verse. Its extent can be gauged from the insignificant number of Catholic priests – fewer than forty in all of Ireland – who took the oath of abjuration prescribed by an act of parliament in 1709, although the penalty specified for refusing to take the oath was banishment from the country. While the priests could plausibly argue that they were unable in conscience to swear that they took the oath 'heartily, willingly and truly' given the severe penalties prescribed for non-jurors, it is clear that the main obstacle lay in the requirement to swear that the son of James II 'hath not any right or title whatsoever to the crown of this realm'. Small though the number of jurors was, it was a cause of concern to one parish priest, William O'Daly of Kilfenora, County Clare, who expressed his views on the subject in verse:

> Mo scíos, mo lagar, mo scairteacha im chlí breoite,
> an tíoradh trasna so ar eaglais chríoch Fódla,
> gan díon dá maithibh is gach teallaire mí-eolach
> ag scríobh gurb d'Anna is ceart sealbh na dtrí gcoróineach.[12]

---

[10] 'An trua libhse faolchoin an éithigh 's an fhill duibh' in P.S. Dinneen and Tadhg O'Donoghue (eds.), *Dánta Aodhagáin Uí Rathaille* (London, 1911), p. 166.
[11] 'A Shéarlais Óig, a mhic rí Shéamais' in Énrí Ó Muirgheasa (ed.), *Céad de Cheoltaibh Uladh* (Dublin, 1915), p. 151.
[12] 'Mo scíos mo lagar mo scairteacha im chlí breoite' in RIA Ms. 23 C 8, p. 127.

(My woe, my weakness, the innards of my body are ailing, this scorching of Ireland's church, with no shelter for its worthies and every ignorant upstart writing that possession of the three crowns is Anne's by right.)

Continuing papal recognition of James III as *de jure* monarch ensured that he retained the power to nominate bishops to Irish sees, a fact which encouraged ambitious members of the clergy to exert their influence on his behalf. It may be noted in passing that Fr O'Daly, the author of the above verse, was promoted to the bishopric of Kilfenora in July 1722.[13]

The Irish regiments in France and Spain represented another link between Catholic Ireland and the exiled dynasty. Although these regiments were in the service of the Bourbon monarchs rather than that of the Stuart pretender, many of their members were politically motivated. State papers record the arguments used by one recruiting agent in 1715:

some of the enlisted then objected that they feared they were to go and serve the French king, or to go to Newfoundland. Luke Ford then assured them that they should serve none but King James the Third, and that he was afraid the king would be in his march for England before they could reach him, that he was sure they should return before the end of harvest and should not fight till they returned.[14]

Prominent officers in the Irish regiments held dual commissions: one from the king in whose army they served and one from the Pretender.[15] The politicised nature of the Irish regiments was noted by a hostile observer writing in 1728 at the height of the Anglo-French détente:

As long as there is a body of Irish Roman Catholic troops abroad, the chevalier [James III] will always make some figure in Europe by the credit they give him; and be considered as a prince that has a brave and well-disciplined army of veterans at his services; though he wants that opportunity to employ them at present, which he expects time and fortune will favour him with.[16]

The existence of this force exerted a considerable influence on the thinking of both Catholics and Protestants in Ireland. While it sustained the hope of a military reversal of the Revolution settlement in the minds of the former, it served to remind the latter of the continuing threat of a Catholic *revanche* and of their ultimate dependence on British power.

The varying fortunes of the Stuart pretender can be traced in the output of Irish Jacobite verse. The flood of poetry and song predicting his

---

[13] T.W. Moody, F.X. Martin and F.J. Byrne, *A New History of Ireland*, IX (Oxford, 1984), p. 362.

[14] PRO, SP 63/373, fo. 34; I have normalised the punctuation. With respect to the political motivation of the Irish regiments, see also Vincent Morley, 'Hugh MacCurtin: an Irish poet in the French army', *Eighteenth-Century Ireland* 8 (1993).

[15] Morley, *An Crann os Coill*, p. 103.

[16] Charles Forman, *A Letter to the Rt. Hon. Sir Robert Sutton for Disbanding the Irish Regiments in the Service of France and Spain* (Dublin, 1728), p. 17.

imminent restoration during the War of Spanish Succession, and again around 1715, declined in subsequent years as the Anglo-French alliance instituted by the regent of France in 1716, the exposure of the Swedish plot of 1717, and the failure of the Spanish expedition of 1719, all combined to lower popular expectations of an early change of régime. None the less, such hopes were deferred rather than abandoned:

> Tiocfaidh bhur Séamas cé gur moilleadh a theacht
> le mioscais na Swedes is Régent cliste na gcleas.[17]

(Your James will come although his arrival was delayed by the spite of the *Swedes* and the cunning *Regent* of the tricks.)

While the Anglo-French alliance endured there could be no hope of a French invasion, with the result that Spain, the weaker of the two Bourbon powers, and its smaller Irish brigade assumed a new prominence in the poetry. The following verse by the County Limerick poet Seán Ó Tuama dates from the 1730s:

> Tá Pilib is Séamas glé is a ngeal-bhuíon
>   ag téacht le gasraí Spáinneach,
> go stoirmeach faobhrach fraochta fras-ghníomh,
>   mar aon le treabh Gael ársa.[18]

(Philip [V] and noble James [III] and their splendid band are coming with detachments of Spaniards, storming, eagerly, angrily, in a hail of deeds, together with a host of veteran Gaels.)

But as France and Britain drifted towards war after more than twenty years of peace the focus of popular attention shifted from Philip V to Louis XV. The County Cork poet Seán Clárach Mac Domhnaill applauded the outbreak of the War of Austrian Succession:

> Tá Laoiseach ina lóchrann go leon-bhuilleach léimeach
> go díoltasach dó-bhriste i ndóchas daingean,
> a mhuintir le dóirsibh Hannover is Bhrémen,
> tá cuing ar an Holónt is ní leomhfaid preabadh;
> tá sé anois ullamh le nochtadh na lann,
> beidh carnadh aige, is coscairt is cogadh na gceann,
> dá shíneadh le Seoirse gan ró-thuirse in aon chor,
> sin críoch ar mo sceól is tá an brón ar Bhreatain.[19]

---

[17] 'Ar thulaigh im aonar ag déanamh cumha is mé im spreas' in Risteárd Ó Foghludha (ed.), *Seán Clárach 1691–1754* (Dublin, 1932), p. 52.

[18] 'Is tuirseach fá dhaorsmacht péine i bhfad sinn' in Risteárd Ó Foghludha (ed.), *Éigse na Máighe* (Dublin, 1952), p. 98.

[19] 'Éistigí lem ghlórtha a mhórshliocht Mhilésius' in Risteárd Ó Foghludha (ed.), *Seán Clárach 1691–1754* (Dublin, 1932), p. 55.

(Louis is a guiding light, striking and audacious, vengeful, invincible, firm in optimism, his men are at the gates of Hanover and Bremen, Holland is hobbled and they won't dare to move; he is ready now to unsheathe the blades, he'll have slaughter and havoc and a war of the chiefs, waging it against George without any respite, there's an end to my story and Britain is in sorrow.)

The course of Prince Charles's Scottish campaign in 1745–46 was closely followed in Ireland. Writing in the interval between the battles of Falkirk, the last Jacobite victory, and Culloden, the County Limerick poet Aindrias Mac Craith ('*an Mangaire Súgach*') exulted:

> *Tá coscar is bascadh orthu roimhe seo,*
> *tá eagla suite ar an gcóip,*
> *ag Falkirk do cailleadh na mílte,*
> *tá Campbells go cloíte agus Cope;*
> *beidh sealbh na Banba ag Gaelaibh,*
> *is na Danair seo choíche gan treoir,*
> *beidh Carolus feasta ina rí againn*
> *is beidh an ainnis go cinnte ar na Seóin!*[20]

(They are already slaughtered and crushed, the whole crew is stricken with terror, thousands were killed at Falkirk, the Campbells are beaten and [General] Cope; the Gaels will have possession of Ireland, and these Danes will be forever powerless, Charles will be our king henceforth and the 'Johns' will surely be afflicted!)

But if the evidence of the vernacular literature leaves no doubt that Jacobite sentiment prevailed among the common people in the 1740s, it is likely that the remnants of the Catholic gentry who risked losing their estates if they gambled incorrectly on the outcome of a French invasion were already more equivocal in their sympathies. When Prince Charles's army withdrew into the Highlands after the battle of Falkirk, Charles O'Conor of Belanagare, a member of the Catholic gentry, made the following dispassionate entry in his diary: '*Ag sin drithle déanach de choinneal taoi dul as re trí fichid bliain, mur dtoirmeascann Dia.*'[21] ('There's the last flicker of a candle that has been going out for sixty years, unless God prevents it.') But only five months earlier, after Prince Charles's entry into Edinburgh, O'Conor had made a more revealing entry: '*Mac Mic Rí Séamais anos in Albain ag buairt na dtrí ríocht. Níl fhios nach amhlaidh as fearr.*'[22] ('The son of King James's son is now in Scotland, unsetting the three kingdoms. One doesn't know that it isn't for the best.') In this cautious double negative one senses the equivocal emotions of a Catholic man

[20] '*A dhalta nár dalladh le dlaoithe*' in Ó Foghludha (ed.), *Éigse na Máighe*, p. 205. 'Seón Buí' or 'Sallow John' was a common pejorative term for the English and the Anglo-Irish.
[21] Síle Ní Chinnéide (ed.), 'Dhá leabhar nótaí le Séarlas Ó Conchubhair', *Galvia* 1 (1954), 39.
[22] *Ibid.*

of property, torn between the hope of his coreligionists for the overthrow of the Revolution settlement, and the fear of fresh political upheavals that he shared with all members of his class.

A year after the restoration of peace Charles O'Conor made his first venture into print with a pamphlet in support of the Dublin-based patriot Charles Lucas that attempted to trace Ireland's parliamentary tradition back to pre-Norman times.[23] In several subsequent publications O'Conor sought not only to rehabilitate the historical reputation of the ancestors of the Catholic community, but also to persuade a Protestant readership that Catholics no longer posed a threat to the Revolution settlement and that Penal legislation only served to damage the economy by depriving Catholic tenants of the incentive to improve properties they could only hold on short-term leases. O'Conor insisted that Catholics were loyal to the established constitution and that a simple oath of allegiance to the reigning monarch was the only requirement which might justly be imposed on them. Writing in the guise of a moderate Protestant in 1755 he argued that Catholics should publicly declare:

That 'they owe all political obedience to the present government, as it hath long been established by law: That they do not owe the pope, or any other foreign potentate, any civil subjection whatsoever . . .' Such a declaration from the Roman Catholics of Ireland, presented by a proper deputation of the whole party, must, undoubtedly, go a great way towards rendering the uprightness of their principles as evident, as the uprightness of their conduct, for near seventy years past, is demonstrable.[24]

But assurances concerning the benign nature of contemporary Catholicism carried little weight with Irish Protestants, who realised that the loyalty of the Catholic population had never been tested. The passivity of a disarmed, untrained and leaderless people during the previous two generations might more plausibly be attributed to their lack of opportunity for rebellion, and to the maintenance in Ireland of a large standing army, than to a new-found enthusiasm for Revolution principles and the Hanoverian succession. An anonymous pamphlet of 1755 made the obvious riposte to O'Conor's protestations of Catholic loyalty:

Suppose 10,000 Frenchmen were landed in this island, either with or without their cat's paw [Prince Charles Edward], (and this it is well known, we had some fears of lately) – I only ask the author of the *Case*, if he does not in his conscience

---

[23] [Charles O'Conor], *A Counter-Appeal, to the People of Ireland* (Dublin, 1749).
[24] [Charles O'Conor], *The Case of the Roman-Catholics of Ireland*, third edition (Dublin, 1756), pp. 33–4.

believe, that some of his friends would be glad to see them – and rejoice to find the good old Catholic cause in so thriving a way.[25]

It was a question that O'Conor could not have answered honestly, but it must be acknowledged that his own publications testify to the emergence of a body of Catholic opinion which hoped to reform rather than overthrow the existing political order. This current was given organisational expression with the formation in July 1756 of a Catholic Committee in Dublin by O'Conor, his fellow pamphleteer John Curry, and others.

In O'Conor's view, the start of the Seven Years War made the need for Catholics publicly to declare their loyalty more pressing than ever but a proposal to this effect met with stiff resistance even among the respectable tradesmen and merchants of the Catholic Committee. O'Conor addressed the arguments of those who opposed such a loyal remonstrance in a letter to his ally, John Curry:

Another objection is deemed strong and very apologetic for our silence, 'That our masters know we hate our bond and consequently must think that our allegiance is forced and unnatural.' But those masters ought to be informed and some I hope may be persuaded that our religion requires of us in such cases to bear patiently what we hate.[26]

It was undoubtedly true that the Catholic bishops counselled obedience to the established authorities and would never have countenanced any attempt at domestic rebellion, but the attitude they would have adopted in the event of a large-scale French landing – a development which would have created an alternative, Catholic, civil authority – must be more doubtful. When the archbishop of Armagh and five other bishops, acting in consultation with Lord Trimblestown, a leading Catholic nobleman, drafted a pastoral letter in September 1757 that would have instructed the clergy to 'offer up a prayer to the Almighty God, beseeching his Divine Majesty to bless our good and gracious sovereign, King George and his royal family' at the end of Mass on Sundays, the opposition of the other archbishops resulted in its suppression.[27] Strongly anti-Hanoverian sentiments were certainly held by members of the lower clergy. News of the French capture of Hanover in July 1757 inspired the following expression

---

[25] *Remarks on a Late Pamphlet, Entituled, the Case of the Roman Catholicks of Ireland* (Dublin, 1755), p. 24.

[26] O'Conor to Curry, 20 August 1756, in R.E. Ward, J.F. Wrynn and C.C. Ward (eds.), *Letters of Charles O'Conor of Belanagare* (Washington, 1988), p. 21.

[27] For the text of the draft pastoral see Patrick Fagan, *Divided Loyalties: The Question of the Oath for Irish Catholics in the Eighteenth Century* (Dublin, 1997), pp. 120–3.

of hostility towards the reigning monarch from Fr Liam Inglis, a member of the Augustinian community in Cork city:

> *Is ró-dhian a screadann an seanduine Seoirse*
> *'Ó, a Dhia, cá rachad? níl agam Hannover*
> *ná fós Hesse-Kassel, mo bhaile beag cóngair,*
> *ná fód mo sheanathrach, táid argtha dóite'.*[28]

(In great anguish old man George [II] screams: 'Oh, my God, where will I go? I don't have Hanover nor Hesse-Kassel either, my little town nearby, nor the land of my grandfather, they've been plundered and scorched.')

Inglis expected that the imminent French victory would free the Catholic clergy from religious oppression and restore the rightful king to his throne:

> *Beidh diadhacht ar maidin ina gceallaibh 's um nóna,*
> *siansa na salm is Aifreann glórmhar,*
> *briathra na n-aspal dá gcanadh go ceolmhar*
> *is an gliaire gan ainm sa bhaile 'gus coróin air.*[29]

(There'll be piety in their cells at matins and nones, the melody of the psalms and of glorious Masses, the words of the apostles being sung in harmony and the unnamed warrior [James III] at home and crowned.)

The fortunes of war soon turned against France but an official announcement in October 1759 that an army of 18,000 men, which included the Irish regiments in the French service, was massing in Brittany for a descent on Ireland renewed the hopes and fears of the various sections of Irish society. An address of loyalty signed by 400 prominent Dublin Catholics was presented to the lord lieutenant while an invasion still threatened but this action aroused strong opposition within the Catholic community. Charles O'Conor reported to a correspondent that his coreligionists in the capital 'who doubtless should take the lead among us, are now divided into two parties, addressers and anti-addressers' and added that 'the clergy are at the head of the latter'.[30] Jacobitism also retained an appeal for Dublin's lower orders: in 1755 rioters sporting white cockades paraded through the streets behind a piper who played a Jacobite air.[31] The threat of a French invasion in 1759 coincided with unprecedented disturbances in Dublin during which a mob burst into the Commons

---

[28] '*Is ró-dhian a screadann an seanduine Seoirse*' in Risteárd Ó Foghludha (ed.), *Cois na Bríde: Liam Inglis, O.S.A., 1709–1778* (Dublin, 1937), p. 35.

[29] *Ibid.*, p. 36.

[30] O'Conor to Hugh Stafford, 21 February 1760, in Ward, Wrynn and Ward (eds.), *Letters of Charles O'Conor of Belanagare*, p. 82.

[31] Thomas Waite to Sir Robert Wilmot, 26 August 1755, in James Walton (ed.), '*The King's Business*': *Letters on the Administration of Ireland, 1740–1761, from the Papers of Sir Robert Wilmot* (New York, 1996), p. 120.

chamber while the house was in session. The irruption was sparked by unfounded rumours of an imminent legislative union with Britain and it is clear that both Catholic and Protestant artisans were involved, but some contemporaries noted the coincidence of the riot with the invasion threat and portrayed it as part of a Catholic plot:

PROTESTANT. I have, within three or four days last past, looked often for you, to transact some business with you, but could not meet you at home; which being so contrary to your custom, I could not but wonder at – Where have you been?
PAP[IST]. I have been every day, at Col[le]ge Gr[ee]n.
PROT. What called you thither?
PAP. I went with most of my neighbours to prevent an union, between Great Britain and Ireland.
PROT. How did you find out it was intended?
PAP. Father___went through his flock, and assured us all, it would be done forthwith, and we should be all undone, if we did not terrify the undertakers.[32]

In reality, the Catholic clergy had directed their flock to take no part in the disturbances, but the fact that such an intervention was thought necessary is itself an indication of the politicisation of the capital's Catholic artisans.[33]

It has been argued in recent years that eighteenth-century Ireland should be seen as an *ancien régime* society in the sense in which Jonathan Clark used the term in his seminal study of pre-1832 England.[34] The comparison is more misleading than most. For Clark, *ancien régime* England was a society in which 'gentlemen, the Church of England, and the crown commanded an intellectual and social hegemony'.[35] In Ireland, by contrast, the bulk of the population regarded the gentry as alien upstarts, the clergy of the established church as preachers of heresy, and the reigning dynasty as usurpers. While eighteenth-century Ireland possessed the typical structure of an *ancien régime* state – a monarch, a hierarchically ordered society and an established church – this superficially imposing edifice was a hollow façade which lacked an essential feature of normal *ancien régime* states: that is, a sense of legitimacy grounded on immemorial usage and sanctified by a church commanding the allegiance

---

[32] *A Dialogue between a Protestant and a Papist, Concerning Some Late Strange Reports about an Union and the Seditious Consequences of them* (n.p., n.d. – 1759?), p. 1.
[33] See Sean Murphy, 'The Dublin anti-union riot of 3 December 1759' in Gerard O'Brien (ed.), *Parliament, Politics and People: Essays in Eighteenth-Century Irish History* (Dublin, 1989). The author concludes that the riot was the work of a mainly Protestant mob (p. 68) but also cites evidence of Catholic involvement (pp. 62–4).
[34] S.J. Connolly, *Religion, Law and Power: The Making of Protestant Ireland 1660–1760* (Oxford, 1992), p. 2.
[35] J.C.D. Clark, *English Society 1688–1832: Ideology, Social Structure and Political Practice during the Ancien Régime* (Cambridge, 1985), p. 7.

of the people. In Ireland, uniquely in western Europe, the religious sentiment of a large majority of the population served to undermine rather than to validate the constitutional status quo. Rev. James Pulleine, dean of the diocese of Dromore in County Down, in the foreword to a catechism first published in 1748 and reprinted in 1782, compared the condition of Irish Catholics after the Revolution with that of the Jewish people during the Babylonian captivity:

Créad fá ar fhulaing Dia an pobal Eabhra, a mhuintir féin, á mbreith go broid na Babiloin ann a raibh siad i ndaoirse faoi smacht agus faoi léan dhá bhliain déag agus trí fichid? Rinne chionn go ndearnadar dearmad an dlí agus an reacht a thug sé dóibh, a theagasc, a mhúineadh agus a chleachtadh dóibh féin agus dá gclainn. Ar an ábhar chéanna, atáimidne inniu faoi smacht, agus faoi dhaoirse, faoi léan agus faoi leatrom ag allúraigh choimhtheacha.[36]

(Why did God tolerate the Hebrew people, his own people, being taken into Babylonian captivity where they remained in bondage, suppressed and grieving, for three score years and twelve? He did so because they had forgotten to instruct, to teach and to apply to themselves and their children the law and the statute he had given them. For the same reason, we today are suppressed and in bondage, grieving and oppressed by alien foreigners.)

By casting the native Irish and Great Britain in the roles of the children of Israel and Babylon respectively, Pulleine implied that, in the fullness of time, another power would step forward in the role of Persia. The same imagery and the same promise of deliverance is found in the secular literature. Thus the County Armagh poet Art Mac Cumhaigh concluded a lament for the fallen power of the O'Neills of the Fews by assuring his audience that the fate which had befallen the last king of Babylon awaited 'Wully' and 'Jane' – stereotypical planter names:

Básadh Baltasar agus ceangladh é i mbraighdibh dlúth,
tiocfaidh an lá sin ar Bhullaigh a mbeidh cumhaidh air is Jane faoi smúid.[37]

(Belshazzar was killed and bound in tight fetters, that day will come to Wully when he'll be sorry and Jane will be desolate.)

Breandán Ó Buachalla has argued in his magisterial study of Irish Jacobite literature that it was Jacobitism rather than republicanism or deism which delegitimised the *ancien régime* in Ireland.[38] The point is well made since the existence of a Stuart court-in-exile effectively ensured that the post-Revolution establishment would not be legitimised by the passage of time

---

[36] James Pulleine, *An Teagasg Criosdaidhe a nGoidhleig* (n.p., 1782), pp. iv–v. I have normalised both the spelling and punctuation.
[37] Tomás Ó Fiaich (ed.), *Art Mac Cumhaigh: Dánta* (Dublin, 1973), p. 83. King Bel-shar-usur was known as 'Baltasar' in Greek and as 'Belshazzar' in Hebrew.
[38] Ó Buachalla, *Aisling Ghéar*, p. 658.

as might otherwise have happened, but the ultimate agent of delegitimation was the Williamite Revolution itself. The Irish *ancien régime* was swept away in 1691 and was never restored. In eighteenth-century Ireland a substantial standing army – reinforced at times of heightened tension (1715, 1745 and 1756) by an exclusively Protestant militia – was a permanent pillar of the state. Even so, the Irish garrison was barely adequate. At the time of the threatened invasion in 1759 the chief secretary advised a correspondent in Whitehall that an additional army would have to be sent from England in the event of a French landing since 'the one we have is about sufficient to keep the papists from rising to join them'.[39] As late as 1775, at the start of the American war, the nominal strength of the Irish garrison was 12,533 men, or 28 per cent of the total strength of the British army throughout the empire.[40]

None the less, tentative signs of convergence with English and Anglo-Irish political norms could be discerned among élite sections of Catholic society by the end of George II's reign. While the rural masses, mostly Irish-speaking and illiterate, remained wedded to the hope of Catholic and Stuart restorations in the context of an Ireland freed from British control by a successful French or Spanish invasion, the residual Catholic gentry and many members of the expanding merchant class had concluded that nothing less than frequent public professions of Catholic loyalty to the house of Hanover would be effective in allaying Protestant fears and in opening the way to a gradual relaxation of Penal legislation. Leading members of the clergy had also publicly signalled their support for a strategy of *rapprochement* with the existing constitutional order, although their freedom of manœuvre was restricted by the papacy's continuing recognition of the Stuart claimant as *de jure* king of Ireland.

Anglican opinion

If the political outlook of the Catholic community in the early eighteenth century has been neglected by historians, a great deal of attention has been devoted to the study of Anglican opinion during the same period. This contrast is partly a reflection of the undue emphasis that was formerly placed on high politics, but the inordinate interest of historians in the operation of the executive at Dublin Castle and the legislature at College Green has also been influenced by the Anglocentric outlook of the historical profession: those aspects of the Irish past that conformed most

---

[39] Richard Rigby to Sir Robert Wilmot, 19 October 1759, in Walton (ed.), 'The King's Business', p. 195.
[40] Edward E. Curtis, *The Organization of the British Army in the American Revolution* (New Haven and London, 1926), p. 3.

closely to English models have been intensively studied while those that were aberrant, such as the Scottish background of the Presbyterian community in Ulster, or, *sui generis*, such as the Gaelic culture of the majority of the population, have been relegated to the historiographical margins when they have not been ignored completely.[41] Yet this concentration of effort on the Anglo-Irish community has failed to produce a consensus on the nature of its political consciousness.

Early writers tended to view the political nation that emerged from the Revolution as an English colony *tout court*. For W.E.H. Lecky, that section of the parliamentary opposition which pretended to represent the 'Irish interest' had in fact 'no sympathy or connection with the great majority of the Irish people' but merely 'represented the English colony'.[42] The image presented by R.B. McDowell in his study of Anglo-Irish opinion in the eighteenth century was equally unequivocal: for McDowell, the Anglo-Irish 'preserved the spiritual and intellectual make-up of colonists' throughout the century and at all times modelled themselves on the 'intellectual, political, and cultural habits of the motherland'.[43] *Colonial Nationalism*, a slight work by J.G. Simms published in connection with the bicentenary of American independence, is the *locus classicus* of an alternative interpretation. Simms sketched a tradition of 'colonial nationalism' – which he defined as 'the demand for domestic self-government within an imperial framework' – extending from William Molyneux, through Jonathan Swift and Charles Lucas, to Henry Grattan.[44] Simms's thesis has undoubtedly been influential and it achieved the status of an orthodoxy with the publication of the eighteenth-century volume of the Royal Irish Academy's *New History of Ireland* in 1986.[45] But the concept of 'colonial nationalism' has been vigorously criticised in recent years. S.J. Connolly has rejected both legs of Simms's thesis, arguing that Ireland was not a colony and that Irish Protestants were not nationalists.[46] Instead, following the lead of Joep Leerssen, Connolly has proposed the concept of 'patriotism' as the one that best represents the outlook of those opposition figures whom Simms described as colonial nationalists. According to this view, a patriot was 'a defender

---

[41] For a recent example, see Neil Longley York, 'The impact of the American Revolution on Ireland' in H.T. Dickinson (ed.), *Britain and the American Revolution* (London and New York, 1998). Despite its title, this study is narrowly focused on the Anglo-Irish community.

[42] Lecky, *Ireland in the Eighteenth Century*, I, p. 439.

[43] McDowell, *Irish Public Opinion*, p. 24.

[44] J.G. Simms, *Colonial Nationalism 1698–1776* (Cork, 1976), p. 9.

[45] T.W. Moody and W.E. Vaughan (eds.), *New History of Ireland, IV: Eighteenth-Century Ireland* (Oxford, 1986).

[46] Connolly, *Religion, Law and Power*, p. 123.

of the rights of parliament against those of the crown' and was inspired by universally applicable principles rather than by national particularism.[47] Jacqueline Hill concurs and, with both Molyneux and Swift in mind, has noted that Anglo-Irish patriotism had a unionist rather than a nationalist orientation.[48]

It will be argued below that it is indeed anachronistic to attribute a 'demand for domestic self-government' to Molyneux, Swift, or any substantial body of Anglo-Irish opinion prior to the 1740s, but that evidence does exist for the gradual emergence of such a demand from the 1740s onwards. This development was far from universal, however, and was vigorously contested from within the Anglican community by those who continued to adhere to older perspectives.

When William III's first parliament assembled in October 1692 its members already displayed many of the attitudes that were to characterise the parliamentary opposition of the eighteenth century. A call was made for a habeas corpus act based on the English model; a government-sponsored mutiny bill was rejected because, unlike the English equivalent, it was perpetual; and, most importantly, a supply bill was rejected because it did not take its rise in the House of Commons. This ideologically motivated opposition to government measures reflected, not incipient 'colonial nationalism' or even 'patriotism', but simple Whiggery. As James McGuire, the historian of the 1692 parliament, has explained, parliament's rejection of the official measures was 'tantamount to an assertion that the Englishman in Ireland was in no sense an inferior Englishman, exempt from the benefits of living in England itself'.[49] It was this principle – the belief that the members of the Anglo-Irish community, as loyal Protestant Englishmen, were entitled to all the rights of their kith and kin who had remained in the mother country – that inspired the constitutional arguments of such putative nationalists as Molyneux and Swift. The identity of the Anglo-Irish community in the late seventeenth and early eighteenth centuries *was* unequivocally colonial in the primary sense of the word 'colony': that is, a 'body of people who settle in a new locality, forming a community subject to or connected with their parent state'.[50]

---

[47] J.Th. Leerssen, 'Anglo-Irish patriotism and its European context: notes towards a reassessment', *Eighteenth-Century Ireland* 3 (1988), 10.
[48] Jacqueline Hill, *From Patriots to Unionists: Dublin Civic Politics and Irish Protestant Patriotism, 1660–1840* (Oxford, 1997), p. 14.
[49] James McGuire, 'The Irish parliament of 1692' in Thomas Bartlett and D.W. Hayton (eds.), *Penal Era and Golden Age: Essays in Irish History, 1690–1800* (Belfast, 1979), p. 18.
[50] The definition is that of the *Oxford English Dictionary*, second edition (Oxford, 1989).

This colonial identity is evident in apologias for the Revolution written by two prominent churchmen, Edward Wetenhall, bishop of Cork, and William King, bishop of Derry. Both men declared that James II had forfeited the allegiance due to him by betraying the trust which must subsist between ruler and ruled. But crucially, both men also resorted to the argument that Ireland was a conquered country. In King's words:

if blood and treasure, or a possession of five hundred years can give a right to a country, England is justly intitled to the government of Ireland. And which, if it had no other exception against King James's government, but his carriage towards Ireland, and his attempts to separate it from its dependance on England, must be justified by all the world, in laying him aside as a destroyer of his people, and a disinheritor of the crown of his ancestors.[51]

Wetenhall was blunter still:

God has now put us under the power of the second William the Conqueror, whom I must affirm (besides his being, more ways than one, otherwise justly intitled) to have *a right to our allegiance by conquest*; that which gave the King of England the first (and still avowed) title to Ireland. I do aver us in Ireland *conquered*, and with my heart bless God for it.[52]

The characterisation of Ireland as a conquered country establishes the colonial nature of Anglo-Irish identity in the late seventeenth century beyond doubt, and William King's views on the question were still being quoted with approval by Anglican polemicists in the middle of the following century.[53]

William Molyneux's celebrated *Case of Ireland* combined historical precedents with arguments based on natural rights in a work which was, in part, a defence of the corporate privileges of the Irish parliament such as might have been penned by an *ancien régime* jurist defending the privileges of a French *parlement* and, in part, an application to Irish conditions of the Lockean principle that every law must have 'its sanction from that legislative which the public has chosen and appointed'.[54] In Molyneux's words, 'the right of being subject only to such laws to which men give their own consent, is so inherent to all mankind, and founded on such immutable laws of nature and reason, that 'tis not to be aliened or given

---

[51] [William King], *The State of the Protestants under the late King James's Government* (London, 1691), pp. 95–6.
[52] [Edward Wetenhall], *The Case of the Irish Protestants: in relation to Recognising, or Swearing Allegiance to, and Praying for King William and Queen Mary, Stated and Resolved* (London, 1691), p. 6.
[53] See, for example, *The Tryal of Mr. Charles Lucas, on Certain Articles of Impeachment* (Dublin, 1749), p. 12, and [Rev. William Henry], *An Appeal to the People of Ireland* (Dublin, 1749), p. 12.
[54] Locke, *Two Treatises of Government*, book II, §134.

up, by any body of men whatsoever'.[55] It was an obvious corollary of this principle that the English parliament, as it contained no representatives from Ireland, could not legislate for that country. But there was a second corollary which Molyneux explicitly acknowledged:

> If...it be concluded that the parliament of England may bind Ireland; it must also be allowed that the people of Ireland ought to have their representatives in the parliament of England. And this I believe we should be willing enough to embrace; but this is an happiness we can hardly hope for.[56]

Molyneux's views on the unsatisfactory nature of Ireland's constitutional position *vis-à-vis* the English parliament and on the desirability of a legislative union appear to have been representative of thinking in the Anglican community as a whole. In 1703 the Irish Commons, citing English acts which prohibited the export of Irish woollens to third countries and appointed trustees for the disposal of forfeited estates in Ireland, petitioned Queen Anne either to restore the powers of the Irish parliament or to institute a 'more firm and strict union' with England.[57] When rejection of these overtures was followed by the union between England and Scotland, Jonathan Swift expressed the dismay felt by the Anglo-Irish colony in an allegorical fable in which Ireland was portrayed as a woman who had been jilted by her lover in favour of a less desirable rival.[58] Swift too has been posthumously enrolled in the ranks of colonial nationalists on the basis of his opposition to the English parliament's power of legislating for Ireland, but his opposition, far from reflecting a demand for domestic self-government, was based on the principle previously invoked by Molyneux – the principle that 'all government without the consent of the governed, is the very definition of slavery'.[59] In 1738, Samuel Madden, a nephew of Molyneux's, reiterated his uncle's appeal for the members of the Anglo-Irish colony to be accorded the privileges of Englishmen in the most emphatic terms: 'may not the children of those Englishmen, who have planted in our colonies in America, be as justly reckoned Indians and savages, as such families, who are settled here, can be considered and treated as mere Irishmen and aliens?'[60] For Madden, the Anglo-Irish

---

[55] William Molyneux, *The Case of Ireland's being Bound by Acts of Parliament in England, Stated* (Belfast, 1776), p. 64.

[56] *Ibid.*, p. 56.

[57] A. Browning (ed.), *English Historical Documents*, VIII (London, 1953), p. 781.

[58] See 'The story of the injured lady' in Joseph McMinn (ed.), *Swift's Irish Pamphlets* (Gerrard's Cross, 1991), pp. 23–8.

[59] The fourth of the Drapier's letters, in McMinn (ed.), *Swift's Irish Pamphlets*, p. 80.

[60] Samuel Madden, *Reflections and Resolutions Proper for the Gentlemen of Ireland* (Dublin, 1738), p. 107.

were 'in the truest sense of the word, Englishmen, as well as English subjects'.[61]

The closeness, both psychological and geographical, of the Anglo-Irish community to its mother country ensured that English intellectual trends diffused quickly and easily in Irish colonial society. Many of the ideas of the English country opposition, such as opposition to placemen and pensioners sitting in parliament and the demand for shorter parliaments, were equally attractive to the members of the Irish political nation – although English misgivings about the maintenance of a standing army held less appeal for obvious reasons. At the most radical end of the opposition spectrum the ideas expounded in publications such as *The Independent Whig* and *Cato's Letters* found an able Irish advocate in the person of Charles Lucas, another figure who has been described as a 'colonial nationalist'.[62] Lucas came to national prominence when he contested a Dublin by-election in 1748–49 and publicised his views in a series of outspoken election addresses. As with his English neo-Harringtonian or 'real Whig' models, issues of corruption and virtue loomed large in Lucas's world-view. Ireland, he claimed, had suffered 'under oppressive and tyrannical governors, usurping and lawless magistrates, dependent and iniquitous judges, and spurious and corrupt parliaments', while he described himself as 'most perfectly contented with being cast among the lower class of men, with regard to station and grandeur: for, there, in all nations, at this, nay, at all times, do we find most freedom and virtue'.[63] Likewise, Lucas emphasised the mixed nature of the British and Irish governments, each consisting of three estates 'so framed and attempered, as to be checks, the one upon the other', while laying particular stress on their democratic component: 'From monarchy, our wise forefathers contented themselves with taking little more, than the name and form.'[64] But Lucas's perspective remained firmly colonial. He argued in one election address that it was unnecessary 'to consider what policy, or what kinds, or forms of government were instituted, by any other people, than those of our mother nation, Britain', while in another he assured the voters of Dublin that he had 'neither consanguinity or affinity, nor even fosterhood, with any Irish family, in the kingdom'.[65] In the dedication to a London edition of his collected election addresses he invited the mayor, aldermen and Common Council of the British capital 'to consider the

---

[61] *Ibid.*

[62] Sean Murphy, 'Municipal politics and popular disturbances: 1660–1800' in Art Cosgrove (ed.), *Dublin through the Ages* (Dublin, 1988), p. 85.

[63] Charles Lucas, *The Political Constitutions of Great-Britain and Ireland, Asserted and Vindicated* (London, 1751), pp. i and 7 respectively.

[64] *Ibid.*, pp. 23 and 33.   [65] *Ibid.*, pp. 23 and 132.

subjects of these confederate kingdoms, or commonwealths, whether individual persons, or bodies corporate, as one and the same people, under one and the same head, though under distinct, yet similar modes of government, and having but one and the same common interest, civil and religious, to attend'.[66] As Molyneux had done before him, Lucas cited Locke as the source of his ideas, 'that our antagonists may not be able to charge us with introducing any innovation',[67] and grounded his rejection of the British parliament's authority to legislate for Ireland on the principle that 'no people may be bound by laws, to which they did not give their assent'.[68]

None the less, it must be acknowledged that Lucas sounded an anti-English note which was new to Anglo-Irish political discourse. It was normal, he wrote, for a lord lieutenant to arrive in Ireland with 'a brood of starved rooks, wretched, worthless dependents, of every class, along with him; who are to be crowded into every vacant place, in the state, in the church, or in the army, without the least regard to merit or qualification'.[69] Such complaints undoubtedly reflected 'real Whig' fears about the corruption of the body politic, but one also detects a sense of resentment at the preference shown to those who were born in England. Lucas's view of Irish history was more remarkable still and he claimed that 'there was no general rebellion in Ireland, since the first British invasion, that was not raised or fomented, by the oppression, instigation, evil influence, or connivance of the English'.[70] By advancing such an all-embracing apologia for Irish rebellions Lucas departed from the general sense of the political nation, and a motion of censure referring to his justification of 'the several horrid and bloody rebellions which have been raised in this kingdom' was passed without opposition in the House of Commons.[71] Lucas left the country hurriedly to avoid arrest but the extent of his popular support can be gauged from the fact that James Digges La Touche, his less outspoken running-mate, was returned (although subsequently unseated) for one of two vacant seats in the Dublin by-election. During his exile in London Lucas published a work which suggested a union between Ireland and Britain as a means of preserving the liberty of the Anglo-Irish community. But in contrast to the earlier authors noted above, such a union was not the preferred solution for Lucas. It was, on the contrary, an option that should be resorted to only if Britain proved unwilling to restore the legislative independence of the Irish parliament:

---

[66] *Ibid.*, p. xii.   [67] *Ibid.*, p. 24.   [68] *Ibid.*, p. 122.   [69] *Ibid.*, p. 221.
[70] *Ibid.*, p. 123.
[71] *A Letter from a Member of the House of Commons, to a Chief Magistrate of a Borough* (Dublin, 1749), pp. 3, 22.

If that parliament may not be entrusted with the government of that people ... Will it not rather be more wise and just, while any sense of liberty remains among the people to intitule them to enrol with the family of Britain, with the same care to rescue them from domestic as from foreign destruction, and unite them effectually, as Scotland has been, with this kingdom?[72]

The intense interest aroused by Lucas's campaign among the Dublin electorate indicates that some Anglicans had begun to reassess traditional political attitudes by the middle of the century. Although Lucas's views were those of a minority in the Anglo-Irish community as a whole, his tireless propaganda had the useful effect of obliging supporters of the constitutional status quo to defend their position in print.

The anonymous author of one anti-Lucas pamphlet justified the legislative supremacy of the British parliament in terms that would become familiar during the American crisis. It was essential, he argued, that there should be one supreme legislature capable of regulating the affairs of the entire British empire and it was natural that this superintending power should reside with the mother country since it was 'much more becoming, that the mother, who protects, should give laws to the daughter, who is protected'.[73] Far from imposing a disability on Irish Protestants, the country's status as a dependent kingdom secured them the rights of 'free-born Britons' in Great Britain – 'far greater privileges than his Majesty's subjects in Hanover are possessed of, or the Scotch before the Union had any pretensions to' – without the need for naturalisation.[74] The same author reminded his readers that only the legislative supremacy of the English parliament had preserved the Anglo-Irish political nation on two occasions in the previous century.[75] Rev. William Henry, author of another anti-Lucas pamphlet, argued that it was a moot point whether a kingdom that must 'in some way be annexed to, and dependant on another' would be 'in happier circumstances by depending only upon the king of that neighbouring kingdom; or by depending upon the king, lords and commons'.[76] In any event, the distinction between the members of the Anglo-Irish colony and the English themselves was merely a geographical one since both groups constituted a single people: 'We are now one people; nor is there any material difference between a free Briton born in England, and one born in Ireland, more than between a man of Yorkshire and a man of Kent.'[77] The colonial nature of Anglo-Irish identity is also evident from the forthright assertion by Sir Richard Cox

---

[72] Charles Lucas, *An Appeal to the Commons and Citizens of London* (London, 1756), p. 6.
[73] *The Tryal of Mr. Charles Lucas, on Certain Articles of Impeachment, Exhibited against him, before the Citizens of Dublin*, p. 7.
[74] *Ibid.*, p. 9.   [75] *Ibid.*, p. 8.
[76] [Rev. William Henry], *An Appeal to the People of Ireland*, p. 7.   [77] *Ibid.*, p. 10.

that 'we are dependant... We know it sufficiently: and we rejoice in it. It is our strength, our marrow, our sinews. We have no safety without it.'[78] Cox teased out the implications of Lucas's argument that Ireland was an independent kingdom linked to Great Britain only by a personal union of the crowns and identified this view of Ireland's constitutional status as a dangerous Catholic and Jacobite doctrine:

No man can dispute, but infinitely the greater number of the people of Ireland denied that King James had abdicated, or that their throne was vacant; but the English convention knew full well their right to Ireland, if they could reduce it, and so disposed of England and that [country] altogether. The dependant Protestants were delighted; but the independent papists held a parliament in Ireland under their king, repealed the act of settlement, Poynings' law... this independence has ever been a popish doctrine.[79]

For Cox also, Irish Protestants and the British were a single people: 'we are', he wrote, 'bone of their bone and flesh of their flesh; and have no interest distinct from theirs'. Supporters of Lucas rejected the suggestion that they aspired to independence. One pamphleteer responded to Cox by claiming that Britain was itself increasing the danger of Irish independence by pursuing policies which not only weakened the Anglo-Irish community but also had the potential to strengthen centrifugal tendencies in other parts of the empire:

all the Protestants of the kingdom, in a few years more, will leave it for New-England, a country much more likely at present to shake off its dependence on the crown of England than ever we were. The papists will then be left masters of Ireland, and, if unassisted, may perhaps employ the English another 400 years before they are subdued; if supported by a foreign power, as it is probable they will be, it will be improbable they should be resubdued at all.[80]

While few of those who read the above passage in 1749 would have dismissed the possibility of a Catholic resurgence, most would probably have regarded the reference to American independence as an instance of patriotic hyperbole.

Two years later the idea of a legislative union between Ireland and Great Britain was again canvassed in a pamphlet by Wills Hill, Lord Hillsborough, who argued that Ireland's status as a kingdom was more apparent than real: 'At present Ireland hath no character, not even a name

---

[78] [Sir Richard Cox] 'Anthony Litten', *The Cork Surgeon's Antidote against the Dublin Apothecary's Poyson*, number II (Dublin, 1749), p. 10.

[79] *Ibid.*, p. 11.

[80] *A Second Letter to the Citizens of Dublin* (Dublin, 1749), p. 13.

in the affairs of Europe ... No nation is truly free, that cannot resent the insults, and repel the violence of her enemies; but Ireland hath really no being, as a nation; neither domestic trade, nor foreign influence, but under the protection of Great Britain.'[81] The present shadow of statehood, Hill proposed, should be exchanged for the substance of influence over British policy that representation at Westminster would confer. Such a proposition would have found general acceptance among Irish Protestants only a generation previously but the largely negative response on this occasion confirms the emergence of a new outlook signalled in Lucas's writings. One anonymous critic of Hill's proposal argued that, however imperfect Ireland's position might be, it was still preferable to Scotland's. Swift's image of the jilted lover was replaced with that of a self-confident woman wary of losing her independence in marriage:

At present Ireland hath no character, not even a name in the affairs of Europe. How will she have a greater name if united? Is not Scotland lost in the name Great Britain? She will resemble a married woman, who gives up her fortune, her name and her liberty for an husband and the prospect of a jointure.[82]

This inverted imagery testifies to the development of a heightened sense of collective identity among the members of the Anglo-Irish political nation – an identity which the writer was concerned to preserve and which would have been lost had the Irish parliament been subsumed into that at Westminster. Nicholas Archdall, a member of parliament who signed his anti-union pamphlet – itself an indicator of the popular mood in an age when it was usual for pamphleteers to shelter behind pseudonyms – also rejected Hill's view of Ireland's status. While accepting that the country was, in practice, dependent on Great Britain, Archdall maintained that the two kingdoms were, in principle, equal. He distinguished between Ireland's constitutional status and that of the American colonies:

Great Britain may be considered as the mother of many children, and all her colonies settled in America, or elsewhere, as so many daughters, to whom she has given portions, and put in a way to shift for themselves; yet subject to the same laws by which her own family is governed. But Ireland should be looked upon rather as a sister, whom England has taken under her protection, on condition she complies with the oeconomy of the family; yet with such distinction and deference, as to shew they were originally upon an equality.[83]

[81] [Wills Hill], *A Proposal for Uniting the Kingdoms of Great Britain and Ireland* (Dublin, 1751), pp. 37–8.
[82] *An Answer to the Late Proposal for Uniting the Kingdoms of Great Britain and Ireland* (Dublin, 1751), p. 33.
[83] Nicholas Archdall, *An Alarum to the People of Great-Britain, and Ireland: In Answer to a Late Proposal for Uniting these Kingdoms* (Dublin, 1751), p. 5.

This growing sense of community, the emerging belief that the descendants of seventeenth-century English colonists constituted a distinct polity, was reflected in a new willingness to distinguish between Irishborn Anglicans and those who were immigrants from England.

From the early 1750s onwards a power struggle developed between two parliamentary factions: one headed by Henry Boyle, the speaker of the Commons, who had been charged with the management of official business since the 1730s, and a second group of aspiring power brokers led by Archbishop George Stone, the English-born primate. Stone's English birth allowed the speaker's faction to portray the contest as one between Irish-based and cross-channel interests. Control of the House of Commons by an English faction, an early pamphlet argued, would reduce Ireland to a state indistinguishable from slavery by opening the door to taxation without consent:

Jack: A people, a nation are then slaves when power no longer resides in the *natives*; when their government (that is the *legislative* part of it) is taken out of their hands, the *executive* part may be vested in *others*, and the people be still free, and as independent as their constitution designed them; but whenever it happens that their *natural* liberties are restrained by laws they had no hand in making, when they are not allowed to tax themselves, and give their own money, but people of a different nation, and perhaps in a different country do it for them, I suppose you will grant me they are not free; and whoever says they are not slaves, must have a better talent at distinguishing than I pretend to.

Sim[on]: And do you think they will ever lay taxes upon us in Eng[lan]d without letting us know how much they are pleased to charge us, or asking our advice about it?

Jack: Truly, Simon, I think not; but it is no way material on what spot of ground the thing is done, if it be done by others, and not by ourselves. It may be done in D[u]bl[i]n as effectually as at W[e]stm[inste]r, if a majority of our p[ar]l[ia]m[en]t consists of E[n]gl[is]h men.[84]

The simmering parliamentary conflict boiled over on 17 December 1753 when the Commons voted to reject a bill for applying surplus revenue to the reduction of the national debt on the grounds that a clause referring to the king's prior consent had been inserted in England.

Such an arcane dispute was an unlikely object of popular enthusiasm but the speaker's party had prepared the ground well. Lord George Sackville – the future Lord George Germain but for the moment Irish chief secretary – informed a correspondent in Whitehall that: 'The cry of the country is "Ireland forever," and sometimes with the addition of "Down with the English," and people were so assured that all the money

---

[84] *A Dialogue between Jack Lane and Simon Curtin Freemen of Cork, concerning P—l—m—t Men* (Cork, 1751), pp. 7–8.

in the treasury was to be carried to England if the bill passed that several members were instructed by their constituents to oppose it.'[85] A contemporary newspaper report described the scene that followed the opposition's narrow victory in the division on the money bill:

The populace, who impatiently waited the important decision, carried the patriot tribune [Henry Boyle] to his coach, and conducted their glorious defender home, amidst repeated acclamations, and the joyful shouts of protected liberty. The sound of the trumpet was not wanting to proclaim the glad tidings, which, as in an instant, reached the most distant parts of the city; joy sparkled in every honest countenance, and gladdened every honest heart. The blaze of more than 1000 bonefires illumined our streets, which resounded with the grateful voice of multitudes, whose rejoicings were only suspended by the approach of day.[86]

The argument that acceptance of the 'prior consent' clause would have struck at the existing powers of the Commons in relation to taxation was widely canvassed. One pamphleteer wrote that the members could not have accepted the amended bill without surrendering a power that it was 'absolutely necessary they should continue to possess, so long as we are to continue a free government, namely, the principal power over the purse of the nation'.[87] This partly accounts for the high level of public interest in the fate of the bill, but opposition propagandists also emphasised the rights of Ireland and portrayed their opponents as the agents of an English ministry. Appeals by supporters of the primate for unity among the members of the political nation on the basis of their shared English origin produced replies which reveal the extent to which the intrusion of English office-holders had alienated some Irish Anglicans: 'though the majority of us are descended from English families', wrote one anonymous pamphleteer, 'yet, I believe, few will be brought to think that it is of no consequence whether we have come sooner or later from thence; they, who fall under the last predicament, have signalized themselves too much for us easily to forget the distinction'.[88] In response to opposition propaganda the 'court' party stressed the virtues of order and loyalty, emphasised the need for Protestant unity and the maintenance of the English connection, drew attention to the material interests of leading patriots, and insinuated that crypto-Catholics had instigated the dispute – a charge

[85] George Sackville to Sir Robert Wilmot, 18 December 1753, in Walton (ed.), 'The King's Business', p. 80.
[86] Universal Advertiser, 22 December 1753. Allowance must be made for an element of exaggeration as this was an opposition organ.
[87] Truth against Craft: or, Sophistry and Falsehood Detected (Dublin, 1754), p. 44.
[88] A Letter to a Person of Distinction in Town, from a Gentleman in the Country (Dublin, 1753), p. 13.

lent some credibility by the prominence in opposition counsels of the prime serjeant, Anthony Malone, who was a convert from Catholicism. The toasts given at a banquet held by supporters of the ministry included the following:

Liberty without licentiousness . . . May party never wear the mask of patriotism, without its being pulled off . . . May his Majesty preserve the connections of England and Ireland by continuing his Grace the Duke of Dorset our chief governor, in support of the Protestant interest of this kingdom. May all those who court popular applause for their own private emolument, be ever disappointed. That the kingdom of Ireland may never suffer for the errors of a few. May the old Protestant interest of Ireland ever defeat new convert schemes. May the interests of England and Ireland be always inseparable.[89]

In contrast, opposition toasts mixed references to established feasts in the Whig calendar and to more recent events in Ireland. The current dispute was represented as the latest in a series of historical episodes in which Protestant subjects had successfully defended their liberties and resisted unconstitutional exercises of the royal prerogative:

The 16th of April 1746 [Culloden]. The 1st of July 1690 [the Boyne]. The 12th of July 1691 [Aughrim]. The glorious 1st of August 1714 [accession of George I]. The 23rd of Nov. 1753 [vote of censure on the surveyor-general, an ally of Primate Stone]. The ever memorable 17th of Dec. 1753 [rejection of the money bill]. The memory of the exclusioners with Lord Russell. The Middlesex Grand Jury who presented the Duke of York for being a papist . . . The 7th of December 1688 [the shutting of the gates of Derry]. The 15th of June 1215 [Magna Carta]. May the enemies of Ireland never eat the bread of it. The memory of John Hampden.[90]

It was inevitable in such circumstances that the arguments of the primate's supporters would have a Tory ring: 'however fashionable it is become to declaim against prerogative', one clerical pamphleteer wrote, it was still 'the only sure barrier we have against sedition and anarchy'.[91] Archbishop Stone's leadership of the court party provided the opportunity for an outpouring of anticlerical rhetoric on the patriot side reminiscent of Whig attacks on high churchmen in Queen Anne's reign. The primate was dubbed 'the high priest Caiphas' in patriot pamphlets and caricatured as a latter-day Cardinal Wolsey, but the depth of feeling aroused by the dispute is perhaps most clearly seen in thinly veiled references to Stone's rumoured homosexuality:

---

[89] *Universal Advertiser*, 5 February 1754.   [90] *Ibid.*, 16 March 1754.
[91] [John Brett], *To All the Serious, Honest, and Well-meaning People of Ireland* (Dublin, 1754), p. 31.

May the island of saints never turn to Sodom and Gomorrah. Speedy exportation of rotten Stone, duty free. May Back-lane never get the better of Bride-street.[92]

May the h[igh] p[riest]'s Ganymede be catched in his bestiality.[93]

Such unrestrained and unprecedented abuse directed against one section of the political élite by another could hardly fail to attract the attention and arouse the interest of many who were excluded from formal participation in the political nation.

While a change of lord lieutenant, the ennoblement of the speaker, and generous pensions for other leading figures in the opposition effected a reconciliation between the two parliamentary factions in 1756, the money-bill dispute permanently raised the political temperature throughout Ireland as Charles Lucas's election campaign had already done in Dublin. Henry Boyle and his fellow patriots in the Commons were happy to be cheered through the streets of the capital in December 1753, but in December 1759 a mob rioted and invaded the Commons chamber on hearing unfounded rumours of an intended union with Great Britain. The chief secretary linked the two episodes in a letter to an English correspondent. 'These disturbances', he wrote, 'are the effects of those wicked insinuations to the prejudice of government in 1753, which, with the national dislike to English rule, has rendered the people easy of belief of all suggestions to its prejudice.'[94] As in the Catholic community, old political orthodoxies were beginning to break down among Irish Anglicans by 1760. Serious divisions had opened within the political nation, ministerial policy had been successfully opposed by a self-styled patriot party, and a minority had begun to question long-standing assumptions concerning Ireland's constitutional dependence on Great Britain.

Presbyterian opinion

Protestant Dissenters of the early eighteenth century, like their Catholic contemporaries, have received comparatively little attention from historians; such attention as they have received has also tended to focus on their religious rather than their political beliefs – although it would be a mistake to believe that the two are entirely unconnected. The neglect of the political outlook of the Presbyterian community has begun

---

[92] *Universal Advertiser*, 19 February 1754.
[93] *An Address from the Independent Freeholders of the P—v—ce of M—ns—r, to Sir R—C— Baronet* (London, 1754), p. 16.
[94] Richard Rigby to Sir Robert Wilmot, 27 December 1759, in John Russell (ed.), *Correspondence of John, Fourth Duke of Bedford*, II (London, 1843), p. xxviii.

to be redressed but, in a further similarity with the historiography of the Catholic community, the influence of teleology has been apparent in the choice of themes: because no Jacobite rebellion ever occurred in Ireland the political outlook of the majority of the population during the greater part of the eighteenth century has scarcely featured in the historiography; conversely, because a major republican rebellion in which Presbyterians were prominent really did take place, republicanism has loomed large in studies of Presbyterian political attitudes.[95] The desire to identify and to trace those aspects of Presbyterian thought which disposed members of the community to embrace republicanism in the 1790s is entirely legitimate, but many historians have gone beyond this and have posited the existence of a substantial body of republican opinion long before the era of the French revolution. Writing of the 1790s, J.A. Froude described the northern Presbyterians as 'hereditary republicans'; his great rival W.E.H. Lecky for once agreed and claimed that the 'Presbyterianism of the North, and especially of Belfast, had been long inclined to republicanism'.[96] Referring to the outbreak of the American war, J.C. Beckett claimed that Ulster Presbyterians were viewed by government as being particularly dangerous because of the existence of a republican element in the community.[97] More recently, Roy Foster has noted a Presbyterian tradition of 'libertarian republicanism' that long predated either the American or the French revolutions.[98] On the other hand, R.B. McDowell has argued that respect for constitutional order was a strong element in Presbyterianism and that Presbyterians, by virtue of their concentration in east Ulster, their receipt of *regium donum* (an official subsidy for ministers), and their close links with the established Church of

---

[95] See, for example, A.T.Q. Stewart, ' "A stable unseen power": Dr William Drennan and the origins of the United Irishmen' in J. Bossy and P. Jupp (eds.), *Essays Presented to Michael Roberts* (Belfast, 1976); Stewart, *A Deeper Silence: The Hidden Origins of the United Irishmen* (London and Boston, 1993); Stewart, 'The Enlightenment: Francis Hutcheson, Irish Presbyterians and the Scottish Enlightenment' in D.G. Boyce, R. Eccleshall and V. Geoghegan (eds.), *Political Thought in Ireland* (London, 1993); McBride, 'William Drennan and the dissenting tradition' in D. Dickson, D. Keogh and K. Whelan (eds.), *The United Irishmen: Republicanism, Radicalism and Rebellion* (Dublin, 1993); McBride, 'Presbyterians in the Penal era', *Bullán* 1 (1994); McBride, ' "When Ulster joined Ireland": anti-popery, Presbyterian radicalism and Irish republicanism in the 1790s', *Past and Present* 157 (1997); McBride, *Scripture Politics: Ulster Presbyterians and Irish Radicalism in the Late Eighteenth Century* (Oxford, 1998); Pieter Tesch, 'Presbyterian Radicalism' in Dickson, Keogh and Whelan (eds.), *United Irishmen*. On the other hand, republicanism is noticeable by its absence from Kevin Herlihy (ed.), *The Politics of Irish Dissent 1650–1800* (Dublin, 1997).

[96] J.A. Froude, *The English in Ireland in the Eighteenth Century*, II (London, 1873), p. 6 and Lecky, *Ireland in the Eighteenth Century*, III, p. 8.

[97] J.C. Beckett, *Protestant Dissent in Ireland 1687–1780* (London, 1948), p. 101.

[98] R.F. Foster, *Modern Ireland 1600–1972* (London, 1988), p. 265.

Scotland, had a 'strong tendency to see themselves as part of the established order'.[99]

It must be acknowledged that the association of Presbyterianism with republicanism – unlike 'colonial nationalism' – is not a mere artefact of modern historiography. But although this association was frequently made by contemporary members of the established church, there is little to suggest that the Presbyterian community harboured any sizable body of republican sentiment in the first half of the eighteenth century. As early as 1713, Rev. James Kirkpatrick published a long and still useful 'historical essay' to defend his coreligionists against allegations of past and present disloyalty that had been levelled against them by William Tisdall, the Anglican vicar of Belfast. Kirkpatrick pointed out that, far from supporting the establishment of the Commonwealth in 1649, a Presbyterian council of war had defiantly informed the Rump of the English parliament that they would 'demean ourselves as become faithful and loyal subjects to the crown of England, and shall at all times give due obedience to the king and free parliament thereof'.[100] Polemical exchanges between the two main Protestant denominations continued even after the ambitions of high churchmen were curbed by the Hanoverian succession. A pamphlet by an anonymous Presbyterian author published in Dublin around 1719 takes the form of a dialogue in verse between St Patrick's cathedral and a nearby Presbyterian meeting house in the course of which the Anglican cathedral charged its Dissenting rival with regicide and republicanism:

> How ill pronounced is sacred loyalty,
> by thy inhuman, murderous brood and thee?
> What mighty mischiefs heretofore you've done,
> murdered the father, and deposed the son;
> you loyal prove only to gain by stealth
> that hideous ill shaped thing, a commonwealth.[101]

In its turn, the meeting house asserted the loyalty of Presbyterians to the reigning monarch and deplored their continued exclusion from office:

> My sons are all excluded from the court,
> and must not serve a *monarch* they support;
> a *king* they love, a *settlement* they own,
> and did their best to bring him to the *throne*;
> for him they always most devoutly *pray*,

[99] McDowell, *Ireland in the Age of Imperialism*, pp. 172–3.
[100] [James Kirkpatrick], *An Historical Essay upon the Loyalty of Presbyterians in Great Britain and Ireland from the Reformation to this Present Year 1713* (Belfast, 1713), p. 286.
[101] Raymond Gillespie, 'Presbyterian propaganda' in Herlihy (ed.), *The Politics of Irish Dissent*, p. 117.

that heaven would bless, and still direct his way:
I teach my infants his just praise to sing,
for him my lute and trembling harp I string,
and all my sons are loyal to the *king*.[102]

Presbyterians had good reasons, both public and private, for concealing any republican sympathies they may have felt and for professing loyalty to a constitutional order that was threatened, not with the re-establishment of a republic, but with the restoration of a Catholic dynasty. None the less, there are grounds for believing that their expressions of loyalty were not a mere tactical subterfuge.

The essential point to note in relation to contemporary allegations of Presbyterian disaffection in Ireland is that they merely echoed a common-place theme of Anglican controversialists in England. There, as Jonathan Clark has put it, 'the English trinity of king, lords and commons was perceived in the first half of the century as treading a via media between Rome and Geneva, each claiming a deposing power – between a Stuart restoration and a republic'.[103] But English Dissenters differed funda-mentally from their Irish counterparts: in England, Protestant Dissent was largely derived from the Independents and sectaries of the interreg-num, a circumstance which provided a factual basis for the Anglican view that Dissent and republicanism were merely two sides of the same coin. In Ireland, although a few small religious bodies – Quakers, Baptists and, to some extent, the Presbyterian congregation in Dublin – could trace their origins back to groups of English Dissenters, the great ma-jority of Dissenters were Ulster Presbyterians whose roots lay, not in England, but in Scotland. If the Ulster Scots followed their parent state in supporting the English parliament during the first civil war and were divided in their attitude to the Engagement, they refused to recognise the Commonwealth and proclaimed Charles II as king on the execution of his father. The constitutional ideal bequeathed to Presbyterianism in both Scotland and Ulster by the upheavals of the seventeenth century was that of a covenanted monarchy, not a republic, and impressions to the contrary are an effect of the Anglocentric perspective that pervades so much of Irish historiography.

The religious, social and intellectual links between the Presbyterian community and their coreligionists in Scotland remained close through-out the eighteenth century. Indeed, the influence of the Church of Scotland on its daughter church was so strong that Scottish schisms were faithfully reproduced in Ulster even when the cause of those divisions did not exist there – as happened with the Secession of 1733 on the issue of lay

---

[102] *Ibid.*, pp. 116–17.   [103] Clark, *English Society*, p. 292.

patronage and the 1747 split among the Seceders on the question of the burgess oath. Irish Presbyterians, both clerical and lay, were educated in the Scottish universities and, given their high rate of emigration to North America, it is hardly possible to disagree with Ian McBride's assessment that they 'inhabited a transatlantic subculture stretching from Scotland to Ulster to the American colonies'.[104] What is much more difficult to accept is the argument of other authors that these Scottish links fostered support for the American revolution. Nancy Curtin, for example, has detected a high level of sympathy for the American colonists in Ulster which she attributes, not only to familial, commercial and religious ties with the colonies, but also to the acceptance by Presbyterians of 'the radical Whig canon, especially as this was mediated through key figures of the Scottish enlightenment'.[105] While it is true that Francis Hutcheson, a native of County Down who has been described as the father of the Scottish enlightenment, supported the principle of colonial independence at an early date, his views on the matter were not shared by many of the Scottish *philosophes*. Thus William Robertson, principal of the University of Edinburgh and a leader of the Moderate faction in the Church of Scotland, was an advocate of coercion: in 1775 he opined that 'if our leaders do not at once exert the power of the British empire in its full force, the struggle will be long, dubious, and disgraceful'.[106] Adam Ferguson, likewise, authored an anti-American pamphlet that found a Dublin publisher in 1776.[107] Adam Smith, for his part, frankly asserted the right of the British parliament to tax not only the colonies but also the kingdom of Ireland:

It is not contrary to justice that both Ireland and America should contribute towards the discharge of the public debt of Great Britain. That debt has been contracted in support of the government established by the Revolution, a government to which the Protestants of Ireland owe, not only the whole authority which they at present enjoy in their own country, but every security which they possess for their liberty, their property, and their religion.[108]

The views of the Scottish *lumières* on the American question were in broad agreement with mainstream opinion in Scotland. John Witherspoon,

---

[104] McBride, 'The school of virtue', p. 74.
[105] Nancy J. Curtin, *The United Irishmen: Popular Politics in Ulster and Dublin, 1791–1798* (Oxford, 1994), pp. 18–19.
[106] Quoted in Dalphy I. Fagerstrom, 'The American revolutionary movement in Scottish opinion, 1763 to 1783' (PhD thesis, Edinburgh, 1951), pp. 230–1.
[107] [Adam Ferguson], *Remarks on a Pamphlet Lately Published by Dr. Price* (Dublin, 1776).
[108] Adam Smith, *Wealth of Nations*, IV.vii.b.63; quoted in Andrew S. Skinner, 'Adam Smith and America: the political economy of conflict' in R.B. Sher and J.R. Smitten (eds.), *Scotland and America in the Age of Enlightenment* (Edinburgh, 1990), p. 155.

perhaps the most prominent Scottish-born advocate of American independence and a signatory of the declaration of independence, acknowledged his countrymen's loyalty to the crown in a pamphlet reprinted at Belfast, but implausibly laid the blame for this circumstance at the door of John Wilkes whose anti-Scottish prejudice was supposed to have 'produced so general an attachment to the king and ministry, as has not yet spent its force'.[109] Like their counterparts in England, Irish patriots noted the loyal disposition of the Scots long before the outbreak of hostilities in America and frequently portrayed them as crypto-Jacobites, slavish followers of Lord Bute, and enemies of liberty throughout the British empire. When news of the engagements at Lexington and Concord arrived in June 1775, a report in the *Londonderry Journal* claimed that Lord North's ministry was deeply divided over its American policy and attributed the blame for the outbreak of hostilities to the belligerent views of Scottish ministers: 'These Englishmen were for adjusting the disputes in a milder way, while Scotch politics, which were always violent, were for making the appeal to the sword.'[110] Such views were not dispelled by personal experience of the mood in Scotland. In 1778 William Drennan, a native of Belfast who was then a medical student in Edinburgh, informed his sister that: 'Nothing is going on here at present but raising regiments, to be devoted to destruction in America. Every order of men from the highest to the lowest are emptying their pockets (and what more could be asked from Scotchmen?) in the support of the war.'[111] Once hostilities began, the Church of Scotland was forthright in its opposition to the American cause and its views were publicised in Ulster.[112] In view of the strength of loyalist sentiment prevailing in Scotland, it comes as no surprise to find that attitudes in Ulster were more varied than has commonly been represented. Thus, when news arrived in June 1780 of the surrender of Charleston to British forces – the most serious American reverse of the war – Belfast was illuminated amid 'great rejoicings' while in Derry city the local Volunteer battalion paraded and fired a *feu de joie*.[113]

This is not to deny that Presbyterians in general regarded the outbreak of war in America with dismay or that a section of the community hoped for an American victory – the former was the inevitable consequence of large-scale emigration from Ulster to the colonies during the eighteenth

---

[109] John Witherspoon, *Dominion of Providence over the Passions of Men*, fourth edition (Belfast, 1777), pp. 36–7.
[110] *LJ*, 9 June 1775. This was probably reprinted from an English source.
[111] Drennan to Martha McTier, 20 January 1778, in Jean Agnew (ed.), *The Drennan–McTier Letters 1776–1793*, I (Dublin, 1998), p. 32.
[112] See, for example, *LJ*, 13 June 1777 and 16 June 1778.
[113] *BNL*, 27 June 1780, and *LJ*, 27 June 1780, respectively.

century while the latter reflected the sympathy for patriot ideas which existed in the Protestant population as a whole – but a section of the community also supported government in its efforts to re-establish Britain's authority in the colonies. If Presbyterian Ulster is to be situated on a spectrum of which the opposite ends were occupied by the American colonies and Scotland, then it must be said that it lay towards the middle of that spectrum. It is natural that this should have been so. The stratified nature of rural society in Ulster, composed as it was of a large body of tenant farmers and a much smaller group of landlords, many of whom belonged to the gentry or nobility, closely resembled conditions in lowland Scotland and differed greatly from the egalitarian society of freeholders that Presbyterian emigrants from Ulster (the 'Scotch-Irish' of American historiography) encountered in the colonial backcountry. On the other hand, Irish Presbyterians were subject to disabilities which did not exist in Scotland where their church was established. The refusal of ecclesiastical courts to recognise the validity of marriages conducted by non-episcopally ordained ministers had long been felt as a grievance, and the 'Act to Prevent the Further Growth of Popery' of 1704, although primarily directed against Catholics, included a sacramental test that effectively excluded Protestant Dissenters from public office and the municipal corporations. While these grievances were a continual source of friction between Protestant Dissenters and members of the established church, they were more than offset by the central reality of Irish life – the fact that the mass of the population was Catholic in religion, alienated from the state, and looked to France and Spain for succour.

In such circumstances it was inevitable that Presbyterians would seek to minimise the distinction between themselves and Anglicans, between those of Scottish and of English descent, and would stress the need for unity among British Protestants in the face of the Catholic threat. In a pamphlet of 1702 on the marriage question, Rev. John McBride posed the following rhetorical question:

Is this a season for those who ought to be uniting against the common adversary of the Protestant interest in Ireland, to be combining against peaceable men for private interest? Sure we are, none of her Majesty's subjects are under greater obligations to stand by one another than the British Protestants in Ireland; who are neither too many nor too strong to maintain themselves against the common enemy of our religion and civil interest, which are here inseparably linked together.[114]

---

[114] John McBride, *A Vindication of Marriage as Solemnized by Presbyterians, in the North of Ireland* (n.p., 1702), p. iv.

Conditions for Presbyterians improved following the accession of George I: the *regium donum*, suspended under Queen Anne, was restored; when a Jacobite invasion threatened in 1715, Presbyterians were offered commissions in the militia, in violation of the test act; and in 1719 a toleration act exempted Trinitarian Dissenters from the acts of uniformity of 1560 and 1665. This legal toleration did not exempt Presbyterians from the sacramental test which continued to prevent them (some occasional conformers excepted) from holding office, and repeal of the test therefore became the main focus of Presbyterian political demands. Rev. John Abernethy employed a familiar argument, the need for maximum unity among Protestants, in a pamphlet that he wrote on the subject in 1731:

Rather indeed, as its certain the Irish rebellion [of 1641] was in favour of that unhappy prince's [Charles I] unjust proceedings against the parliament and the nations, (whatever orders he might give concerning it) it should direct true Protestants and Britons to look with a jealous eye on the Irish papists, as the tools of arbitrary power, and ready to lay hold on the distracted state of public affairs as a proper opportunity for serving the cause of their church, and committing those barbarities against Protestants which their religious principles incline them to.[115]

At times of emergency Presbyterians readily acknowledged the essential identity of interests of all Protestants, a point emphasised by Samuel Delap, minister of Letterkenny, who claimed in a thanksgiving sermon on the occasion of the Hanoverian victory at Culloden that 'if God, for our sins, had given us a popish king in His wrath, French tyranny, popery, and slavery, would have come in like a deluge'.[116] The realisation that the alternative to the existing Hanoverian régime with its Anglican establishment was a Stuart restoration and an independent Irish parliament dominated by Catholics was one calculated to keep Presbyterian discontent within narrow bounds.

How, then, should the political outlook of Irish Presbyterians in the first half of the eighteenth century be characterised? Certainly not as republican, if by 'republican' one means anti-monarchist. The denial of royal claims to headship of the church in no way implied a rejection of royal authority in the secular sphere. Presbyterian political discourse in the eighteenth century was notably conventional: commonplace Whig shibboleths about the mixed constitution and Revolution principles were reiterated and, in so far as Presbyterian authors diverged from those who were members of the established church, they did so in the greater

[115] [John Abernethy], *The Nature and Consequences of the Sacramental Test Considered* (Dublin, 1731), p. 13.
[116] Quoted in Thomas Witherow (ed.), *Historical and Literary Memorials of Presbyterianism in Ireland (1731–1800)*, second series (Belfast, 1880), p. 46.

emphasis they placed on the contractual nature of government and on the right of subjects to resist unconstitutional innovations. A good illustration of this is found in a sermon preached at Belfast while the outcome of the Jacobite rebellion of 1745 was still uncertain. Citing Locke's second treatise on government, Rev. Gilbert Kennedy argued that 'No man can justly claim any power over me, my person or estate, without my own consent; and only so much, as I voluntarily give him; and whatever is assumed over and above this, is unreasonable and unjust, meer tyranny and usurpation; and what I have a natural inherent right to resist and oppose.'[117]

It is difficult to determine the extent to which the 'new light' belief in the primacy of personal religious judgement influenced, or was influenced by, the political views of Presbyterians, but it is worthy of note that two of the most prominent new-light ministers, James Kirkpatrick and John Abernethy, endorsed in print the right of subjects to rebel against a prince who behaved unlawfully. In 1713, Kirkpatrick argued that opposition to 'arbitrary power' was inherent in the Presbyterian system of church government:

The ecclesiastical constitution of Presbytery does provide such effectual remedies against the usurpations and ambition of the clergy, and lays such foundations for the liberty of the subject in church matters: that it naturally creates in people an aversion from all tyranny and oppression in the state also: which hath always made it odious in the *eyes of such princes*, as have endeavored to stretch the prerogatives above the laws of the nation, and liberties of the subjects.[118]

John Abernethy not only counselled resistance to attempts to extend the royal prerogative but also defined monarchy as an institution of purely human origin. In a sermon preached to mark the 'happy accession' of George I to the throne, he advised his congregation that 'the consent of the people is the only just foundation of government':

I own indeed a limited monarchy is a very happy constitution, and I believe there is none in the world more excellent than our own. May God still graciously preserve it from the invasion of tyranny, usurpation, and anarchy, as He has hitherto most wonderfully done! Yet still it is a human ordinance, which I don't say to lessen the respect that's due to it . . . But it is the ordinance of God, no other ways than in a general sense, as all forms of government are, that are regularly and freely chosen, according to the different genius and circumstances of nations. And as the consent of the people is the only just foundation of government, the right of the person governing must be derived from the same spring.[119]

---

[117] Gilbert Kennedy, *The Wicked Ruler: or, the Mischiefs of Absolute Arbitrary Power* (Belfast, 1745), pp. 16–17.
[118] [Kirkpatrick], *An Historical Essay*, p. 152.
[119] Quoted in Witherow, *Historical and Literary Memorials*, pp. 199–200.

Implicit in the above argument is the idea that the people have the right, not only to withdraw their consent to be governed by a particular monarch, but also to remodel the constitution as they see fit. Evidence exists to link Abernethy and other 'new lights' with a circle of 'real Whig' thinkers influenced by classical republican ideas: the subscribers to a 1737 edition of James Harrington's *Oceana* which was published by William Bruce, a Dublin-based Presbyterian bookseller and pamphleteer, included both John Abernethy and Francis Hutcheson, as well as James Digges La Touche, the electoral ally of Charles Lucas.[120]

Yet if the right of subjects to resist unlawful authority was a common feature of Presbyterian rhetoric, this principle sat happily alongside loyalty to the existing régime, notwithstanding the exclusion of Presbyterians from full participation in the political nation. The thanksgiving sermon preached by Gilbert Kennedy in Belfast on the conclusion of the War of Austrian Succession drew a number of major themes together. The doctrine of resistance was expounded:

We freely own that while he acts as a king, according to the good and wholesome laws which the society has thought proper to establish, he ought cheerfully to be obeyed, and his administration protected against all insults. But when he abuses his power, for *oppressing* instead of *protecting* his subjects, has he not then *unkinged* himself? Is he not to be considered as a *traitor* to the society; and consequently is not all manner of obligation between him and his subjects entirely dissolved?[121]

But Kennedy was careful to emphasise the impeccably constitutional conduct of George II and his concern for the liberties of his subjects:

I live under a mild and equitable government; tender of the rights and liberties of the subject; never dispensing with the laws, nor attempting any undue stretch of prerogative; that collects no ship-money, raises no subsidies without authority of parliament, grants no monopolies to the ruin of trade, imprisons no persons against law; commits none of those violences, which were heretofore so grievous and oppressive.[122]

Kennedy's sanguine assessment of his coreligionists' standing and prospects was probably as representative of the views of his congregation as was his simultaneous attack on the sacramental test:

We suffer no hardships now on account of religion excepting such as are *negative*; I mean, our being put upon a level with the *notorious* and *avowed enemies* of the constitution, by being legally disqualified from serving his majesty and the public

---

[120] These links are detailed in McBride, 'The school of virtue'.
[121] Gilbert Kennedy, *A Sermon Preach'd at Belfast, on Tuesday, April 25th, 1749* (Belfast, 1749), p. 16.
[122] *Ibid.*, pp. 13–14.

in any places of trust; for this reason and no other, because we conscientiously scruple the terms of conformity.[123]

The aspirations of the Presbyterian community for political reform at mid-century appear not to have extended beyond the long-standing demand for admission to the political nation on equal terms with members of the established church.

None the less, the historical experience of the community and the teachings of the church together produced a bias in favour of the parliamentary opposition which was evident during the money-bill dispute of the 1750s. Within two months of the bill's rejection a public meeting of the 'free and independent inhabitants' of Belfast voted an address of thanks to the speaker, Henry Boyle.[124] A pamphlet by William Bruce illustrates the fusion of Whig and Presbyterian principles in support of the 'patriot' party. Bruce took issue with the citation of parliamentary precedents, a tactic resorted to by writers on both sides of the dispute, as such a line of argument implied that 'there is no other measure of human and social rights but what depends upon precedents, and positive acts'.[125] Far from being restricted in their powers by precedents or the statute book, governments had a duty to take whatever steps might be necessary to vindicate the rights of man: 'so far are decrees of this sort from constituting the principal rights of men, that the purpose of securing, more effectually, the enjoyment of those natural, original, inherent rights is the principal, legitimate, and righteous foundation of all the powers, prerogatives, and rights in civil governments'.[126] Among such inherent rights Bruce enumerated 'life, liberty, and the power of acquiring and disposing of property . . . and the exercise of that *unalienable* right of doing homage to his maker in such manner, as from his own inward persuasion, he expects will render him most acceptable'. While the first three of these rights are an echo of Locke, the fourth recalls the right of personal judgement in questions of religion asserted by new-light Presbyterians.[127] Bruce was a cousin of Francis Hutcheson and when he died in 1755 his body was interred in Hutcheson's tomb.[128] He may safely be regarded as one of the most advanced thinkers in the Presbyterian community at mid-century and it is worthy of note that he viewed Ireland as a subordinate province of the British empire. Bruce frankly advised his countrymen that,

---

[123] *Ibid.*, pp. 18–19. [124] *Universal Advertiser*, 14 February 1754.

[125] [William Bruce], *Remarks on a Pamphlet Intitled, Considerations on the Late Bill for Paying the National Debt* (Dublin, 1754), p. 12.

[126] *Ibid.*

[127] *Ibid.*, p. 13; cf. Locke, *Two Treatises of Government*, book II, §123 ('lives, liberties and estates') and §137 ('lives, liberties, and fortunes').

[128] Stewart, *A Deeper Silence*, p. 117.

in the event of a conflict arising between Ireland's economic interests and those of Great Britain, they ought 'voluntarily to acquiesce in the sacrifice of their own, which must be honestly acknowledged, the inferior interest, to that of their mother-country'.[129] The following passage shows how far his views were from those of the American patriots of the revolutionary period:

instead of claiming or wishing to be considered as an entire whole, or community, by itself, this country has long accounted it a circumstance of inestimable value, and the only rational security for our liberty and happiness, 'That Ireland is not a *whole*, but a *part*; an honourable and integral member of the noblest political community now subsisting upon earth; whereof Great Britain is most readily acknowledged to be still so much the greater and more honourable part, that whatever is found essential to the safety and interests of this our parent country, ought, in all justice, to be considered by all her children as essential to the welfare and interests of the whole.'[130]

Popular support for the speaker's faction in the money-bill dispute found expression in the formation of patriot clubs, bodies that were particularly active in Ulster, and a speech delivered to the patriot club of County Armagh endorsed Bruce's views in the most forthright terms, describing the pamphlet quoted above as 'the most useful, indeed, the only sensible paper, I ever read, with regard to stating the just relation that this island stands in to Britain'.[131]

When Henry Boyle and his parliamentary allies made their peace with a new lord lieutenant in 1756 they were condemned for deserting the patriot cause by many of their supporters in the wider political nation. The members of the patriot club of County Antrim were among those who voiced their sense of betrayal at Boyle's reconciliation with the ministry, an intervention which prompted an anonymous pro-government writer to tender the following facetious advice to the members of the club, whom he dubbed the 'Sons of Liberty':

Admit none of your club who are not true Commonwealth's men, of the old stamp, and ready for noble enterprizes . . . may the memory of Andrew Marvell, and of William Bruce, be for ever green among you, and forget not, at every meeting, to celebrate their patriot deeds.

> Drink, in despight of all the blood he spilt,
> Cromwell's grim ghost, and consecrate his guilt.

---

[129] [William Bruce], *Some Facts and Observations Relative to the Fate of the Late Linen Bill, Last Session of Parliament in this Kingdom* (Dublin, 1753), p. 22.
[130] *Ibid.*, pp. 23–4.
[131] *A Layman's Sermon, Preached at the Patriot Club of the County of Armagh, which Met at Armagh, the 3d of September, 1755* (Dublin, 1755), p. 7.

Guilt, in vulgar eyes, but, in those of the Sons of Liberty, the greatest of human achievements; and thus, I think, without a blunder we may say, you will be eternized, both in ancient and modern history.[132]

It was a predictable tactic for erstwhile patriots to portray Protestant Dissenters who ventured to criticise them as Puritan fanatics and potential regicides, but such allegations must be seen as partisan rhetoric with a very slender basis in reality. There is no reason to believe that the ministers of the Synod of Ulster misrepresented the feelings of the Presbyterian community when they addressed George III on the occasion of his accession. The ministers expressed their gratitude to the king for his 'resolution to maintain the toleration inviolable' and pledged that they would 'inculcate principles of the strictest fidelity and attachment to your Majesty's person and government', while making no allusion to any grievance.[133] At the start of the new reign the Presbyterian community, like the Anglican, contained a vocal minority of patriots but, the question of the sacramental test aside, Irish Presbyterians gave no indication that they were any less supportive of the constitutional status quo than their coreligionists in Scotland. None the less, the emphasis that they placed on the right of subjects to resist unconstitutional exactions would render them more susceptible to the arguments of American patriots during the early phases of the revolution than were their Anglican compatriots.

[132] *Advice to the Patriot Club of the County of Antrim on the Present State of Affairs in Ireland, and some Late Changes in the Administration of that Kingdom* (Dublin, 1756), p. 14.
[133] *Records of the General Synod of Ulster*, II (Belfast, 1897), pp. 450–1.

1 Imperial unrest, 1760–1775

The early years of George III's reign were a time of profound change throughout the British empire. The euphoria produced by victories over France in Canada and India in 1759, and over Spain in Cuba and the Philippines in 1762, together with the optimism inspired by the accession of a young 'patriot king' in 1760, faded as the problems of administering an enlarged empire became apparent. In the west, the old Anglophone and Protestant colonies no longer felt constrained by the threat of a French presence in Canada, while the administration of new Francophone and Catholic subjects presented government with novel dilemmas. The acquisition of an eastern empire likewise raised new questions concerning relations between the crown and the East India Company, as well as fears about the corrupting effects of an influx of 'nabob' wealth on the British body politic. In Britain itself, the new monarch's intention of drawing a veil over past dissensions in the interests of national unity successfully integrated the Tory squirearchy into the political establishment after forty-five years of exclusion, but only at the cost of alienating sections of the Whig élite and setting alarm bells ringing in patriot circles. Ironically, the same policy of political inclusiveness facilitated the return of Charles Lucas to Ireland, an event that contributed greatly to the reanimation of the patriot opposition.

The revival of patriotism

The general election of 1761 marked the beginning of a revival of the extra-parliamentary opposition after a period of demoralisation produced by the defection of Henry Boyle and his followers. In 1756 Edmund Sexton Pery, a future speaker of the Commons, informed an English correspondent in 1758 that 'those who were so lately adored by the people are now sunk into the abhorrence of most and contempt of all'.[1]

---

[1] Pery to Lord George Sackville, 5 January 1758; Emly Mss., HMC 8th report, appendix I (1881), p. 182.

But this disillusionment had a radicalising effect in the longer term. Deserted by the parliamentary leaders who reverted to supporting the administration as soon as sufficiently attractive terms were offered, patriot opinion in the country sought more resolute and principled leadership elsewhere. Anonymous verse which excoriated Henry Boyle – now the Earl of Shannon – also praised the exiled Charles Lucas as a truly disinterested friend of his country who had suffered for his beliefs:

> Old Shannon see! who heretofore,
> the name of honest Roger bore;
> but he, whilst at the Legion's steerage,
> betrayed his country for a peerage;
> nay, saith the muse, 'was more, I hear,
> he got two thousand pounds a year.
>   . . .
> A Lucas next deserves your care;
> what wrongs did he from Legion bear?
> an exile made to foreign land,
> because he dared for freedom stand.[2]

When Lucas decided to contest the general election in Dublin city, the issue he emphasised above all others in his address to the voters was the need for an act to limit the duration of parliaments – the previous two had been dissolved only by the death of the monarch. Lucas proposed that candidates should be asked to make a number of pledges as a means of furthering the most cherished object of 'real Whig' ideologues – namely, the restoration of the constitution to its original, mythical, purity. Foremost among these pledges was 'a solemn promise to endeavour to bring parliaments nearer the primitive institution, by making them, instead of perennial, contrary to law and reason, triennial, or quadrennial at the most'.[3] Lucas's proposal was acted upon and candidates were asked to pledge that they would 'to the utmost of their power, oppose every money-bill of longer duration than six months' until a limitation bill was enacted.[4] The tactic proposed, that of limiting grants of money to six months instead of the normal two years, would, if adopted, have required near-continual sessions of parliament. Implicit in the proposal was an assumption that taxation could only be levied with the consent of the elected representatives of the political nation. This belief, the principle that may

---

[2] 'Patriot Freeman', *An Address to Hibernia, on the Late Most Happy Dissolution of that Dread Junto, the Legion Club* (Dublin, 1761), pp. 11 and 18.
[3] Reprinted in Charles Lucas, *A Seasonable Advice to the Electors of Members of Parliament at the Ensuing General Election* (Dublin, 1768), p. 37.
[4] Sir Richard Cox, *Previous Promises Inconsistent with a Free Parliament: and an Ample Vindication of the Last Parliament* (Dublin, 1760), pp. 3–4.

be said to have precipitated the American revolution, was stated explicitly
in patriot tracts:

That branch of the legislature which the people have any power over [the House
of Commons], is the most important in many respects; this justly exercises the
exclusive right of laying taxes on their constituents, and as justly claims a right of
controlling the disposition of the public money, a right to see how it is applied,
and that it is not expended to the people's own destruction, by crafty and wicked
ministers.[5]

The patriots' contention that members of parliament should be account-
able to their constituents was disputed by supporters of the status quo. Sir
Richard Cox, who had played a leading role in driving Lucas from Ireland
in 1749, complained of the 'wild notions of liberty, that have seized some
people' and insisted that it was 'destructive of the constitution, as it was
subversive of the freedom of parliament, to compel the elected, to promise
any thing to the electors'.[6] Lucas himself was returned for Dublin city
and pressure for a limitation act continued to be applied both within and
without the new parliament.

The view that members of the House of Commons ought, properly,
to be deputies of the electorate was reiterated in an anonymous patriotic
pamphlet of 1762: 'If they hold seats in perpetuity, which you ought,
at reasonable periods, to fill with representatives of your own choosing;
they sit, in exclusion of *your* representatives, and *you* have none.'[7] For
the supporters of administration, however, elections merely provided a
dangerous opportunity for demagogues to 'raise an enthusiastic fermen-
tation, to jumble all things, and to throw somewhat upon the surface,
conducive to their purposes'.[8] Ireland's constitutional subordination to
Great Britain, it was argued, ensured that the country already indirectly
enjoyed the benefits of the British septennial act of 1716 without running
any of the risks that regular elections would entail: 'this country is so
closely, and inseparably connected with England . . . that if this law be of
such real benefit to England, Ireland necessarily enjoys all the possible
advantage, which can flow from it, without being exposed, to any one of
the mischiefs, or inconveniences which attend it in that kingdom'.[9] While
opponents of a limitation bill argued that the divisions and acrimony resulting from frequent electoral contests would be especially dangerous
in Irish conditions given the numerical weakness of the loyal Protestant

---

[5] *A Serious and Affectionate Call to the Electors of Ireland* (Dublin, 1761), p. 5.
[6] Cox, *Previous Promises*, pp. 1 and 5.
[7] *The Case of Ireland in 1762* (title page missing; Dublin, 1762?), p. 8.
[8] Cox, *Previous Promises*, p. 45.
[9] *The Speech of a Young Member of Parliament, on the Debate of the Septennial Bill* (Dublin, 1761), pp. 15–16.

population, a patriot propagandist stood this argument on its head and claimed that demographic weakness made it all the more necessary for Irish Protestants to have frequent access to the levers of political power: 'It is objected, that we differ from Great Britain; in abounding with internal enemies. But if this proves any thing, it proves that the power of the people, by means of these divisions, is less in proportion here: Which renders this limitation of parliaments, to increase their power, the more necessary.'[10] This issue remained the focus of patriot attention until the eve of victory, but the debate was won at an early stage and frank opposition to the principle of a limitation bill quickly fell away. In 1766, when Dublin's Common Council (the Corporation's lower house which represented the city's guilds) petitioned the Board of Aldermen (the self-perpetuating upper house which normally supported government) to instruct the city's members of parliament to support a limitation of parliament, the Board rejected the petition because of the 'exceptionable' terms in which it was expressed – suggesting that it was the controversial tactic of instructing members rather than the now widely accepted principle of limited parliaments which deterred the aldermen from lending their support.[11]

If the demand for a limitation act dominated the patriot agenda in the early 1760s it did not entirely obscure other issues, and the growing pension list and restrictions on Irish trade were both common themes in patriot discourse. James Digges La Touche, Lucas's ally in the Dublin by-election campaign of 1749, complained that Ireland was 'debarred from the common and natural benefits of trade' while being 'obliged to support a large national, civil, and military establishment, with a numberless band of strange pensioners, English, Scots, German, as well as Irish'.[12] In a pamphlet of 1763, Alexander McAuley rejected the right of the executive to grant pensions on the Irish establishment without parliamentary approval: 'an unlimited power of granting pensions on that establishment to the full amount of the Irish hereditary revenue, is claimed by ministers on behalf of the crown. If this claim be just, Ireland's existence, as a country of liberty and property, is at an end.'[13] The second (1767) edition of *A List of the Absentees of Ireland* – a work that first appeared in 1729 and

[10] [Alexander McAuley], *Septennial Parliaments Vindicated: or, Freedom against Oligarchy* (Dublin, 1762), p. 8.

[11] Charles Lucas, *A Third Address to the Right Hon. the Lord Mayor, the Board of Aldermen, and the Sheriffs, Commons, and Citizens of Dublin* (Dublin, 1766), p. 21.

[12] [James Digges La Touche], *A Short but True History of the Rise Progress, and Happy Suppression, of Several Late Insurrections Commonly Called Rebellions in Ireland* (Dublin, 1760), p. 11.

[13] Alexander McAuley, *An Inquiry into the Legality of Pensions on the Irish Establishment* (London, 1763), p. 3.

went through further editions in 1769 and 1783 – argued that Irish landlords should be required to reside and to spend their rents in the country if the restrictions on Irish trade were to be maintained; alternatively, if Irish landlords were to be allowed to reside in England, then 'a greater liberty of trade' was 'absolutely necessary ... for the support of the kingdom'.[14] Patriot members of parliament made repeated but unsuccessful attempts to secure the appointment of judges during good behaviour rather than at pleasure, an Irish habeas corpus act, and – that great patriotic shibboleth – the establishment of a national militia.[15] Anglo-Irish patriots continued to assert the exclusive right of the House of Commons to grant supply in the 1760s as they had done during the money-bill dispute of the 1750s, but the widespread mistrust of parliamentarians in the aftermath of the defection of Boyle and his 'legion' to the ministerial camp goes a long way towards explaining the importance they now attached to regular elections as a measure that would make parliament more representative of, and more responsive to, the political nation. Of course, the threat posed by the Catholic and Jacobite masses could not be forgotten and the presence of this internal enemy continued to exercise a restraining influence on patriot demands. An anonymous pamphleteer of 1762 reminded his readers that: 'The condition of this kingdom is, perhaps, the most peculiar on earth. Two thirds of her people, to use their own intimidating words in a late address to the public, sworn enemies to the constitution, as it stands in church and state; ever plotting to weaken the props and pillars that support it.'[16] Yet the comprehensive defeat inflicted on France in the Seven Years War inevitably contributed to a certain relaxation of tension among members of the established church. It may not be coincidental that Patrick Darcy's *Argument* asserting the constitutional equality of the kingdoms of Ireland and England, a work originally published by the Confederate Catholics in 1643, was reprinted for the first time in 1764 – one year after the war ended. An editorial note in the volume expressed the hope that it would be found 'pleasing to all true lovers of liberty and our constitution'.[17] A year before the stamp act of 1765 first drew the attention of Anglo-Irish patriots to the constitutional status of the American colonies, the legislative independence of the Irish parliament was again being asserted in print.

[14] *A List of the Absentees of Ireland* ... (Dublin, 1767), pp. 66–7.
[15] For a summary of such efforts see David Smyth, 'The Volunteer movement in Ulster: background and development 1745–85' (PhD thesis, QUB, 1974), p. 56.
[16] *Some Reasons against Raising an Army of Roman Catholicks in Ireland in a Letter to a Member of Parliament* (Dublin, 1762), p. 7.
[17] Patrick Darcy, *An Argument Delivered by Patricke Darcy, Esquire; by the Expresse Order of the House of Commons in the Parliament of Ireland, 9. Iunii, 1641* (Dublin, 1764), p. 151.

Catholic opinion and the new reign

The accession of George III provided the Catholic Committee (recently reconstituted by John Curry and other residents of the capital) with an opportunity to address the new monarch and to express the condolences of the Catholic community on the death of his grandfather, an event they had deeply regretted because the 'repose' they enjoyed 'entirely proceeded from his royal clemency, and the mild administration of his government in this kingdom'.[18] Such reliance on the grace and favour of the executive rather than the goodwill of the legislature was characteristic of the thinking of the Catholic élite, but differences of opinion existed on the extent of the commitment that should be made to the Hanoverian régime. A more deferential, not to say obsequious, attitude found expression in a text prepared by Lord Trimleston that was presented on behalf of the Catholic 'noblemen and gentlemen' of counties Meath and Westmeath:

And we now raise our flowing eyes from the obsequies of our late good and merciful king to your Majesty's throne, where with unspeakable and heart-felt joy we behold all his shining virtues in your Majesty's royal person as hereditary as his crown . . . faithful hearts and hands, unarmed indeed, but ready, earnest and desirous to exert themselves strenuously and faithfully, whenever your Majesty shall think them worthy to be employed in your and their country's cause.[19]

While the 600 gentlemen and merchants who signed the Dublin committee's address were prepared to affirm their passive allegiance to a dynasty that had reached the apogee of its power in Britain's *annus mirabilis* of 1759, the more aristocratic signatories of the Meath address went further in actively supporting a crown to which they looked for relief. A year later, Lord Trimleston offered to recruit a number of Catholic regiments for service in the on-going war. He informed Lord Halifax, the lord lieutenant, that 'what the Roman Catholics of Ireland most wished for was to serve his Majesty as elector of Hanover, since they could not serve him as king'.[20] Halifax transmitted the offer to the secretary of state, advising him that Trimleston was 'the most sensible man belonging to the Roman Catholic party' and repeating the latter's assurance that 'all impressions in favour of the Stuart family are worn out with the Irish gentlemen of consequence and fortune'.[21]

There is no reason to doubt the accuracy of Trimleston's representation of the sentiments of the most affluent sections of Catholic society.

[18] *London Gazette*, 7 February 1761; reprinted in J. Brady (ed.), *Catholics and Catholicism in the Eighteenth Century Press* (Maynooth, 1965), p. 100.
[19] *London Gazette*, 3 February 1761; reprinted in *ibid.*, p. 99.
[20] Halifax to Egremont, February 1762, in *Calendar of Home Office Papers 1760–1765* (London, 1878), p. 154.
[21] *Ibid.*

The period following the peace of Paris was a time of painful reassessment for some formerly committed Jacobites. Piaras Mac Gearailt, a minor member of the east Cork gentry and author of the perennially popular Jacobite anthem '*Rosc Catha na Mumhan*', had revised his expectations by 1769. When transcribing another Jacobite song in that year, Mac Gearailt added the following observation of his own: '*Is iomdha glór díomhaoin i gceann an tí a chum an t-amhrán so, 's go bhfóire Dia air gan chiall!*'[22] ('Many are the idle utterances in the head of the one who composed this song, and may God help him in his stupidity!'). But the evolution of opinion among the Catholic élite barely impinged on the political attitudes of the mass of the population. A work composed by Fr Liam Ó hIarlaithe, a west Cork priest, on the death of George II testifies to the narrowness of the social base on which the Catholic Committee's professions of loyalty rested:

> *Sin é an Seoirse ceannais bhí inné acu i stát*
> *i gcoróin na Sacsan is i réim go hard,*
> *gan treoir gan tapa le tréine an bháis,*
> *sin fógairt fearthainne is éiclips.*
>
> *Biaidh mórchuid scamall ar Éirinn spás*
> *ag tóir, ag taisteal, tar Téitis tráth,*
> *foirneart fearachon faobhair ar fás*
> *go dtógfar sealbh don réx ceart.*[23]

(There is the mighty George whom they had in splendour yesterday, in the crown of England and ruling on high, without movement or vigour through the power of death, that's an omen of storm and eclipse. There'll be a great mass of clouds over Ireland some time, chasing and voyaging over the sea for a while, the violence of armed warriors growing, until possession is taken for the rightful king.)

Although the rightful king was left unnamed, none of Ó hIarlaithe's audience can have imagined that George III was intended. The Catholic clergy were, however, sharply divided in their political attitudes. When Friday 12 March 1762 was designated an official day of fasting and prayer, a Dublin newspaper reported that in all of the city's Catholic churches there were 'exhortations for a religious and strict observance of the fast and humiliation on Friday next' in order to 'implore of heaven success by sea and land on the arms of our most gracious sovereign'.[24] This report was exaggerated, from whatever motive, and the letter from Archbishop Lincoln that was read in the capital's churches did not go so far as to call

---

[22] Risteárd Ó Foghludha (ed.), *Amhráin Phiarais Mhic Gearailt* (Dublin, 1905), p. 17.

[23] '*Sin é an Seoirse ceannais bhí inné acu i stát*' in RIA Ms. 23 C 18, p. 231; edited in Diarmuid Ó Muirithe (ed.), *Cois an Ghaorthaidh: Filíocht ó Mhúscraí 1700–1840* (Dublin, 1987).

[24] *Sleator's Public Gazeteer*, 9 March 1762; reprinted in Brady (ed.), *Catholics and Catholicism*, p. 103.

for prayers for the success of British arms. It did, however, remind congregations of Christ's exhortation to 'give unto Caesar what belongeth to
Caesar, and unto God what belongeth to God' and urged them to 'offer
up your prayers for the spiritual happiness of his gracious Majesty King
George the Third, and his royal consort, beseeching the Almighty God to
assist his councils, of restoring a solid, lasting, and advantageous peace,
and so put a stop to the further effusion of Christian blood'.[25] For some
Catholics this was a minimal and unexceptional step towards recognising political realities. Charles O'Conor had urged the archbishop to seize
the opportunity of endorsing the official fast, pointing out in a letter to
him that the fast, 'falling on one of our Fridays in Lent, requires nothing but what the Church commands already, fasting and prayer on that
day'.[26] But for other Catholics, lower on the social scale than O'Conor,
clerical support for the fast represented an act of political treachery.
Liam Dall Ó hIfearnáin, a poet who had applauded the French landing
at Carrickfergus in 1760, had not revised his views in the intervening
period:

> An bhuíon úd do dhíbir mo charaid romhamsa
> faoi dhaoirse le dlíthibh na nGalla-chóbach,
> ní shílim im smaointe gur peaca dhomhsa
> gan guíochan Dé hAoine le haicme den tsórt sin.
>   . . .
> Bídís sin ag Laoiseach dá ngreadadh i gcomhrac
> is ríthe gach críche uile ag teacht i gcomhar leis,
> mo phíobsa dá síneadh le reamhar-chórda
> dá nguífinn ar slí ar bith ar mhaithe leo sin.[27]

(That gang who drove my friend [James III or Prince Charles Edward] away from
me, oppressed by the laws of the foreign boors, I don't believe in conscience that
it's a sin for me, not to pray on Friday for a gang of that sort ... Let them be
hammered in battle by Louis [XV], with the kings of all the countries coming to
assist him, may my windpipe be stretched by a thick rope, were I to pray in any
way on their behalf.)

The political attitudes of the Catholic élite, clerical as well as lay, had been
diverging from those of the general population for more than a decade;
by 1762 the emerging pro-Hanoverian stance of the former was apparent
even to a blind poet in County Tipperary.

---

[25] *Pue's Occurrences*, 13 March 1762; reprinted in Brady (ed.), *Catholics and Catholicism*,
p. 104.
[26] O'Conor to Archbishop Richard Lincoln, 10 February 1762, in C.C. Ward and R.E.
Ward (eds.), *The Letters of Charles O'Conor of Belanagare* (Ann Arbor, 1980), p. 126.
[27] '*Carbh ionadh taoiseach nó easpag comhachtach*' in RIA Ms. 24 L 22, fo. 35; edited
in Risteárd Ó Foghludha (ed.), *Ar Bhruach na Coille Muaire* (Dublin, 1939). For
Ó hIfearnáin's celebration of the Carrickfergus invasion, see pp. 58–9 in the same
anthology.

Rural agitation

The emergence of an organised body of Catholic opinion that was prepared publicly to support the established dynasty in the hope of future
relief was quickly followed by the first large-scale agitation by the rural
Catholic masses for the redress of their grievances. Between 1761 and
1765, and again between 1769 and 1776, a large part of east Munster and
south Leinster was disturbed by the Whiteboys. The nocturnal assemblies and depredations of large bodies of white-clad men were undoubtedly sparked by specific local factors such as the enclosure of commons
and the more vigorous collection of tithes. Advocates of Catholic relief
were anxious to explain the unrest in purely economic terms; a pamphlet
published under the name of Count Nicholas Taaffe, an Irish emigrant
who had been ennobled for his services to the Austrian court, but which
was largely the work of Charles O'Conor, argued that it was unfair to
charge Catholics in general with responsibility for the 'madness of a rout
of peasants, wearied with life, and desperate from invincible poverty'.[28]
Similar views were argued at length by John Curry in a pamphlet published at London.[29] Protestant commentators, in contrast, interpreted
the Whiteboys' activities as evidence of a rebellion in gestation. This was
the view expressed by an anonymous author who replied to Lord Taaffe's
pamphlet:

And how can any man, indeed, believe otherwise of it, who knows that they had at
first a camp upon the Galtee mountains, where no horse could come at them; that
they were regularly paid, carefully trained by one Bourke, their adjutant general,
an experienced foreign officer, and kept to such a severity of discipline, that some
of them died of the whippings which they received for breach of duty.[30]

The coincidence of the Whiteboy agitation with Lord Trimleston's proposal to raise Catholic regiments for service overseas – a proposal which
was accepted by the administration but rendered unnecessary by the
conclusion of peace – served only to intensify the suspicions of Irish
Protestants. One anonymous pamphleteer, who expressed 'equal surprise
and indignation' at Trimleston's proposal and its favourable reception by
government, stated that France remained an object of 'blind love, and
implicit adoration' for Catholics. He posed and answered the following

---

[28] [Nicholas Taaffe], *Observations on Affairs in Ireland from the Settlement in 1691, to the Present Time*, third edition (Dublin, 1767), p. 19.
[29] [John Curry], *A Candid Enquiry into the Causes and Motives of the Late Riots in the Province of Munster* (London, 1766).
[30] *Lord Taaffe's Observations upon the Affairs of Ireland Examined and Confuted* (Dublin, 1767), pp. 26–7.

rhetorical question: 'did they ever or could they conceal their joy when any success has attended the arms of France? They who live among them know they cannot, whatever awkward professions of the contrary, the more artful and disguised among them may make.'[31] Fears about the improvement in relations between administration and the Catholic élite were expressed with increasing frequency in patriot propaganda as the decade advanced. In 1766, for example, the prominent patriot Sir Edward Newenham, speaking in his capacity as sheriff of County Dublin, warned the grand jury of the county that although 'the lenity of our government makes them wink at the papists exercising their religion publicly, yet they will not remain quiet, notwithstanding that indulgence. The late trials [of Whiteboys] at Clonmel and Kilkenny, are sufficient evidences of their bad intentions.'[32] The Catholic gentry and merchants could not fail to notice the contrast between the civility or mild encouragement that their spokesmen met with from government and many of its parliamentary supporters on the one hand, and the intemperate hostility that they typically encountered from the patriot opposition on the other.

Historians from Lecky onwards have largely agreed in portraying the organised rural violence of the Whiteboys as having an 'unsectarian and unpolitical character'[33] and in discounting contemporary assertions to the contrary as 'the paranoia of Protestant zealots'.[34] But the vernacular literature associated with the Whiteboy agitation confirms neither the argument of the Catholic élite that it was an apolitical reaction to economic grievances nor the contemporary Protestant fear of an organised conspiracy to overthrow the existing political order in concert with a foreign power. Instead, the image that emerges is one of a chronically alienated and disloyal population goaded into action by economic distress. Verses composed in the aftermath of a skirmish that took place at Newmarket, County Kilkenny, on 29 September 1764 in which eight civilians and two soldiers were killed leave no doubt that a sense of abandonment by the Catholic powers could coexist with a millenarian belief in the ultimate overthrow of the existing social and political order:

> Ní chreidfinnse ón Phápa, ó shagart ná bráthair
> go bhfuil an Francach nó an Spáinneach ina mbeatha –
> ach níl cabhair dá n-áireamh, agus nár thóga Dia slán iad!
> nó an trua leo na Fir Bhána dá leagan?

[31] Some Reasons against Raising an Army of Roman Catholicks in Ireland, p. 7.
[32] FJ, 9 September 1766; reprinted in Brady (ed.), Catholics and Catholicism, p. 122.
[33] Lecky, A History of Ireland in the Eighteenth Century, II, p. 32.
[34] J.S. Donnelly, 'The Whiteboy movement, 1761–5', IHS 21 (1978), 54.

> *Tá mo shúilse le Máire agus ar chuaigh uainn thar sáile*
> *go mbeimidne lá éigin faoi ghradam –*
> *ár gcampaí go láidir, agus* Light Horse *dá gcarnadh*
> *agus 'hurú' aige Fir Bhána á dtreascairt.*[35]

(I wouldn't believe from the pope, a priest or a friar, that the Frenchman or
Spaniard lives – but we don't count on their help, and may God not save them!
or have they no pity for the Whiteboys who are being felled? My hope is in Mary
and in all who departed from us overseas [the Irish brigades] that we will some
day have status – our camps powerful, with the *Light Horse* falling in heaps and
the Whiteboys hurrooing as they destroy them.)

While a historian of the Whiteboys has argued that the movement's mythical leader, the fairy queen Sadhbh, should not be viewed 'as a symbol of
Ireland in a consciously nationalistic sense',[36] just such a symbol is found
in a lament for Nicholas Sheehy, a priest who was executed at Clonmel in
March 1766 for Whiteboy activities. Addressing Fódla, a female personification of Ireland, the poet Seán Cundún attributed his own wretched
and degraded condition to the effects of foreign oppression:

> *Gur neart namhad ó thriúchaibh caoitheach*
> *le fórsa is feall re cam is éitheach*
> *d'fhúig mo chéadfa gan tromacht céille*
> *is do rinn' donnsa gan leabhar gan léann díom.*[37]

(That it was the power of enemies from foreign regions, by force and treachery,
with deceit and perjury, which left my understanding without the weight of sense,
and made a dunce without books or learning of me.)

The use of Jacobite symbols – white cockades and flags, and the playing of the Jacobite air 'The White Cockade' – has also been noted but
discounted by a modern historian.[38] While a systematic search of Irish
literary manuscripts for material associated with the Whiteboys would be
outside the scope of this work, it is evident that conclusions concerning
the political complexion of the movement cannot be safely grounded on
a study of English-language sources alone.

The summer of 1763 witnessed an outbreak of popular agitation which
began in County Armagh and spread throughout much of south and
mid-Ulster. The 'Oakboy' or 'Hearts of Oak' movement took the form
of mass mobilisations of several hundreds – in some cases thousands –
of people from the lower classes of rural society who congregated at the
homes of members of the gentry and of the Anglican clergy to demand

---

[35] 'Lá Fhéil Michíl an tórraimh aige doras tigh an ósta' in Dáithí Ó hÓgáin (ed.), *Duanaire
Osraíoch* (Dublin, 1980), p. 35.
[36] Donnelly, 'The Whiteboy movement', p. 28.
[37] 'Ag taisteal liom fá smúit im aonar' in RIA Ms. 23 C 5, p. 187.
[38] Donnelly, 'The Whiteboy movement', p. 29.

the reduction of local taxes levied by county grand juries, and the abolition of 'small dues' – the fees for births, marriages and deaths that were payable to the clergy of the established church by persons of all denominations.[39] While Dissenters were heavily involved in this agitation, it was also supported by Catholics, and Art Mac Cumhaigh, an author of Jacobite verse from County Armagh, made a sympathetic reference to the movement in one of his poems.[40] Order was quickly restored on the arrival of troops in the affected areas but the fears aroused by the episode among members of the established church were out of all proportion to the scale of the danger. The speeches delivered by the judges at the Armagh assizes in July 1763 were considered to be of sufficient importance to be published in pamphlet form. Mr Justice Tenison noted that since the time of the Revolution, 'when the liberty of the subject, was thought to be settled on a firm and durable basis', until the outbreak of the Oakboy disturbances, it had never 'entered into the heads of any loyal subjects, that they had a right to rise and redress public grievances, by such violent and tumultuous methods'.[41] The intervention of his colleague on the bench, Mr Justice Robinson, was equally politicised and stressed the necessity for Ireland's constitutional dependence on Great Britain: 'By birth, by education and principles, by all my relations in domestic life, my affections are firmly and warmly engaged to the well-being of this kingdom, which, I am most certain, exists, under God, in its connection with, and constitutional dependence upon, our mother-country, Great Britain.'[42] It is not at all obvious why an agitation directed against local taxes and clerical dues should have prompted appeals for loyalty to Revolution principles and the British connection, neither of which had been called into question by the Oakboys. One plausible explanation is that the leading role of Presbyterians in a movement which also attracted the support of Catholics had raised the spectre of serious divisions within the Protestant bloc – particularly in view of the Oakboys' opposition to the payment of small dues – and that it was the possible consequences of such a division rather than the substance of the Oakboys' demands which caused the most alarm. However apolitical the movement may have been in reality, its opposition to even a minor aspect of the religious establishment seems to have caused nervous Anglicans to

---

[39] For an account of the Oakboy movement, see J.S. Donnelly, 'Hearts of oak, hearts of steel', *Studia Hib.* 21 (1981), pp. 7–22.

[40] '*Tar éis mo shiúil fríd chúigibh Éireann*', lines 79–84, in Ó Fiaich (ed.), *Art Mac Cumhaigh*, p. 120.

[41] Christopher Robinson and Thomas Tenison, *The Respective Charges; Given to the Grand Jury of the County of Armagh, at the General Assizes Held there, July 23, 1763* (Dublin, 1763), p. 13.

[42] *Ibid.*, p. 33.

question the loyalty of the Presbyterian community. In 1771, eight years after the suppression of the Oakboys, a pro-administration pamphleteer cited the agitation in support of the argument that a militia could not be safely established anywhere in Ireland: in the three southern provinces Protestants were too thin on the ground, and in Ulster they were mostly Dissenters of doubtful reliability.[43]

The American stamp act

Parallels were drawn between the position of the American colonies and that of Ireland from the beginning of the stamp act dispute. As early as March 1765 William Hamilton, who had been chief secretary to the lord lieutenant until the previous year, wrote to Edmund Sexton Pery to reassure the Irish MP that 'there is not at present, whatever there may be in prospect, the faintest idea of taxing Ireland by authority of the British legislature'. He explained how such an erroneous idea had arisen:

When the proposal for imposing a stamp duty in America was first made, Alderman Beckford, the Dr. Lucas of the English House of Commons, apprehended he should increase considerably the number of opponents to that measure, if he could contrive to convey an impression that the taxation of America was not desired merely for its own sake, but as a preliminary also to the taxation of Ireland.[44]

Hamilton described the response of the ministry in terms that were intended to reassure his Irish correspondent but which are likely to have had the opposite effect:

both Mr Grenville and Mr Yorke [the attorney general], I profess I thought very unnecessarily, took an opportunity of asserting strongly, and without any reserve, the power of the British legislature to impose taxes upon Ireland. But while they maintained that, in point of mere right, the jurisdiction of the British parliament was the same over Ireland as it was over America, they not only admitted but explained very much at large that in point of policy and propriety they were very different questions.[45]

Reports of developments in America began to appear regularly in the Irish press from this time and the treatment of events in most publications was dispassionate and even-handed, tending to consist of factual accounts with a minimum of partisan commentary. The arguments employed on both sides of the question contained few novelties for an Irish audience. From the assertion by Francis Bernard, governor of Massachusetts, that in an empire 'extended and diversified as that of Great Britain, there must be a supreme legislature, to which all other powers must be subordinate'

---

[43] [Sir James Caldwell], *An Address to the House of Commons of Ireland* (Dublin, 1771), p. 28.
[44] Hamilton to Pery, 7 March 1765, in HMC Emly Mss., p. 190.   [45] *Ibid.*

on the one hand, to the resolution of the Pennsylvania assembly that it was 'the indubitable privilege of every British subject, to be taxed only by his own consent, or that of his legal representatives' on the other, Irish readers had heard it before.[46]

If colonial polemics contained little that was original, some of the events unfolding in America were more remarkable. The 'resolves' of the Virginia House of Burgesses which condemned the taxation of the colony in the British parliament as 'illegal, unconstitutional and unjust' and as having 'a manifest tendency to destroy British, as well as American freedom' galvanised opposition to the stamp act throughout North America but are unlikely to have raised many eyebrows in Ireland. However, the same letter that furnished readers of the *Freeman's Journal*, the leading opposition organ, with the text of the Virginia resolves also reported that an offended governor had reacted by dissolving the colony's assembly – an exercise of the royal prerogative that had no parallel in Ireland since Lord Sidney's prorogation of parliament in 1692.[47] If this development was a cause of concern for Irish patriots, readers of the solidly pro-administration *Faulkner's Dublin Journal* may have been equally disturbed by reports that merchants were preparing to leave New York and New England because of the 'anarchy and devastation, which was universally expected to result from the licentiousness of the populace'.[48] The rapid growth and success of the non-importation movement in the colonies was even more striking. As early as January 1766 it was reported that English manufacturers were beginning 'greatly to feel the effects' of the American action.[49] By February the value of duties lost to the crown through the interruption of trade with America was estimated at £120,000 and the Irish press was already beginning to anticipate the repeal of the stamp act.[50] Although the act's repeal in March was greeted with demonstrations of joy in London, the event appears to have passed off without any overt display of public interest in Ireland.

This indifference may have been partly the result of restrictions placed on Irish trade with the colonies by British legislation, but – as will be seen below – it may also have been partly due to the distraction occasioned by a constitutional dispute of domestic origin. In addition, it should be noted that some American propagandists had shown little regard for the sensibilities of the Anglo-Irish political nation. James Otis, in a pamphlet entitled *The Rights of the British Colonies Asserted and Proved* which was first published at Boston in 1764, contrasted Ireland's constitutional position unfavourably with that of the colonies: 'I am aware

[46] *BNL*, 17 September 1765, and *FDJ*, 7 December 1765, respectively. For comparable statements in an Irish context, see pages 21 and 24 above.
[47] *FJ*, 26 October 1765. [48] *FDJ*, 16 November 1765. [49] *Ibid.*, 18 January 1766.
[50] *Ibid.*, 25 and 11 February 1766 respectively.

it will be objected, that the parliament of England, and of Great-Britain, since the Union, have from early days to this time, made acts to bind if not to tax Ireland: I answer, Ireland is a *conquered* country.'[51] However convenient this argument may have been from an American perspective, it ran counter to what was now the preferred self-image of the Irish political nation as ever-loyal colonists who had prevailed over rebellious natives – with some assistance from the mother country – in 1691.

The corn export bill

Despite such differences in perspective, the Irish opposition displayed its sympathy for the American patriots when a new constitutional dispute arose at the end of 1765. Because of a threatened famine the House of Commons adopted the heads of a bill to prohibit the exportation of grain. A clause gave the Irish Privy Council the right to suspend the embargo should the food shortage ease but when the bill returned from England it was found to have been amended to give the same suspending power to the *British* Privy Council. Charles Lucas was quick to denounce the proposed transfer of 'the executive or the dispensing power from this kingdom, to that of Great Britain'[52] and to deny the right of either the Irish or British Councils 'to alter any bill or heads of a bill sent from either house of parliament in this kingdom, for the king's sanction in England'.[53] In Lucas's view, the return of the amended bill from England had presented the Irish parliament with a 'horrid alternative, famine or the subversion of our constitution'.[54] He placed this ministerial attack on the Irish constitution in the context of a wider conspiracy that had first attacked the liberties of the American colonists:

The refugees who fled from the horrid lawless oppressions of the detested Stuart race, to the inhospitable wilds and deserts of America, after obtaining the fullest assurances of the sanction and protection of a British constitution transplanted to those colonies, have of late had those badges of slavery fixed upon them, which their wise and free ancestors formerly fled from in England. Though a Britannic constitution and laws had been granted them, they are now fatally bound by laws, to which they neither did, nor could assent or consent. And when by such means, the asylum for the oppressed in this or the neighbouring kingdom was thus cut off in America; Ireland was avowedly and openly threatened with the like measures by the same hand.[55]

The pages of the *Freeman's Journal* reveal the extent to which Lucas's argument struck a chord with the population of Dublin, with one guild after

---

[51] James Otis, *The Rights of the British Colonies Asserted and Proved* (London, 1765), p. 65.
[52] Charles Lucas, *To the Right Honourable the Lord-Mayor, the Alderman, Sheriffs, Commons, Citizens, and Freeholders of Dublin* (Dublin, 1765), p. 8.
[53] *Ibid.*, p. 13.   [54] *Ibid.*, p. 12.   [55] *Ibid.*, p. 6.

another adopting resolutions in support of his stance on the corn export bill. During the months of December 1765 and January 1766, the cutlers, saddlers, weavers, barbers, joiners, carpenters, brewers, chandlers, vintners, shoemakers, hosiers, merchants, goldsmiths, smiths, butchers and bricklayers all publicly declared their support.[56] Such sentiments were not confined to the capital. The corporation of Ennis in Lucas's native county of Clare conferred the freedom of the borough on him, describing the honour as one of 'the manifold marks of applause which a conduct uniformly patriotic has so long merited'.[57] In Dublin, the important guild of merchants, as well as commending Lucas, also conferred its freedom on Henry Flood, the rising star of the patriot party in parliament, for having 'exerted the utmost force of eloquence and argument in maintaining our most gracious sovereign's sole and undoubted right of exercising, as king of Ireland, the executive power constitutionally lodged in his Majesty's hands, by his viceregents and Privy Council of this realm, without consulting or advising with his Privy Council of Great Britain'.[58] However disingenuous this and similar declarations of zeal for the defence of the prerogatives of the Irish crown against encroachments by the British Privy Council may appear, they anticipated the subsequent enthusiasm of American patriots for defending the prerogatives of the crown even as they rejected the claims of the crown in parliament to legislate for the colonies.[59] But the position of the Anglo-Irish patriots was the more advanced: when an American patriot asserted in 1774 that 'the only dependency which [the colonies] ought to acknowledge is a dependency on the crown', the crown he referred to was the British crown, not a distinct imperial crown in a mere personal union with that of Great Britain.[60]

The controversy continued unabated even after the amended corn export bill became law, fuelled by continuing criticism of Lucas by supporters of the administration. The patriots' success in exciting the interest of the public was acknowledged by one ministerial writer who explained that he took up his pen because opposition pamphleteers had caused 'more dissatisfaction and uneasinesses than any real friend to society would wish to see'.[61] A personalised attack on Lucas in another anonymous pamphlet

---

[56] *FJ*, 31 December 1765; 4, 11, 14, 18, 21, 25 and 28 January 1766.
[57] *Ibid.*, 1 February 1766.   [58] *Ibid.*, 18 January 1766.
[59] For American examples of this genre, all dating from 1771 or later, see Bernard Bailyn, *The Ideological Origins of the American Revolution*, second edition (Cambridge, Mass. and London, 1992), pp. 221–5 and Theodore Draper, *A Struggle for Power: The American Revolution* (London, 1996), pp. 381–6.
[60] James Iredell, *Address to the Inhabitants of Great Britain* (n.p., 1774), quoted in Bailyn, *Ideological Origins*, p. 225.
[61] *The Case Fairly Stated, Relative to an Act Lately Passed in this Kingdom against the Exportation of Corn* (Dublin, 1766), p. 3.

is indicative of the resentment aroused by his action in appealing 'out of doors' to the general public:

If a majority do not coincide with the opinion of a single member, he must no longer endeavour to do his duty, in speaking and acting agreeable to his judgment and conscience in the House; but must turn *author*, and communicate his sentiments to the people at large, that every one may pass his and her opinion upon the propriety of parliamentary measures and national affairs; and that every cobbler, butcher, tinker, and coal-heaver may be enabled to dispute on ways and means, Poynings' law, liberty and property, patriotism and public spirit, and such like topics; as the popular and patriotic Charles Lucas, M.D. used to do in the celebrated atheistical and deistical society of the Robin-Hood, in the Butcher Row, London, when he was banished his country.[62]

Pro-government writers countered patriot objections to the suspending power that had been given to the British Council by arguing that the Irish parliament was free to delegate its powers to any individual or body within or without the kingdom as it saw fit. This line of reasoning in turn obliged opposition writers to deny the sovereignty of the crown in parliament – even that of the Irish crown in the Irish parliament. One anonymous patriot took issue with Sir James Taylor, the lord mayor of Dublin and a supporter of the amended corn bill, in the following forthright manner:

Is an act of parliament omnipotent? Can it overturn the established constitution of the nation? Is not all the power, pre-eminence, privilege and authority possessed by parliament, derived from and held in trust for the people? Can they forfeit that trust? Are they not delegates, and can they delegate or share their power or authority? Can they abolish the institution of parliaments, and set up anarchy or tyranny?[63]

Essentially the same point was made by Charles Lucas in the second of three addresses which he published during the corn-bill controversy:

The whole parliamentary power, in all its estates and branches, is derived from, and held in trust for those, who instituted parliaments, and established the national constitution, before parliaments were framed or thought of. Those undoubtedly were the people, the origin of all power and authority... But by Poynings's law, the legislature shared, transferred, and in effect, alienated their delegated power and authority.[64]

---

[62] *A Letter to Charles Lucas, M.D. Relative to the Annual Stipend of Three Hundred and Sixty-five Pounds, Proposed to be Paid him, during the City's Pleasure* (Dublin, n.d. – 1766?), p. 6. The Robin Hood Society was subsequently noted for the pro-American views of its members, see John Sainsbury, *Disaffected Patriots: London Supporters of Revolutionary America 1769–1782* (Montreal and Gloucester, 1987), pp. 23–4.

[63] *An Answer to the Counter Address of a Pretended Free-Citizen* (Dublin, 1766), p. 9.

[64] Charles Lucas, *A Second Address to the Right Hon. the Lord Mayor, the Aldermen, Sheriffs, Commons, Citizens, and Freeholders of the City of Dublin* (Dublin, 1766), pp. 9–10.

Irish patriots were familiar with American attacks on the doctrine of parliamentary sovereignty. In January 1766, for example, while the corn bill controversy was at its most intense, the *Freeman's Journal* printed the reply of the Massachusetts assembly to Governor Bernard's opening speech. The assembly asserted that the colonists had rights 'belonging to the people, which the parliament itself cannot divest them of, consistent with their own constitution: among these is the right of representation in the same body which exercises the power of taxation'.[65] Both American and Anglo-Irish patriots rejected the theory of the sovereignty of the crown in parliament, but the position of the Anglo-Irish was the more radical in two respects: first, because they sought to limit the legislative competence, not of a distant parliament in which they were unrepresented, but of the Irish parliament itself; second, because implicit in their rejection of the suspending power conferred on the British Privy Council – a power which they readily accepted when it was conferred on the Irish Privy Council – was the principle that the two kingdoms were not merely separate, but equal. This outlook can be clearly seen in a rhetorical question posed by Charles Lucas:

How would the British subjects like having orders conceived to rule them in the Council of Hanover, when some of our kings resided in that part of their dominions? or by orders made in the Council of Ireland, if his Majesty should reside in this kingdom? These I shall leave to the cool reflection of... the reader, without offering any answer of mine own.[66]

This assertion of Ireland's constitutional parity with Great Britain was considerably in advance of contemporary American thinking which still sought only to exclude the British parliament from the internal affairs of the colonies while accepting its superintending role in matters of imperial concern such as trade and defence. Thus the stamp act congress of October 1765 acknowledged that the colonies owed 'all due subordination to that august body the parliament of Great Britain' without attempting to define precisely what was encompassed by the term 'due subordination'.[67] In contrast, the position adopted by the patriot opposition during the corn bill dispute showed that a new stage had been reached in the evolution of Anglo-Irish patriotism. While recognition of the Irish parliament's exclusive power of legislation would have effected a real change in the condition of the country by, for example, abolishing the restrictions imposed on Irish trade by British legislation, it could be of no practical concern whether orders were made in the British or the Irish

[65] *FJ*, 4 January 1766.
[66] Lucas, *A Second Address to the Right Hon. the Lord Mayor*, p. 27.
[67] Draper, *A Struggle for Power*, p. 268.

Privy Council as both were organs of the same executive. The issue was of symbolic importance and its ability to arouse popular interest indicates that, for a substantial section of the Anglo-Irish community, the assertion of the constitutional equality of the two kingdoms no longer was merely a *means* of securing the rights of Englishmen but had become an *end* in itself. This new position was an unacknowledged reversion to the constitutional views of the Catholic Confederates of the 1640s and of the Jacobite parliament of 1689.

Augmentation of the army

The attention given to American events in the Irish press declined once the stamp act was repealed in March 1766 and the concerns of the Irish opposition were further assuaged by the formation of the Chatham ministry in July of the same year. A pamphlet published in London but evidently intended for an Irish audience claimed that Chatham, by his opposition to the stamp act, had 'shown himself to be a watchful guardian of the liberties and properties of even the most insignificant appendages of Great Britain'.[68] Had the attempts of the Grenville ministry to tax America succeeded, similar measures would surely have followed in Ireland:

if it was possible, that this spirited people [the Americans] could have been brought to have submitted to this unconstitutional measure, it would have led, in all human probability, to the like attempt upon the kingdom of Ireland: For it has been thrown out, during a certain administration, in a certain assembly, that Ireland was no more than a colony; that it might be taxed without its consent; that it was a dependent country.[69]

The new administration had, in fact, decided to make a major change in the government of Ireland: the lord lieutenant would in future be required to reside in the country permanently and not merely during the biennial sessions of parliament. This measure was designed to undercut the power and patronage of the established factional interests in the Irish parliament and was conceived as part of Chatham's wider policy of abolishing party divisions – 'measures not men'. The pamphlet quoted from above confidently predicted that a limitation bill and a habeas corpus bill would be promoted by Lord Bristol, the new lord lieutenant, and more tentatively suggested the possibility of a place bill, a qualification bill, a militia bill, a relaxation of restrictions on the export of woollen goods, and the appointment of judges during good behaviour – all measures which

---

[68] *A Letter to the Right Honourable J[ohn] P[onsonby], S[peake]r of the H[ous]e of C[ommon]s in I[relan]d*, third edition (London, 1767), p. 22.
[69] *Ibid.*

had been advocated by the patriot opposition. Irish patriots were urged to 'profit of this tide of pleasing circumstances, while there is a patriot king upon the throne, a patriot minister at the helm, and a patriot lord lieutenant, three of the greatest phaenomenons that ever appeared'.[70]

The moment quickly passed. Chatham's nervous collapse was followed by the resignation of his protégé, Bristol, in August 1767 – before he had set foot in Ireland. The post was immediately offered to Lord George Townshend, brother of Charles Townshend – the chancellor of the exchequer who three months earlier had introduced duties on a range of imports to the American colonies. The new chief governor could not possibly have been described as a 'patriot lord lieutenant'. He was, on the contrary, a close associate of the patriots' *bête noire*, Lord Bute, whom he described as 'the first friend I ever met with in public life'.[71] He appointed Bute's son-in-law, George Macartney, to the important position of chief secretary and continued to correspond with Bute after his appointment as lord lieutenant, advising him that his aim would be to 'suppress the rage of factionalism' in Ireland.[72] George Townshend was also a close political ally of his brother, Charles, to whom he owed his appointment. None the less, the new lord lieutenant enjoyed a brief political honeymoon following his arrival in Ireland. A promise in the king's speech of official support for a bill to appoint judges during good behaviour won Townshend some early popularity. More important still from a patriot perspective was the return of a septennial bill from England – albeit altered to provide for octennial elections. The patriots' principal organ, the *Freeman's Journal*, exulted:

Let the grateful people all rejoice while George sways the sceptre of these heaven-favoured realms and Townshend truly represents the sovereign of this isle. We must now be convinced, though against long-rooted suspicions, that the councils of a neighbouring kingdom begin to consider us in a light different from what we too long apprehended. They now look upon us as a part of themselves. They judge we should be free.[73]

This atmosphere of goodwill did not last for long. The judges bill was returned from England with an additional clause permitting the removal of judges on the address of both houses of the *British* parliament – the heads had provided for the removal of judges on the address of both houses of the Irish parliament and the advice of the Irish Privy Council. The amendment implied that the kingdom of Ireland was constitutionally subordinate to Great Britain and raised the prospect of another patriotic

---

[70] *Ibid.*, p. 42.
[71] Townshend to Bute, 2 January 1770. Quoted in Thomas Bartlett, 'The Townshend viceroyalty 1767–72' (PhD thesis, QUB, 1976), p. 50.
[72] Townshend to Bute, 9 July 1768, *ibid.*, p. 50.   [73] *FJ*, 11 February 1768.

agitation along similar lines to that of the corn export bill. Parliamentary managers moved to nip the controversy in the bud and the bill was rejected without a division on 13 May 1768, but the episode had raised patriot hopes only to dash them.

A more serious conflict between the executive and the opposition was occasioned by a proposal to increase the number of troops on the Irish establishment from 12,000, a maximum figure that had been fixed by an English act in the reign of William III, to more than 15,000. This proposal was inspired by a desire to bring the smaller Irish regiments up to the same strength as British regiments, thereby facilitating the rotation of units throughout the empire. Although the garrison in Ireland had been reinforced at times of crisis by a militia, this local force had been allowed to atrophy after the end of the Seven Years War and the proposed augmentation was a signal for the opposition to demand its revival as a 'constitutional' alternative to that great bugbear of patriots in all parts of the British empire, a standing army: 'There can be no real security, no safe limitation of monarchy, where the sword is not held by the people; and although the people have the power of granting money, where there is a large standing army kept up in time of peace, it is it that properly holds the purse; for how can the people unarmed, defend it?'[74]

By this time American affairs had returned to prominence in the Irish press. The *Freeman's Journal* began serialising John Dickinson's *Letters from a Farmer in Pennsylvania, to the Inhabitants of the British Colonies* in January 1768, and attention increasingly focused on colonial opposition to the Townshend duties and the growth of a new non-importation movement. On the other hand, the resistance of the New York legislature to the 1765 quartering act does not appear to have been a factor in inspiring opposition to the proposed augmentation of the army in Ireland, although one patriot pamphlet characterised the latter as an attempt 'to put this kingdom in the meanest light of subjection, to make us worse than the little charter governments of America' – wording which suggests scant respect for the colonial legislatures.[75] A series of letters purporting to be from a correspondent in Ireland to his friend in Pennsylvania that appeared in the *Freeman's Journal* from January 1768 onwards portrayed Ireland as a laboratory for new experiments in ministerial despotism:

You are, happily, at too great a distance from ministerial tyranny, to fall an immediate sacrifice to the politics of despotism; therefore, the essay has been commenced nearer home. We have been treated, of late, not as the *children*, but the

---

[74] [Sir Charles Bingham], *An Essay on the Use and Necessity of Establishing a Militia in Ireland, and Some Hints towards a Plan for that Purpose* (Dublin, 1767), p. 12.

[75] *Considerations on the Present State of the Military Establishment of this Kingdom, Addressed to the Knights, Citizens, Burgesses of Ireland in Parliament Assembled* (Dublin, 1768), p. 42.

bastards of our mother country; and all our expectations of an equal distribution of inheritance, are considered, not as claims of right, but as pretences of contumacy, and presumption. Your circumstances, and ours, then, being exactly the same, the difference of our situations can possibly gain you but the poor respite of Ulysses's petition to Polyphemus, of being devoured the last.[76]

The Irish opposition evidently felt that it had little to learn from the American. Consequently, domestic issues dominated the pamphlet debate on the question. While Charles Lucas sought to link military augmentation with the patriots' most notable success to date by arguing that 'standing parliaments and standing armies have ever proved the most dangerous enemies to civil liberty',[77] supporters of the proposal played on fears of a different kind by reminding the members of the political nation of their uniquely vulnerable position as a comparatively small minority living among a disloyal population:

The number of her [England's] people constitute her national strength... It is an invidious task to enlarge upon the very different circumstances of our own country... circumstances which all tend to invite an enemy to attack Ireland, preferable to any part of the British dominions, if they had hopes of finding us unprepared to receive them; and doubtless we have every reason to expect that they would meet with assistance from our own discontented and disaffected fellow subjects.[78]

The Irish regiments in the armies of the Bourbon powers were referred to in support of the contention that a reversal of the Revolution settlement was still possible:

Men born and educated in every province, in every town, in every corner and spot of this island, are to be found in the dominions and under the allegiance of France and Spain... Ireland they still consider as their natural inheritance, and the claim of original possession is transmitted amongst them from generation to generation. To revisit the land of their forefathers, and to enjoy again the property they have forfeited, is the favourite topic of their discourses, and the object ever present to their hopes... Innovators and robbers are the characters we are described under; and, as such, should the fatal opportunity happen, we must expect to be treated.[79]

Irish political and demographic realities were such that a large standing army, which might indeed pose a threat to liberty in other circumstances, was essential for the very existence of a Protestant state in Ireland. The

---

[76] *FJ*, 16 January 1768.
[77] Charles Lucas, *To the Right Honorable the Lord Mayor... upon the Proposed Augmentation of the Military Establishment* (Dublin, 1768), p. 36.
[78] *Reasons for an Augmentation of the Army on the Irish Establishment, Offered to the Consideration of the Public* (Dublin, 1768), p. 12.
[79] *Considerations upon the Augmentation of the Army. Address'd to the Publick* (Dublin, 1768), pp. 12–14.

same considerations rendered the formation of a militia, the favoured project of the patriot opposition, impracticable under Irish conditions:

> Whatever may be the case in Great Britain, it is otherwise in Ireland; our properties and our lives demand security here as much as our liberties; and of two dangers, that which is the most pressing and urgent requires our attention before that which is more remote. We cannot spare our Protestants from our manufactures in sufficient numbers to form a well regulated militia.[80]

The opposition could not convincingly refute such arguments, but they proved to be even more successful than the administration had intended.

Concerned that augmentation of the army would merely facilitate the withdrawal of regiments from Ireland for service overseas, parliamentarians who were disposed to support government measures sought assurances that the number of troops remaining in the country would not be reduced below 12,000 unless an invasion or rebellion took place in Britain itself. In the absence of such an assurance, patriots who advocated a militia, and independent country gentlemen who opposed a larger army on financial grounds, were joined in opposition by members who were fearful that augmentation might be a prelude to redeployment of much of the Irish garrison overseas and the Commons narrowly rejected the proposed augmentation by 105 votes to 101 on 2 May 1768. Before the end of the month, parliament was dissolved under the terms of the octennial act. The administration had been frustrated in one of its principal aims, but it had been defeated by a temporary coalition in which patriots were a minority. Two regiments were transferred from Ireland to America during the summer of 1768 and reports of conflict between the military and the residents of Boston appeared in the Irish press during 1769, but the administration's belated agreement that a force of 12,000 men would be permanently stationed in Ireland allayed fears sufficiently to ensure the passage of a revised augmentation bill by a large majority when it came before the new parliament in October 1769.[81] The low priority attached to America by the opposition at this comparatively late date is evident from the protest against the bill entered in the journal of the House of Lords. The protesting lords gave priority to the dangers that a standing army posed for the liberty of the subject and the undue expense of an enlarged military establishment, and relegated the American dimension to eighth place in their list of objections: 'Because, from an use that was made of a part of the Irish army in North America, immediately after

---

[80] *Some Impartial Observations on the Proposed Augmentation* (Dublin, 1768), p. 7.

[81] For reports of military misbehaviour in Boston and exchanges between the Massachusetts assembly and governor on the stationing of military in the town, see *FJ*, 18 March, 22 July and 29 August 1769.

the late proposal of an augmentation, we are apprehensive of a design of administration, extremely injurious to the great commercial interests of the British empire.'[82]

The evolution of Catholic opinion

In order to secure parliamentary approval for the augmentation of the army Lord Townshend's administration had emphasised the military threat to the political and religious establishment posed by Catholics – as enemies of the Protestant interest who had 'always been so ready to show themselves, when they have had any foreign assistance to support them'.[83] However, pro-administration writers were careful to give some recognition to the recently developed loyalty of Catholics from the higher social strata, even as they stressed the implacable hostility of the bulk of the Catholic population:

In the first place the French are all apprised that the lower class of the Roman Catholics in Ireland, which out-number the Protestants at least three to one, would join and support them with the utmost alacrity and joy, at the same time they must with the greatest reason be convinced, that the most sensible of the titular bishops and priests, as well as the Roman Catholics of landed interest and in trade, would be most averse to any attempt made by the French to distress this their native country.[84]

This statement was an accurate reflection of official thinking on the critical question of Catholic loyalty. In a memorandum which he drafted in 1770 when war with Spain appeared imminent, Lord Townshend wrote that the security of the three southern provinces had, until the recent augmentation of the army, depended upon two factors: 'the constant protection of the British fleet and the submission of the wealthy Roman Catholics to his Majesty's government'. None the less, the lord lieutenant harboured no illusions about the sympathies of the Catholic population as a whole in the event of war: he described the Bourbon powers as 'a restless enemy in constant correspondence with the disinherited and bigoted inhabitants of their own religion' and noted the existence in Cork and Kerry of the 'remains of the old popish clans who keep up a constant correspondence with France and Spain for smuggling for recruits and for our deserters'.[85] This was an essentially accurate picture that took account of the caution and political evolution of the Catholic élite while recognising the underlying problem of popular disaffection.

---

[82] *A Collection of the Protests of the Lords of Ireland, from 1634 to 1771* (Dublin, 1772), p. 102.
[83] *Reasons for an Augmentation of the Army*, p. 12.
[84] [Sir James Caldwell], *An Address to the House of Commons of Ireland*, p. 10.
[85] Memo by Townshend dated 16 October 1770, BL Add. Ms. 33,118, fos. 2r, 5v, 13r.

The death of James III, the Stuart pretender, in 1766 and the refusal of the papacy to recognise his son as *de jure* king of Ireland freed members of the Catholic clergy to recognise the legitimacy of George III's title to the crown. Press reports noted that prayers were offered for the royal family in some dioceses – indicating both the novelty of such events and the change that was taking place in clerical attitudes.[86] But it should not be imagined that either the example of the Roman court or exhortations from the pulpit transformed the deep-seated political outlook of the wider Catholic community. Prince Charles Edward had long occupied a more prominent place than his father in popular consciousness, and the authors of vernacular verse did not hesitate to acclaim him as king. The transfer of allegiance from the Old to the Young Pretender is attested by an anonymous Munster song associated with the Whiteboys:

> *Rachmas is sástacht ar mórmhuir is ar bhánchnoic,*
> *is is suairc linn a ngártha is a misneach;*
> *níl luascadh air aon árthach ná buaireamh san lá so,*
> *ó chuan Cheanna tSáile go Doire;*
> *is buacach na blátha go fuadrach ag fásadh,*
> *ar dhualladh na mbánta gan mhilleadh,*
> *le huaill is le háthas na mBuachaillí Bána,*
> *faoi thuairim Rí Seárlas go dtiocfadh.*[87]

(There's plenty and contentment on the wide sea and the bright hillsides, and joyous to us are their shouts and their courage, no vessels are tossed and this day is untroubled, from the harbour of Kinsale to Derry; sprightly are the flowers which are vigorously growing, unspoiled on the sward of the meadows, because of the cries and delight of the Whiteboys at the thought that King Charles [III] will come.)

A poem composed by the County Armagh poet Art Mac Cumhaigh sometime between 1767 and 1771 provides comparatively rare literary evidence of popular Catholic sentiment in Ulster, and its agreement with the attitudes expressed by southern authors is striking. Mac Cumhaigh's work takes the form of a dialogue between a medieval Catholic ruin and a newly built Protestant church. The latter speaks in English in some versions of the text:

> In Hibernia fair and Scotland we reign,
>   in England and great Hanover,
> and what need we care for France or for Spain,
>   or Charley that rakish rover.[88]

---

[86] See *FLJ*, 9 January 1768 and *FJ*, 6 February 1768; reprinted in Brady (ed.), *Catholics and Catholicism*, pp. 129–30.

[87] '*Rachmas is sástacht ar mórmhuir is ar bhánchnoic*' in RIA Ms. 23 O 77, fo. 46. The song is quoted more fully in Ó Buachalla, *Aisling Ghéar*, p. 634.

[88] '*Eadar Foirceal na cléire is Fochairt na nGael*' in RIA Ms. 23 L 7, p. 254; edited in Énrí Ó Muirgheasa, *Dánta Diadha Uladh* (Dublin, 1936).

The ruined Catholic church, which speaks in Irish in all versions of the work, responds to its modern rival as follows:

> *Níl gar damh bheith 'dréim le creideamh gan chéill,*
> *nach ngabhann uaim scéal nó comhairle,*
> *nó go dtiocfaidh na méir do chonairc an tréan*
> *Baltasar ar thaobh a lóistín,*
> *'s do mhionnaigh dhuit féin 'réir cuirthe mo scéil*
> *gurbh easpaí an* beagle *Seórsa,*
> *is ar bheartaibh Mhic Dé, nár mhairidh sé i gcéim,*
> *nó go gcuirfidh Rí Séarlas brón air.*[89]

(It's futile for me to contend with a senseless religion, that will accept no report or advice from me, until the fingers appear which were seen by the mighty one, Belshazzar on the side of his dwelling, and affirm to you according to the statement of my story, that George [III] was a needy hound, and by the deeds of God's Son, may he not live in pomp, but may King Charles [III] plunge him into sorrow.)

The image of south Ulster which emerges from such compositions is of a society divided into two coherent and antagonistic blocs – the one Protestant, English-speaking and loyal to the existing political order; the other Catholic, Irish-speaking and resolutely unreconciled to the post-Revolution establishment. A similar situation pertained in north Leinster which formed part of the same cultural province. In Kells, County Meath, more than a hundred people wearing the Jacobite white rose assembled behind a fiddler and 'paraded through the town' on 12 July 1772 when the anniversary of the battle of the Boyne happened to fall on a Sunday. The crowd verbally and physically abused some persons 'whom they deemed not of their profession', prompting the town's corporation and a local landlord to offer substantial rewards for information leading to the arrest of the culprits.[90]

Catholics were aware of patriot criticisms of George III's supposed absolutist tendencies and some elements of the patriots' critique were suitable for incorporation in Jacobite propaganda. Thus Conchubhar Ó Ríordáin, a County Cork schoolmaster, recycled allegations of an adulterous liaison between Lord Bute and the dowager Princess of Wales that may have originated with supporters of John Wilkes.[91] On a real or imagined visit to London, Ó Ríordáin noticed the conjoined images of Hibernia and Britannia on the sign over a tavern and engaged the former in conversation, entreating her to return home with him and to take

---

[89] *Ibid.* For the biblical reference, see Daniel 5:5.   [90] *HM*, August 1772, 456.
[91] For the background to the allegations, see John Brewer, 'The misfortunes of Lord Bute: a case-study in eighteenth-century political argument and public opinion', *Hist. Jn.* 16 (1973).

'*an prionsa ceart chugat i gceannas céile*' ('the true prince to you in wedded
authority'). The following is part of their dialogue:

The poet:
Seo an chúis fá deara dhúinne teacht tar tonntaibh mara ad éileamh,
ag tnúth tú chasadh chuchu abhaile id dhúthaigh chneasta féinig,
a rúin mo scart ná diúltaigh teacht is is umhal do gheobhair géilleadh,
is cé hiomaí fear do dhlúthaigh leat sa drúis ná meas gur baol duit.
Hibernia:
An chúis do chasais liom le fala chugam mar scanaill shaolta,
d'iompaigh beart dá shúirt isteach san chúirt i measc a mbéithe,
atá ár siúir dá dhamnú le dearbhú is liom ná meastar bréagach,
i Londain gheobhair ciontach acu Bute is an ainnir aosta.[92]

(This is the reason for our journey over the billowing sea to claim you, in the hope
of taking you back home to them in your own kindly land. O love of my heart
don't refuse to come and humbly you'll be deferred to, and though many a man
has coupled with you in lust don't think you're in danger.

The charge you've brought against me from spite, approaching me like a public
scandal, a caper of that sort took place in the court amongst their ladies. Our sister
[Britannia] condemns it on oath, and may it not be thought false by me, in London
you'll find they've convicted Bute and the old girl.)

Salacious rumours have always had an appreciative audience, but patriot
paranoia about Bute's influence 'behind the curtain' could hold little interest for plebeian Catholics who were politicised in the world-view of
Irish Jacobitism – a view which regarded George III as a usurper and
assumed the constant malevolence of England towards Ireland. Their
own differences with the régime were at once deeper than, and profoundly different from, those of patriots throughout the English-speaking
world.

In sharp contrast to such expressions of popular alienation from the political establishment, the pro-government sympathies expressed by members of the Catholic élite became more pronounced after 1766. James
Hoey, printer to the Catholic Committee in Dublin, was also, from 1766,
publisher of the *Dublin Mercury* – a newspaper that catered for an élite
Catholic readership and was outspoken in its support for the administrations in Dublin and London. This unusual perspective could result in
unlikely juxtapositions in the columns of the paper. While the *Mercury's*
first issue reported the death sentence passed on Fr Nicholas Sheehy without comment, the second contained a report from London endorsing the
government's handling of American opposition to the stamp act:

[92] '*A chúileann tais is clúmhail cneasta múinte blasta béasach*' in RIA Ms. 23 O 26, p. 94;
edited in Ó Muirithe, *Cois an Ghaorthaidh*.

It's imagined that full compensation will be made by the colonies to such persons as have suffered injury or damage by their aiding or assisting in the execution of the American stamp-act; and that the authority of Great Britain to make laws and statutes of sufficient force and validity to bind the British colonies in all cases whatever, will be fully ascertained and acknowledged.[93]

The third issue of Hoey's paper contained news of Prince Charles Edward's declaration of his Catholicism in an interview with three cardinals at Rome.[94] Unequivocal in its support for Lord Townshend's administration, the *Mercury* portrayed the patriot opposition as free-thinkers and republicans – enemies of the establishment in both church and state. The following mock confession was attributed to the publisher of the *Freeman's Journal*, the principal patriot organ:

We set out upon a principle, that religion was priestcraft, and civil government was tyranny. Every man was born free, and has a liberty of doing what he pleases, without any arbitrary restraint of law. We drew all our maxims from Hobbs, Tindal, Toland, Machival, Trenchard and Gordon; and Cromwell was our pattern of heroism. We pretended to be most zealous champions for the present constitution in church and state, though, in reality, we would wish to overturn it, as we are levellers by principle.[95]

For John Curry, likewise, the earl of Shaftesbury, arguably the founding father of the Whig party, was 'a republican by principle' who had been 'deeply engaged in the rebellion against Charles the First', and his campaign to exclude the future James II from the succession was an attempt 'to reduce the British monarchy, to the state of a commonwealth'.[96] Whatever its merits in the abstract, this line of argument can only have strengthened patriots' belief in the Jacobite sympathies of the entire Catholic population. A bias towards the executive and a corresponding hostility towards the opposition characterised the outlook of those Catholics who were willing to accept the existing political order. Charles O'Conor, in a private letter to Curry, detected signs of ministerial goodwill in the lord lieutenant's speech from the throne:

I find a disposition in some to reform old errors if they dared. Can anything tend ... to such an end more than the sense of government in the following lines which you have read? I must recommend 'to your consideration such laws as may be salutary for the benefit of the lower orders of the community, for these have ever been found the most effective means of binding their affections to their

---

[93] *Dublin Mercury*, 22 March 1766.   [94] *Ibid.*, 25 March 1766.
[95] *Ibid.*, 4 February 1769.
[96] [John Curry], *A Parallel between the Pretended Plot in 1762, and the Forgery of Titus Oates in 1679* (Cork, 1767), p. 29.

country and securing their allegiance to one common parent' – Nothing can more plausibly show the good intentions of the executive power.[97]

The expression of such views by members of the Catholic élite would have tended to confirm the patriot opposition in its belief that Catholicism and 'arbitrary government' were inextricably linked. The response of the *Freeman's Journal* to an account of Prince Charles Edward's wedding published by James Hoey in the *Dublin Mercury* underlines the depth of the mistrust that existed between the two groups:

> The great virtues of the Pretender and the Princess of Stolberg, he calls them the most illustrious pair, he declares that they are adored by all ranks of people, and says that foreign courts seem hearty in their cause. Hitherto the writers of Hoey's paper have proved themselves steady adherents to the principles of arbitrary government, and now prove that their ultimate wishes centre in expecting the French, looking for the arrival of the Pretender and his princess, with an undisguised longing for the revival of popery.[98]

Developments in America would further deepen the mutual hostility with which Protestant supporters of the patriot opposition and those Catholics who were anxious to assert their new-found loyalty to the House of Hanover regarded each other.

The money bill dispute

Augmentation of the army had been Lord Townshend's principal object when he arrived in Ireland and he interpreted its rejection by the Commons as a challenge to English authority – a perception that reveals more about the thinking of British ministers than it does about the outlook of members of the Irish parliament. Writing to the prime minister, the Duke of Grafton, Townshend argued that if 'English government loses this opportunity to re-establish itself and is deceived by any specious medium of private gratification and public necessity, it must remain an eternal suitor to the factions of this kingdom in the future course of public business'.[99] At the time, however, government was preoccupied with the repercussions of John Wilkes's election, the St George's Fields 'massacre', and on-going American opposition to the Townshend duties. There was a corresponding lack of enthusiasm for Townshend's proposal

---

[97] O'Conor to Curry, 16 October 1771; in Ward and Ward (eds.), *The Letters of Charles O'Conor of Belanagare*, p. 287.

[98] *FJ*, 17 October 1772.

[99] Townshend to George Macartney, 20 May 1769; quoted in Bartlett, 'The Townshend viceroyalty', p. 128.

to dispense with the services of the parliamentary managers and to build a new ministerial party to be directly managed by the lord lieutenant and the chief secretary – a course which, however attractive it might have been in the longer term, would inevitably have driven the most powerful men in the House of Commons into opposition in the short term. The balance of convenience finally changed in November 1769 when the newly elected House of Commons rejected a government money bill. The bill was one that had been drafted in the Irish Privy Council, certified by the Council and lord lieutenant as being a proper cause for summoning parliament, and agreed in the British Privy Council – a procedure required by Poynings' law before a new parliament could meet. The inclusion of a money bill among those drafted by the Council was regarded by patriots as an infringement of the 'sole right' of the Commons to grant supply. None the less, the money bill would certainly have been accepted by the Commons, as a similar bill had been in 1761, had the main faction leaders not chosen it as a suitable issue on which to demonstrate how essential their support was for the conduct of government business. Amid much patriotic oratory and enthusiasm the Commons rejected the bill because it did not take its rise in the House: 'The moment this latter resolution was proposed, it was received by the House with a degree of ardour that totally precluded deliberation, or debate.'[100] In his report to the secretary of state, Townshend presented the vote as final proof that the opposition intended to 'possess the government of this country and to lower the authority of English government'.[101] Rejection of the money bill persuaded the cabinet to back Townshend's plans to remodel the government of Ireland and firm measures were approved by the king. Townshend entered a protest in the journal of the House of Commons, prorogued parliament, and dismissed office-holders who had opposed the money bill. In the following months he wrested control of the revenue board, the principal source of patronage in Ireland, from the parliamentary leaders.

Opposition reaction to the prorogation was predictable in its general thrust and was grounded on the long-standing claim that the members of the House of Commons 'possess the sole right of originating money bills'.[102] The Commons, and they alone, had the right to tax the people:

[100] *A Letter to Sir L—s O—n, Bart. on the Late Prorogation; and in Answer to his Letter to Mr Faulkner, on the Subject of the Rejected Money-Bill* (Dublin, 1770), p. 12.
[101] Townshend to Weymouth, 21 November 1769; quoted in Bartlett, 'The Townshend viceroyalty', p. 163.
[102] *A Letter to a Noble Lord, in Answer to his Address to the People of Ireland, with some Interesting Reflections on the Present State of Affairs, and a Short Address to Lord T—ns—d* (Dublin, 1770), p. 20.

'If the lieutenant and Council could frame a money bill, and transmit it, previous to the meeting of parliament, they, and not the Commons, would be the givers of that money and the taxers of the people.'[103] But if there was nothing original in the patriots' arguments a new shrillness was evident in their tone: 'the deep laid system of tyranny and oppression is now clearly discerned, and we can now no longer doubt of the plan being formed to reduce this kingdom to the most abject state of subjection and dependence, and annex it as a province to the absolute sway of the British minister'.[104] The lord lieutenant's prorogation of parliament as a sign of official displeasure had no precedent in Ireland since 1692 but it was strikingly similar to the manner in which American governors had dissolved the assemblies of Massachusetts and Virginia in 1768 and 1769 because of their opposition to the Townshend duties. Charles Lucas noted the parallels between events in Ireland and those in America. Under the circumstances, it was not surprising that he reversed the argument of the anonymous author who two years before had predicted that the colonists would enjoy the privilege 'of being devoured the last' by virtue of their remoteness. Instead, Lucas portrayed Ireland as the victim of measures that had already been employed elsewhere and claimed that 'those who have turned the rest of the British Empire topsy-turvy, are come here also'.[105] Ministerial writers made no attempt to mollify the opposition by drawing flattering distinctions between the ancient parliament of the kingdom of Ireland and the 'little charter governments' of America. Instead, questions of constitutional theory were passed over in favour of appeals for prudence in view of Ireland's weak and exposed position:

Is it not an illusion to compare us with the colonies? . . . Have we the same connections with the people of England which the colonies have, to induce them to espouse us? Are we at as great a distance from England as they are? Could we retain in our hands millions of the money of England, until we compelled the doing of that which we would wish to have done?[106]

This was a realistic appraisal of the weakness of the Anglo-Irish opposition. Although the opposition succeeded in mobilising a large and unruly crowd which surrounded parliament on 27 February 1771 under the belief 'that the lord lieutenant had got a great majority, and was

---

[103] [Richard French], *The Constitution of Ireland, and Poynings' Laws Explained* (Dublin, 1770), p. 17.
[104] *A Letter to a Noble Lord*, p. 22.
[105] Charles Lucas, *The Rights and Privileges of Parlements Asserted upon Constitutional Principles* (Dublin, 1770), p. 74.
[106] [Gorges Edmond Howard], *Some Questions upon the Legislative Constitution of Ireland* (Dublin, 1770), p. 18.

going to carry away their parliament',[107] convinced patriots remained a small minority and the widespread mobilisation of the political nation that had been achieved during the 'prior consent' dispute of the 1750s was not repeated on this occasion. Opportunistic opponents of the ministry quickly made their peace with the lord lieutenant as his determination to build a 'castle party', a ministerial bloc that would give him control of the Commons without the need to bargain with the faction leaders, became apparent. By the time parliament reconvened in February 1771 Townshend had constructed a government majority by the judicious use of carrot and stick. The apocalyptic note struck by the *Freeman's Journal* in the same month was hardly coincidental:

Despotism is the idol of the present ministry; to which they mean to sacrifice the birth-right privilege of British subjects: The axe has been already lifted up, in America; England is defiled, with the blood of wounded victims; they are now meditating the fatal blow, against this injured country; and *arbitrary taxation* is the instrument contrived for the fall of liberty, through the whole British empire.[108]

Underlying this dramatic imagery was a realisation of the impotence of Irish patriot opinion.

Patriot opinion and America

As early as 1768 Charles Lucas drew an explicit comparison between the conditions of the colonies and Ireland in an election address. The Americans, 'though intituled to all the rights and privileges of Englishmen', were so oppressed as to have been 'driven from their loyalty and allegiance, for want of the due protection and benefit of the laws' – just as the 'constitution of Ireland, by law equal to that of Britain' was 'in many points invaded and broken'.[109] At that time, however, Lucas still referred to the colonial question in an apologetic manner, explaining that he would not have mentioned the American colonists, 'this brave unfortunate people' as he called them, 'did I not apprehend this kingdom as well as that of England, involved in the fate of the free and loyal subjects of America'.[110] The parallels between Ireland and America were also noted by colonial commentators and some of their writings were

---

[107] Townshend to Rochford, 28 February 1771 in *Calendar of Home Office Papers 1760–1765* (London, 1878), p. 211. See also Séamus Cummins, 'Extra-parliamentary agitation in Dublin in the 1760s' in R.V. Comerford, Mary Cullen, Jacqueline Hill and Colm Lennon (eds.), *Religious Conflict and Coexistence in Ireland* (Dublin, 1990), pp. 131–3.
[108] *FJ*, 21 February 1771.
[109] Charles Lucas, *Seasonable Advice to the Electors of Members of Parlement at the Ensuing General Election*, part II (Dublin, 1768), p. 7.
[110] *Ibid.*, p. 13.

republished in Ireland. For example, the *Freeman's Journal* republished the tenth of John Dickinson's *Letters from a Farmer* in which he urged the inhabitants of the colonies to learn from the misfortunes of others: 'We may perceive by the example of Ireland, how eager ministers are to seize upon any settled revenue, and apply it in supporting their own power.'[111] American recognition of the efforts of Anglo-Irish patriots was reported in the local press. The *Freeman's Journal* noted that the toasts drunk by the members of the Massachusetts House of Representatives on the occasion of the king's birthday in 1769 included one to 'Dr Lucas and the patriots of Ireland'.[112] Further evidence of colonial respect for the most prominent Irish patriot came in March 1770 when a public meeting of the inhabitants of Boston directed that a printed report on 'the late horrid massacre in Boston by the soldiery' be sent to Lucas.[113] The report of the Boston committee was reprinted in Dublin and Lucas's reply was in turn published in the pages of the *Freeman's Journal*. In this, he again pointed to the similarity between American and Irish conditions, assuring the Bostonians that 'as for military execution, your more immediate grievance, it has long been carried to the greatest excess here', but he did not seek to disguise the fact that 'the want of union in religious and political sentiments, among the people of this country, has reconciled them, in a great measure, to military rule'.[114] This was a frank acknowledgement – one which might not have been expected from Lucas – that the precarious position of the Anglo-Irish community, placed as it was among a hostile population that rejected the reigning monarch, the established church, and Ireland's subordination to Great Britain, regarded a strong standing army as a necessary protection for, rather than a threat to, the constitutional status quo. Lucas recognised that there was not the remotest possibility of the Irish parliament's emulating the demand of the Massachusetts assembly for the withdrawal of all land and naval forces from Boston.[115]

Two other members of parliament who were identified with the opposition viewpoint made more reflective and less polemical contributions to the pamphlet literature on the developing American crisis. Hercules Langrishe, in a 1769 pamphlet published anonymously in both Dublin and London, urged Britain to retain control over the colonies' external relations while renouncing all power to tax them or to legislate for their internal affairs: 'keep them dependent in every external relation, but let

---

[111] *FJ*, 27 December 1768.   [112] *Ibid.*, 21 October 1769.
[113] *A Letter from the Town of Boston, to C. Lucas, Esq.* (Dublin, n.d. – 1770?), p. 3.
[114] *FJ*, 19 September 1771.
[115] For the Assembly's address to Governor Bernard see *FJ*, 22 July 1769.

them experience internal liberty, and a security in their acquisitions'.[116] Langrishe argued that the navigation acts alone would be sufficient to ensure a steady transfer of wealth from the colonies to their mother country. He accepted the right of the British parliament to regulate Irish trade in a similar manner, although this may have been a tactical position intended to appeal to a British readership:

Let Ireland and the colonies enjoy every degree of commerce, compatible with the trade of England. – I wish for no more: and their acquisitions, after a progress conferring benefits as they flow, will finally settle in England. – This will result from the natural course of things: if it did not, it might be so directed by the external superintendency and commercial policy of the British legislature. – And this is the utmost extent of taxation, that one people can exercise over another.[117]

Gervase Parker Bushe was the author of a second pamphlet which, while published in both London and Dublin, was addressed to an English audience. The similarity between Bushe's solution and that proposed by Langrishe is striking: 'The Americans must relinquish many rights of property; that is, many rights of *acquiring* property; for they must be subject to British navigation laws, and trade-regulations; but the right of *granting* property, already acquired and vested, should be sacred. This should be theirs, safe and entire.'[118] Both of these authors are likely to have benefited from the advice of a prominent American: when the Connecticut agent in London dined with Benjamin Franklin on 12 May 1769 he found three Irish guests in the company – Bushe, Langrishe, and Lord Mountmorres, one of the lords who had entered a protest against the augmentation of the army.[119] In 1771 Franklin himself made a short trip to Dublin 'to visit some American friends or rather friends of America'.[120] In a letter to James Bowdoin, subsequently a Massachusetts delegate to the first Continental Congress, Franklin remarked on the solidarity of Lucas and Irish patriots generally with the colonists: 'among the patriots I dined with Dr. Lucas. They are all friends of America, in which I said everything I could think of to confirm them.'[121] Franklin gave a similar account of his reception to Thomas Cushing, another Massachusetts delegate to Congress:

---

[116] [Sir Hercules Langrishe], *Considerations on the Dependencies of Great Britain* (London 1769), p. 79.
[117] *Ibid.*, pp. 90–1.
[118] [Gervase Parker Bushe], *The Case of Great Britain and America, Addressed to the King, and Both Houses of Parliament*, third edition (Dublin, 1769), p. 21 (footnote).
[119] J. Bennett Nolan (ed.), *Benjamin Franklin in Scotland and Ireland* (Philadelphia, 1938), p. 132.
[120] Franklin to Jonathan Williams, 25 August 1771, *ibid.*, p. 138.
[121] Franklin to James Bowdoin, 13 January 1772, *ibid.*, p. 148.

Before leaving Ireland I must mention, that, being desirous of seeing the principal patriots there, I stayed till the opening of their parliament. I found them disposed to be friends of America, in which I endeavoured to confirm them, with the expectation that our growing weight might in time be thrown into their scale, and, by joining our interest with theirs might be obtained for them as well as for us, a more equitable treatment from this nation [Britain].[122]

From 1769, the exclusion of John Wilkes from the British House of Commons tended to be conflated in patriot propaganda with American and Irish grievances and to be cited as evidence of a ministerial conspiracy against liberty throughout the empire. The appointment of Colonel Henry Lawes Luttrell (the candidate in the Middlesex election who was declared elected when Wilkes was debarred from taking his seat) to the position of adjutant general on the Irish establishment was interpreted as a further evidence of ministerial perfidy:

Would they [the ministry] over-bear the freedom of election, or over-awe the spirit of liberty in England; he [Luttrell] can be better supported now, than when he appeared their champion at Brentford [where the Middlesex poll was held]: Would they enforce a British tax in America, or the decrees of a Privy Council in Ireland; he cannot hazard fame, or honour, in the enterprise.[123]

In this imperial perspective Ireland was portrayed, not as uniquely oppressed, but as 'equally oppressed with the other parts of the British Empire'. England itself had experienced such outrages as 'The daring violation of the rights of election: The support given to the Brentford ruffians: The massacre in St. George's Fields: The unjust and unconstitutional attacks on the liberty of the press', while the 'arbitrary taxation of our fellow subjects in America ... has drawn on the most spirited associations; a continuance in which must insure them their liberty, against the attempts of a despotic ministry'.[124] One piece of patriotic doggerel characterised Lord Townshend as the 'tool of Lord Bute' and viewed the increasingly serious situation in the American colonies as merely one consequence of a concerted policy that was also being pursued closer to home:

This rascally herd, to the Devil I pitch 'em!
(must we toil, and labour, and sweat, to enrich 'em?)
to serve their own purpose, and mischievous ends,
first strove to enslave our American friends.

Nor even of our brethren of England afraid,
with Star Chamber warrants their rights they invade;
and to bring all their villainous schemes to perfection,
they strike at the root, and the right of election.

---

[122] Franklin to Thomas Cushing, 13 January 1772, *ibid.*, p. 157.
[123] *FJ*, 25 September 1770.   [124] *Ibid.*, 13 October 1770.

And next at poor Ireland they level their blows;
poor Ireland, that still has been led by the nose:
and to shew they resolved both to ruin and fool her,
they send over Townshend, that blockhead, to rule her.[125]

Such allegations, however amplified with local references for an Irish readership, were not of Irish origin; rather, they reflected a belief in the existence of a conspiracy to undermine the British constitution which was widely held in opposition circles in Britain and was perhaps most memorably expressed in Edmund Burke's *Thoughts on the Cause of the Present Discontents* – a pamphlet which went through several Dublin editions in 1770. In America, this conspiracy theory won widespread acceptance and was a major factor in the drift towards war.[126]

In Ireland, by contrast, such ideas failed to diffuse beyond the most committed patriot circles and were easily ridiculed as a product of the overheated imagination of ideologues in thrall to the theories of Gordon, Trenchard, Bolingbroke and Wilkes. One satirical pamphlet had an addle-brained demagogue named Phlogos (from φλόγεος – Greek for 'inflamed' but clearly intended to remind readers of 'Lucas') declare that the sources of his political ideas were 'too numerous to be easily recounted, or indeed recollected; but the most irradiating, whom I would chiefly recommend, are the *Independent Whig, Cato's Letters,* the *Craftsman,* the *North Briton, Junius's Letters'*.[127] Patriot rhetoric was largely confined to the pages of the *Freeman's Journal,* the *Hibernian Journal,* and pamphlets where it was read by the converted. Those members of the opposition who sought the support of the wider political nation found it expedient to emphasise practical reforms rather than the finer points of constitutional theory. When, in October 1773, the Dublin patriots established the Society of Free Citizens (a title inspired by the pen-name of Charles Lucas who had died in November 1771) there was a discernible contrast between the preamble and the body of the society's founding declaration. While the preamble expressed concern at the 'settled scheme of usurpation and corruption' that had been 'systematically and obstinately carried on' for some years 'against public liberty, in violation of Magna Charta and the Bill of Rights' – a revealing reference to English rather than to Irish legislation – the body of the declaration embodied a more soberly worded programme of reform:

we will use our utmost legal endeavors to restore and preserve the constitutional rights, liberties, and privileges of our fellow subjects; and to promote the trade

---

[125] *Baratariana: A Select Collection of Fugitive Political Pieces Published during the Administration of Lord Townshend in Ireland* (Dublin, 1772), pp. 292–3.
[126] See, for example, Bailyn, *Ideological Origins,* pp. 144–59.
[127] *The Principles of Modern Patriotism* (Dublin, 1770? – title page missing), p. 9.

and manufactures of our country . . . to repeal the late unconstitutional riot-act; to procure an act for suppressing useless employments, an effectual place and qualification act, and to reduce the exorbitant list of pensions, so destructive to this overloaded nation: and that we will, on every proper occasion, be ready at a call, to support the authority of the civil magistrates, in our respective counties and districts, without the aid of military force.[128]

When Sir Edward Newenham, who hoped to represent County Dublin in the next parliament, convened a meeting of the county's freeholders the resolutions that were adopted focused on measures of immediate concern to the electorate by rejecting a land tax, 'all useless employments and pensions', and a proposed stamp duty on legal documents and newspapers, while calling for additional taxes on 'the luxuries and superfluities of life'.[129] Again, when a by-election occurred in Dublin city in December 1773, Redmond Morres, the opposition candidate who was supported by the Society of Free Citizens and an older Whiggish club, the Aldermen of Skinner's Alley, adopted a modest election address in which he restricted himself to promising to be 'ever ready to accept the instructions of my constituents' and to work for the exclusion of placemen and pensioners from parliament.[130] In the event, Morres only narrowly defeated his aldermanic rival by a margin of eighty-five votes in a total poll of 3,043 – in the by-elections of 1767 and 1771 the candidates favoured by the opposition had secured majorities of 139 and 442 respectively.[131] The election of 1773 was warmly contested and the passions it aroused are indicated both by an attempt to intimidate voters which will be discussed below, and by a duel fought between Sir Edward Newenham and the defeated candidate.[132] The fact that Morres's opponent, Alderman Benjamin Geale, secured the votes of a large majority of his fellow merchants was a factor in reducing the opposition's majority on this occasion, but the closeness of the result in one of the most open and politically sophisticated constituencies in the country indicates the continued weakness of Anglo-Irish patriotism.[133]

For patriots, as for the population generally, American affairs continued to be overshadowed by events closer to home. It was only when reports of the Boston 'tea party' arrived in February 1774 that the magnitude of the crisis appears to have been fully appreciated and transatlantic developments thereafter received greater attention in the press than events in Poland or Turkey. In September 1774 the *Hibernian Magazine* inaugurated a regular column on American events with the observation that 'nothing can be more interesting than a clear view of the affairs of

---

[128] *FJ*, 14 October 1773.   [129] *FLJ*, 13 November 1773.
[130] *SNL*, 8 December 1773.   [131] *Ibid.*, 5 January 1774.   [132] *Ibid.*   [133] *Ibid.*

America'.[134] Yet as late as March 1775, when Sir Edward Newenham replied to an address from the Aldermen of Skinner's Alley pledging the support of that club for his candidacy in the next general election, his main concern was to emphasise the need for patriotic candidates to pledge that they would not 'accept of place, pension, or employment' if returned. He referred to the American crisis only to underline the growth of parliamentary corruption, which he considered to be a more serious problem in Britain than in Ireland:

Let them prove, that any placeman or pensioner opposed those acts which robbed the brave Americans of their chartered rights . . . At present the Irish (and more so, the British) House of Commons cannot be justly styled the representatives of the people:– they are a meeting of placemen and pensioners; under the form of a parliament.[135]

A few militant pronouncements supporting the position of the colonists appeared in the opposition press on the eve of the American war but they reflected the ideological commitment of a minority rather than the general sense of the Anglo-Irish community. For example, four days before the first shots were fired at Lexington a correspondent of the *Freeman's Journal* using the pseudonym 'Locke' wrote that 'There are certain unalienable rights and privileges which it must be our glory to maintain, and every man is born with a commission from heaven to defend them.'[136] When news of the outbreak of hostilities reached Ireland a leading article in the same paper sided unequivocally with the colonists and quoted Lord Chatham in support of the assertion that this was the view of Protestant Ireland as a whole:

It is hoped that as a civil war is commenced, and the first attack already made by the King's troops, on loyal, suffering subjects, bravely defending their rights, that our chief magistrate and aldermen will not longer defer addressing his Majesty on their behalf . . . Lord Chatham, in his late glorious speech, (which must strike terror to the hearts of guilty ministers, and is very prophetic of their fate) speaking of the Americans, says, 'Ireland they have to a man!' Meaning, I suppose, our true Whig and Protestant inhabitants. May the truth of this now appear![137]

But Chatham's assertion was far from being the truth. The loyal response of the Irish political nation on the outbreak of hostilities would again confirm that Anglo-Irish patriotism, advanced though it was in its ideas, remained the viewpoint of a minority of the political nation – a fact that had been obvious since the opposition's failure to organise widespread protests against Townshend's prorogation of parliament. The Anglo-Irish community, geographically close to its mother country and dependent

---

[134] *HM*, September 1774, 555.   [135] *FLJ*, 15 March 1775.   [136] *FJ*, 15 April 1775.
[137] *Ibid.*, 13 June 1775.

upon it for the maintenance of its position in Ireland, could not afford the luxury of supporting the American colonists, however much the policies that precipitated their rebellion may have been deplored. At a less rational and more emotional level, the majority of the Irish political nation, deeply Anglican, hierarchical and royalist in outlook, identified more readily with their British counterparts than with American Dissenters who were suspected of harbouring democratic ideas and who, with the passage of time, provided mounting evidence of their disloyalty to the crown. The impact of events in America on such supporters of the constitutional status quo will now be considered.

Loyalist opinion and America

Unrest in the colonies accentuated the concern felt by supporters of government about events closer to home. Their unease was expressed with clarity by John Hely-Hutchinson, a prominent member of the House of Commons. In Hutchinson's opinion, 'a virulent spirit of licentiousness' had broken out in Ireland which threatened 'the destruction of all order and subordination' and the patriot's greatest success – the octennial act of 1768 – had 'added great weight to the democratical scale and will raise the lever of false popularity higher than before'. He viewed the conflict with the colonies and the Wilkes agitation in England as destabilising factors which increased the need for vigilance by 'honest men' in Ireland: 'The situation of affairs in America and the late disturbances in England ought to be strong inducements to the friends of Ireland to exert themselves in supporting the king's measures with all the ability of their country.'[138] Similar sentiments were expressed in anti-patriot pamphlets of the period. 'Have not the revolutions which have happened in most states, been set on foot by a single incendiary?', asked one anonymous pamphleteer, who alluded to Wilkes in a second pointed question: 'is there not such a character at present in a neighbouring nation?'[139] The same author dismissed 'Poynings' law, pensions, the restraint on the woollen trade of the kingdom, and an union' as 'the hackneyed baits which every new professor of patriotism throws out to hook the sorry gudgeons, that are ever ready to swallow them'.[140] The pamphlet concluded by asking 'have not the wild and extravagant notions of liberty, freedom of writing and independency, which of late years have been so much propagated amongst us, been of the greatest detriment to the kingdom?'[141] The threat posed by

---

[138] Undated draft letter from Hutchinson to [Charles?] O'Hara; Donoughmore Mss., HMC 12th report, appendix IX (1891), p. 264.

[139] *Queries upon Liberty, the Freedom of the Press, Independency, & c.* (Dublin, 1768), p. 14.

[140] *Ibid.*, p. 20.   [141] *Ibid.*, p. 27.

patriot ideas and the example of the American colonies to the stability of the empire in general and of Ireland in particular was noted by George Macartney, Irish-born son-in-law of Lord Bute and chief secretary during the Townshend viceroyalty, in his book on the state of the country. Macartney asserted the legislative supremacy of the British parliament over all parts of the empire and recognised the potential of American ideas to attract a wide following in Ireland, while recognising that such a situation had not yet been reached:

In this vast empire, on which the sun never sets, and whose bounds nature has not yet ascertained, one great superintending and controlling dominion must exist somewhere; and where can that dominion reside with so much dignity, propriety and safety, as in the British legislature?... Of late years, indeed, the licence and turbulence of the times have countenanced the denial of this principle; in America it has been loudly exploded, and, if great wisdom and address are not used in the administration of Ireland, there are many who may be led to dispute or disown it.[142]

Macartney's belief in the need for an ultimate centre of sovereignty if the unity and stability of the empire were to be preserved was shared by British opponents of colonial claims and by American Tories, but as a proposition it was both questionable and abstract and is unlikely to have swayed the opinions of many who were undecided. But supporters of the existing political order had a more compelling argument in their armoury – one which appealed to the fears rather than the reason of the Anglo-Irish community and which subverted the myopic view held by some Anglo-Irish patriots that their community constituted the 'Irish nation'. An anti-Lucas satire stated unpalatable facts with unusual frankness and deflated the patriotic pretence that Ireland was an independent kingdom. It was, argued the anonymous author, either a conquered province or an English colony:

in respect to the real Irish, its early inhabitants, it is certainly a conquered province: in respect to the English, who have been sent hither from time to time, to preside, manage and direct, it is as plainly a colony; consider it then in what sense you will, it can have no claim of independancy: that claim if it could be asserted with any prospect, or probability of success, can belong only to that class of its people, the native Irish, who still make up the major part, and by the law of nations, have some right to throw off the yoke if it were in their power.[143]

This was an opinion that few members of the Anglo-Irish community can have wished to hear articulated, yet precisely because of its sensitivity it cannot have been very far from their minds.

[142] [Sir George Macartney], *An Account of Ireland in 1773* (London, 1773), p. 55.
[143] *The Principles of Modern Patriotism*, p. 27.

Between the opposing political camps, men who identified with the American colonists and the supporters of Wilkes in England on the one hand, or those who opposed all challenges to established authority throughout the empire on the other, a middle ground was occupied by those in whose minds an appreciation of American grievances was balanced or outweighed by the fear of civil unrest or worse. When unfounded reports arrived that Governor Hutchinson of Massachusetts had been deposed by 'the mob of Boston' and replaced by a ten-member council, the development was condemned as 'absolute rebellion' by a writer who regretted that 'those brave asserters of freedom' would now be 'liable to the severest chastisement by pursuing such desperate and unconstitutional methods of redress'.[144] As early as 1768 the editor of a Dublin edition of John Dickinson's *Letters from a Farmer in Pennsylvania*, who was himself sympathetic to the American cause, deplored the fact that 'a very unfavourable opinion of the people of America has, I know not how, crept abroad' and urged that 'we, who are united under the same head should be very cautious how we entertain illiberal prejudices against our fellow subjects'. He concluded with the anodyne hope that 'America, on her part, may ever adhere to that dutiful dependence, which, to do her justice, she continues respectfully to acknowledge; and that Great Britain, on hers, may reassume her wonted generosity and good nature'.[145] Six years later, an equally dissatisfied patriot who claimed that the 'eyes of all Europe are now fixed with admiration on the noble struggles of the brave Americans' regretted the fact that 'in this general glow of patriotism, with grief and indignation I behold our unhappy country alone frigid, spiritless and unconcerned'.[146]

Dr Philip Skelton, rector of Fintona, County Tyrone, was a well-informed observer with official connections who treated the claims of both government and opposition with some scepticism. In a letter of January 1772 to William Knox, the Irish-born under-secretary of the colonial department, he commented that 'The patriots, odious appellation, say all the ministerial men are robbers and oppressors of the country; the ministerial men say all the patriots are rebels and only want to be ministers.'[147] Skelton readily admitted that, in this instance, he was inclined to believe the claims of both parties. In another letter to the same correspondent, written in October 1774 when the likelihood of war was obvious to all, he expressed his ambivalent feelings as follows: 'I think

---

[144] *FLJ*, 14 August 1773.
[145] [John Dickinson], *Letters from a Farmer in Pennsylvania, to the Inhabitants of the British Colonies* (Dublin, 1768), pp. iii–iv and vii.
[146] *FLJ*, 5 November 1774.
[147] Skelton to Knox, 30 January 1772; Knox Mss., HMC, Report on Manuscripts in Various Collections, VI (1909), p. 442.

these Americans are downright rebels, and yet, if they are to be taxed by the parliament of England, they may bid adieu to the thing called property. How wisdom shall make its way between the horns of this dilemma, with justice in tow, I am too far off to see.'[148] Implicit in this statement is a poorly formulated distinction between the British parliament's powers of legislation and of taxation in the colonies – the former of which Skelton seemed to allow and the latter of which he questioned. Precisely the same view was taken by Alderman William Forbes, lord mayor of Dublin in 1771 and 1772, and John Forbes, his nephew and a future associate of Henry Grattan. Writing to his nephew in March 1775, the older man expressed his agreement with the 'line you have drawn between England and their American subjects, which shews that the Americans are insisting on privileges they are not entitled to, and have nothing to claim but the constitutional right of taxing themselves, which I hope will be allowed them, provided it be adequate and what is necessary, and that our contests will end'.[149] This viewpoint would be frequently expressed by members of the Irish political nation in the early years of the war. A similar reluctance to lay all the blame for the crisis at either the American or the British door is evident in an anonymous piece that appeared in the columns of *Finn's Leinster Journal* during the short interval between the commencement of hostilities in America and the arrival of the first reports in Ireland. The author appeared to censure the ministry for initiating the conflict with the colonies but confessed his own inability to see any easy way out of the impasse that had been created by the progress of events:

How justly ... may every good subject and sincere well wisher to the prosperity and happiness of this empire and its colonies, execrate that blundering head, or that wicked heart which first kindled the coals of dissension amongst us, and brought both to a crisis which makes it difficult for the wisest man to determine how far the one can relax, or the other submit with propriety.[150]

This may be as close as one can now come to an expression of majority opinion in the Anglo-Irish community. The Irish political nation would support the crown in its efforts to suppress the American rebellion, but not without considerable misgivings.

Presbyterian opinion and America

Although east Ulster was particularly active in supporting the patriot opposition during the money bill controversy of the 1750s, the region

---

148 Skelton to Knox, 26 October 1774; *ibid.*, p. 444.
149 William Forbes to John Forbes, 7 March 1775, in T.J. Kiernan (ed.), 'Forbes letters', *Anal. Hib.* 8 (1938), 319.
150 *FLJ*, 20 May 1775.

appears to have been slow to recover from the slump in patriot morale that followed the defection of Henry Boyle and his followers, and opposition there was muted during the 1760s. Events in other parts of the empire were noted, however, and the 'numerous and respectable' assembly that met in Belfast in April 1770 to celebrate the release of John Wilkes from prison was an early sign of a patriot revival in the north. The toasts drunk on that occasion shed some light on the outlook then prevailing among Presbyterian patriots:

The wooden walls of England. – Increase of spirit, of liberty; and importance to the people of Ireland. – The 16th of February 1768 [the octennial act]. – The American colonies, and may the descendants of those who fled from tyranny in one country, never be forced to submit to its galling yoke in another. – The memory of John Hampden... May the sacred elective rights of the people ever be preserved, and no attempt to violate them escape with impunity. – As Britain hath ever disdained to submit to the tyranny of one, may she successfully resist the still more odious tyranny of many... May oppression never be carried so far, as to make it necessary for the people to resume the powers delegated to the magistrate for their good; but if it should, may their efforts for the restoration of liberty, prove irresistible.[151]

An emphasis on parliamentary issues (limitation, the rights of electors, the rejection of the unlimited sovereignty of the crown in parliament) is apparent, but this may have been accentuated by the nature of the event being celebrated. On the other hand, the explicit declaration of the right of the people to resist oppression struck a characteristically Presbyterian note. The imperial perspective displayed in the toasts was one shared by Irish patriots generally and, notwithstanding the substantial emigration that took place from Ulster to the North American colonies during the 1760s, the attention given by the Belfast patriots to transatlantic events was no greater than might have been found at a similar gathering in Dublin.

Emigration from Ulster ports to America, which had continued at a steady rate since the conclusion of peace in 1763, increased abruptly in 1771 and continued thereafter at a level averaging nearly twice that of the earlier period until the outflow was again halted by war in 1775.[152] This increased emigration can be explained by economic factors. A recession in the linen industry and a succession of poor harvests together with increasing rents impelled many who had the necessary resources to make a fresh start in a new country. The same factors also sparked a serious outbreak of agrarian unrest in the form of the 'Hearts of Steel'

[151] Henry Joy, *Historical Collections Relative to the Town of Belfast: from the Earliest Period to the Union with Great Britain* (Belfast, 1817), pp. 110–11.

[152] R.J. Dickson, *Ulster Emigration to Colonial America 1718–1775* (London, 1966), p. 60.

or 'Steelboy' movement. While the Hearts of Steel, like the Hearts of Oak before them, would appear to have been motivated by purely economic factors – most notably by the increased rents that were demanded as leases fell due for renewal on Lord Donegall's large estate in south Antrim – they showed a degree of militancy comparable to that of the Whiteboys in the south.[153] The Steelboys first came to national prominence in December 1770 when 500 armed men marched into Belfast and released an imprisoned comrade from the town's barracks despite the resistance of the garrison. The agitation flared up intermittently and spread from south Antrim into counties Down and Derry before being brought under control by military action in 1772 when a good harvest also facilitated a return to normality in the affected areas. The violence associated with the movement and the resulting repression added to the flow of emigrants to the colonies but had little political impact. Despite the violence of the Steelboys and their Presbyterian composition, their narrow focus on the question of rents appears to have been less alarming for members of the established church than the Oakboys' opposition to clerical dues. One effect of the agitation was to drive many of those who were most deeply involved, an appreciable proportion of whom had prior military experience,[154] to emigrate to America just as the chronic crisis there was about to enter its acute phase. The scale of this outflow is apparent from the advertisements in the Ulster press for passenger sailings to America. For example, the *Belfast News-Letter* of 19 April 1774 contained no fewer than sixteen notices for vessels that were preparing to sail for Philadelphia, New York or Charleston.

Such emigrants would form a personal link between Ulster Presbyterians and the rebellious colonies in future years, but in the immediate pre-war period the Irish parliament may have done more to concentrate Presbyterian minds on the central point in dispute between the British parliament and the colonies – the issue of taxation without representation. In 1774 an act (13 & 14 Geo. III, c.10) was passed that restricted the right to vote at meetings of parish vestries, bodies empowered to raise local taxes for the repair of churches. Sir Edward Newenham condemned the act in a letter to the *Belfast News-Letter* for 'depriving the Dissenters of this kingdom of their birth-right in matters of taxation'.[155] The parallel with the case of the American colonists was obvious and a flood of petitions against the measure poured into the House of Commons from Ulster constituencies.[156] When a dinner was held in Belfast in August 1774 to

---

153 For an account of the Steelboy movement, see Donnelly, 'Hearts of oak, hearts of steel', pp. 23–73.
154 *Ibid.*, pp. 49–50.   155 *BNL*, 28 June 1774.
156 See Smyth, 'The Volunteer movement in Ulster', p. 12, n. 4.

honour two members of parliament for their 'spirited defence of those constitutional and inherent rights of Protestants of every denomination' in opposing the vestry act, the toasts mentioned, but did not dwell on, the American crisis:

The Revolution of 1688, and may we never need another...Religion without priestcraft...A farther progress to the Reformation...The memory of Mr Locke...The memory of John Hampden. February 1768, and a further limitation to parliaments...Wisdom and firmness to the American assemblies, justice and moderation to the legislature of Britain, that their disputes may be happily settled...May the tyranny and persecution the fathers fled from in Europe, never fasten on the sons in America...Lord and Lady Donegall. – Sir Edward Newenham...[157]

The advocacy of a further limitation of parliament and the toast to Sir Edward Newenham are indicative of the patriotic orientation of the attendance, yet the inclusion of Lord and Lady Donegall among those toasted cautions us against regarding the diners as an assembly of radicals. It is suggestive that such a group displayed a balanced attitude towards the contending parties in the American crisis. If the wish for American 'firmness' and British 'justice' reveals a belief that the colonists were correct in principle, the wish for American 'wisdom' and British 'moderation' equally implies that the resistance of the colonists had already exceeded the bounds of propriety – a view which may have been inspired by recent events in Boston.

The *Belfast News-Letter* and the *Londonderry Journal* both maintained a fairly even-handed approach in their coverage during the months preceding the outbreak of hostilities. Statements on behalf of administration, the Continental Congress, and the colonial assemblies were all given extensive coverage, as were individual contributions reprinted from the London, Dublin and American press – the latter reflecting both patriot and loyalist viewpoints. In the immediate aftermath of the Boston port act the *Belfast News-Letter* carried an appeal for a compromise solution that may have been written locally. Britain, it was proposed, should 'confirm to America her original privileges and immunities without blemish' while America should 'by her own special act, bear a proportional part of the expense of government'.[158] When an early general election was unexpectedly called in Britain, the same paper published an 'epitaph' for the dissolved parliament which claimed that it had 'died struggling for the just superiority of the mother country over her rebellious offspring in America'.[159] Even the fundamental patriot principle of 'no taxation

[157] Joy, *Historical Collections*, p. 115.   [158] *BNL*, 8 April 1774.
[159] *Ibid.*, 1 November 1774.

without representation' was controverted: the two principal Ulster newspapers copied a letter of English origin which proposed that the Americans should acknowledge the right of the British parliament to extend any taxes levied in Britain to the colonies also, while Westminster should reciprocate by undertaking not to impose taxes specific to the colonies.[160] On the other hand, the issue of the *Londonderry Journal* in which this proposal appeared also reprinted an article from the *Freeman's Journal* which argued that 'by the same authority which the British parliament assumes to tax America, it may also, and with equal justice presume to tax Ireland without the concurrence or consent of the Irish parliament'.[161] In January 1775 the *Londonderry Journal* gave details of the brutal treatment of slaves in North America, a repugnant feature of colonial life that had recently been publicised by John Wesley, and drew attention to the 'notable inconsistency' of the colonists: 'It seems, indeed, wondrous strange, that those very people who so fondly complain of infringements of their liberties, and so speciously complain about the natural rights of mankind, should themselves have so little consideration for the sufferings of such of their fellow creatures who have the misfortune to fall into their power.'[162] It is difficult not to see the wide range of pro- and anti-American views that were published in the Ulster press – irrespective of where the pieces may have originated – as a reflection of the variety of opinions that existed in the largely Presbyterian districts where the papers circulated.

Catholic opinion and America

It might reasonably be expected that the wide measure of toleration allowed to all religious groups in North America would have secured the Americans a large measure of sympathy from the Catholic élite as relations between Britain and the colonies worsened. The potential for such a development can be glimpsed in Charles O'Conor's argument that Penal legislation not only prevented Catholics from contributing to the economic development of Ireland but was also driving them to emigrate to America: 'More improvements have been made in North America, within these ninety years, than in Ireland, in the course of five hundred; and it should excite shame, as it must one day provoke indignation, to reflect, that so fine an island as this, should become a nursery of labourers and manufacturers for that thriving continent.'[163] That sympathy for the colonists did not develop among the Catholic élite was, no doubt, largely due to that group's reliance on the goodwill of administration for future

---

[160] The letter signed 'Moderatus' in *BNL*, 6 January 1775, and *LJ*, 13 January 1775.
[161] *LJ*, 13 January 1775.   [162] *Ibid.*, 24 January 1775.
[163] [Charles O'Conor], *Observations on the Popery Laws* (Dublin, 1771), p. 53.

measures of relief, but the evolution of British policy in Canada must also have played a part. The religious tolerance enjoyed by Catholics in the older colonies paled in comparison with the virtual establishment of the Catholic church and the full equality accorded to the Catholic laity in recently conquered Quebec. Inevitably, Catholic polemicists drew attention to the stark contrast between their own legal position in Ireland and that of their Canadian coreligionists:

> The Catholics there, though habituated to a Catholic government, have reconciled themselves to the government of a Protestant monarch, who permits them to worship God in their own way, and abridges them of no civil privileges for so doing. – What have Irish Catholics, born under the present establishment, and ever obedient under it; what, I say, have such men done, or what civil guilt can be produced against them, to distinguish their case from that of their brethren in Canada?[164]

The novel religious policy being pursued in Canada provided firm evidence that attitudes towards Catholicism were softening at the highest level of government. Furthermore, the willingness of the British ministry to grant religious freedom to Canadian Catholics suggested that it was the Irish parliament, and the wider Protestant community from which its members were drawn, rather than the executive in either Dublin or London, that constituted the real obstacle to Catholic relief in Ireland.

The Quebec act of 1774 met with intense opposition from patriots on both sides of the Atlantic. While this was partly due to provisions that extended the borders of the colony southwards and provided for a nominated rather than an elected legislature, the statutory recognition given to the existing status of the Catholic church was the principal target of opposition attacks and a torrent of anti-Catholic invective was unleashed throughout the British empire. In Britain, a petition presented by the lord mayor, aldermen and commons of London complained that 'the Roman Catholic religion, which is known to be idolatrous and bloody, is established by this bill'.[165] In Ireland, Dublin's Society of Free Citizens included 'a repeal to the unconstitutional Quebec bill, which establishes popery' among their toasts at a quarterly assembly chaired by Sir Edward Newenham.[166] The *Hibernian Magazine* noted the 'universal indignation, which seems to prevail through these kingdoms, at the sanction given to popery'.[167] Such sentiments were fully shared by American patriots. The 'Suffolk resolves', adopted by the residents of the county in which Boston is located, were reprinted in the Irish press and contained the following assertion:

---

[164] Taaffe, *Observations on Affairs in Ireland*, pp. 28–9.   [165] *BNL*, 28 June 1774.
[166] *HJ*, 14 October 1774.   [167] *HM*, August 1774, 451.

That the late act of parliament for establishing the Roman Catholic religion, and the French laws in that extensive country, now called Canada, is dangerous in an extreme degree to the Protestant religion and to the civil rights and liberties of all America, and therefore as men and Protestant Christians, we are indispensably obliged to take all proper measures for our security.[168]

While the views of the delegates to one Massachusetts county convention might be dismissed as unrepresentative of American opinion as a whole, the same could not be said of the address to the British people adopted by the Continental Congress, an address which characterised Catholicism as 'a religion that has deluged your island in blood, and dispersed impiety, bigotry, persecution, murder and rebellion through every part of the world'.[169]

The attitudes of some government supporters contrasted sharply with the crude anti-Catholicism that was general among the opposition. For example, a pro-government member of the House of Commons, Colonel Browne, ventured to assert that:

In my opinion papists can be, and are, as loyal as any others; of which I will give an instance. In the time of the late war I recruited the regiment in which I served with above two hundred papists raised about Cork. They went to Canada, behaved bravely; and when in garrison, in a popish town, and surrounded with papists, whilst many Protestants deserted, not one of these papists ran away.[170]

Browne was speaking in favour of a bill which proposed to give Catholics the right to take unlimited leases on building lots within corporate towns. It was a very modest measure of relief, but the opposition which it aroused demonstrates that penal legislation still enjoyed considerable support among Irish Protestants on the eve of the American war. Speaking in the same debate, the prominent patriot Barry Barry declared that 'the popery laws did not spring from persecution, but from necessity and self-defence'.[171] The bill was heavily defeated by 126 votes to 77. Significantly, it has been calculated that government supporters split almost evenly on this private measure, 60 voting against and 51 in favour, while opposition members rejected it by the emphatic margin of 60 to 18.[172]

Colonel Browne's praise for the reliability of Catholic troops is of interest as an indication of the views of a professional soldier on the

---

[168] *FJ*, 10 November 1774.
[169] *An Address to the People of Great-Britain, from the Delegates . . . in General Congress, at Philadelphia, September 5, 1774* (Dublin, 1775), p. 12.
[170] *FJ*, 15 February 1774; reprinted in Brady, *Catholics and Catholicism*, p. 159.
[171] *Ibid.*
[172] John Patrick Day, 'The Catholic question in the Irish parliament 1760–82' (MA thesis, UCD, 1978), p. 104.

potential importance of Catholic recruitment and, in so far as it was uttered on the floor of the Commons by a habitual supporter of government, it is also suggestive of an evolution in official policy on the question. It cannot, however, be accepted as an accurate reflection of the political sentiment of the general Catholic population, whose relations with the military were characterised by frequent outbreaks of violence. Just three weeks after Browne's speech *Finn's Leinster Journal* reported that the mayor of Kilkenny had offered a reward of ten guineas for information leading to the apprehension of two men who had attacked and fatally injured a member of the local garrison, and described a 'desperate affray' between a party of soldiers and 'a vast number of country people' at a *pátrún* (a festival in honour of a local patron saint) at Ballyellin, County Carlow – a clash which ended when the soldiers fired on the crowd, two of whom were wounded 'in a most desperate manner'.[173] It may be relevant that the unit involved was the 27th regiment of foot, better known as the Enniskillen Foot, which contained an unusually high proportion of Irish Protestants in its ranks. But if such episodes point to the disaffection of lower-class Catholics – both in rural areas and, as will be seen below, in the cities – they took place alongside increasingly vocal expressions of loyalty by Catholics of higher social standing.

The depth of the social and political divisions which had emerged within the Catholic community are evident from a battle fought at Ballyragget, County Kilkenny, on 22 February 1775, in which at least three Whiteboys were killed. The opposing force on this occasion was not a military party but an anti-Whiteboy association organised by the local parish priest, Alexander Cahill, with the encouragement of Archbishop Butler of Cashel, that had been issued with firearms by the authorities in violation of the law against Catholics bearing arms.[174] In an open letter addressed to Fr Cahill in the aftermath of the battle the archbishop defended his own and the priest's conduct and placed it in the wider context of the need to demonstrate the loyalty of Catholics: 'the association we formed at Ballyragget of all its inhabitants had no other view than to wipe off the foul aspersion cast on a Roman Catholic town; to convince the whole kingdom that Roman Catholics, by being Roman Catholics, were only the more zealous for its peace and prosperity'.[175] The perspective of the rural populace was quite different. Notwithstanding the prominent role played by a local priest in forming the anti-Whiteboy association and the public support given him by his bishop, a contemporary lament

---

[173] *FLJ*, 5 March 1774.
[174] See Ó hÓgáin, *Duanaire Osraíoch*, pp. 91–3 and J.S. Donnelly, 'Irish agrarian rebellion: the Whiteboys of 1769–76', *Proc. RIA* 83 C (1983), 322–3.
[175] *FLJ*, 8 March 1775.

for the dead Whiteboys identified their enemies as alien Protestants who despised the Virgin Mary:

> *A Aon-Mhic Mhuire, ar dh'fhulaing tú féin an pháis,*
> *an bhfeiceann tú na Gallaibh ag seasamh is a ngunnaí ina láimh,*
> *ag síorthabhairt tarcaisne do bhanaltra an Uain ghil bháin –*
> *is gan a céad míle beannacht níl flaitheas Mhic Dé le fáil?*[176]

(O only Son of Mary, did you suffer the passion yourself, do you see the *Gaill* standing with their guns in their hands, forever cursing the nurse of the shining white Lamb – and without her hundred thousand blessings God's paradise is not attainable?)

On the eve of the outbreak of hostilities in America, violent social conflict between Irish Catholics was still interpreted within the old and familiar ideological framework of religious and national oppression that had been inherited from the seventeenth century:

> *Liomsa níorbh ionadh 'á loscfadh an ghrian an t-aer,*
> *ná an ghrian nó an ghealach a dh'fheiscint le saol na saol,*
> *tríos na fearaibh do leagadh gan choir gan chúis, mo léan –*
> *ach is minic do fealladh ar chlanna bocht' cráite Gael!*[177]

(It would be no surprise to me if the sun were to scorch the sky, or if the sun or the moon were never again seen, because of the men who were struck down without fault or cause, my woe – but it's often the poor oppressed children of the Gael have been betrayed!)

But by 1775 the political outlook of the more affluent sections of Catholic society could scarcely have differed more from that which is found in the vernacular literature. When Robert Butler, the Catholic landlord of the Ballyragget estate, returned from England in November 1775, seven months after the battle at Concord and nine months after that at Ballyragget, he invited his principal tenants to a celebration at which the toasts included 'the king and royal family, and success to his Majesty's arms; Lord Harcourt [the lord lieutenant], and prosperity to Ireland; the 22nd of February 1775, and the brave garrison of Ballyragget'.[178] An implicit comparison can be seen in this juxtaposition of 'his Majesty's arms' with 'the brave garrison of Ballyragget'. But if Butler and his confrères in the Catholic gentry were capable of drawing a favourable parallel between the forces of law and order in America and those in Ireland, it was equally open to the mass of plebeian Catholics, with their very different world-view, to apply the same reasoning in reverse and to take the novel

---

[176] 'I gContae Chill Chainnigh is ea rinneadh an t-ár go léir' in Ó hÓgáin, *Duanaire Osraíoch*, p. 36.
[177] *Ibid.*, p. 37.   [178] *FLJ*, 29 November 1775.

step of identifying with the cause of rebellious Protestant Dissenters in the colonies.

Army and populace

From 1773, at the latest, military personnel in urban areas were subjected to a sustained campaign of physical assaults of a very specific type. Typically, unaccompanied soldiers were attacked by two or more persons who knocked them to the ground and cut one of their hamstrings – an operation that left the victim permanently lame and unfit for further military service. It is impossible to read the newspapers of the period without being struck by the frequency of these semi-ritualistic mutilations but the phenomenon has been strangely neglected by historians. Lecky noted the occurrence of such attacks in Dublin in 1784 but associated them with economic distress arising from the post-war depression.[179] Froude remarked on the houghing of soldiers four years earlier, in 1780, but implausibly linked them with patriot opposition to the perpetual mutiny bill enacted in that year.[180] Both of these explanations lose much – and perhaps all – of their force when it is realised that the attacks began long before a shot was fired in America or an Irish mutiny bill was ever thought of.

The earliest reference to the houghing of soldiers that I have found dates from 1772 and is associated with the Steelboy agitation in Ulster:

Charles Glass, a soldier of the 57th regiment of foot, now quartered in the barracks of Belfast, was most inhumanely and barbarously maimed by the back sinews of his leg being cut through, on Thursday last 15th day of May 1772 at 3 o'clock as he lay asleep in a field near the barracks, with his face downwards, by two men, one of whom stated they treated him thus because one of the soldiers had given evidence against some of the Hearts of Steel.[181]

This attack is geographically exceptional as it is the only one of which I am aware that took place north of a line from Galway to Dublin. None the less, it points to a possible source of inspiration for such attacks – the practice of 'houghing' livestock employed by both Whiteboys and Steelboys. In a metropolitan context, the Catholic 'Ormond Boys', many of whom were journeymen butchers from the capital's Ormond market, had employed the same tactic against their rivals, the Protestant 'Liberty Boys', during the sectarian riots which punctuated the life of the city

---

[179] Lecky, *Ireland in the Eighteenth Century*, II, p. 392. The same explanation is repeated in Jim Smyth, *The Men of No Property: Irish Radicals and Popular Politics in the Late Eighteenth Century* (Dublin, 1992), p. 136.

[180] Froude, *The English in Ireland in the Eighteenth Century*, II, p. 268.

[181] Quoted in F.J. Bigger, *The Ulster Land War of 1770* (Dublin, 1910), pp. 145–6.

between the early 1730s and the late 1760s.[182] There is some evidence that tensions between members of the Dublin garrison and the civilian population were rising during the course of 1773. A threat to hough members of the city guard was made as early as January 1773 and in April of the same year a 'dreadful affray' took place between a large body of soldiers from the barracks and the residents of Stoneybatter – a neighbouring area which was also adjacent to the Ormond market.[183] In June, a soldier in the city had the sinews of his hand cut in what appears to have been a planned attack.[184] By January 1774 special precautions had been instituted to guard against attacks on members of the Dublin garrison:

It is with very great concern we complain of the cruelty of some atrocious villains, who cut and chalk soldiers after nightfall, when they are going to and from the barracks or lodgings, by which many have lost the use of their limbs, [and] others have been terribly gashed and disfig[ured on] their faces; upon which occasion, we [are in]formed, that orders have been given, th[at sol]diers are to walk two and two together [carrying] side arms, to defend and secure the[mselves against] being attacked and murdered.[185]

'Chalking' was Dublin slang for the practice of slashing a victim's face with the intention of leaving permanent scars – apparently motiveless criminal behaviour that was not uncommon at the time. Some of those engaged in chalking revealed their political sympathies during the by-election of November 1773 contested by Redmond Morres, a patriot in the Lucas tradition, and Benjamin Geale, representative of the city's aldermen. The chalkers attempted to intimidate supporters of the aldermanic candidate, to the great embarrassment of the patriot camp:

The real friends of liberty and the constitution, feel the highest indignation at the late intervention of a set of armed ruffians ... an ill compliment to the cause, or personal interest, of the popular candidate, who stands on too fair a ground in the affections and good opinion of his fellow-citizens, to need the lawless and violent partisans of riot and disorder. As these sons of rapine are the same as have been distinguished by the title of light-horse or chalkers, public thanks are due to the activity of the sheriffs, in lodging one of their number in Newgate.[186]

---

[182] For the Ormond Boys, see Murphy, 'Municipal politics and popular disturbances'; for their use of houghing, see [John Edward Walsh], *Sketches of Ireland Sixty Years Ago* (Dublin, 1847), p. 4.

[183] R.M. Gilbert (ed.), *Calendar of Ancient Records of Dublin*, XII (Dublin, 1905), p. 245 and *FLJ*, 7 April 1773 respectively.

[184] *FLJ*, 19 June 1773.

[185] *Ibid.*, 12 January 1774; the original copy is torn and the bracketed letters represent my reconstruction of missing text.

[186] *SNL*, 15 December 1773.

There is nothing in these early reports to indicate either the social or religious background of the chalkers and it is possible that the 'light-horse' mentioned above may not have been involved in the attacks on military personnel. However, the identity of those who were becomes clearer when reports of the series of assaults on soldiers that took place during August and September 1774 are taken into account.

During a four-week period, eight separate attacks took place on soldiers from four different regiments – seven of whom had the sinews of their legs and one the sinews of his hand cut.[187] It is clear that these attacks formed part of a concerted campaign: the men who houghed William Silles, a soldier in the 57th regiment of foot, on 30 August shouted to waiting associates 'that they had houghed him, and that they would soon have more of them'; when Patrick Downey, a soldier in the same regiment, was houghed on 7 September one of the attackers told him 'they would serve the whole regiment in the same manner'.[188] Two retaliatory attacks on butchers working in the Ormond market by parties of soldiers – attacks in which 'many on both sides were wounded, and several weapons taken from the military' – confirm suspicions about the identity of some, at least, of the houghers.[189] The situation in the capital was viewed with such concern by government that the privy council issued a proclamation detailing the attacks that had taken place to date and offering a reward of £200 for each offender convicted.[190] In a further tightening of security, members of the garrison were confined to barracks after evening roll-call.[191] A lull in the campaign of attacks on the military took place following the arrest of one Neale Lamb who, having behaved with 'uncommon insolence' throughout his trial, was convicted of houghing a soldier and was executed on 9 November.[192] None the less, attacks resumed early in the new year. The first incident for which I have found a report took place on 10 January: 'The same evening a corporal of foot was attacked by some chalkers, who most inhumanly and cruelly cut the sinews of his hams.'[193] A report of another attack on 28 January refers to a coincident factor which may have contributed to the fresh wave of anti-military violence:

A recruiting party beat up through this city, for volunteers to fill up the regiments going to America. At night Thomas Thompson, private soldier in the 24th regiment, and Charles Dowley, soldier in the 35th regiment, were houghed, and otherwise so cruelly used, in the neighbourhood of the barracks, that they are rendered incapable of ever earning their bread.[194]

---

[187] *BNL*, 23 September 1774.   [188] *Ibid.*   [189] *FLJ*, 7 and 10 September 1774.
[190] For the text of this proclamation, see *BNL*, 23 September 1774.
[191] *FLJ*, 17 September 1774.   [192] *Ibid.*, 29 October and 12 November 1774.
[193] *Ibid.*, 14 January 1775.   [194] *Ibid.*, 1 February 1775.

Two more members of the Dublin garrison were houghed on 1 and 6 February, with the assailants on the former occasion being identified in the press as butchers.[195] The report above in which a reference to recruitment for the American service immediately precedes the account of attacks on two soldiers suggests (to put it no more strongly) that this may have been a factor in triggering the attacks. As early as May of the previous year two regiments of foot sent from Ireland to reinforce General Gage at Boston were brought up to strength before their departure by a recruiting campaign which appears to have been restricted to Munster.[196] Recruitment efforts became more intensive in January 1775 when a further three regiments of foot and one of light dragoons were ordered to be ready to embark from Cork for Boston on 1 March, with the infantry regiments being 'completed to their full number by recruits to be raised in Ireland previous to their departure'.[197] Later in the same month it was decided that 500 men would be despatched to Boston to bring the regiments already stationed there up to strength: of these 500 men, 200 were to be drafted from regiments remaining in Ireland, 60 were to be drafted from regiments remaining in England, and 240 were to be recruited in Ireland.[198] The suspicion that tensions aroused by the recruitment campaign may have contributed to attacks on the military is consistent with incidents in Cork city, where recruiting parties were particularly active. On 18 February a local man who refused to enlist was shot and seriously wounded by a member of a recruiting party and a month later, on 26 March, a soldier in the city was attacked by a group of men who knocked him down and cut off two of his fingers.[199] In fact, recruitment was proceding very slowly. In March the officer in charge of raising the 240 recruits for General Gage's command reported from Cork that 'our success will not answer his excellency the lord lieutenant's expectations' and stated that only sixty-nine recruits had been raised – little more than a quarter of the target – a failure which he attributed to the inadequate bounty money offered to recruits.[200]

On 8 March two men, James Hand and John Murphy, were executed at St Stephen's Green for houghing soldiers in Dublin, and on 23 March a

---

[195] *Ibid.*, 8 February 1775 and *BNL*, 14 February 1775 respectively.
[196] PRO SP 63/445, fos. 92 and 94; the 5th and 38th regiments were thirty-five and forty-one men under strength respectively before recruitment began.
[197] Rochford, secretary of state, to Harcourt, 19 January 1775, PRO SP 63/445, fo. 17.
[198] Lord Barrington, secretary at war, to Major Bruce, 28 January 1775, PRO SP 63/445, fo. 59.
[199] *FLJ*, 25 February and 1 April 1775.
[200] Major Bruce to Thomas Waite, 6 March 1775, PRO SP 63/445, fo. 259, and attached list of recruits, fo. 262.

butcher named Laurence Coleman was convicted of the same offence.[201]
These measures failed to intimidate the Dublin houghers, however, and
yet another soldier was houghed in the capital on 26 March.[202] Further
evidence linking the butchers of the Ormond markets with the spate of
attacks on the military is provided by an assault of a different kind which
took place on 29 March: 'As Major Boyle Roche, was going to the barracks, passing by Ormond-market on Ormond quay, a paving stone of
a pound and a half weight was thrown at him from the market.'[203] This
attack, committed on a prominent officer in one of the busiest thorough-
fares of the city, may have been the final factor in determining Archbishop
John Carpenter to issue a pastoral letter that was read to all Catholic
congregations in the city on Sunday 2 April 1775. This letter establishes
the Catholic background of the houghers beyond reasonable doubt and is
of interest, not only as another example (alongside that of Bishop Butler
noted previously) of the willingness of the higher clergy to assist the civil
authorities in suppressing unrest, but also because it clearly intimates
that the attacks on the military had commenced quite recently and were
unprecedented in nature:

As frequent injuries of the most atrocious kind have, for some time past, been
committed on some of the military in this city, we think it expedient to express our
utmost horror and detestation of all such unchristian and barbarous doings. And
we do hereby forbid all those of our communion, under the severest censures that
the church can denounce, to be in any wise concerned in cutting or wounding,
or maiming any one whomsoever. – At present we shall only observe, that the
vengeance of heaven, together with the highest punishment that the laws can
inflict, must necessarily and justly pursue the miscreants who are capable of
perpetrating such a horrid and unheard-of species of villainy.[204]

Whether because of this clerical condemnation, the deterrent effect of
executions, or a reduction in the army's recruitment effort, serious attacks on military personnel in Dublin appear to have ceased for several
months. The example of the capital was taken up elsewhere, however,
and another soldier was houghed in Cork city on 7 May.[205] Such serious
and premeditated attacks on military personnel indicate that many urban
Catholics were as disaffected as their rural coreligionists on the eve of the
American war. A serious riot 'wherein several on both sides were desperately wounded' that took place between soldiers and quarry workers in
Carlow on 7 June is less easy to characterise and may have been entirely
non-political in origin, yet it is suggestive that the clash took place just

[201] *FLJ*, 11 March 1775 and *BNL*, 28 March 1775.   [202] *FLJ*, 1 April 1775.
[203] *Ibid.*, 5 April 1775.   [204] *Ibid.*, 8 April 1775.   [205] *Ibid.*, 13 May 1775.

as the first reports of the engagements at Lexington and Concord were arriving in Ireland.[206]

Conclusion

The unrest in the American colonies during the agitation against the stamp act in 1765–66 and the Townshend duties in 1767–70, and the mounting resistance to the 'intolerable acts' in 1774–75, were followed with interest by Irish Protestants who, whether they were members of the established church or Dissenters, belonged to a single north Atlantic cultural province united by a shared language and by common religious, political and legal traditions. Indeed, the unrest in the colonies was widely regarded as part of a general political malaise affecting the British empire as a whole. For supporters of government, American unrest, the disturbances associated with John Wilkes in England, and patriotic agitation in Ireland during the 1760s could all be seen as products of patriotic demagoguery in the tradition of Trenchard and Gordon. In the same period, patriots in all three countries came to believe that their liberties were threatened by the perceived absolutist tendencies of George III and his neo-Tory favourite, the Earl of Bute. But while there are obvious similarities between the concerns of the Irish opposition and the issues that engaged the attention of American patriots in the years between the accession of George III and the outbreak of hostilities – powers of taxation, the size of the military establishment, the independence of the judiciary, the legislative supremacy claimed by the British parliament – the existence of such similarities does not imply that developments in America directly influenced either the evolution of ideas or the course of events in Ireland. On the contrary, the intellectual inheritance shared by the patriot opposition in both countries, their common subordination to the British parliament, and the impact of political developments in Great Britain on the empire as a whole, provide a sufficient explanation for the emergence of broadly similar patriot programmes in America and Ireland.

On the eve of the American war, Irish Protestants were divided between a minority of vociferous patriots who proclaimed their support for the colonists, a more traditional and conservative body which instinctively supported the mother country's assertion of its authority, and a third section of opinion, perhaps the largest, which continued to hope that some compromise would avert a conflict which seemed increasingly likely. However it would be a mistake to think that American affairs

---

[206] *Ibid.*, 10 June 1775. A report of the outbreak of hostilities in America appeared in *SNL*, 5 June 1775.

loomed particularly large in the consciousness of the Irish political nation. Although the patriot opposition – scarcely any stronger in 1775 than it had been twenty years earlier – drew parallels between the circumstances of Ireland and America and postulated the existence of a concerted ministerial plan to strengthen royal authority throughout the empire, the attention of the opposition remained focused on a programme of long-standing 'real Whig' demands (limitation of parliament, exclusion of pensioners and placemen from parliament, reduction of the pension list, establishment of a militia, independence of the judiciary, a habeas corpus act) which owed little or nothing to American example. Anglo-Irish patriots had been increasingly forthright in asserting Ireland's constitutional equality with Great Britain during the 1760s, but this development also emerged from the internal dynamic of Irish politics and had been signalled as early as 1749 in the writings of Charles Lucas. Direct contact between Irish and American patriots was fitful and transatlantic solidarity never progressed beyond the level of rhetoric.

Throughout this period, the Catholic community remained divided between prosperous landed and commercial interests anxious to assert their loyalty to the house of Hanover, and the bulk of the population whose long-standing hostility towards the existing political order showed no sign of waning. The support expressed by the former for the ministry's American policy would have been forthcoming in any event but was facilitated by the clamorous anti-Catholicism of the patriot opposition on both sides of the Atlantic. While the death of James III in 1766 finally allowed the Catholic clergy to give their unequivocal support to the reigning dynasty, Prince Charles Edward had long been the principal focus of popular affection and was hailed as king in the vernacular literature. The world-view of the Irish-speaking masses in which *Gaeil* and *Gaill*, Catholics and Protestants, Ireland and England, were locked in Manichaean opposition left them ill-equipped to appreciate the depth of the political gulf that had opened up between the *Gaill* of America and those of Great Britain during the reign of George III. The hopes of Irish Jacobites continued to be focused on the Bourbon powers, and there is no evidence to suggest that the colonial crisis had any impact on popular consciousness until its nature was transformed by the 'shot heard round the world'.

2 Colonial rebellion, 1775–1778

The first news that the Irish public received of war in America came from a report in a Massachusetts newspaper, the *Essex Gazette*, which crossed the Atlantic several days ahead of official despatches and was reprinted in the Irish press in the first week of June 1775, more than a week before the official account of the actions at Lexington and Concord was carried by the pro-government press. This factor is likely to have influenced the pro-American stance adopted by newspapers that could not normally be described as organs of patriot opinion. In Dublin, *Saunders' News-Letter* reprinted the *Essex Gazette*'s account of the engagements verbatim: 'Last Wednesday the 19th of April, the troops of his Britannic Majesty commenced hostilities upon the people of this province, attended with circumstances of cruelty not less brutal than what our venerable ancestors received from the vilest savages of the wilderness.'[1] A comment in the next issue of the same paper was more balanced but still attributed most of the blame for the violent turn of events to government: 'A correspondent, who calls the Americans obstinate, warmly censures the want of judgment, as well as humanity, in the conduct of our ministry towards the colonies. A small knowledge of history would teach them that the sword is as little likely to subdue an enthusiastic spirit of liberty, as fire and faggot are to suppress bigotry in religion.'[2] In Kilkenny, *Finn's Leinster Journal* sympathised with the military personnel involved in the actions but blamed the ministry for the outbreak of hostilities: 'a very essential, and a very glorious victory has been obtained by the brave Americans over the poor heart-broken soldiers, who were obliged to fight against, justice, their conscience, liberty, and their country'.[3] The expression of such outspoken opinions in the columns of normally staid papers may be less significant than it appears: the London press was the principal source of both information and comment on American affairs for Irish papers and a modern investigator has concluded that 'not only was the London press in the hands of the opposition, it was in the hands of the most

[1] *SNL*, 5 June 1775.   [2] *Ibid.*, 7 June 1775.   [3] *FLJ*, 21 June 1775.

radical elements of the opposition'.[4] It follows that the reportage and commentary on the American conflict in the Irish press cannot be taken at face value as a reflection of thinking in the Anglo-Irish community.

Although publications from all sources helped to shape political attitudes in Ireland, the present study will focus on material that bears internal evidence of Irish authorship and the few exceptions to this rule will be indicated. The extant files of contemporary Irish papers are far from complete, but those for which substantial runs survive include the official *Dublin Gazette*, which confined its coverage of the war to communiqués reprinted from the *London Gazette*; established commercial publications such as *Faulkner's Dublin Journal*, which was strongly pro-government, and *Saunders' News-Letter*, also pro-government but less markedly so; the patriot press represented by the *Freeman's Journal* and the *Hibernian Journal*; and regional papers (such as *Finn's Leinster Journal* in Kilkenny, the *Hibernian Chronicle* in Cork, the *Belfast News-Letter* and the *Londonderry Journal*) which, perhaps attempting to satisfy all strands of local opinion, tended to be less partisan in their coverage of American affairs than the Dublin press. Few provincial journals are extant, however, and the newspapers known to have been published during the period of the American war that have been largely or completely lost include the *Clonmel Gazette*, *Connaught Journal* (Galway), *Drogheda Journal*, *Galway Evening Post*, *Munster Journal* (Limerick), *Newry Chronicle*, *Waterford Chronicle*, *Westmeath Journal*, *Sligo Journal*, *Strabane Journal*, *Ulster Journal* (Monaghan) and the *Wexford Journal*. A notable publication that has not survived is the Catholic and pro-government *Dublin Mercury*, for knowledge of which we must depend on occasional hostile references in the patriot press.

Anglican opinion and the American war

The *Essex Gazette*'s interpretation of the actions at Lexington and Concord was whole-heartedly endorsed by the patriot press, which proceeded to explore the implications of this latest essay in ministerial tyranny for the Anglo-Irish community. For the *Freeman's Journal* the American conflict presented the component parts of the British empire with a stark choice between freedom and slavery: 'If the butchery goes forward in America, the question will be very short with us, whether we are to be freemen or slaves here; but to the American virtue will we probably be indebted at length for our salvation, but without deserving such a boon on our

---

[4] Solomon Lutnick, *The American Revolution and the British Press 1775–1783* (Columbia, Missouri, 1987), pp. 12–13.

part from indulgent providence.'[5] Lord Chatham's speech to the British
House of Lords, in which he pointed to Ireland's constitutional position
as a precedent which should be observed by the ministry in its dealings
with the American colonies, was reprinted: 'Ireland they [the Americans]
have to a man. In that country, joined as it is to the cause of the colonies,
and placed at their head, the distinction I contend for is, and must be
observed: this country superintends and controls their trade and navigation, but they *tax themselves*.'[6] Chatham, a victorious war leader and
Whig icon, was assured of a respectful hearing in patriot circles under
any circumstances, and could not fail to receive it when he called for
the removal of British forces from Boston and rejected the competence
of the British parliament to tax those who were not represented therein.
His assertion of unanimous Irish support for the colonists would also
have flattered local patriots, but they must have viewed other parts of his
speech with reservations: they had come to regard Ireland, not as first
among the colonies and a legitimate object of the British navigation acts,
but as a kingdom with an independent legislature of its own.

It may not be entirely coincidental that this perspective was reiterated in
the pages of the *Freeman's Journal* only a week after Chatham's speech was
reported in the columns of the same paper. The author, striking an anti-
Jacobite note which was a common feature of patriot rhetoric in England
but had a particularly strong resonance among Irish Protestants,[7] claimed
that the throne was 'surrounded by none but wicked, detested Jacobites,
by the well known friends of slavery, popery and oppression'. Invoking
the authority of William Molyneux, he argued that the exclusive right of
the Irish parliament to levy taxes in Ireland was at stake in the American
conflict:

Under a reign [William III's] far more favourable to liberty than the present,
an attempt was made to bind us by the laws made in the British parliament; it
was then the learned Molyneux took up his pen in our cause, and demonstrated,
in a treatise which will ever preserve his memory, that we are an independent
nation, and having a parliament of our own, are subject to laws only made in that
parliament, and to which we consent. If then at a time when, in other respects,
our rights are most severely struck at, the British parliament can obtain the power
of taxing the Americans without their consent, is it not reasonable to imagine they
may attempt to exercise the same unjust authority upon us?[8]

It may be doubted how widely this view of the Irish parliament's right
to legislative independence was shared by members of the Anglo-Irish
community, but it is clear that the authority of the British parliament to

[5] *FJ*, 6 June 1775.   [6] *Ibid.*, 10 June 1775. The emphasis is in the original.
[7] For England, see Lutnick, *The American Revolution and the British Press*, p. 115.
[8] *FJ*, 17 June 1775.

tax Ireland was generally rejected and that the assertion of such a power in relation to the colonies was a source of widespread concern.

Surviving private correspondence gives some indication of the initial reaction of Irish Anglicans to the outbreak of war. Charles O'Hara, an independent rather than an opposition member of parliament, memorably informed Edmund Burke that 'here we sympathize more or less with the Americans; we are in water colours, what they are in fresco' – a comment prompted by the claim of persons close to the British ministry that the Westminster parliament enjoyed the same authority over Ireland as it did over the colonies: 'The language of your ministerlings have made us what we are; for till [Charles] Jenkinson and company told us we were slaves, we never knew it; and might have gone on in the same happy ignorance.'[9] Another of Burke's correspondents, the Dublin lawyer John Ridge, informed him that 'all the Protestants as far as I can see, especially the Presbyterians, except a few who have connections in the army at Boston and a few military geniuses (such as Lord Bellamont) are here with us, friends to the American cause'.[10] Burke's views on the American crisis were well known and the objectivity of his correspondents' assessments of the mood in Ireland must therefore be doubted, but the records of debates held by the Trinity College Historical Society provide some quantitative evidence of the political attitudes of younger members of the Anglo-Irish élite at this time. Before the outbreak of war, in November 1774, the Society had answered the question 'Whether the Athenian colonies in Sicily should have been subject to the laws of taxation imposed on them by the Athenians?' in the negative.[11] Unusually, the numbers voting on each side of the question were not recorded on that occasion. A year later, in November 1775, the issue of colonial taxation was again considered – this time without any classical camouflage. To the question 'Whether taxation without consent of the person taxed or his legal representative be consistent with real liberty?', eight members answered 'yes' and ten 'no' – a narrow margin in favour of the American position.[12] In March 1776, when the related but distinct question 'Whether a colony should have an equal share in the legislature with the parent state?' was considered, the result was reversed and colonial claims were rejected by the more substantial margin of fourteen votes to five.[13] There are obvious reasons why too much weight should not be attached to these straw polls. Apart from the small numbers involved, the results must also be treated with caution because of the presence of English students among those voting; because

---

[9] O'Hara to Burke, 5 June 1775, in Hoffman, *Edmund Burke*, p. 585.
[10] Ridge to Burke, 25 September 1775, in *ibid.*, p. 600.
[11] Historical Society minutes, 9 November 1774, TCD Mun. Soc./Hist. 2, p. 152.
[12] *Ibid.*, 8 November 1775, pp. 298–9.   [13] *Ibid.*, 27 March 1776, pp. 374–5.

of the exclusive social background of the student body; and, of course, because the voting must to some extent have been a judgement on the abilities of the speakers rather than the merits of the question. None the less, the evidence of the student debates suggests the existence of widespread sympathy for the Americans on the specific issue of taxation, together with a more sceptical – or even hostile – attitude towards evolving colonial demands in the legislative sphere. The prevalence of such an ambivalent viewpoint in the wider Anglo-Irish community is confirmed by the positions adopted by both government and opposition speakers in parliament.

It is not my intention to provide an account of the parliamentary manœuvrings of either government or opposition in relation to the American crisis. However, it seems reasonable to assume that speakers on both sides of the house would have emphasised the arguments they considered most likely to elicit the sympathy of the political nation out of doors. To the extent that parliamentary orators were playing to the gallery, their speeches may shed some light on the attitudes of the Anglo-Irish community as a whole and will therefore be considered here.

Sir John Blaquiere, the chief secretary, outlined the strategy adopted by the parliamentary opposition in a letter to the secretary of state:

[the opposition] meant to connect the discontents of Ireland with those of Great Britain and America, and standing upon the breach of our law for the 12,000 men, by addresses from different parts of the country, by laying hold of party expressions thrown out in your House of Commons touching your right of taxing Ireland, which embarrasses Irish government more than I can possibly tell you, they meant, by these and such other means after the recess, to cast such a set of resolutions as must have injured you, and perhaps have ruined us entirely.[14]

Evidently, these two issues – the need to maintain a strong garrison (the strength of which had fallen slightly below the 12,000 required by law as troops were withdrawn for service in America) and the danger that the British parliament would proceed to tax Ireland if colonial resistance were overcome – were identified as the strongest cards in the hand of the opposition. Taxation was thought to be of such importance by Lord Harcourt, the lord lieutenant, that he wrote to Lord North to complain about the conduct of government speakers in the British parliament:

When, for example, it is asserted here that Great Britain has no intention of taxing Ireland, is it necessary to proclaim in your House of Commons an absolute right of taxing Ireland – not, I presume, intended to be exercised – or to inflame the minds of a loyal people at a time most critical to Great Britain . . . by vaunting and unprovoked declarations of superiority and menace?[15]

---

[14] Blaquiere to Rochford, 12 October 1775, Gilbert Library Ms. 93, p. 261.
[15] Harcourt to North, 12 November 1775, *ibid.*, p. 284. I have normalised the punctuation.

In spite of such obstacles, the administration won a crucial victory over an opposition weakened by the recent defection of Henry Flood to the government benches when it succeeded in having a condemnation of the American 'rebellion' inserted in the reply of the Commons to the speech from the throne by the comfortable margin of ninety votes to fifty-four. Harcourt informed Whitehall that he had considered an early test of strength on the American question to be advisable in view of the growing strength of the opposition: 'I saw the moment approaching, when this important question, would have been pressed upon me by the opposition to the king's government in this country, who were daily gaining strength upon this ground with such advantages, that I should have had great difficulty in resisting it.'[16] Almost without exception, opposition speakers in the debate focused on the question of taxation. Redmond Morres, representing Dublin city, openly justified American resistance:

If any power on earth, except our own legislature, should tax me, or attempt to alter our constitution, I would oppose them – I would resist. I am the firmer in this opinion, because I know my constituents, in this great metropolis are of the same sentiments: And shall we then, Sir, condemn the Americans who act on the same principles?[17]

Barry Yelverton, another patriot member, echoed this position, saying that 'he could not call the Americans rebels, without at the same time allowing the right and authority of the British parliament to tax them; and no slavery can be more perfect, than to be taxed where men are not represented'.[18] Thomas Conolly, a member for County Londonderry and normally a government supporter, made the same point, arguing that 'the next step would be to tax Ireland in the British parliament; for it had been already asserted there, that they had an absolute right to do so'.[19] John Ponsonby, the former speaker, argued in favour of reconciliation but added that if the Americans refused a conciliatory offer – the outlines of which he did not attempt to trace – the war effort should be supported.[20] Luke Gardiner, member for County Dublin and a frequent though not invariable supporter of government, expressed his 'abhorrence' of the ministry's actions in America and likened ministers to 'those rash practitioners who prescribe immediate amputation, when any inflammation or gangrene comes on, which might be cured by gentler means'.[21] The contribution of Walter Hussey Burgh, a prominent member of the opposition and one of the Duke of Leinster's connection, was exceptional in looking beyond the immediate question in dispute and in

---

[16] Harcourt to Rochford, 11 October 1775, PRO SP 63/449, fo. 87v.
[17] *HM*, October 1775, 609.   [18] *Ibid.*   [19] *Ibid.*   [20] *Ibid.*   [21] *Ibid.*, p. 612.

echoing the conspiracy theories of the most extreme extra-parliamentary patriots:

It is evident Britain has not relinquished her design of destroying the rights of this kingdom; she has torn off already one of the valuable privileges of a free nation, an appeal to the House of Lords: and the book written by Molyneux, in defence of Irish rights, was burnt by the hands of the common hangman.[22]

It seems likely that opposition speakers concentrated on the narrow issue of taxation, not only because they viewed it as the fundamental cause of the conflict between Great Britain and the colonies, but also because they were conscious of a widespread apprehension in the Irish political nation as a whole that the successful taxation of America by the British parliament would serve as a precedent for the taxation of Ireland by the same body.

This impression is strengthened by the response of government speakers in the debate. Sir John Blaquiere allayed the concerns of wavering members by formally dissociating government from the suggestion that the British parliament enjoyed the power to tax Ireland: 'any mention in the English House of a right to tax Ireland, was only the rash opinion of some individuals, not authorized or adopted by government, and was wrong founded'.[23] This was an authoritative statement which not only disavowed any intention of taxing Ireland at Westminster but also placed on record an official declaration that any such action would be impolitic, if not unconstitutional. Likewise, the attorney general, James Dennis, readily conceded that 'if the British parliament's taxing America could in some sort infer a similar right in them to tax Ireland, the arguments used by the opponents to this part of the address would be unanswerable', a position which clearly implied that Ireland was not merely 'at the head' of the colonies, as Lord Chatham had stated, but was a polity of a different and higher order – a kingdom that could only be taxed by its own parliament.[24] This line of argument must have assuaged the fears of many, both within and without the doors of parliament. It was, moreover, a position that could be held even by those who were sympathetic to colonial demands. Thus the author of a pamphlet advocating Catholic relief digressed from his subject to argue, first, that the colonies were not subject to the British legislature and, second, that even if *they* were, Ireland certainly was not:

Ireland is not to be compared with Virginia, St. Christopher's, Nevis, Montserrat, or any other island or place in the American seas, or elsewhere, that have been

---

[22] *Ibid.*   [23] *Ibid.*, p. 610.
[24] John Ridge to Edmund Burke, 11 October 1775, in Hoffman, *Edmund Burke*, p. 605.

conquered by or planted at the cost of and settled by the people and authority of the British nation; if even all or any of those circumstances make a people once received into the bosom of the laws, and the consequent enjoyment of the liberty and privileges of Great Britain, any way dependent upon or subordinate to a legislature in which they have no representatives; the negative of which I have not for myself a doubt of adopting . . .[25]

If ministerial assurances on the taxation issue drew the members of parliament in one direction, opinion 'out of doors' exerted an opposite effect on the minority of members who represented counties and open boroughs. The existence of a substantial body of pro-American opinion in the country is confirmed by the chief secretary's admission that the inveterate opponents of administration had been joined in the vote on the reply to the speech from the throne by 'some county members frightened with the apprehension of rotten eggs and the approaching election'.[26]

Government's initial success was followed in November 1775 by a resolution authorising the withdrawal of 4,000 of the 12,000 troops on the Irish establishment for service overseas. In order to allay the anxiety that this weakening of the garrison would inevitably provoke among the Protestant population it was proposed to replace the withdrawn troops with an equal number of Germans. Both proposals were vigorously attacked by the opposition, the latter with more effect than the former: while the withdrawal of 4,000 men was approved by 121 votes to 76, their replacement with Germans was rejected by 106 votes to 68. As in the earlier debate, opposition speakers identified taxation as the key issue. John Ponsonby expressed his confidence that the British parliament's waiving the right to tax the colonies would be sufficient to end the conflict:

the Americans were dutiful and contented till the stamp act was passed for the purpose of internal taxation. At this they murmured, this they opposed; but as soon as it was repealed they cheerfully returned to their duty, and so would they do now, if the same expedient was used. To take a part against America will likewise be contrary to prudence, for if we assist to punish them for resisting against being taxed by the British parliament, we furnish a precedent against ourselves, if ever the like occasion should happen.[27]

Barry Yelverton – arguably the most prominent patriot in parliament since Flood's defection – claimed that the proposed troop withdrawal was intended to 'aid the arbitrary designs of a despotic ministry' and forcefully reiterated the central message of the opposition: 'Great Britain pretends to a supreme authority over all her dominions, as well in regard

---

[25] [Arthur Brooke], *An Inquiry into the Policy of the Laws, Affecting the Popish Inhabitants of Ireland* (Dublin, 1775), pp. 125–6.
[26] Blaquiere to Rochford, 12 October 1775, in Gilbert Library Ms. 93, p. 261.
[27] *FJ*, 28 November 1775.

to internal taxation, as to commercial regulations. Does this assertion not include Ireland? It certainly does; and nothing is wanting but a plausible pretext, or a proper opportunity to enforce it.'[28] He echoed contemporary debates in Britain by rejecting the theory of 'virtual representation' ('Representation is not a representation of persons, but of property . . . not one American blade of grass is represented in the British parliament, therefore it cannot be justly taxed there') and by endorsing the view that the American colonists had been unaffected by corrupting influences which had sapped the spirit of liberty in England itself: 'English men surely did not lose their spirit as well as their rights by crossing the Atlantic? No; they did not; they carried thither their free born spirit before it was contaminated with an influx of Asiatic wealth.'[29] George Ogle, who sat for County Wexford, discerned an alarming connection between the taxation question and the proposed introduction of German troops, two issues which might have been regarded as unrelated: 'A land tax will probably be attempted here; and if it does not succeed, (as certainly it cannot) then it will be laid on by the British parliament, and the foreign troops will be left here to enforce obedience.'[30] Opposing the sending of troops to 'cut the throats of their American brethren', he revived a familiar patriot theme in proposing a militia ('our natural, our constitutional defence') as the proper replacement should the proposed withdrawal of troops take place. Sir Edward Newenham, probably the most outspoken supporter of the American cause in parliament, opposed the introduction of German troops as he believed that 'the designs of the ministry ultimately tended to erect a military government'.[31] Walter Hussey Burgh harped on fears that were shared by many members of the established church outside the House. The withdrawal of 4,000 troops would, he declared, leave the country 'open to the insurrections of the White Boys in the south, and the Steel Boys in the north'.[32] Taxation was also emphasised in the protest entered in the journal of the House of Lords by six peers. The protesting peers, who were headed by the Duke of Leinster, declared that since the 'arbitrary levying of money is contrary to all freedom, and particularly to all English ideas of freedom' it was no surprise to them that it should be resisted by 'a nation born of Britain, warmed by her principles, and taught by her example'.[33]

If the arguments advanced by the opposition in the debate were entirely predictable, a mixture of old and new themes was employed by pro-government speakers. Hercules Langrishe, formerly a pro-American pamphleteer but now a supporter of administration, once again laboured

---

[28] *SNL*, 29 November 1775.   [29] *Ibid.*   [30] *FJ*, 28 November 1775.   [31] *Ibid.*
[32] *Ibid.*   [33] *HJ*, 1 December 1775.

the essential constitutional distinction between the ancient kingdom of
Ireland and Britain's North American colonies. He hoped that no member of parliament 'would suffer himself to be impressed with apprehensions arising from loose or unguarded expressions thrown out by rash
or inconsiderate men in another kingdom' because Ireland's rights were
'founded on an antient and firm basis, and its constitution was coeval
with that of Great Britain itself'.[34] Somewhat more imaginative was an
attempt to stimulate anti-American sentiment in response to an embargo
placed on the importation of Irish goods by Congress.[35] It is clear, however, that the threat posed to the unity of the empire by events in America
now formed the principal theme of pro-government speakers. Opening
the debate, Sir John Blaquiere posed the question 'Whether at a time
when the empire of Britain was shaken to its foundations, Ireland should
take part with England or with America?'[36] The issue of taxation was portrayed as a mere pretext for the rebellion – the colonists' true goal which
they were not yet ready to avow openly was independence. In the words
of John Foster, member for County Louth, 'It was clear that the wish of
America was a total independence; and if we refuse to send these troops
we prevent a reconciliation, by hindering Great Britain from enforcing
reasonable terms, which, if properly enforced, the Americans might agree
to.'[37] Luke Gardiner, the member for County Dublin who had opposed
the inclusion of any reference to America in the reply to the speech from
the throne, now supported the administration's proposal and argued that
'the question is not, whether America resisted first, or whether she was
oppressed first; but at present it stands only, whether America shall be
forever lost to Great Britain, or not?'[38] If the patriots believed that the
majority of the Irish political nation rejected the right of the British parliament to tax the colonies, supporters of administration seem to have
been equally confident that the Anglo-Irish community as a whole would
deplore any threat to the unity of the empire. Both were probably correct, and the example of Luke Gardiner indicates that imperial unity
outweighed other considerations in the minds of some.

The Catholic masses and the American war

The attitude of lower-class Catholics towards the American conflict, as it
is reflected in the vernacular literature of the period, owed nothing to arcane constitutional arguments about the powers of the British parliament.

[34] *HM*, December 1775, 752.
[35] See the report of Denham Jephson's speech in *FJ*, 28 November 1775.
[36] *HM*, December 1775, 750.   [37] *FDJ*, 28 November 1775.
[38] *FJ*, 28 November 1775.

Instead, the conflict was interpreted in the light of a long-standing world-view that assumed the persecution of Catholics by the established church, the oppression of Ireland by England, and the illegitimacy of the Revolution settlement. The prevalence of such an outlook did not imply that Catholics would necessarily sympathise with the American rebels but it did preclude the possibility of widespread support for Britain.

A poem composed by Uilliam an Chreatháin Ó Dábhoireann, a County Clare author, during the first months of the war when General Gage's army was besieged in Boston illustrates the intensity of popular hostility to Britain but contains no overt indication of sympathy for the colonists, whom it describes as 'Presbyterians'. The piece begins with an ironical expression of concern for the British forces in Boston:

> *Is trua liom na scéalta do chuala go déanach*
> *im' chluasa do chéas me le sealad*
> *ar scuaine seo an Bhéarla do ghluais uaim le tréimhse*
> *as cuanta na hÉireann go Boston,*
> *le fuadar le faobhar dá bhfuadach le chéile*
> *is dá scuabadh ins na spéarthaibh 'na gceathaibh*
> *le fuaim torann piléaraibh ag slua* Presbytérian
> *cé gur mhór ar féasta iad 's ar bainis.*[39]

(Grieved am I by the stories I've lately heard, that have pained my ears for some time, about this English-speaking herd which set out some time ago, from the harbours of Ireland for Boston, with energy and arms being driven together, and being blown to the sky in showers, to the sound of roaring bullets by a *Presbyterian* army – though they'd be great at a feast or banquet.)

Ó Dabhoireann made no distinction between the English and the Anglo-Irish and identified the besieged army with the oppressors of the Irish ('*ba bhuartha agaibh Gaelaibh*' – 'the Gaels were tormented by you'). Amid much non-specific rhetoric about the oppression to which the Gaels were subjected ('*dá suaitheadh le claonadh is le cleasaibh*' – 'being shaken by deceit and trickery'; '*i gcrua-shnaidhm an daorbhroid*' – 'in the harsh fetter of bondage') the Penal prohibition on Catholics leasing land for long terms was selected for particular mention ('*gan buaineacht 'na saolaibh / a lua do na Gaelaibh ar thalamh*' – 'with no permanence in their lives assigned to Gaels on land').[40] Ó Dabhoireann showed no interest in the matters at issue between Britain and its colonies and his work gives no indication of any sympathy for the Americans *per se*, but the mere fact that the unrelenting enemies of the Irish had suffered heavy casualties at the battles of Concord and Bunker Hill and were now hemmed

---

[39] '*Is trua liom na scéalta do chuala go déanach*' in BL Egerton Ms. 160, fo. 157b.
[40] *Ibid.*, fos. 158, 158b.

into the town of Boston was itself cause for celebration and for hope – irrespective of either the merits of the dispute or the identity of Britain's enemy. Confirmation that this attitude was not confined to Munster is provided in a rare manuscript of Connacht origin written by Brian Ó Fearghail, a scribe who was resident in County Galway in the 1770s. A bilingual entry in his hand reads as follows:

Cogadh an dá Ghall, probably now beginning between his Majesty King George, and the Americans,

> *An uair do cloífear an leon, agus chaillfeas an fothannán a bhrí*
> *is binn binn do sheinnfeas an chláirseach, idir a hocht agus a naoi.*

1777
The lion, for England, the thistle for Scotland, the harp for Ireland.[41]

('The war of the two *Gaill*', probably now beginning between his Majesty King George, and the Americans, 'When the lion is defeated, and the thistle loses its vigour, most melodiously will the harp play, between eight and nine.' 1777. The lion, for England, the thistle for Scotland, the harp for Ireland.)

'*Cogadh an dá Ghall*' (the 'war of the two *Gaill*') recalls two earlier conflicts that changed the course of Irish history: '*cogadh an dá Aodh*' (the 'war of the two Hughs', 1594–1603) and '*cogadh an dá rí*' (the 'war of the two kings', 1689–91). The word '*Gall*' originally signified any non-Gael but by the eighteenth century it had come to be associated with English speakers, whether Irish Catholics of Anglo-Norman descent, more recent Protestant settlers, the English themselves, lowland Scots or American colonists. Prophetic references to *cogadh an dá Ghall* long predate the American revolution[42] and persisted long after it: the verse that Ó Fearghail associated with the American war would be used in the 1840s to forecast an imminent repeal of the act of union, and again in the 1850s to predict a British defeat in the Crimean War.[43] It is likely that the prediction originally envisaged either a civil war in England or an Anglo-Scottish conflict which would again provide favourable circumstances for rebellion in Ireland, but the American war was easily explicable within the same prophetic framework – especially as English-language

[41] RIA Ms. 23 O 35, p. 91.
[42] See, for example, '*Tráth chogaios an dá Ghall*' in RIA Ms. 23 M 4, p. 154, a manuscript that was written about 1725.
[43] See Colm Beckett, *Aodh Mac Domhnaill: Dánta* (n.p., 1987), p. 30 and Nicholas O'Kearney, *The Prophecies of Saints Columbkille, Maeltamlacht, Ultan, Seadhna, Coireall, Bearcan, &c.* (Dublin, 1856), p. 200. For use of the phrase by Ulster and Connacht authors in twentieth-century literature see Séamus Ó Grianna, *Caisleáin Óir* (Cork, 1976), p. 26 and Máirtín Ó Cadhain, *Cré na Cille* (Dublin, 1949), p. 219.

authors commonly described it as a civil war. The nationalist character of the message is evident: England and Scotland will be weakened by the present struggle and Ireland will have an opportunity to assert its rights in 1778 and 1779. The American war was also identified as '*cogadh an dá Ghall*' in a later anonymous song from west Ulster composed some time after General Burgoyne's surrender at Saratoga, news of which reached Ireland in December 1777.[44] This northern composition establishes that the view of the conflict as an Anglo-Saxon civil war which should be welcomed by Irish Catholics was geographically widespread.

A Munster author named Seán Mac Cathail reworked the well-known Jacobite song '*Síle Ní Ghadhra*' (one of the many personifications of Ireland in the vernacular verse of the period) in the early days of the war by incorporating contemporary references, not only to American events, but, more importantly from his perspective, to well-publicised Spanish preparations for an overseas expedition. This song was as forthright as Ó Dábhoireann's composition in its hostility to Britain but its attitude towards the Americans was more ambiguous:

> *Tá an fhoireann so Liútair dá dturnamh i ngach bóthar,*
> Prussia *agus a chomplacht ag tnúth le Hannover,*
> *Gage bocht i gcoimheascar dá bhrú ag* Bostonians
> *Putnam dá rúscadh agus gan súil le teacht beo aige.*
> *Ar bóchna tá an gasra in arm agus i bhfaobhar*
> *a seolta ar leathadh agus is maiseach a scéimh*
> *chun fóirthin ar Bhanba ó anbhroid dhaor,*
> *taoiseach ceart Gael orthu b'shin* Captain Reilly
> *agus beidh an lá leis an mbuíon seo ag Síle Ní Ghadhra.*[45]

(This crew of Luther's is being vanquished on all sides, *Prussia* and its forces are longing for Hanover, poor Gage is in battle and being crushed by *Bostonians*, Putnam is being pelted and he doesn't expect to escape alive. At sea the soldiers are armed and keen, their sails are spread and beautiful is their appearance, to rescue Ireland from cruel oppression, a true chieftain of the Gaels commands them, that's *Captain Reilly*, and victory will belong to this band of Síle Ní Ghadhra's.)

This Spanish expedition was described by the *Annual Register* as 'the most formidable in its preparations, of any in the present age' and was commanded by General Alexander O'Reilly, a County Meath-born veteran of the Hibernia regiment in the Spanish service.[46] Mac Cathail's hope that the force might be intended for Ireland was not entirely unreasonable – Britain and Spain had come close to war over the Falkland Islands in

---

[44] See '*Dar Cogadh an dá Ghall a thosaigh go mall*' in Breandán Ó Buachalla (ed.), *Cathal Buí: Amhráin* (Dublin, 1975), p. 59.
[45] '*Tráth dom ag smaoineamh ar chríochaibh an tsaoil seo*' in UCD Ferriter Ms. 4, p. 288.
[46] *Annual Register*, 1775, p. 146.

1770 – but the expedition was in fact directed against Algiers. His up-dated version of '*Síle Ní Ghadhra*' illustrates both the continuing vigour and relevance of popular Jacobite politics and the prevalence of the idea that 'England's difficulty is Ireland's opportunity'. A literal reading of the only copy of the work that I have located would suggest that the author regarded the commander of American forces at the battle of Bunker Hill, Colonel Israel Putnam, with as little favour as he did the British com-mander in North America, General Thomas Gage. Such a 'plague on both their houses' stance is quite conceivable and many Catholics may have contented themselves with gloating at British reverses while remain-ing indifferent to the fate of their Whiggish, Dissenting and increasingly republican opponents. It should be noted, however, that the song's ap-parent neutrality may be an artefact of careless orthography: the phrase '*dá rúscadh*' is commonly pronounced '*á rúscadh*' and substitution of the latter in the verse above would transform its meaning from 'Putnam is being pelted' to 'Putnam is pelting him [Gage].'

What is clear is that the possibility of war in Europe, rather than the existing rebellion in North America, remained the principal theme of popular political song – predictably enough as the Bourbon powers alone seemed capable of ending British rule in Ireland. While the Kerry-born poet Eoghan Rua Ó Súilleabháin lauded Benedict Arnold's advance into Canada at the head of an American army in one of his many Jacobite *aislingí* (vision-poems), his reference to the American conflict was little more than a rhetorical device to increase the credibility of the predicted overthrow of the existing régime:

> Le sámh-thoil Dé fuair páis is péin
> tá an báire ag téacht 'na gcoinne ar buile
> fágfaid séanfaid rithfid sin
>   as caomh-chríoch Eoghain,
> atá Arnold laoch nár stán i mbaol
> ag fáil an lae ar an bhfoireann uile
> an mál so ag maodhmadh, ag milleadh-bhriseadh
>   an chlaon-dlí nó.
> Tá ag téacht i mbarcaibh sár-dhín go magh mhín Chuailnge
> ag traochadh an tsleachta chráigh sinn, na táinte rí-ghas óg,
> cloífear créimfear díscfear tréad
>   an fhill is an Bhéarla in iomaidh an tsiosma
> is chífear Gaeil 'na n-ionad suite
>   i saor-shlí só.[47]

---

[47] RIA Ms. 23 B 14 contains copies of '*Tráth inné is mé tnáite i bpéin*' on pp. 164 and 244; the first of these omits the reference to Arnold – a reflection of popular disillusionment with his subsequent career – but I have used it to supply some words that are unclear in the second copy. The song has been edited in Risteárd Ó Foghludha (ed.), *Eoghan Ruadh Ó Súilleabháin 1748–1784* (Dublin, 1937).

(By the calm will of God who suffered passion and torment, the contest is turning against them [the British] rapidly, they'll leave, they'll quit, they'll flee the beautiful land of Eoghan [Ireland]; Arnold, a hero who never shirked danger, is vanquishing the entire crew, this hero is bursting and shattering the perverse new law; they are coming in stout ships to the smooth plain of Cuailnge [Ireland], wearing down the race which tormented us, hosts of majestic young warriors; they'll be crushed, ground down, destroyed – the herd of treachery and of the English language in the schismatic contest – and Gaels will be seen installed in their place in comfortable liberty.)

In the final verse the inevitable female personification of Ireland delivered once again the oft-repeated prophesy that her lover, the Stuart pretender, would be restored to his crown by invading heroes: '*Réabfaid reacht is rátaí an táir-rí thuathail / méirleach meabhail tá faoi bhláth i ríocht mo stóir*'[48] ('They'll tear up the legislation and taxes of the false base king, a fraudulent plunderer who flourishes in the kingship of my beloved'). A faint echo of contemporary constitutional arguments about the powers of legislation and taxation may be detectable in this traditional message.

From early in the war, therefore, American successes were celebrated and colonial generals appeared as heroes of vernacular song. This fusion of anti-British and pro-American sentiments is also found in a drinking song composed by Tomás Ó Míocháin, a County Clare schoolmaster, in celebration of General Howe's evacuation of Boston on 17 March 1776. George Washington, the commander of the besieging American army, was naturally cast in the heroic role played by Benedict Arnold in Ó Súilleabháin's *aisling*:

> *Is fonn 's is aiteas liom Howe is na Sasanaigh*
> *tabhartha, treascartha choíche,*
> *is an crobhaire, Washington, cabharthach, calma,*
> *i gceann is i gceannas a ríochta;*
> *sin amhais ag screadadh gan chúil, gan chathair,*
> *gan trúip, gan barcaibh ar taoide,*
> *is fá Shamhain go dearfa búir na Breataine*
> *i bponc fá thearmainn Laoisigh.*[49]

(It's a joy and a pleasure to me that Howe and the English, are spent and destroyed for ever, and stalwart Washington, supporting, courageous, is at the helm and in command of his realm; behold the mercenaries screaming without a refuge or city, without troops, without ships on the sea, and by Halloween it's certain that the British boors, will be trapped and in the custody of Louis [XVI].)

Like his Kerry-born contemporary, Ó Míocháin predicted that Britain's defeat would lead inevitably to a Stuart restoration. However warmly they

---

[48] *Ibid.*
[49] '*A ghéaga cumainn na nGael gcumais*' in RIA Ms. 23 L 35, p. 128; edited in Ó Muirithe (ed.), *Tomás Ó Míocháin.*

applauded American victories, Catholic authors gave no indication of support for the Whig ideology of the colonial patriots – military commanders such as Arnold and Washington might be lauded, but political leaders such as Hancock or Adams were passed over in silence. When the County Limerick poet Séamas Ó Dálaigh responded in verse to Ó Míocháin's song he made only the most cursory reference to the American conflict, citing it in support of his assertion that the long-prophesied return of the 'wild geese' was finally at hand:

> D'fhág na flaithibh is na fáidhibh feasach
> bhí tráth i bhfearann Loirc líonmhar
> le fáil a marbhna i bpár 's go beachtaithe
> sárcheart tarranta scríofa,
> ar dháil an chatha seo 'chairde Chailvin
> tharla i mBoston i gcoimheascar,
> gan spás go gcasfadh go bláth i mbaile poirt
> cáidhshliocht calma Ghaoil Ghlais.[50]

(They've left – the princes and learned prophets who once were numerous in Lorc's land [Ireland] – their elegies available in parchment, correctly and most accurately drafted and written, [which predict] that on the outbreak of this battle among Calvin's friends which took place in the fight at Boston, there quickly would return in splendour to port the pure valiant progeny of Gael Glas.)

As poets had done for three generations, Ó Dálaigh predicted that the Irish regiments would be accompanied by 'an mál gan ainm' – 'the nameless prince' – a thinly veiled reference to the Stuart pretender which would have been readily understood by his audience. These early responses to the American war confirm that the political culture of the Irish-speaking population remained firmly grounded in Catholicism, nationalism and Jacobitism, as it had been since the Revolution. The sympathy of lower-class Catholics for the American rebels was superficial and rested on nothing more profound than the pragmatic calculation that 'my enemy's enemy is my friend'.

In view of both the practical difficulties and the risk of prosecution involved, it is not surprising that the seditious sentiments which characterise the vernacular verse of the period seldom found expression in print, but a pamphlet by Thomas O'Brien McMahon, a Catholic priest from County Clare, published at London in 1777, is a rare exception. The pamphlet is primarily a work of religious controversy in which McMahon poured scorn on the irreligion of the English, but he also gave free rein to his

---

[50] 'D'fhág na flaithibh is na fáidhibh feasach' in Maynooth Ms. C 15, p. 27; edited in Diarmuid Ó Muirithe, 'Amhráin i dtaobh Cogadh Saoirse Mheiriceá'. Gael Glas was an ancestor of Milesius, mythological ancestor of the Irish.

nationalism and informed the 'unfortunate natives of Ireland' that they had endured 'long and unparalleled sufferings' under the English yoke:

Your fertile country uncultivated, through their industry-chilling discourage-ment – your trade, notwithstanding your advantageous situation, cramped and insignificant, through their restraining laws. Every branch of trade – particularly those most beneficial to agriculture, English influence has doomed to decay.[51]

McMahon was equally outspoken in his Jacobitism. English menda-city and perfidy were clearly revealed in the work of Whig propagandists who propagated 'throughout the three kingdoms the villainous tale of the warming-pan . . . making it serve for a corner-stone, to support the black citadel of rebellion, and the perjured transfer of their allegiance'.[52] He also expounded a rudimentary theory of imperialist exploitation: the English had developed an 'accursed system of policy', that of 'reducing to beggary every nation subject to their realm'.[53] The poverty of the Scots and Irish who barely survived on 'a scanty allowance of oaten-meal and water, or potatoes and water' was the result 'not of their sloth, but of the jealous and unheard of tyranny with which they are treated by some good-natured na-tion that enslaved them'.[54] McMahon did not dwell on the American con-flict, but in a passing reference he interpreted the rebellion there as further evidence of English exploitation and oppression: 'certain colonies, [by] their actions have discovered abundantly the deep sense they entertain of the moderation, freedom from tyrannical insolence, disinterestedness, good-nature, and humanity of – Englishmen'.[55] This singular work ex-pressed a political outlook which pervades the vernacular literature of the period but which seldom found its way into either print or the English lan-guage. Inevitably, it attracted hostile attention. Sir Edward Newenham, prominent patriot, anti-Catholic and supporter of America, informed the House of Commons that 300 copies of a 'dangerous treasonable book' which was intended to 'advance popish tenets' had been shipped from London to Limerick.[56] Similarly, an anonymous letter received by the chief secretary linked McMahon's pamphlet with an imaginary Catholic conspiracy in which the Limerick-based antiquary Sylvester O'Halloran and the Clare-born but French-based antiquary Thomas O'Gorman were also implicated.[57]

The absence of principled support for the rebellious colonies is hardly surprising given the prominence of anti-Catholic rhetoric in the pro-nouncements of American patriots. In a speech delivered at the state

---

[51] [Thomas O'Brien McMahon], *Remarks on the English and Irish Nations* (reprinted Dublin, 1792), p. 63.
[52] *Ibid.*, p. 83. [53] *Ibid.*, pp. 63–4. [54] *Ibid.*, p. 188. [55] *Ibid.*, p. 67.
[56] *HM*, March 1778, 184 and *HJ*, 30 January 1778.
[57] Anonymous and undated letter to Sir Richard Heron, NLI Ms. 13,057.

house in Philadelphia and published as a pamphlet at Dublin in 1776, Samuel Adams assured an audience which included fellow members of Congress that 'Our fore-fathers threw off the yoke of popery in religion; for you is reserved the honour of levelling the popery of politics . . . This day, I trust, the reign of political Protestantism will commence.'[58] He implicitly associated Catholics with Indian 'savages' and black slaves when he charged that the British ministry were '*Men* who have let loose the merciless savages to riot in the blood of their brethren – who have dared to establish popery triumphant in our land; who have taught treachery to your *slaves*, and courted them to assassinate your wives and children.'[59] Much of the American literature that was reprinted in Ireland in the early stages of the war portrayed the conflict in religious terms. A sermon preached at Philadelphia in July 1775 to mark a day of fasting proclaimed by Congress, and which was reprinted in Belfast, called on God to hear 'the prayers which are this day offered up unto thee, by the whole family of Protestant people throughout this American continent'.[60] In August of the same year the *Freeman's Journal* reprinted a report from the *Essex Gazette* of Salem, Massachusetts, which equated Catholicism with sectarian butchery: 'We hear that one Porter, an attorney at Salem, was lately detected at Cohoss, in conveying a letter from [General] T. Gage [commander of the British army at Boston] to Governor Carleton at Quebec, requiring his very good friends, the Catholics, may be forthwith sent to assist him in cutting the throats of all heretics.'[61] Yet the signals coming from America were confused and contradictory enough to ensure that the rebellion was not viewed in Ireland as an essentially anti-Catholic movement. The issue of the *Freeman's Journal* which carried the above report also reprinted an address from Congress to the inhabitants of Canada in which the importance of religious differences between the inhabitants of Britain's North American colonies was discounted: 'We perceive the fate of the Protestant and Catholic colonies to be strongly linked together, and therefore invite you to join with us in resolving to be free by rejecting with disdain the fetters of slavery, however artfully polished.'[62] Even Hoey's *Dublin Mercury*, which consistently sought to attract a Catholic readership while extending uncritical support to the administration, was obliged to note the more tolerant stance adopted by Congress, while casting doubt on the sincerity of the new approach: 'the high stile of the

---

[58] Samuel Adams, *An Oration Delivered at the State-House, in Philadelphia, to a Very Numerous Audience; on Thursday the 1st of August, 1776* (Dublin, 1776), pp. 6–7.
[59] *Ibid.*, p. 44.
[60] Thomas Coombe, *A Sermon Preached before the Congregation of Christ Church and St Peter's Philadelphia, on Thursday, July 20, 1775* (Belfast, 1775), p. 23.
[61] *FJ*, 12 August 1775.   [62] *Ibid.*

intolerant Continental Congress is already happily changed, and the popish Canadians are now most tenderly addressed as friends, countrymen and fellow-sufferers; and even invited to a share in the (new) constitution. This, doubtless, is good policy.'[63] Impressions of American tolerance can only have been strengthened when the terms extended by the Donegal-born Brigadier Richard Montgomery to the inhabitants of Montreal on the capitulation of that city became known, including as they did a provision that 'the inhabitants, whether English, French or others, shall be maintained in the free exercise of their religion'.[64]

Montgomery was a Presbyterian and the brother of Alexander Montgomery, a member of parliament for County Donegal, but Catholics cannot have been unaware that they too had kinsmen among the rebels. A list of the 148 colonels commanding American infantry regiments published by the *Freeman's Journal* included such distinctively Irish surnames as McCabe, Ryan, O'Sullivan, Daly, O'Hara, Walsh, O'Mara, O'Dermott, O'Madden, Fitzpatrick, Nowlan, Molloy, Dermot, Gannon and McGuire.[65] If little positive support for the political principles of the colonial patriots was forthcoming from the Catholic masses, it is equally true that they had every reason to welcome a conflict which, whether it resulted in a British defeat or in the reconquest of sullen and alienated colonies, appeared likely to weaken the existing political and ecclesiastical order throughout the British empire.

Presbyterian opinion and the American war

Many contemporary observers attributed strong pro-American sentiments to the Presbyterian community. In late 1775 Sir John Blaquiere, the chief secretary, referred to the 'natural fanaticism of the northern province' in a letter to the secretary of state and, writing to the prime minister, described Ireland as 'a country principally inhabited by papists connected by interest, and Dissenters attached by principle to America'.[66] At about the same time Lord Harcourt mentioned the 'Presbyterians in the north, (who in their hearts are Americans)' in a letter to the secretary of state.[67] Nor was this merely the view of outside or hostile observers. In June 1775, as the first reports of the battle at Concord were being studied, the prominent patriot Lord Charlemont, a major landowner in County Armagh, noted that 'a proper and unusual spirit seemed to be

[63] Quoted in *FLJ*, 7 August 1775.   [64] *Ibid.*, 18 January 1776.
[65] *Ibid.*, 14 September 1776.
[66] Blaquiere to Rochford, 12 October 1775, and North, 17 December 1775, in Gilbert Library Ms. 93, pp. 261 and 307 respectively.
[67] Harcourt to Rochford, 11 October 1775, PRO SP 63/449, fo. 87v.

rising in the country, especially in the northern parts'.[68] As late as 1777, and writing from a very different political viewpoint, Lord Hillsborough, who was a member of the British parliament, a former secretary of state for America and a major landowner in County Down, informed the then lord lieutenant that the 'Dissenters are almost all Americans, their parsons, (many of them) preach against the duty due to government, and pray for the success of the rebels and their common people universally adopt these principles.'[69] But very different views can also be found. In August 1775 Lord Bellamont offered to raise 500 recruits in Ulster, declaring himself impatient to 'disprove a bold and unwarranted assertion touching that respectable district, with which I have too intimate a communication not to know to a certainty that every attempt to alienate their affections will prove abortive, and that even the nearest tie of blood will find themselves dissolved, where those of loyalty have been violated'.[70] Lord Bellamont's estate was in County Cavan where the Protestant population tended to be Anglican rather than Presbyterian, but similar views were expressed by Lord Antrim, a major landowner in the county of the same name, who advised the lord lieutenant in October 1775 that he lived 'in the midst of a very Protestant tenantry, which might enable him to be serviceable either in raising a new corps, or in forwarding the recruiting service'.[71] Recruitment will be discussed later in this chapter, but at this point it can be said that the numbers enlisting were low throughout Ireland and that Ulster was no exception. The *Freeman's Journal* expected that 'in the north of Ireland, particularly, the same general aversion will continue to shew itself, that none however great in title and promises, may be able to induce them from virtuous employments, to fight against their friends and cousins in America'.[72] Northern Dissenters undoubtedly had much closer links than any other section of the Irish population with America. As one Presbyterian minister put it, 'there is scarcely a Protestant family, of the middle and lower classes among us, who does not reckon kindred with the inhabitants of that extensive continent'.[73] The contribution made by immigrants from Ulster to the American cause was immediately apparent in one of the opening campaigns of the war – the invasion of Canada.

---

[68] Charlemont to Henry Flood, 15 June 1775, in BL Add. Ms. 22,930, fo. 57v.
[69] Hillsborough to Lord Buckinghamshire, 25 October 1777, in NLI Ms. 13,035 (13).
[70] Bellamont to Blaquiere, 15 August 1775, in PRO SP 63/448, fo. 109r.
[71] Harcourt to Rochford, 27 October 1775, in W.E. Harcourt (ed.), *The Harcourt Papers*, IX (n.p., n.d.), pp. 17–18.
[72] *FJ*, 9 September 1775.
[73] William Steel Dickson, 'On the ruinous effects of civil war' in Brendan Clifford (ed.), *Scripture Politics: Selections from the Writings of William Steel Dickson* (Belfast, 1991), p. 48.

General Richard Montgomery, who captured Montreal in November 1775 and was killed when leading an unsuccessful attack on Quebec in the following month, has already been mentioned, and it is clear that immigrants from Ulster comprised a large part of the army under his command. During the course of the British counter-offensive that cleared Canada of American forces in the summer of 1776 more than 200 prisoners were captured in the battle of Trois Rivières. A register which records their names and, in most cases, their country of origin, has survived. It reveals that at least eighty-nine of the captured rebels were natives of Ireland – a figure which considerably exceeds the fifty-four prisoners from the thirteen united colonies, the fifteen from England, the four from Scotland, and the twenty from other specified countries. No place of birth was recorded for forty-three men. In short, 48 per cent of the Trois Rivières prisoners whose place of birth is known were from Ireland. An examination of their names suggests that about twenty-six were from a Catholic background; the great majority of the remainder, or about one third of the total, are likely to have been Presbyterians.[74] The interest taken by the Ulster public in the Canadian campaign is evident from the publication in Belfast of an oration delivered by William Smith, the Scottish-born educational theorist and episcopalian divine, in memory of General Montgomery at the request of the Continental Congress.[75] In view of the close personal ties which existed between Ulster and the American colonies, it is safe to assume that the outbreak of hostilities in America was deplored with near unanimity by the Presbyterian community. But lack of enthusiasm for the war effort should not be equated with support for the American cause, nor should one lose sight of the fact that Ulstermen also served in the British forces. Guy Carleton, the governor of Canada who repulsed the attack on Quebec with a motley force of Canadian militia, sailors and Scottish immigrants, was a native of Strabane, County Tyrone. In July 1776, the *Londonderry Journal* informed its readers, with every appearance of pride, that 'two thirds of the sailors who defended Quebec, were Irish'.[76] While Carleton was a member of the established church, this cannot have been true of all the Irish-born sailors under his command.

[74] The following names are suggestive of a Catholic background (the original spellings are preserved): Timothy Mading, Dennis Murphy, Felix Muckilheany, Patrick McGlochlan, Patrick Teagert, Thomas Kelly, John Docherty, Patrick Fitzpatrick, John McGinnis, Neal Hardin, Daniel Riggin, Cornelius Crawley, Patrick Dier, Daniel Troy, Dominic Cook, Michael McConnor, Charles McLaughlan, Thomas Welch, Hugh McCarty, John Maloney, Thomas Delaney, James Kelly, John Curran, Thomas Curran, John Riely, Patrick Doyle. See PRO CO 42/35, fos. 133–6.
[75] Smith's oration was delivered at Philadelphia on 19 February 1776 and was advertised for sale in *BNL*, 7 May 1776.
[76] *LJ*, 9 July 1776.

Only contemporary texts produced by, and for, Presbyterians can establish the views of that community on the issues posed by the American war with any degree of confidence. Unfortunately, there is a dearth of such primary sources from the early years of the conflict. While complete files of two Ulster papers, the *Belfast News-Letter* and the *Londonderry Journal*, have survived, only a small proportion of the war-related material that they contain was written locally. Neither journal displayed any marked bias, either in its reporting of the war or in its treatment of the underlying issues. But although the towns where the papers were published were predominantly Presbyterian, they did not cater for an exclusively Presbyterian readership. The catchment areas of both papers contained considerable numbers of Anglicans who, in view of their generally higher social status and the high cost of newspapers (which were subject to stamp duty after 1774), are likely to have formed a greater proportion of the newspaper-buying public than they did of the general population. The output of political pamphlets in the northern province was small and few such productions appeared during the early years of the war. Sparse though the extant sources are in comparison with what is available for the Catholic and Anglican communities, they convey the impression of a community which was anxious for peace, which contained within it a substantial body of opinion sympathetic to the American cause, but which confined its criticisms of the ministry within the conventional bounds of Anglo-Irish patriotic discourse.

Although the Common Council of Dublin called for an aggregate meeting of the citizens to consider the American crisis as early as June 1775 – a meeting which took place in October – it was not until the 4 November 1775 that a similar meeting was held in Belfast. Chaired by the sovereign of the town, the meeting adopted a 'humble address and petition of the merchants, traders, and other principal inhabitants' which, unlike the Dublin equivalent, was 'agreed to without a dissenting voice' and was 'signed by almost every person present'.[77] The address noted the adverse effect of the conflict on the city's linen exports and, blending Irish with American grievances, argued that 'limited and restrained as the commerce of this country is by the policy of the British legislature' the disruption of transatlantic trade would have a particularly severe effect on Ireland. The address was forthright in its condemnation of the war but was more equivocal in relation to the political issues involved, requesting the king to intervene to halt the bloodshed on the grounds that the Americans had been

[77] *FLJ*, 22 November 1775.

driven to extremities by sanguinary men, for the mere suspicion of political error; and that in questions so involved and dubious, that many of the greatest names, many of the wisest and best men who have ever adorned these lands, together with large important communities of the people, are firm in their opinion, that the error is not chargeable on them.[78]

A plea for the restoration of 'that old constitutional system, under which Great Britain and her colonies, united in affection as in interest, grew in strength, till they became the admiration and envy of other nations' establishes that the Belfast meeting placed the blame for the outbreak of war on constitutional innovations introduced by the British ministry and there can be little doubt that the power of taxation claimed by the Westminster parliament was uppermost in the minds of those who signed the petition. This emphasis on taxation is evident in various statements which emanated from patriotic circles in Ulster. In July 1775, for example, the following toasts were drunk at a gathering of freeholders held in Coleraine, County Derry, to support John Richardson, an 'independent' candidate who proposed to stand for one of the county's seats in the next general election: 'May Protestant Dissenters always enjoy the full benefit of a constitution, of which they have ever been the steady supporters. – May we and our fellow subjects every where enjoy the invaluable right of disposing of our own money.'[79] An implicit comparison was made here between the vestry act and the efforts of the British parliament to tax the Americans. The vestry act was repealed in 1776 and it was hardly coincidental that the motion for its repeal was moved by one of the sitting members for the same county.

In the event, Richardson's election bid was unsuccessful but the patriots had a notable success in County Antrim where two 'independent' candidates and two candidates supported by major landowners split the vote almost equally, with one from each party being elected. The successful independent, James Wilson, took a typically patriotic pledge in which he promised to support a habeas corpus bill; the establishment of 'a more fair and equal representation of the people in parliament'; the exclusion of pensioners from, and a reduction in the number of placemen in, the House of Commons; and the amendment or repeal of Poynings' Law in order 'to restore to Ireland her rights as a free country'. In addition, the candidate undertook not to accept any 'place, pension, title, or emolument' if elected.[80] However no mention was made of the authority of the British parliament to legislate for Ireland and the criticism of Poynings' law in the Antrim pledge must therefore be seen as an

---

[78] For the text of the address see Joy, *Historical Collections*, pp. 119–20.
[79] *FJ*, 12 August 1775.   [80] *BNL*, 31 May 1776.

assertion of the right of parliament, and of the Commons in particular, to initiate legislation, to have bills transmitted unaltered to England, and to have them returned unaltered if they received the royal assent. That is to say, it asserted the rights of the legislature against the pretensions of the executive, rather than the rights of Ireland against the pretensions of Great Britain. The County Antrim pledge contained no reference or allusion to the American conflict, but in March 1776 James Wilson resigned his commission as a marine captain on half-pay in order to avoid, as he put it, having to 'disobey the commands of his sovereign, or adopt the horrid alternative of stifling every impulse of humanity, and rushing into the blood of his kindred fellow-subjects and countrymen'.[81] That Wilson should express his views so bluntly only three months before the general election strongly suggests that he considered it likely to increase his following among the electorate; at the very least, one can assume that he believed such an anti-war declaration would be unlikely to harm his electoral prospects. Some years later a hostile commentator wrote that Wilson had 'resigned his half-pay as captain to devote himself entirely to the popular and Presbyterian interest'.[82] When a dinner was held in Belfast to celebrate Wilson's election victory the toasts included 'equal liberty to all parts of the British empire' and 'reformation to those who established popery in Canada' – the former could be read as a reference to either Irish or American grievances or to both, and the latter repeated a frequently voiced grievance of American patriots which held a particular appeal in the atmosphere of Presbyterian Ulster. But a pious aspiration for 'a speedy and happy reconciliation between Great Britain and America' was the only explicit reference to the war. A toast to Lord Chatham, 'increase of health to him, and may his wisdom again save us', was probably inspired by the conflict and is worthy of note because Chatham consistently asserted the right of the British parliament to regulate the trade of the colonies – and of Ireland – while rejecting its right to tax those territories: 'this distinction between external and internal control is sacred and insurmountable' he declared in the British House of Lords.[83] The Belfast patriots toasted candidates in four other constituencies: 'Mr Dawson, and the independent electors of Armagh. Mr Richardson and the independent electors of Derry. Mr Tennison, and the independent electors of Monaghan. Mr Edward Newenham, and the independent electors of the county of Dublin.'[84] All of these except Richardson were elected, but the small number of candidates named is indicative of

[81] Joy, *Historical Collections*, pp. 127–8.
[82] G.O. Sayles (ed.), 'Contemporary sketches of the members of the Irish parliament in 1782', *Proc. RIA* 56 C (1954), 233.
[83] *FJ*, 10 June 1775.   [84] *BNL*, 25 June 1776.

the weakness of the patriot opposition as an electoral force in Ulster as a whole. A similar celebratory dinner was held at Dundonald, County Down, where Lord Chatham was again toasted, as were 'A speedy and happy agreement between Great Britain and America' and the 'Memory of Gen. Montgomery'.[85] Ulster patriots, like their counterparts in the capital, continued to believe that the status quo *ante bellum* would be restored if only the British parliament could be induced to drop its claim to tax the colonies.

During the course of the Antrim election campaign the *Belfast News-Letter* published a series of anonymous 'Letters' by Hugh Boyd in support of Wilson's candidacy. Boyd employed a radical rhetoric and urged his readers 'never to lose sight of the great fundamental principle, that *you are the origin of power*. Government was constituted *by*, and *for*, the people.'[86] While the 'Letters' as published in the *Belfast News-Letter* made no overt reference to the American conflict, when they were subsequently issued in pamphlet form a preface was added which explicitly linked Ireland's fate with that of the colonies. If Britain defeated the Americans, Boyd predicted that 'This unhappy country will then feel, and will lament too late, the mischiefs of her voluntary folly, in abetting the tyranny of the parent-state over her dependencies. For, what better name than tyranny can be given to a system of arbitrary exaction, supported by the sword?'[87] Further evidence of support for the American cause in Ulster was provided by the publication in Belfast in August 1776 of *A Congratulatory Poem on the Late Successes of the British Arms; Particularly the Triumphant Evacuation of Boston*, a satirical work by William Preston that had previously been published in Dublin.[88]

The same edition of the *Belfast News-Letter* which announced the appearance of a local edition of Preston's poem also carried the text of the American declaration of independence. This development had the potential to disrupt what had hitherto been, if not a pro-American consensus, at least an anti-war consensus in the Presbyterian community. The claim that independence was the true goal of the Americans had been the central argument advanced by supporters of the ministry since the early days of the war. As early as July 1775 an anti-American article in the *Londonderry Journal* had stated that 'independence is no longer the concealed object of many in the colonies', adding for good measure that the 'system of a Chatham is spurned at with as much detestation as a North's'.[89]

[85] *Ibid.*   [86] *Ibid.*, 27 February 1776.
[87] [Hugh Boyd], *Letters Addressed to the Freeholders of the County of Antrim* (Belfast, 1776), p. x.
[88] See the notice of publication in *BNL*, 27 August 1776.
[89] *LJ*, 4 July 1775. This was probably reprinted from a British source.

Supporters of the colonies had been equally emphatic in denying such claims. Hugh Boyd, in the preface to the pamphlet mentioned above, asserted that 'To check the independent views of America, was not the motive [for the war]; because no such views were entertained, and therefore no such motive could exist. But liberty existed, flourished, in that great continent; and that is a crime of the deepest dye in the ethics of modern polity.'[90] Similarly, an article which appeared in the *Londonderry Journal* just two days before the declaration of independence was signed rejected the idea that the 'odious name of rebels' could properly be applied to the Americans since they 'are neither disaffected to his Majesty, nor dispute his title, as was the case in the rebellions of 1715 and 45'.[91] Now, however, the claims of government had been fully vindicated and it was inevitable that support for the Americans would decline as a result. There is anecdotal evidence that the decline may have been less marked among Ulster Presbyterians than it was in the case of their neighbours who were members of the established church. One man later recalled how the declaration of independence shattered the unity of a patriotic club in the Coleraine of his childhood:

On hearing news from America favourable to their cause, indeed the entire village seemed but as one family, united in praying for the success of their efforts. This continued until the famous declaration of 4 July 1776 arrived, when Mr Lecky withdrew from the club, and his brethren of the village who were members of the established church thought it incumbent on them to join in the hue and cry against the rebels.[92]

Reports of similar divisions among the colonists themselves must have further undermined local support for the American cause.

Even before news of the declaration of independence arrived in Ireland the publisher of the *Londonderry Journal* advertised two very different publications in the same notice. One was *Common Sense*, Thomas Paine's powerful polemic in favour of independence; the other was *Plain Truth*, a coherent rebuttal of Paine's arguments by the same William Smith who just a few months previously had eulogised General Richard Montgomery at the request of Congress.[93] Support for the colonists may also have been eroded in the second half of 1776 by reports of an uninterrupted series of British victories as Carleton expelled the Americans from Canada, and Howe seized New York and pursued Washington's army across New Jersey. In October the *Belfast News-Letter* published an optimistic letter which a resident of Belfast had received from an officer serving with Howe's army:

---

[90] [Boyd], *Letters Addressed to the Freeholders of the County of Antrim*, p. xvii.
[91] *LJ*, 2 July 1776. This article was reprinted from the *Freeman's Journal*.
[92] Quoted in Stewart, *A Deeper Silence*, p. 54.   [93] *LJ*, 19 July 1776.

The independent declaration has produced great discord among themselves, and many (who heartily wished it) will now make it a pretext for a retreat, as they must be pretty well convinced we shall conquer... I am convinced that the plan of accommodation most likely to last, would be to banish all taxes, and regulate the support, which it is fair and necessary the colonies should afford to the empire, by the sums and proportions which Britain pays; but not to lose sight of the acts for the regulation of trade... I pronounce that the Congress will be annihilated, and the British laws restored by the first of December.[94]

Around the same time, the *Londonderry Journal* published an anonymous poem entitled 'Hope Revived' in which the figure of Britannia, recovering from an illness, rose from her couch and declaimed as follows:

> But now me thinks a gladdening ray appears,
> to soothe my sorrows, to dry up my tears;
> and make my laurels, which I thought would fade,
> bud out a fresh, and spread an ampler shade
> my Howe's victorious arms achieve the deed,
> may glory after glory still succeed;
> bid smiling peace at length expand her door,
> with greater joy than e'er she knew before![95]

Many who had previously sympathised with the colonists may have considered neutrality to be the wisest stance to adopt in the changed political and military circumstances. In a published sermon preached to the Presbyterian congregation at Ballyhalbert, County Down, on 13 December 1776, Rev. William Steel Dickson outlined the destructive effects of the war and continued: 'Nor, are we to charge these effects, *wholly*, either upon destructive counsels at home, or rebellious dispositions abroad. Moderation will readily admit there may be, and indeed have been, errors on both sides.'[96] The argument that there were 'errors on both sides' would seem to imply the need for concessions on both sides and a settlement far short of independence for the colonies. By late 1776 Lord Harcourt felt able to give the prime minister a reasonably sanguine, if somewhat cynical, assessment of the political attitudes of the Presbyterian community:

The Presbyterians in general are a discontented people, but not more so than they have been for many years. That many of them bear a good will to their brethren in N. America I make no doubt, but from any thing that has hitherto appeared, there is no reason to suspect that their infatuation will carry them further than to supply the Americans in a clandestine manner and at a very dear rate with such

[94] *BNL*, 29 October 1776.
[95] *LJ*, 8 November 1776. This was probably reprinted from a British source.
[96] William Steel Dickson, 'On the advantages of national repentance' in Clifford, *Scripture Politics*, p. 43.

necessaries as they may stand in need of, which is too frequently the case among trading people.[97]

The climate of opinion must also have been influenced by the close cultural, religious, and educational ties between Presbyterian Ulster and Scotland. In June 1777, for example, the General Assembly of the Church of Scotland condemned the American rebellion in the most forthright terms in an address to the king which was reprinted in the local press:

> We observed with deep concern the first appearance of a turbulent and ungovernable spirit among the people of North America. We have contemplated its alarming progress with astonishment, and beheld fellow subjects, who enjoyed, in common with us, the blessings of your Majesty's mild administration, take arms in opposition to your just authority, disclaim the supremacy of the British legislature, reject with disdain the means of conciliation generously held out to them by your Majesty, and labour to erect their unlawful confederacies into independent states.[98]

When, later in the same month, 'a respectable number of the delegates and other freeholders of the county of Antrim' met in Belfast to celebrate the first anniversary of the County Antrim election the resolutions adopted contained no reference to the American conflict.[99]

Yet the declaration of independence and British successes on the battlefield did not entirely silence the supporters of America in Ulster. In November 1776 a new edition of Molyneux's *Case of Ireland* appeared at Belfast, the publisher's advertisement declaring that its publication had been prompted by 'the principles inimical to the liberties of Ireland, held out by members of the present British parliament'.[100] It might be thought that this referred only to the belief of some supporters of the ministry that the British parliament had the same powers of taxation in Ireland as in the colonies, but the foreword to the new edition was more sweeping. It described Molyneux's book as 'a work highly useful to be read and understood, by all who glory in the freedom and independence of this kingdom' and condemned the mercantilist restrictions on Irish trade by which the 'parliament of Britain assumed a privilege to prescribe limits to our trade, and attempted ('tis to be feared too successfully) to blast a part of that general liberty, restored to the empire, on the accession of William the third (of immortal memory) to the crown of those kingdoms'.[101] An explicit comparison between the situation of Ireland and the American colonies underlined the contemporary relevance of Molyneux's work:

---

[97] Harcourt to North, 21 October 1776, in Gilbert Library Ms. 93, pp. 469–70.
[98] *BNL*, 10 June 1777; *LJ*, 13 June 1777.   [99] *Ibid.*, 24 June 1777.
[100] *BNL*, 1 November 1776.
[101] Molyneux, *The Case of Ireland's Being Bound by Acts of Parliament in England*, [p. i].

How should the doctrines contained in this work be now esteemed, when that body [the British parliament], have attempted to trample on the most valuable privileges of one country, and threaten to usurp an authority over the liberties of this? The same lust of domination, which hath led them to encroach on the constitutional rights of our fellow subjects in America, may (if their attempt shall succeed) lead them to desire to bind Ireland also, by their laws, 'in all cases whatsoever'.[102]

Similarly, a Belfast edition of a pamphlet by John Witherspoon, the Scottish-born signatory of the declaration of independence, was published in 1777. In it, Witherspoon explained that the Americans had 'resolved that they will be both free and independent, because they cannot be the one without the other' and justified this contention with an argument which would have been of particular interest to Irish readers:

The king of England, living in his English dominions, would not, and indeed durst not, assent to any act of an American legislature, that was, or was supposed to be hurtful to his English subjects. This is not founded on conjecture, but experience. There is not (at least Dean Swift affirms it) any dependence of Ireland upon England, except an act of the Irish parliament, that the king of England shall be the king of Ireland. This last has a separate independent legislature, and in every thing else, but the above circumstance seems to be perfectly free; yet if any man should assert, that the one kingdom is not truly subject to the other, he would, in my opinion, know very little of the state and history of either.[103]

In Belfast, as in Dublin, a core of radical patriots continued to support the American cause and to assert that the fate of Ireland was linked to that of the colonies, but the impression persists that such views were more rarely voiced in the period after the declaration of independence.

Pro-American agitation

Among the members of the Protestant political nation generally, the superior organisation of the opposition to that of government supporters is indisputable. As early as 13 June, only a week after the news of Lexington and Concord had reached Ireland and before any official account of the engagements had been published, the Common Council of Dublin called by 'a large majority' on the city's sheriffs to convene an aggregate meeting of citizens to consider an address to the king on the subject of events in America.[104] The meeting was not held until 24 October but it then adopted, by the emphatic margin of 278 to 43, an address 'greatly lamenting the present civil war; and humbly entreating his Majesty's interposition to heal the breach'. Among those who spoke in favour of the

---

[102] *Ibid.*, [pp. i–ii].   [103] Witherspoon, *Dominion of Providence*, p. 40.
[104] *FJ*, 20 June 1775.

address were Sir Edward Newenham and James Napper Tandy.[105] Copies of the address were left in the city's coffee houses, where it was expected that it would be signed 'by at least two thousand Protestants' – an expectation which was not disappointed as, by the time it was presented to the lord lieutenant in December, it was said to bear 'near three thousand names'.[106] On the opposition side, the Society of Free Citizens provided a forum where like-minded patriots could concert their actions. The members dined together periodically and at the first such gathering after the outbreak of war, with James Napper Tandy in the chair, the toasts included several that referred to the American crisis, either directly or by commending prominent opponents of the ministry's American policy. The toasts of the Free Citizens constitute a virtual litany of Whig heroes and anniversaries and demonstrate the essentially colonial, Anglocentric and Protestant character of their patriotism:

Our fellow subjects in America, now suffering persecution for attempting to assert their rights and liberties. – The Continental Congress; unanimity to their councils, and success to their resolves. – The glorious memory of the great King William. – The memory of the incorruptible Charles Lucas. – The patriotic lord mayor and livery of London. – The Earl of Chatham; and may he soon appear at the head of an honest administration... The 19th of April, 1775 [Lexington and Concord]; and the memory of the brave Americans who fell in defending the liberties of their country... 1st of July, 1690. [the Boyne] – 12th of July, 1691 [Aughrim]... – 5th of June 1215. [Magna Carta] – 26th of February, 1768. [the octennial act] – 16th of April 1746 [Culloden]; and the memory of the Duke of Cumberland. – The two Protestant bishops, Exeter and St. Asaph. – Laud's fate to every bishop that voted for the establishment of popery in Quebec. – A speedy downfall to the present Jacobite administration... The xxxth of January, 1648–9 [execution of Charles I]; and the memory of Oliver Cromwell.[107]

Efforts to mobilise pro-administration sentiment in the capital were less successful. An attempt to convene a meeting of government supporters in the music hall at Fishamble Street on 10 November was frustrated by a large attendance of patriots. According to the *Hibernian Journal* – which also commented favourably on the absence of Catholics from the event – only seventeen persons appeared to support an address that expressed 'disapprobation of sundry unjust, unnatural and ungrateful measures, adopted by some of the American colonies'.[108] It is not necessary to rely on the accuracy of this report in an opposition journal to conclude that the bulk of politically active Anglicans in the capital reacted with dismay to news of the American war and attached most of the blame for its commencement to the British ministry.

[105] *Ibid.*, 26 October 1775.
[106] *HJ*, 15 December 1775, which also gives the text of the address.
[107] *Ibid.*, 19 July 1775.   [108] *Ibid.*, 15 November 1775.

While Anglo-Irish patriots were drinking to the success of the Continental Congress, other sections of Irish society were manifesting their sympathy for the American cause in more practical ways. As early as September 1775 Lord Harcourt advised the secretary of state that 'Intelligence has been sent me from Cork and Limerick that there are vessels now lying at each of those places bound for America, having on board numbers of young men, to the amount of nearly one hundred, indented, as is given out, for servants; but who may possibly be intended for the rebel army.'[109] The source provides no information on the religious affiliations of the men – who may, in any event, have been genuine indentured servants – but the Munster locations strongly suggest that those involved were predominantly Catholic, while the viceroy's action in informing Whitehall of the matter indicates a high level of official concern. Practical support for the American rebellion was shown by Presbyterian merchants in the Ulster ports. In November 1775 a treasury official wrote that 'Newry, Belfast and Larne are [the Irish] ports which succour America most', with linen and woollen goods being shipped to the island of Providence in the Bahamas from where they were reshipped to the rebel colonies.[110] More seriously, in May of the following year the lord lieutenant informed the secretary of state of an attempt by two merchants, James Lecky and Andrew Thompson of Dublin and Newry respectively, to ship gunpowder to the rebels; an American vessel disguised as a French ship was impounded.[111] In the same month a British agent reported that Irish merchants operating out of Nantes – a group which would have been largely, if not entirely, Catholic in composition – 'trade with America via French West Indies. *Experiment* from Dublin is now loading with gunpowder.'[112]

Pro-American sympathies were also manifested by Dubliners of lower social rank. In September 1776 as Lord Harcourt was preparing to leave Ireland he commended the magistrates of Dublin for their role in 'defeating and crushing at the peril of their lives and to the manifest prejudice of their properties the many popular commotions which at different times have been endeavoured to be excited by turbulent people in this metropolis in favour of the cause of the American rebels'.[113] In the same letter he referred to the practice of houghing off-duty soldiers as they walked through the streets of the capital. A wave of such attacks had taken place in late 1774 and early 1775 but a lull followed until 12 August when

---

[109] Harcourt to Rochford, 1 September 1775, PRO SP 63/448, fo. 159.
[110] John Robinson to John Pownall, 25 November 1775, in K.G. Davies (ed.), *Documents of the American Revolution 1770–1783 (Colonial Office Series)*, X (Dublin, 1976), p. 137.
[111] Harcourt to Weymouth, 17 May 1776, in PRO SP 63/454, fos. 34–36r.
[112] Theodore Canon to Lieutenant-Governor Irving of Guernsey, 5 May 1776, in Davies (ed.), *Documents of the American Revolution*, X, p. 303.
[113] Harcourt to North, 11 September 1776, Gilbert Library Ms. 93, p. 442.

another member of the garrison was houghed. There is evidence that this attack may have been associated with a strike by journeymen skinners but it prompted the archbishop of Dublin to urge Catholics in his diocese to behave 'in a manner perfectly becoming peaceable neighbours, edifying Christians and faithful subjects' in a letter read at all Masses on the following Sunday.[114] None the less, a further concentrated series of attacks followed within two months: one soldier was houghed in Dublin on 14 October, two on 15 October, and one 18 October.[115] Attacks in the capital then appear to have halted until mid-1777 but they continued in other garrison towns. Soldiers were houghed in Cork city in November 1775 and in July 1776, when the latter attack prompted the mayor to offer a reward of £50 for information leading to the apprehension of those responsible.[116] A series of attacks took place in Waterford in January 1776 in which two soldiers were houghed and an attempt was made to hough a third, as a result of which the enormous sum of £600 was subscribed by the inhabitants for information leading to the conviction of the 'monsters of barbarity' responsible for the attacks.[117] In October 1777 the Dublin-published *Magee's Weekly Packet* reported that 'the infernal practice of houghing is again revived in this city' and described attacks which had taken place on two soldiers, one of whom was houghed and the other stabbed in the stomach.[118] Further houghings of military personnel in the capital took place on 6 October, 16 October and 26 October – the last incident involving a sentry in the yard of Dublin Castle.[119] In the same month, the lord mayor issued a proclamation offering a reward of £30 for information leading to the apprehension of those responsible.[120] This mayoral proclamation was ineffective and in early December it was reported that a soldier had been houghed 'within ten yards of the barrack gate'.[121] At the end of the year a government proclamation offered the more substantial reward of £300 for information leading to the arrest of each of the first three persons convicted of houghing twelve named soldiers from four different regiments in Dublin city between the months of July and December.[122] The high number of victims detailed in the proclamation serves as a useful reminder of the inadequacies of the eighteenth-century press: I have located press reports of

---

[114] *Dublin Gazette*, 19 August and 22 August 1775.
[115] *Ibid.*, 19 October and 21 October 1775.
[116] *FLJ*, 25 November 1775 and 3 August 1776.
[117] *Ibid.*, 3, 24, 27 January and 3 February 1776.
[118] *Magee's Weekly Packet*, 4 October 1777.   [119] *FDJ*, 11, 18 and 28 October 1777.
[120] Proclamation dated 17 October 1777; see, for example, *FDJ*, 24 January 1778.
[121] *Magee's Weekly Packet*, 6 December 1777.
[122] Proclamation dated 22 December 1777; see, for example, *Dublin Gazette*, 24 December 1777.

only five of the twelve attacks described in the proclamation and it seems
reasonable to assume that newspapers would have been less efficient still
in recording such incidents when they took place outside the capital. It
has already been seen that there is evidence to link the butchers of the
Ormond markets with the wave of attacks on members of the military
which took place in 1774–75 and the same is true of the fresh outbreak.
In January 1778 the *Freeman's Journal* published an anonymous letter
which called on legislators to turn their attention to 'the state of warfare in which the soldiery and the inhabitants of this kingdom (but more
particularly those of the city of Dublin) have for some years lived' and
claimed that the campaign of houghing was carried out by men who were
'hardened by their occupation against the feelings of humanity' – a phrase
which points to the butchers.[123] It is possible that the Dublin houghers
employed the tactic, at least in part, as a gesture of solidarity with the
Whiteboys. Certainly, it is clear that sympathy for the Whiteboys existed
in the capital and that it could find violent expression. For example, when
a Whiteboy from County Tipperary was executed at St Stephen's Green
in February 1778 for his part in the killing of an unpopular magistrate
the hangman had his skull fractured by the hail of missiles thrown at him
by an enraged crowd.[124]

The loyalty of the Catholic élite

It has already been seen that members of the Catholic élite – the surviving
members of the gentry, the prosperous merchants of the Dublin-based
Catholic Committee and, since the death of James III, leading members of the clergy – moved towards a position of support for the existing political order during the 1760s. This body of opinion was given an
opportunity to make a formal declaration of its principles in 1774 when
the Irish parliament passed an act to permit 'his Majesty's subjects of
whatever persuasion to testify their allegiance to him'.[125] The oath prescribed by the act contained a pledge of allegiance to George III and his
successors, an abjuration of the person 'said to have assumed the stile
and title of king of Great Britain and Ireland, by the name of Charles
the Third', a repudiation of the power of the pope to depose princes,
and a declaration that no foreign prince, including the pope, had 'or
ought to have any temporal or civil jurisdiction' in Ireland. The oath
provoked a lively controversy among both the Catholic clergy and laity,
with even some of those who had been instrumental in its introduction

---

[123] *FJ*, 22 January 1778.   [124] *Ibid.*, 10 February 1778.
[125] 13 & 14 George III c. 35. The text of the oath is reprinted in Fagan, *Divided Loyalties*,
  p. 143.

being reluctant to take it. No Catholics had subscribed to the oath by the beginning of 1775[126] and it seems likely that the oath was the subject under discussion at a 'mixed meeting of Catholics' held under the aegis of the Catholic Committee in the following June – a meeting which failed to reach a decision.[127]

The arguments put forward by both opponents and supporters of the oath provide an insight into the political beliefs of members of the higher strata of Catholic society at this time and indicate the persistence of Jacobite sentiment even among members of the social élite. An anonymous author, writing in the unlikely forum of the patriot-inclined *Hibernian Magazine*, advanced the following reason for declining to take the oath: 'Because the words "ought to have" seem to have a retrospect to the Revolution, by which James IId. was deprived of the throne because he was a Roman Catholic, and made attempts to re-establish the Roman Catholic religion'.[128] This was a purely historical argument, and the belief that it was proper to have supported James II in his efforts to retain his crowns in 1689–91 did not necessarily imply that future attempts by his grandson to recover them should also be supported. But some objections to the oath related to future contingencies. Charles O'Conor confided to a clerical correspondent that:

On my own part (and it is the case of many others) I have long hesitated on the paragraph: 'That no power whatsoever can dispense with the obligation of the allegiance sworn to', though certainly the sense of the legislature refers to nothing more or less than the allegiance which is due to the executive power while *it can afford* that protection, or *withdraws not* that protection which the constitution requires for the security of the public. In any other sense the oath would be absurd.[129]

What O'Conor envisaged here was nothing less than the overthrow of the existing constitutional order, although it is unclear whether he was anticipating another revolution in England or a foreign invasion of Ireland. He made it clear to his correspondent that he would not consider himself to be bound by an oath of allegiance in such circumstances: George III might depend on his loyalty for just so long as his ministers were in effective control of Ireland but it would be 'absurd' to maintain one's allegiance to the king once a new régime had been installed.

The arguments advanced by those who supported the oath are still more revealing. The author of an anonymous pamphlet written to rebut

[126] *Ibid.*, p. 145.
[127] Maureen McGeehin, 'The activities and personnel of the General Committee of the Catholics of Ireland, 1767–84' (MA thesis, UCD, 1952), pp. 67–8.
[128] 'Catholicks' reasons against taking the oath of allegiance' in *HM*, October 1775, 606.
[129] O'Conor to Mr Sherlock, 2 October 1778 in Ward and Ward (eds.), *The Letters of Charles O'Conor*, II, p. 127.

the *Hibernian Magazine* article referred to above said that he had taken up his pen, 'Whilst the flames of discord and jealousy are raging through many parts of his Majesty's American dominions, and whilst the horrid sound of rebellion is tingling in our ears . . . In hopes of preventing . . . the ignorant and unwary from catching the infectious breath of faction and sedition.'[130] It might be thought from this that the author feared the spread of the revolutionary contagion from America, but it is clear from the body of the work that his concern was with the persistence of Jacobitism among the general Catholic population. Yet if the enemy was old, the writer was willing to deploy modern arguments in the battle against it. He borrowed the principle of parliamentary sovereignty from Sir William Blackstone: 'Parliament is the place where that absolute despotic power, which must, in all government, reside somewhere, is entrusted by the constitution of these kingdoms. It can regulate or new model the succession of the crown.'[131] Catholics with traditional beliefs were reassured that the 'new test, now in question, expresses no approbation of the principles, measures or motives of the Revolution', while an attempt was made to allay Protestant fears with the assertion that 'Upon the whole . . . the present Roman Catholics of Ireland are too much employed and connected in trade with their Protestant fellow-subjects, to wish for, or entertain any idle thoughts of a pretender.'[132] The polemical talents of Fr Arthur O'Leary, a Capuchin and leading Catholic controversialist, were also brought to bear in favour of the oath. It is noteworthy that he considered it necessary to devote no fewer than twenty-five pages in a pamphlet of 107 pages to a refutation of the Pretender's right to the throne. O'Leary pointed out to his readers that scripture commands 'obedience to the prince whose image is stamped on his coin'.[133] He sought to undermine popular loyalty to the deposed dynasty by reminding his readers that 'James the first signalized his generosity in our favour, by giving, under the finesse of laws, six counties in Ulster to Scotch planters.'[134] None the less, he did not venture to dispute the belief that it was 'the duty of the Irish to fight for their king' in 1689–91.[135] O'Leary also asserted the legislative supremacy of the crown in parliament:

the law both in present, and past times is, and has been, that the crown is hereditary in the wearer: that the king and both houses of parliament can defeat this hereditary right, and by particular limitation exclude the immediate heir, and vest the inheritance in any one else. Thus not only the Pretender, but even the present

---

[130] *A Vindication of the New Oath of Allegiance, Proposed to the Roman Catholics of Ireland*, second edition (Dublin, 1775), p. 7.
[131] *Ibid.*, pp. 11–12.   [132] *Ibid.*, pp. 20 and 22.
[133] Arthur O'Leary, *Loyalty Asserted, or, the New Test Oath, Vindicated* (Cork, 1776), p. 9.
[134] *Ibid.*, p. 15.   [135] *Ibid.*, p. 22.

Prince of Wales can be excluded from the throne with the consent of the king, lords and commons.[136]

This line of argument was open to the obvious objection that James II had never consented either to his deposition or the alteration of the succession, but O'Leary made a more telling point when he questioned the benefit Catholics might expect from a Stuart restoration:

> In my humble opinion, Charles the third would have removed pope and popery out of his way to the throne . . . Perhaps I pass a rash judgement on this cherished twig of the Stuart stock: If so, I retract. But all we expect from him is the liberty to fast and pray; this we enjoy without his mediation, and it would be madness to forfeit it.[137]

Substantially the same point was made more trenchantly by the anonymous author of a third pamphlet written in support of the oath – a work which devoted eighteen of its sixty-eight pages to an effort to prove the legitimacy of the house of Hanover:

> I ask if any man can be in his senses, and persevere in his fruitless wishes to place on the throne a man [Prince Charles Edward] of near sixty years old, who enjoys affluently the comforts of life; and by this obstinacy, endanger the civil existence of millions, and suffer them to pine in hunger and infamy, for the sake of one only man, to whom his attachment can be of no value?[138]

The fact that such arguments were advanced at such length in English-language pamphlets confirms that Jacobite sentiment was far from extinct even among those prosperous, educated and anglicised Catholics who might have been expected to take the oath without compunction.

From the middle of 1775 reports appeared in the newspapers of groups of Catholics taking the oath in various localities, beginning in Dublin with 'a very numerous and respectable body of Roman Catholic gentlemen of property' headed by Lord Trimblestown who presented themselves at the court of King's Bench on 28 June.[139] Some months later, Lords Fingal and Gormanstown together with prominent members of the Catholic gentry took the oath before the same court.[140] Yet the social prominence of the jurors could not disguise the fact that the numbers taking the oath were small and amounted to a total of only 1,500 in the period before Luke Gardiner's relief act of 1778 provided Catholic landowners with a strong material incentive to swear allegiance.[141] This

---

[136] *Ibid.*, pp. 29–30.   [137] *Ibid.*, p. 27.
[138] *Historical Remarks on the Pope's Temporal and Deposing Power. With some Anecdotes of the Court of Rome, and Observations on the Oath of Allegiance* (Dublin, 1778), p. 26.
[139] *FDJ*, 3 July 1775. For similar reports see Brady, *Catholics and Catholicism*, pp. 173–80.
[140] *FJ*, 18 November 1775.   [141] Fagan, *Divided Loyalties*, p. 178.

figure includes five bishops, 115 priests and about 350 members of the gentry, with large farmers, members of the professions and merchants accounting for the bulk of the remainder.[142] The figure of 1,500 Catholics who took the oath in Ireland may be contrasted with the 5,600 inhabitants of Manhattan, Staten Island and Long Island who swore allegiance to George III after royal government was restored in those areas in the autumn of 1776.[143] There was, undoubtedly, a greater pressure on the inhabitants of districts that had lately been in rebellion to signify their loyalty to the crown, but it is none the less striking that the number of jurors in the city of New York and its immediate environs was almost four times greater than the number furnished by the entire population of Catholic Ireland.

While the Catholic masses maintained their attitude of sullen hostility towards the establishment in church and state, the high social standing of the minority that was pursuing a strategy of accommodation, together with the greater accessibility to the ruling élite of the manner in which they expressed their views – pamphlets and loyal addresses in English rather than songs and verse in Irish – combined to ensure that they would receive attention disproportionate to their numbers. In 1775 John Curry felt confident enough to make the following public assertion: 'We do not think we have any disaffected papists at this day in Ireland. The number, at least must be very inconsiderable.'[144] Repudiating a claim made by Lord Chatham in the British House of Lords, James Hoey's *Dublin Mercury* asserted that 'It is a false assertion, that all Ireland, to a man, is for the American rebels; for it is well known that the *flower* of upwards of *two million* of loyal old inhabitants are ready to join the military and well affected in support of the king and constitution, against all republicans and innovations whatsoever.'[145] In September of the same year a loyal address signed by members of the gentry and by prominent members of the Catholic Committee (including Lords Fingal and Trimleston, John Curry and James Reynolds) was quietly presented to the lord lieutenant. The signatories offered to raise a fund to promote enlistment, expressed their abhorrence of the 'unnatural rebellion' that had broken out in America, and purported to lay at the king's feet 'two millions of loyal, faithful and affectionate hearts and hands, unarmed indeed, but zealous, ready and desirous to exert themselves strenuously in defence of H.M.'s most sacred person and government'.[146] Similar sentiments were

---

[142] *Ibid.*, p. 179.   [143] *HM*, April 1777, 288–9.
[144] [John Curry], *An Historical and Critical Review of the Civil Wars in Ireland, from the Reign of Queen Elizabeth, to the Settlement under King William* (Dublin, 1775), p. v.
[145] *Dublin Mercury*, 12 August 1775, as quoted in *FJ*, 29 August 1775.
[146] Enclosed with a letter from Harcourt to Rochford, 30 September 1775, in Gilbert Library Ms. 93, p. 257.

expressed publicly in the humble address presented to Lord Harcourt on the occasion of his departure:

It is also matter of peculiar exultation to us to find, that whilst this kingdom hath been occasionally disturbed by tumultuous risings of promiscuous miscreants from every denomination of religion, and whilst an unnatural rebellion hath distracted his Majesty's colonies, your Excellency has seen the body of Irish Roman Catholics, uniformly peaceable in their deportment, obedient to the laws, and loyal to his Majesty.[147]

The twelve signatories included Lords Gormanstown, Fingal and Trimleston. That such declarations really did reflect the views of an élite grouping cannot be doubted. In private correspondence with his associates on the Catholic Committee, Charles O'Conor expressed the hope that after the defeat of the American rebellion Maryland might be re-established as a Catholic colony: 'Would not the repossessing Maryland with Catholics be a bridle hereafter on the republican provinces north and south of them?'[148] He also anticipated that rewards for good behaviour would be bestowed on the Catholic population nearer home: 'Government should, indirectly, be confirmed in the important idea that a passive party among us deserve protection, not only from the *moral* injustice [recte: 'justice'] due to all parties but the *political* justice due to the nation who must be interested in some counter-balance to our modern republicans.'[149] Yet fulsome declarations of Catholic loyalty could cause unease in unexpected quarters. Writing to a brother bishop around the time of Lord Harcourt's departure, the Catholic bishop of Ossory observed that 'many of our people, by their ill-timed expressions and declarations exasperate the Presbyterians without rendering any real service to government'.[150] It is likely that the term 'Presbyterian' was used here as a synonym for 'republican' – interesting evidence that at least one southern prelate associated Dissent with disaffection. The 'tautological and unmeaning jargon' of the address to Lord Harcourt was also subjected to ridicule in the pages of the *Hibernian Journal* by a correspondent calling himself 'Aristus' who may have been a former member of the Catholic Committee disenchanted with the pro-administration policy of its aristocratic leadership.[151]

---

[147] *FJ*, 1 February 1777.
[148] O'Conor to Charles Ryan, October 1777, in Ward and Ward (eds.), *The Letters of Charles O'Conor*, II, p. 110. See also his letters to John Curry of 28 October 1777 and to Charles Ryan of 11 November 1777, *ibid.*, pp. 114–15.
[149] O'Conor to Curry, *ibid.*, pp. 90–1.
[150] Bishop John Troy to Bishop Fallon of Elphin, 10 January 1778; quoted in Eamon O'Flaherty 'Ecclesiastical politics and the dismantling of the penal laws in Ireland, 1774–82', *IHS* 26 (1988), 39.
[151] *HJ*, 10 February 1777. See McGeehin, 'The activities and personnel of the General Committee of the Catholics of Ireland', pp. 88–92.

The unease generated by the address to Lord Harcourt among sections of the Catholic community may have influenced the wording of the address that was presented shortly afterwards to the new lord lieutenant, Lord Buckinghamshire, by essentially the same group of signatories. This address pledged the 'real and permanent loyalty' of the Catholic population but avoided all mention of transatlantic events.[152] Notwithstanding his private reservations about the prudence of presenting addresses of loyalty to government, the bishop of Ossory saw fit to endorse the official day of fast and prayer called in the aftermath of General Burgoyne's defeat at Saratoga, and the pastoral letter read in all the churches of his diocese was as outspoken as any of the lay addressers had been in its support for the administration's American policy. Citing the divine injunction to 'give unto Caesar, what belongeth to Caesar', Bishop Troy instructed his flock that:

A cheerful compliance with this important obligation is particularly requisite in these days of discord, and calamity, when our American fellow-subjects, seduced by specious notions of liberty, and illusive expectations of sovereignty, disclaim any dependence on Great Britain, and endeavour by force of arms to distress their mother country, which has cherished and protected them.[153]

Catholic declarations of loyalty acquired a new importance as Britain and France drifted towards war. Thus James Fortescue, member of parliament for County Louth, emphasised the effect that such addresses might have in discouraging a French landing when forwarding a loyal address from the principal Catholics of his locality to the lord lieutenant, and the Louth address was indeed published.[154] None the less, the Dublin administration continued to counsel against any relaxation of anti-Catholic legislation on the grounds that 'it would most probably occasion a flame in this country' – advice which was accepted in Whitehall.[155]

Between the celebration of British defeats which characterised the popular political verse of the period on the one hand, and the equally unrestrained condemnations of an 'unnatural rebellion' which featured in the addresses of the Catholic gentry and merchants on the other, a narrow middle ground can be discerned in a small number of newspaper articles and pamphlets written by Catholic authors. Arthur O'Leary, while anxious to stress the loyalty of the Catholic population to the established

---

[152] *FJ*, 11 March 1777.
[153] *Dublin Evening Journal*, 28 February 1778. Interestingly, the quoted passage was omitted when this pastoral was reprinted in a hagiographical article in 1897; see N. Murphy, 'Dr Troy, as bishop of Ossory, 1776–1786', *Irish Ecclesiastical Record*, 4th series, 2 (1897), 420.
[154] HMC Lothian Mss. (1905), pp. 327–8; *FJ*, 7 April 1778.
[155] Buckinghamshire to Weymouth, 4 March 1778 and Weymouth to Buckinghamshire, 28 March 1778, PRO SP 63/459, fos. 109 and 177.

order – or perhaps to any political order that might ever happen to be established – was also careful to avoid condemning the colonists. When seeking to defend the Irish rebels of 1641 in the patriotic lion's den of the *Freeman's Journal* he questioned whether there had really been any rebellion in that year: 'For rebellion implies an immediate and direct opposition to the king or to the supreme authority of the state; and no sophistry can prove that the Catholics came under the description.' He then invited the patriotic readership of the paper to apply a principle that was often invoked in relation to contemporary events in America to the Confederate Catholics of the 1640s – the principle that resistance to oppression does not constitute rebellion: 'As the present unhappy contest between Great Britain and her colonies has turned the attention of men to the discrimination between rebellion and justifiable resistance to established government, we are at this day better enabled to judge with propriety by which name the conduct of the Irish in 1641 ought to be described.'[156] An anonymous pamphlet entitled *A Humble Remonstrance, for the Repeal of the Laws against the Roman Catholics* provides further insight into Catholic attitudes. The author, who was clearly uncomfortable writing in English, stressed the loyalty of Catholics to the house of Hanover – a house which, like many other royal lines, had its origins in usurpation but had been legitimised by the passage of time. Just as Arthur O'Leary had justified the rebellion of 1641, the author of this pamphlet defended the loyalty of the Irish to James II at the time of the Revolution, a loyalty which he contrasted favourably with the disloyalty of contemporary Americans:

There is no comparison of the war that is now with the colonies, with the war that was in Ireland at the time of the Dutch Revolution, when the Irish had not as yet professed allegiance to King William, declared against the invaders, and for the king that reigned by the antient laws of these realms, that were at that time, whereby the opposition they made was evidently lawful by the law of the land.[157]

The author argued that even now a 'due observance of the capitulation of Limerick may dispose the colonies to confide to a proclamation of general oblivion by the king's royal mercy'.[158] Having broached the topic of the American conflict, he outlined his own proposals for a settlement. The colonists should 'return to their allegiance, become loyal to the crown, and acknowledge the chief jurisdiction of parliament to revise the laws of the colonies', however the colonial assemblies should enjoy the same exclusive power of taxation as the Irish parliament:

[156] *FJ*, 8 November 1777.
[157] *A Humble Remonstrance, for the Repeal of the Laws against the Roman Catholics* (Dublin, 1778), p. 10.
[158] *Ibid.*, p. 11.

But the jurisdiction of the general assemblies of the colonies, with regard to laws and taxes, and even of the general congress of the united colonies in case of invasions, should be guaranteed by parliament, to be equally secure (which may be expressed in a law to that intent) as the jurisdiction that the parliament of Ireland ... always had of legislation and taxation.[159]

Implicit in this proposal was the principle that, although Irish legislation could be overruled at Westminster, the country could only be taxed by its own parliament.

Recruitment

The relative failure of efforts to raise Irish recruits for service in America during 1774 and early 1775 has already been noted. Two months before hostilities began, Lord Harcourt was given unprecedented permission by the secretary of state to recruit locally for the Irish garrison itself: 'I am, in this private and confidential manner, to acquaint your Excellency that, in order to fill up the vacancies with more speed, his Majesty is pleased to grant you a discretionary leave to connive, on the present emergency, at the regiments that remain in Ireland taking Irish recruits.'[160] The illegal recruitment of Catholics was not explicitly authorised, but it was recognised on all sides that recruitment of Irish troops would inevitably involve some intake of Catholics. Government was initially optimistic about the prospects for recruitment in Ireland. In August 1775 Harcourt cited the example of three students from Trinity College who volunteered for service in America as an example of 'the spirit that begins to prevail'.[161] At the beginning of September he reported to the secretary of state that the recruiting service 'seems now to be in a very promising way' and referred to the 'laudable zeal' of the mayor and magistrates of Limerick in offering an additional bounty of 10/6 to local men who enlisted, as well as to the actions of Lords Crosbie, Kenmare (a Catholic) and Shannon who were all offering additional bounties to recruits from their localities.[162] But despite such inducements, all sections of the population showed a marked reluctance to enlist. As early as August 1775 *Finn's Leinster Journal* noted that the recruiting parties operating in Kilkenny were not meeting 'with so much success, as they did in the late war'.[163] Later in the same month the paper reported that Major Boyle Roche's recruitment effort was meeting with 'great success' at Limerick, where he was dispensing 'large quantities

---

[159] *Ibid.*, p. 12.
[160] Rochford to Harcourt, 6 February 1775, in Harcourt, *The Harcourt Papers*, IX, p. 303.
[161] Letter of 21 August 1775 in *ibid.*, p. 347.
[162] Harcourt to Rochford, 1 September 1775, Gilbert Library Ms. 93, pp. 249–50.
[163] *FLJ*, 19 August 1775.

of beer, enlivened with whiskey' to the populace and where prominent Catholics were offering an additional bounty to the first 200 men who enlisted. None the less, when the major left the city in the middle of September he was accompanied by only 100 'likely young fellows' and suffered the further embarrassment of having forty-two of these recruits rejected by the commanding officer at Kinsale as being 'totally unfit for service'.[164] A letter written in the same month by an officer at Cork to a fellow officer serving with the besieged army at Boston drew a clear distinction between the loyalty of the Catholic élite and the disaffection of lower-class Catholics:

> Though the principal Romanists in Cork and Limerick have formed associations and offered bounties to such recruits as shall list on this occasion, yet they have very little success; for though the heads of that communion are in the interest of government, the lower class, who have not sagacity enough to make proper distinctions, are, to a man, attached to the Americans, and say plainly the Irish ought to follow their example. Even Lord Kenmare, who on this occasion took the lead, had his recruiting party severely beat up in Tralee, and their drums broken to pieces.[165]

Government did not remain unaware of such realities for long. Only a week after the above account was written, Lord George Germain remarked on the slowness of Catholic recruitment in a letter to the commander of the army in Ireland.[166] On 20 September, the chief secretary informed Whitehall that a recruitment campaign undertaken by Major Boyle Roche and supported by Lord Kenmare which had the wildly optimistic aim of raising 'two thousand or more recruits' in Kerry and the adjoining counties, was progressing 'but indifferently after such vast expectation raised'; the failure of Catholics to enlist was described as 'a matter of surprise and concern'.[167]

David Dickson, in his survey of eighteenth-century Ireland, has claimed that opposition to the American war was of such intensity in Ulster that 'any recruitment in the province in 1775–6 was avoided'.[168] The basis for

---

[164] *Ibid.*, 30 August; 2, 23 and 27 September 1775.
[165] The letter, dated 8 September 1775, was intercepted and published by order of Congress in the *Philadelphia Packet* of 27 November 1775; it is quoted in Michael O'Brien, *A Hidden Phase of American History: Ireland's Part in America's Struggle for Liberty* (New York, 1921), p. 48.
[166] Germain to General Irwin, 13 September 1775, in HMC Stopford-Sackville Mss., I (1904), p. 137.
[167] For the plan see Rochford to Harcourt, 2 August 1775, PRO SP 63/448, fo. 16; for the report on its lack of success see Blaquiere to Rochford, 20 September 1775, Gilbert Library Ms. 93, pp. 255–6.
[168] David Dickson, *New Foundations: Ireland 1660–1800*, second edition (Dublin, 2000), p. 160.

this statement was not disclosed, but it may have been inspired by a letter of 1 March 1775 in which Lord Harcourt recommended that recruiting parties should be 'restricted to the raising of men in the provinces of Leinster, Munster and Connaught only'.[169] If this is the case, it represents a serious misunderstanding of the viceroy's motives. An identical request had been made by Lord Townshend five years previously, at a time when recruits were urgently needed because of a threatened war with Spain over the Falkland Islands, but on that occasion the lord lieutenant had explained the rationale for his request:

it has ever been considered of infinite prejudice to the kingdom to take away any considerable number of Protestants, upon which account they have always been spared; and when there has been an absolute necessity for augmenting the forces in Ireland by levies in the kingdom, it has mostly been upon condition of their being obliged to serve in Ireland only.[170]

Subsequent correspondence leaves no doubt that Lord Harcourt's reluctance to authorise recruitment in Ulster was inspired by the same motive as his predecessor's. When the secretary of state insisted that recruiting parties should be permitted to beat up 'in Ireland at large' because of the urgency of the military situation, Harcourt responded by submitting a plan for 'raising the *greater number* of the 600 recruits in the province of Ulster' – a proposal which duly received the approbation of the king.[171] I have not located the plan in question, but the only plausible explanation for Harcourt's *volte face* is that he now proposed to draft soldiers from existing regiments for the American service and to replace them with Protestant recruits from Ulster, thereby retaining the latter in Ireland. In the event, recruiting parties had little more success in the north than in the south. A proposal made by Colonel William Style in September 1775 to raise recruits on his County Donegal estate was accepted, but in March of the following year his agent advised that 'I am in hopes of raising one hundred men by the first of June. I find they are not so easily raised as I at first apprehended and communicated to you.'[172] The numbers enlisting were small and tended, if anything, to diminish with the passage of time. A year later, in July 1777, Colonel Style complained that recruitment, which had been 'till late tolerably successful', was now 'very bad'.[173]

---

[169] Harcourt to Rochford, 1 March 1775, in PRO SP 63/445, fo. 213.
[170] Townshend to Rochford, 27 December 1770, in *Calendar of Home Office Papers, 1773–75* (London, 1899), p. 123.
[171] Rochford to Harcourt, 16 and 31 March 1775, in PRO SP 63/445, fo. 265 and PRO SP 63/446, fo. 138 respectively. The emphasis is mine.
[172] Knox to Style, 28 March 1776, National Archives Ms. M. 600 (a); for the recruitment proposal see PRO SP 63/448, fo. 173.
[173] Style to Col. William Amherst, 25 July 1777, National Archives Ms. M. 600 (f).

The difficulty of persuading Catholics to enlist drove one officer who was engaged in recruiting for a new regiment to describe it as 'the Queen's Loyal Catholic Volunteers' and to issue a handbill which announced that the unit would 'consist of Roman Catholics, who are to have the free use of their own religion, as a priest is to be chaplain'.[174] The officer concerned was arrested as soon as these illegal promises were brought to official attention but his tactic of appealing openly to the religious convictions of Catholics appears to have had little effect. Some 500 recruits were procured for the new corps but when they were inspected by the Earl of Cavan it was found that only 200 were fit for service and that many of these were deserters from other regiments who were availing of an amnesty. Cavan's report was scathing: 'as to the other remaining 300 men, which I rejected, I found them mostly to be, some old and infirm, some blind of an eye, some decrepit and with broken distorted limbs, some weak and feeble with a great number of boys'.[175] It is an indication of the desperate need which existed for recruits that a subsequent inspection of substantially the same body of men found the great majority of them fit for service and in August 1776 the regiment was shipped to Jamaica, a colony which seemed unlikely to become a theatre of war.[176] A contemporary press report commenting on the unit's departure stated that 'so much precaution in the embarkation of a regiment, perhaps, never before seemed more necessary; many very desperate, daring, profligate fellows, in and about Dublin, having enlisted therein'.[177] It was not an exceptional case. The officer commanding at Cork likewise complained in a letter to the secretary-at-war about the difficulty of raising Irish recruits and described those who came forward as 'the very scum of the earth', adding that they 'do their utmost to desert, the moment they are clothed'.[178]

As late as January 1776 the lord lieutenant informed Whitehall that proposals had been received from Lords Antrim, Granard and Ross for raising infantry battalions.[179] By this time, however, it was evident that recruits would not be forthcoming in anything like the numbers originally expected and Lord North, in the same month, referred to 'the present difficulty of recruiting the infantry' in correspondence with the viceroy.[180] In early February Harcourt forwarded proposals that originated within the army for a reduction in the minimum height of recruits from 5 ft 6 in. to 5 ft 5 in., an increase in the upper age limit from thirty to thirty-five,

---

[174] PRO SP 63/452, fo. 144.
[175] Lord Cavan's inspection report, 19 April 1776, PRO SP 63/453, fo. 195.
[176] PRO SP 63/454, fos. 280 and 293.   [177] *FLJ*, 12 October 1776.
[178] Major-General Cunningham to Lord Barrington, 19 May 1776, PRO WO 1/991, fo. 9.
[179] Harcourt to Weymouth, 18 and 31 January 1776, PRO SP 63/451, fos. 120v and 196r.
[180] North to Harcourt, 16 January 1776, NLI Ms. 755, p. 78.

and an amnesty for any of the 'numerous deserters who swarm over the face of this country' who surrendered voluntarily.[181] Later in February the viceroy admitted that the numbers of men required for America could not be supplied by recruiting 'as it goes on so very slowly' and informed the secretary of state that he had ordered drafts for the American service to be taken from the regiments that were to remain in Ireland, with the places of the draftees being filled by Kilmainham pensioners – elderly or invalid veterans who were in receipt of army pensions.[182] Not only was the number of Irish recruits unexpectedly low, their quality was also poor: in March 1776 Lord George Germain admitted to General Howe that 'recruiting for some time went on very slowly and the men raised in Ireland will be of little use to you', but reassured the general that 'since the [recruiting] parties have been removed [from Ireland] to England we have had better success and the recruits raised may make soldiers'.[183] Further expedients followed. In the same month, Harcourt proposed that those prisoners under sentence of transportation who agreed to enlist in the army or navy should be pardoned, a proposal which was accepted, and in May he recommended a second amnesty for deserters who returned to the colours as the first one had not 'been attended with the consequences which might have been expected from his Majesty's royal clemency' – although on this occasion the proposal was rejected by the king.[184]

Inevitably, the carrot was replaced by the stick and in August Harcourt reported that a court martial had sentenced three deserters to death; he recommended that one man who was aged only eighteen should be reprieved but that the other executions should proceed since, in the opinion of the commander-in-chief, they might 'prove effectual in putting a stop to the very great desertion which has prevailed of late thro' His Majesty's army in this kingdom', a recommendation which was confirmed by the secretary of state.[185] The extent of the problem is clear from the records of the five regiments that embarked at Cove for North America in early 1776: the 9th, 20th, 24th, 34th and 62nd regiments of foot lost more than 400 men by desertion between the time of their receiving orders for foreign service and their embarkation.[186] A large majority of those

---

[181] Harcourt to Weymouth, 5 February 1776, PRO SP 63/451, fos. 248–9.
[182] Harcourt to Weymouth, 23 February 1776, PRO SP 63/452, fo. 119.
[183] Germain to Howe, 28 March 1776, in Davies (ed.), *Documents of the American Revolution*, XII, p. 94.
[184] Harcourt to Weymouth, 30 March 1776, PRO SP 63/452, fo. 37v; Weymouth to Harcourt, 23 April 1776, PRO SP 63/453, fo. 184; Harcourt to Weymouth, 22 May 1776, PRO SP 63/454, fo. 122.
[185] Harcourt to Weymouth, 29 August and Weymouth to Harcourt, 20 September 1776, PRO SP 63/455, fo. 43.
[186] Lists of deserters are found in PRO SP 63/453, fos. 164, 165, 167, 170 and 173.

deserting – more than 300 – were Irish, although this may reflect nothing more than the ease with which Irish deserters could evade capture. In March 1776 the War Office reported that 'about 450 recruits for North America' had been raised in Ireland since the war began – a figure barely sufficient to replace those who deserted on being ordered overseas.[187]

An attack on a recruiting party in Tralee has been mentioned above and similar clashes were reported regularly in the press. In one incident, four men enlisted in Dublin city but, having obtained their bounty money, they 'knocked down the serjeant and two of his companions, and then made off, with a loud huzza for America'.[188] Common footpads would have chosen an easier target than a party of soldiers and the attack must be seen as an expression of political disaffection. Clashes in which crowds of civilians sought to help recruits or deserters escape are more difficult to characterise but are at least indicative of strained relations between the army and populace. For example, in March 1776, one civilian was killed in a skirmish with a military party which was trying to apprehend deserters near Youghal.[189] In the following October a 'riotous mob' in Kilcullen, County Kildare, rescued two recruits and beat the recruiting party 'in so cruel a manner that they were not able to return to their quarters'.[190] In March 1777 a party of five soldiers was attacked and overpowered by a group of men near Cappoquin, County Waterford, who rescued two deserters who had been taken into custody.[191] In the same month a 'great mob arose' in an unsuccessful attempt to rescue a deserter in Dublin; the leader of the crowd on this occasion, a coal-porter named Charles Connor, was himself captured and promptly impressed as a 'warning to the other porters, not to interfere with what does not concern them'.[192] Another violent clash which took place in the capital in April 1777 is suggestive of a link between such spontaneous assaults on the military and the more concerted threat posed by the houghers:

as a recruiting serjeant and two corporals belonging to the marine service were passing by the markets on Ormond-quay, a recruit they had with them cried out that they had trepanned him by putting a shilling in his pocket, upon which a number of butchers came out of the market armed with long knives and clubs, and cutting them in a cruel manner, set the man at liberty.[193]

Incidents such as the above left the Irish administration in no doubt that enthusiasm for the war and the royal service, though readily expressed by the self-appointed spokesmen of the Catholic laity, was not shared by

[187] Lord Barrington to Germain, 6 March 1776, in Davies, *Documents of the American Revolution*, X, p. 233, no. 1140.
[188] *FLJ*, 6 September 1775.
[189] *Ibid.*, 10 April 1776.   [190] *Ibid.*, 5 October 1776.   [191] *FDJ*, 18 March 1777.
[192] *Ibid.*, 20 March 1777.   [193] *Hibernian Chronicle*, 17 April 1777.

the bulk of the community. When Sir Richard Heron, the chief secretary, travelled to London in December 1777 he took with him a memo by the lord lieutenant which, as well as referring to the difficulty of procuring recruits and the high rate of desertion, also noted the disaffection of both northern Presbyterians and southern Catholics: 'The inclination to favour the Americans which appears in the north of Ireland. Ld Shannon is of opinion that the Catholics in his neighbourhood are also their well wishers.'[194] Within days of his arrival in London, Heron wrote to assure the viceroy that he had 'convinced Lord George [Germain] and Lord North, as I believe, that the plan of raising Roman Catholic troops is impracticable'.[195] This was indeed the prime minister's view. By the time that war with the Bourbon powers became a real prospect in the aftermath of Saratoga, government had been disabused of its earlier hopes of securing widespread Catholic support for the war effort. Referring to Ireland, Lord North advised the king frankly that the 'utmost that can be expected from the papists would be neutrality, but, probably, a large body would be easily induced to join an invader'.[196]

If recruits for the army were in short supply the same was true of the navy. In November 1776 Harcourt told the secretary of state that the officer responsible for naval recruitment in Ireland had received a press warrant from the Admiralty but, on presenting his warrant to the lord mayor of Dublin, the latter had refused to provide municipal employees to assist him – an action which mirrored the response of the lord mayor of London in similar circumstances.[197] Shortly thereafter, Harcourt received a representation from the lord mayor in which he claimed that 'from fear of being impressed the fishermen by whom this city is constantly supplied with fish have left their boats and absconded into the country by which means the inhabitants in general are deprived of a principal part of their food'.[198] In Dublin, as in London, the issue of impressment was taken up by the patriot opposition. A series of letters on the subject appeared in the *Hibernian Journal* during March and April 1777, of which the following is typical:

A press gang, publicly parading the streets of Dublin at noon-day, and seizing not only seamen but landsmen, in the centre of our city, between the custom-house, the exchange, and the castle, ought surely to open our eyes, awaken our attention,

---

[194] Memo by Buckinghamshire to Sir Richard Heron, 26 December 1777, NLI Ms. 13,035 (16).
[195] Heron to Buckinghamshire, 2 January 1778, NLI Ms. 13,036 (1).
[196] Lord North to George III, 30 December 1777, in John Fortescue (ed.), *The Correspondence of King George the Third*, III (London, 1928), p. 530.
[197] Harcourt to Weymouth, PRO SP 63/455, fo. 172; for London, see Sainsbury, *Dissaffected Patriots*, p. 135.
[198] Harcourt to Weymouth, 12 December 1776, PRO SP 63/455, fo. 212.

and ask if we are freemen, protected by laws, or slaves, at the mercy and disposal of a lawless set of men-stealers, with no shadow of authority, but the warrants of the lords of the Admiralty, who are not warranted by any law to issue it.[199]

Impressment was a frequent cause of serious violence. In January 1777 a press gang that attempted to impress a sailor on Dublin's Aston Quay was 'roughly treated by the populace' and one member was killed.[200] In April of the same year a mob rescued a sailor who had been seized by a press gang on Essex bridge and laid siege to a house in which members of the gang took refuge. The city sheriffs were unable to restore order and only the arrival of a military party from Dublin Castle persuaded the crowd to disperse.[201] Despite such opposition the press gangs continued to operate and by May 1777 the *Freeman's Journal* could report that a total of 225 men had been impressed in the port of Dublin alone prior to that date.[202] The opinion of the political nation on the practice would appear to have been finely balanced: when the Trinity College Historical Society debated 'Whether impressing men into the king's service is agreeable to the liberty of the subject?' the question was carried in the affirmative, but only on the casting vote of the chairman.[203]

Popular interest in the American war

A substantial level of interest in the American conflict is apparent from the number of publications dealing with the subject that were reprinted in Ireland. A comparison between the number of titles supporting the ministry and the colonists – admittedly a crude gauge of opinion – suggests that both viewpoints enjoyed a sizable following among the reading public. Some of the publications relating to America are likely to have predated the outbreak of hostilities: a speech by Lord Chatham to the British House of Lords, the Continental Congress's address to the people of Great Britain, and Edmund Burke's speeches to the British Commons on the history of American taxation and in favour of conciliation all fall into this category.[204] Interest in America increased with the outbreak of war. A speech by Samuel Adams, a sermon delivered by a patriotic minister to a Philadelphia congregation, Richard Price's impassioned statement

---

[199] *HJ*, 9 April 1777; see also the issues of 21, 24 and 31 March 1777.
[200] *FDJ*, 21 January 1777.   [201] *Ibid.*, 8 April 1777.   [202] *FJ*, 27 May 1777.
[203] Historical Society minutes, 19 November 1777, TCD Mun. Soc./Hist. 2, pp. 128–9.
[204] William Pitt, earl of Chatham, *The Speech of the Right Honourable the Earl of Chatham, in the House of Lords, on Friday the 20th of January, 1775* (Dublin, n.d.); *An Address to the People of Great-Britain*; Edmund Burke, *The History of American Taxation from the Year 1763* (Dublin, 1775); *The Speech of Edmund Burke, Esq., on Moving his Resolutions for Conciliation with the Colonies, March 22, 1775* (Dublin, 1775).

of 'real Whig' views on the corruption of Britain's body politic, Edmund Burke's letter to the sheriffs of Bristol, and Lord Abingdon's reflections on the latter, were pro-American polemics from a variety of perspectives which found Dublin publishers.[205] Perhaps the most celebrated pamphlet to emerge from the American revolution, Thomas Paine's *Common Sense*, first published at Philadelphia in January 1776, was reprinted in London in April and was being hawked on the streets of Dublin before the end of May.[206] Lengthy excerpts from *Common Sense* appeared in the June number of the *Hibernian Magazine* and its serialisation in the *Freeman's Journal* began, by a fitting coincidence, on 4 July 1776. However, Paine's frank republicanism was too extreme for some who sympathised with the American cause. The editor of the *Hibernian Magazine* – a periodical which normally displayed a pro-American bias – thought it advisable to omit Paine's strictures on the institution of monarchy, although he summarised them for the benefit of his readers and seemed to imply that they might be justified in an American context:

monarchy he looks upon as *an evil*, and a degradation and lessening of ourselves, and hereditary succession as *an insult and imposition on posterity*. His arguments occupy no less than fifteen pages, and can tend only to make men disgusted with their situation under a monarchy, whether absolute or limited. As such is the situation of this kingdom, we forbear to transcribe this part since it could answer, *here* no one desirable end.[207]

Publications expressing a ministerial viewpoint are less numerous but it would seem that a sufficient market existed to justify Dublin editions of William Smith's answer to *Common Sense*; a reply to the declaration of independence by James Macpherson, the author of *Fingal*; and an appeal by a group of Pennsylvania Quakers who were detained by the authorities of that state on suspicion of harbouring pro-British sympathies.[208] Lord North's conciliation proposals were reflected in the reply to Price's *Observations* by Adam Ferguson, who argued that the British parliament

---

[205] Adams, *An Oration Delivered at the State-House*; William Smith, *A Sermon on the Present Situation of American Affairs, Preached in Christ Church, June 23, 1775* (Dublin, 1775); [Richard Price], *Observations on the Nature of Civil Liberty, the Principles of Government and the Justice and Policy of the War with America* (Dublin, 1776); Edmund Burke, *A Letter from Edmund Burke, Esq. to John Farr and John Harris, Esqrs on the Affairs of America* (Dublin, 1777); Earl of Abingdon, *Thoughts on the Letter of Edmund Burke, Esq. to the Sheriffs of Bristol, on the Affairs of America. By the Earl of Abingdon* (Dublin, 1777).

[206] For Dublin, see the advertisement in *FJ*, 23 May 1776.

[207] *HM*, June 1776, 363. Emphasis in the original.

[208] [William Smith] 'Candidus', *Plain Truth: Addressed to the Inhabitants of America* (Dublin, 1776); [James Macpherson], *The Rights of Great Britain Asserted against the Claims of America* (Dublin, 1776); *An Address to the Inhabitants of Pennsylvania, by those Freemen of the City of Philadelphia who are now Confined in the Masons Lodge* (Dublin, 1777).

should waive its undoubted right to tax the colonies if they agreed to establish a permanent mechanism for raising a sufficient revenue to support the expenses of government.[209]

The space devoted to the opposition and ministerial viewpoints in a periodical such as the *Hibernian Magazine* – which, although published by the proprietor of the patriotic *Hibernian Journal*, was aimed at a more general readership – may be a better guide to the scale and nature of public interest in American issues than partisan pamphlets which may have been subsidised by either the government or opposition. The pro-American material carried by the *Hibernian Magazine* during 1775 included Congress's non-importation resolution; its addresses to the British and the Irish peoples; Lord Chatham's speech of January 1775; the humble address of the livery of London ('the power contended for over the colonies, under the specious name of dignity, is to all intents and purposes, despotism'); and Burke's two speeches on American taxation and conciliation.[210] On the other side of the debate, Samuel Johnson's *Taxation no Tyranny* and John Wesley's address to the American colonies put the British case.[211] The pro-American bias of the *Hibernian Magazine* became, if anything, more pronounced during 1776: a biographical notice and portrait of the president of Congress, John Hancock; an American reply to John Wesley's letter; a biographical notice of Samuel Adams; Price's *Observations*; the 'Articles of Confederation'; excerpts from Paine's *Common Sense*; an account of the life of General Richard Montgomery; the declaration of independence; and laudatory biographies of Generals Washington and Lee would have been welcomed by those who sympathised with the American cause.[212] The following comment by Richard Price must have caused readers of the *Hibernian Magazine* to reflect on Irish rather than American grievances: 'a country that is subject to the legislature of another country, in which it has no voice, and over which it has no control, cannot be said to be governed by its own will. Such a country, therefore, is in a state of slavery.'[213] This pro-American material was only partly balanced by excerpts from Smith's *Plain Truth*; a biographical sketch of General Howe; and an account of the case of James Rivington – a prominent New York printer whose press had been

---

[209] [Ferguson], *Remarks on a Pamphlet Lately Published by Dr Price.*
[210] *HM*, January 1775; January and October 1775; February 1775; July 1775; February–March and June–July 1775 respectively.
[211] *Ibid.*, April and November 1775 respectively.
[212] *Ibid.*, January; January; February; February; February–May; June; July; September; October and December 1776 respectively.
[213] *Ibid.*, February 1776, p. 78.

confiscated by patriots because of his publication of material considered to be pro-British.[214] It may be significant that two of these three loyalist items appeared after September 1776 – the month in which the magazine published the declaration of independence.

The ebb and flow of the tide of battle in America was reflected in the tone and content of the Irish press. During 1775 and much of 1776 the mood of patriot commentators was buoyant owing to the pyrrhic victory of royal forces at Bunker Hill, the Americans' investment of Boston, and their advance into Canada. An Armagh-based correspondent of the *Freeman's Journal* was moved to verse by General Gage's difficulties in Massachusetts:

> Vain were his *looks* and vain his skill
> at Lexington and Bunker's Hill:
> there freedom's chosen sons
> did soon convince him, to his cost,
> with many a gallant soldier lost,
> they'd stand – and fight like Britons.[215]

The news of the successful defence of Quebec and of General Montgomery's death during the attack was greeted with disbelief by Irish patriots and the *Freeman's Journal* assured its readers that 'the report circulated yesterday, in all the public prints, respecting the defeat of Montgomery's army before Quebec . . . is attended with so many improbable circumstances that it scarcely deserves credit'.[216] Three months later the newspaper was still refusing to regard the Americans' failure as anything more than a temporary setback: 'Quebec is by *nature* strongly fortified. The provincials have not, as yet, taken it. This is the whole of what the *Gazette* informs us.'[217] Whatever dismay the British victory in Canada may have caused in patriot circles was more than offset by General Howe's evacuation of Boston, news of which reached Ireland in May 1776 and inspired the publication of a long humorous poem by William Preston, a graduate of Trinity College.[218] The bad news for government continued with the failure of a naval attack on Charleston in June, but thereafter the fortunes of war changed again as General Howe drove Washington from New York, an operation which provided the patriot press with an opportunity to condemn 'the fierceness and slaughter that marked the Highlanders and Hessians' – English (and Irish) members of the royal

---

[214] *Ibid.*, July, November and December 1776 respectively.
[215] *FJ*, 6 January 1776.   [216] *Ibid.*, 2 March 1776.   [217] *Ibid.*, 18 June 1776.
[218] [William Preston], *A Congratulatory Poem on the Late Successes of the British Arms, Particularly the Triumphant Evacuation of Boston* (Dublin, 1776).

army, it was implied, fought in a more civilised manner than the Scots and Germans.[219]

American independence

Just as the recovery of New York was depressing patriot spirits the political significance of the conflict was transformed by the American declaration of independence. The colonists could no longer credibly be represented as loyal subjects resisting unconstitutional exactions. On the contrary, the principal argument relied on by supporters of government since the start of the war – that it was being fought to preserve the unity of the empire – was given retrospective justification. This argument had previously been vehemently rejected by Irish patriots. At the beginning of 1776, for example, a letter in the *Freeman's Journal* described the colonists as 'legal revolutionists' and rejected the ministerial allegation that they aimed at independence: 'If our ministers could give satisfactory proof of any such design, doubtless great numbers in both realms [Ireland and Britain] who are warmly attached to constitutional supremacy, would approve coercive measures; but nothing can be more foreign to truth than this assertion.'[220] In the event, the principal patriot organs received the news of the declaration of independence with outward equanimity. An article in the *Hibernian Journal*, which may have been reprinted from a British source, argued that independence 'was certainly the wisest step they [the Americans] could have taken in their present circumstances; since thereby they will have a regular state of government established, and a kind of legal authority to reward and punish'.[221] A front-page letter in the *Freeman's Journal* praised the content of the declaration as conveying 'sentiments of civil liberty and government just and truly constitutional; they are chiefly those of Cicero, Sallust, Harrington, Sidney, and Locke'.[222] Some patriots had foreseen the likelihood of American independence in the early days of the war. An easily deciphered allegory which appeared in the *Freeman's Journal* as early as October 1775 not only anticipated American independence but even predicted that it would be a prelude to Irish independence:

When the Dutch [American] Whigs resisted that obstinate, destructive despot, Philip the 2d [George III], born and bred a Spaniard [Englishman], and the corrupt Cortes of Spain [parliament of England]; his viceroy of the appendant kingdom of Portugal [Ireland] procured from their venal Cortes [parliament] an address to support his bloody measures against their oppressed fellow subjects

[219] *FJ*, 5 November 1776.   [220] *Ibid.*, 11 January 1776.   [221] *HJ*, 28 August 1776.
[222] *FJ*, 29 August 1776.

of Holland: the cause of liberty notwithstanding prevailed, and the brave Dutch threw off the Spanish yoke for ever. The Spanish pride and ambition which had before tyrannized over Portugal with some degree of moderation, having no other object left to prey upon, redoubled their usurpations, and provoked the whole Portuguese nation to become Whigs, and roused them into unavoidable resistance. The Spaniards being exhausted by the Dutch, their lust of power became impotent, and Portugal shook off the galling yoke of Spain for ever.[223]

On the other hand, the *Hibernian Magazine* was circumspect in its discussion of the declaration: 'Whether those grievances were real or imaginary, or whether they did or did not deserve a parliamentary enquiry, we will not presume to decide. The ball is now struck, and time only can shew where it will rest.'[224] Such a non-committal assessment may have reflected the misgivings felt by many members of the Anglo-Irish community who had formerly sympathised with the American patriots.

The *Hibernian Magazine* appears to have changed its editorial policy following the declaration of independence and more space was given to pro-British material in 1777. For the first time, material sympathetic to the American cause (a hostile account of Lord North, Burke's letter to the sheriffs of Bristol, and an engraving of the late General Montgomery)[225] was more than offset by loyalist material. This included a biographical notice of Lord Howe; a report of George Washington's alleged philandering; hostile accounts of the trial of 'John the painter' (an American agent who attempted to burn Portsmouth dock-yard); a report from New York by the reinstated royal governor, William Tryon; and a biographical notice and portrait of General John Burgoyne.[226] The reduced coverage given to American affairs during 1777 suggests that the swing in opinion described in the February issue of the *Hibernian Magazine* may have been common among members of the Anglo-Irish community: 'the success of our arms in North America made many converts of the nominal patriots who had espoused their [the Americans'] cause; and numbers who had declared themselves the warm advocates of the colonists, pretended no longer to defend them, after they had avowedly thrown off their dependency upon Great Britain'.[227] A recent study of Dublin municipal politics has indeed found that pro-American protests by the Common Council and the guilds of the city 'died down' in the aftermath of the declaration of independence.[228]

---

[223] *Ibid.*, 14 October 1775.   [224] *HM*, September 1776.
[225] *Ibid.*, June; June; and August 1776 respectively.
[226] *Ibid.*, January; January; April–May; April; and October 1777 respectively.
[227] *HM*, February 1777, 110–11. This comment refers to Europe rather than Ireland, and may have been reprinted from a British publication.
[228] Hill, *From Patriots to Unionists*, p. 144.

But if the more lukewarm supporters of the American cause fell away, the sympathies of committed patriots were unshaken by either British victories on the battlefield or the decision of the colonies to sever all links with the mother country. At their quarterly dinner in January 1777 the members of the Society of Free Citizens drank 'Success to our friends in America', 'The thirteen sisters and their sponsors; unanimity and success to them' and '28th of June 1776' (the date of the unsuccessful British attack on Charleston). Other toasts illustrate the Irish patriots' high regard for leaders of the British opposition ('The Earl of Chatham and better health to him', 'The asserter of British liberty, John Wilkes, Esq.'), the essential linkage between their political and religious loyalties ('The Protestant interest over all the world'), the importance they attached to maintaining the exclusive power of the House of Commons over taxation ('May the Commons of Ireland ever hold the purse of the nation'), and their continuing support for parliamentary reform ('A revolutionary ferret to all rotten boroughs', 'May the present House of Commons be as virtuous as the last was corrupt', 'A sharp pair of scissors to our scandalous pension list').[229]

The sense of the political nation

In emphasising the exclusive role of the House of Commons in granting supply the Free Citizens undoubtedly reflected the views of a majority of the Irish political nation. In March 1776, as he contemplated the imminent dissolution of parliament under the terms of the octennial act, Lord Harcourt advised the secretary of state against including a money bill among those which were to be drafted by the Privy Council and transmitted as the cause for summoning the new parliament, explaining that the octennial act had made members of parliament 'more dependent upon their constituents, and more afraid of offending the people, the body of whom are, to the last degree, jealous of this power, which alone renders them, they think, of any importance in the state'.[230] A reply from the prime minister made it clear that the crown's right of drafting a money bill in the Privy Council would be insisted upon, although he fully accepted the bill had no prospect of passing into law.[231] Given the dispute it had provoked in 1769, the sensitivity of the money bill issue cannot be attributed to the influence of the American conflict. Outside of parliament, some patriots were willing to cast doubts on the competence of the

[229] *HJ*, 15 January 1777.
[230] Harcourt to Weymouth, 20 March 1776, PRO, SP 63/452, Pos. 3,863, fo. 299.
[231] North to Harcourt, 25 March 1776, NLI Ms. 755, pp. 89–90.

Irish House of Commons – unrepresentative and filled with pensioners and placemen as it was – to consent to taxation:

If the crown *influences* the representatives of the people, in their parliamentary decisions; does not *representation* cease to exist? – And, would it not, therefore, be justifiable in the subjects, to *refuse* submission to the taxes imposed on them by such a legislature, if ever we should be cursed with the like?[232]

It is not necessary to look to America for precedents even for such a potentially revolutionary argument as this: essentially the same point had been made as early as 1751 during the power struggle between Speaker Boyle and Primate Stone.[233] As the general election approached, an anonymous pamphleteer warned electors not to believe ministerial claims that all supposed threats to the liberty of the subject were 'formed by the heated imagination of modern patriotism alone'. There was, on the contrary, abundant evidence of the administration's tyrannical intentions:

Has not the claim of taxation, enforced at the point of the bayonet in America, written a lesson to us in letters of blood, which if we are not lost to all sense of reason and experience, we must read with apprehension and distrust. Did not the very parent of the American stamp act declare, at the instant of its birth, that he hoped to make the haughty Irish bend their necks, when that system should have ripened into maturity?[234]

None the less, the author concluded that the House of Commons – the 'shield to cover us in the day of battle' as he described it – imperfectly constituted though it was, remained sufficiently representative to frustrate the schemes of government:

There are in this kingdom thirty-two counties, and, I compute, at least twelve corporations that return members by the voice of the people; and when to these are added the boroughs under the control of persons whose independence, as well of spirit as of property, have always ranked them with the foremost in support of our real interests and our dearest rights, we shall soon perceive that such a representation, united by the desire of attaining one common object, must overpower even the corruption of modern times.[235]

In keeping with this outlook a public meeting of the 'independent electors of Dublin city' approved a declaration against accepting any 'place, pension or emolument, from the crown' that was to be put to parliamentary candidates in the city, and appointed a committee, which included

[232] *FJ*, 3 February 1776.
[233] *A Dialogue between Jack Lane and Simon Curtin Freemen of Cork*, pp. 7–8, quoted on p. 24 above.
[234] *An Appeal to the Understanding of the Electors of Ireland* (Dublin, 1776), pp. 7–8.
[235] *Ibid.*, pp. 14–15.

the indefatigable James Napper Tandy, to wait on the candidates for that purpose.[236]

The results of the general election of 1776 do not suggest that patriot sentiment had strengthened among the electorate. The defeat of Henry Flood ('the man, who, by his apostasy, has rendered the word patriotism such a term of reproach') in Kilkenny was one of the few results to be celebrated in the patriot press.[237] Annotated parliamentary lists compiled for the use of government, the first by the chief secretary, Sir John Blaquiere, in 1773 and the second by Sir Michael Cromie, member for Ballyshannon, in 1776, estimated that thirty-two of the sixty-four county seats were held by opposition supporters at the earlier date compared with twenty-seven in the House that was elected three years later.[238] Lord Harcourt soon had the satisfaction of reporting that, although the Privy Council's money bill had been defeated, 'by management we procured it to be read before it was rejected ... without assigning any reasons for the rejection'.[239] Patriot dismay at the composition of the new House can be deduced from an article in the Hibernian Journal, published within a month of its first meeting, which listed the parliamentary seats controlled by lords or borough patrons and concluded that 'the free electors in this kingdom may boast of having the favour and the liberty of returning about 60 [members] – if so many'.[240] An English visitor at this period concluded that 'Lord Harcourt now finds the parliament of Ireland full as obsequious as that of Great Britain.'[241] It was a view shared at the highest level of the administration: when the prime minister advised Lord Harcourt of his replacement by Lord Buckinghamshire in November 1776 he commended the departing viceroy for leaving 'the government of Ireland in a state of ease and opulence, which it had not known these twenty years'.[242]

Outside of parliament, patriots maintained a vigorous and unremitting criticism of ministerial measures in terms that would have been recognised by Charles Lucas ten or even twenty-five years previously, but the opposition failed to make the transition from propaganda to agitation. In November 1776 a correspondent of the Freeman's Journal proposed

[236] FJ, 13 February 1776.   [237] Ibid., 18 June 1776.
[238] The former has been published: see M. Bodkin, 'Notes on the Irish parliament in 1773', Proc. RIA 48 C (1942–43); I have counted George Ogle, for whom no note appears, as a member of the opposition. The latter is found in BL Add. Ms. 33,118, fos. 145–67; for the attribution of authorship see David Lammey, 'The growth of the "patriot opposition" in Ireland during the 1770s', Parliamentary History 7 (1988), 264.
[239] Harcourt to Weymouth, 19 June 1776, PRO SP 63/454, fo. 184.
[240] HJ, 9 July 1777.
[241] [Thomas Campbell], A Philosophical Survey of the South of Ireland, in a Series of Letters to John Watkinson, M.D. (Dublin, 1778), p. 59.
[242] North to Harcourt, 24 November 1776, NLI Ms. 755, p. 113.

that general meetings should be convened in all counties, cities and boroughs for the purpose of drawing up addresses calling for reconciliation
with America and the dismissal of the North ministry. The anonymous
author attributed the weakness of the Irish opposition to lack of leadership:
'Great Britain whose ministers have brought those accumulated distresses
on you, claims omnipotence in legislation. You have Floods, Beresfords,
and Boyles ready to acknowledge that presumptuous claim; but, alas!
you have not an Adams, a Hancock, or a Washington, to repel it.'[243]
Yet it is difficult not to feel that the opposition's weakness lay more in
a shortage of followers than of leaders. Nothing came of the proposal
to organise county meetings but the patriotic Cassandra's chorus continued unabated: 'This year is likely to prove the most important æra in
the history of Great Britain. Every victory weakens her, and every hour
her natural enemies are accumulating strength and riches... Oh! fatal
hour, that taxation without representation became an object of government; accursed source whence all our misfortunes have proceeded!'[244]
It was never likely that sympathy for Dissenting and rebellious colonists,
who now declared themselves republicans and sought to dismember the
British empire, would be widespread among the members of an Anglican
and royalist Anglo-Irish community which felt itself considerably more
threatened by the political disaffection of the bulk of the Irish people than
by any arbitrary tendencies that George III or his ministers may have harboured. Radical patriots, fearing the implications which a British victory
and the consequent strengthening of the British parliament's authority
would hold for Ireland, as well as the risk of French or Spanish intervention which a prolongation of the conflict would entail, were driven to
argue that a swift and decisive American victory was the best outcome
that could be hoped for. As an anonymous letter in the *Hibernian Journal*
put it, the 'people of Ireland' were caught in a dilemma 'from which the
defeat of your own arms, and the good fortune of those against whom
they are employed, can alone extricate you':

Every person who has been in their country [England] knows that, from the
highest to the lowest, they all agree in this point of our dependence; some of
them go so far as to assert that we are theirs by the right of conquest. To ask them
to prove this point is an insult. Mr Molyneux's *Case* they have not heard of.[245]

However logical this stance may have been in the abstract, it must have
struck the majority of the Anglo-Irish community which did not wish
for the defeat of its 'own arms' as shamefully disloyal if not actually
treasonable.

[243] *FJ*, 12 November 1776.   [244] *Ibid.*, 4 January 1777.   [245] *HJ*, 8 October 1777.

Patriot opinion and the Catholics

Long-standing patriot fears of the Catholic population were intensified by the outbreak of the American war – a conflict that raised the prospect, not only of the withdrawal from Ireland of military forces necessary for the maintenance of internal security, but also of greatly increased Catholic recruitment, with or without the overt sanction of the authorities. In December 1775 Sir Edward Newenham linked a fresh wave of Whiteboy activity in south Leinster and east Munster with the withdrawal of troops for service in America and revealed some alarming intelligence that had been communicated to him by a correspondent at Clonmel, County Tipperary: 'There is some desperate deed now in view, which if not nipped in the bud, will perhaps spread, once more, into a general massacre of the Protestant subjects in this kingdom.'[246] An earlier '*cogadh an dá Ghall*' had provided an opportunity for the 1641 rising, and history, according to Newenham's correspondent, was about to repeat itself. He was not alone in his fears. Catholic unrest, unlike the constitutional questions posed by the American crisis, was an issue capable of spurring Irish Protestants into action. In March 1776 the *Hibernian Magazine* reported from Roscrea, County Tipperary, that 'a number of Protestant inhabitants of that town have voluntarily agreed to clothe themselves in uniforms, and arm themselves, in defence of their lives and property, and for the preservation of the peace of the country, against those rioters called White Boys, and all other disturbers of the peace and tranquillity of the Protestant inhabitants'.[247] Only a month later a letter in the *Freeman's Journal* claimed that Volunteer associations were spreading 'like wild fire', that they already numbered more than a thousand men, and that corps had been formed in Wexford, Kilkenny, Limerick, Tipperary and Queen's County. Unusually, the author deplored their activities and motivation, exclaiming that 'The very idea they are formed on must prove ruinous to this country. To keep down the Catholics – wretched policy indeed!'[248] This was a small straw in the wind, an early indication that some sections of patriot opinion had begun to question prevailing attitudes towards the Catholic population.

More typical was the characterisation of supporters of the American war as 'Tories, Jacobites, half Protestants' and the heartfelt appeal contained in another letter to the *Freeman's Journal*, signed by 'a Williamite', for a war against Catholic rather than Protestant enemies:

May Britons never more be led against their brethren, or assist in preparing shackles of slavery for their Protestant fellow-subjects! but reserve their strength and

---

[246] *HJ*, 1 December 1775.   [247] *HM*, March 1776, 215.   [248] *FJ*, 16 April 1776.

courage to subdue real enemies, or to maintain their constitutional rights! . . . the cause of King James and of popery was the same; by introducing an intolerant religion, the persecution of Protestants followed.[249]

Protestant fears of Catholic rearmament were sufficiently widespread to persuade the administration that any recruitment of Catholics would have to proceed without official sanction. When leading members of the Catholic Committee offered to subscribe a large sum of money to encourage enlistment shortly after the outbreak of war, Lord Harcourt considered it prudent to decline their offer.[250] The ministry's negative response did not prevent rumours of the proposal from reaching the ears of patriots and being reported in the opposition press: 'Jemmy Reynolds [James Reynolds, treasurer of the Catholic Committee], though a papist, and but a weaver, inflamed with a new and equal zeal in the glorious cause of his king, offered his services to government for the same purpose [recruitment], which were most graciously received.'[251] The issue of Catholic recruitment was debated between the opposition and administration in parliament and some supporters of government were prepared to defend the idea openly:

Mr Barry Barry took notice of a report that papists were to be recruited to fill the regiments going to America. On which colonel Brown replied, that he should always think it were better to export papists than Protestants; for his part he did not much trouble himself about articles of religion, but thought papists the fittest to be sent abroad that we might be defended at home by Protestants.

Mr Barry Barry answered, that if papists were to be trained as soldiers, when they returned back again they would become the more dangerous; – that it was contrary to our laws to arm papists, as they were not permitted to bear arms.[252]

Patriots continued to stress the grave dangers inherent in providing Catholics with military training while government appears to have decided that a blank denial that such a practice existed was the best form of defence. When George Ogle, an outspoken patriot and anti-Catholic, raised the matter in the House of Commons in January 1778, a month after news of Saratoga had reached Ireland, the ensuing exchange differed considerably from that which had taken place two years before:

Mr. Ogle said, a report had prevailed that government intended to make popish levies in this kingdom, and desired to know if there was any foundation for such report? on which Mr. Secretary Heron declared no such orders had been received, nor had he any reason to believe such would be given.[253]

[249] *Ibid.*, 5 November 1776 and 13 July 1776 respectively.
[250] Harcourt to Rochford, 30 September 1775, Gilbert Library Ms. 93, p. 256.
[251] *HJ*, 6 October 1775.
[252] *HM*, November 1775, 687. The exchange took place on 21 October 1775.
[253] *FJ*, 27 January 1778. The exchange took place on 26 January 1775.

The depth of Protestant concern at the prospect of Catholics being armed must have been the principal factor in determining this cautious response, but administration had abandoned its early hopes of widespread Catholic enlistment long before 1778.

The view that Catholics were compliant tools of the ministry derived whatever contemporary force it possessed from the loyal addresses that were regularly submitted to the crown by the Catholic élite, as well as from the none too successful efforts of Catholic gentlemen to encourage recruitment. The fact that prominent members of the Catholic gentry and commercial class had sworn allegiance to George III also allowed patriot writers to represent them as supporters of arbitrary government: 'many of our respectable Roman Catholics in Ireland, have in a manner sworn themselves to be passive obedience men, or to support and defend our British monarchs, be they good or evil maintainers of freedom, and the public welfare, or the contrary! May we never again hear of unconditional oaths in a free country!'[254] More reasonably, it could be argued that Catholics would lend their support to government in the pragmatic hope of obtaining measures of relief from penal legislation as a reward for their assistance. This was the view expressed by a pro-American lawyer in Dublin who informed Edmund Burke that 'The Roman Catholics who receive no favour, no quarter, from their fellow subjects of a different persuasion, and are indebted only to government for some lenity in the execution of the laws again [sic] them, and who have no liberty like the American Dissenters at stake – are ready to give their beggarly assistance to government.'[255] The *Hibernian Journal* reached the same conclusion when commenting on the support lent by the Catholic clergy in Dublin to the official day of fasting and prayer on 13 December 1776: 'the papists have been informed, that on their shewing their loyalty will greatly depend the success of the intended bill next session of parliament, to relax some of the laws against them'.[256] An even more jaundiced assessment of Catholic attitudes – albeit one that had a basis in fact, as is evident from the expression '*cogadh an dá Ghall*' – was expressed by a pro-American correspondent in the *Freeman's Journal* who commented that the 'zeal with which the popish inhabitants of this country espouse, and applaud this most unnatural contest, where Protestants and fellow-subjects are sheathing their swords in each others breasts does not at all surprise me'.[257] Protestant opinion was not deceived by the loyal addresses of the Catholic Committee and remained conscious of the outlook of the wider Catholic community. Indeed, public declarations of Catholic

---

[254] *Ibid.*, 15 August 1775.
[255] John Ridge to the Burkes, 25 September 1775, in Hoffman, *Edmund Burke*, pp. 600–1.
[256] *HJ*, 11 December 1776.   [257] *FJ*, 16 December 1777.

loyalty could easily be represented as part of a twin-track strategy of pressing for reform while keeping the ultimate option of rebellion in reserve for more favourable circumstances, as the *Freeman's Journal* did in the following parody of the Catholic Committee's resolutions:

Resolved, That next to the pope and Pretender, his present Majesty ought to be supported; himself and ministry being the best we have had since 1688.
Resolved, That should our friends, the French and Spaniards land in Ireland, or a few more of the Protestant military be sent from this [country] that something clever may be effected.
Signed by order,
Mercury Hoey, Clerk to the Midnight Committees.[258]

It is difficult to see how such fears could have been allayed: if Catholics took the oath of allegiance to George III they could be represented as supporters of arbitrary government and the coercion of America; if they declined to do so, they could be represented as unreconstructed Jacobites and allies of the Bourbon powers.

The embargo controversy

What the opposition required was an issue that would direct popular anger against the administration – not an arcane constitutional dispute suitable for debate in parliament and analysis in the columns of the patriot press, but a matter of pressing concern to a large section of the Protestant population and capable of effecting a popular mobilisation comparable in scale to that provoked by the Whiteboy disturbances. Only one issue – the embargo on the export of provisions imposed by proclamation on 3 February 1776 – looked as if it might have such a potential, and patriots made what use they could of it. Three days after the proclamation the embargo was denounced by opposition members of parliament on both economic and constitutional grounds. Robert French, representing Galway city, declared it 'was a great hurt to commerce, and was an assuming of a power by the British Privy Council to suspend the laws of this kingdom'. Barry Barry, a member for County Cavan, expanded the latter point by explaining that the embargo 'was in effect repealing the act for allowing a bounty on the exportation of corn, meal and flour' – a rather unconvincing argument since the proclamation suspended the export of corn rather than payment of the bounty.[259] Weak though it was, this formed the main point of the opposition's case when the embargo was debated on 22 February. Walter Hussey Burgh opened the debate and argued that the embargo was 'a claim of dispensing power, which kind of claim

[258] *Ibid.*, 2 September 1775.　　　[259] *FJ*, 8 February 1776.

had struck the crown off one king, and the head off from another' before moving that 'every attempt to suspend the law, under colour of the prerogative of the crown, is illegal'. Opposition to the embargo extended to some of the independent members, as is clear from the fact that the motion was seconded by Luke Gardiner, and its final defeat by the narrow margin of 89 votes to 66 suggests that many regular government supporters considered it prudent to absent themselves from the vote.[260]

Given the possibility of adverse effects on the economy the embargo on the provisions trade had the potential to stimulate extra-parliamentary opposition, but patriot hopes in this direction were largely disappointed. As early as 9 May 1776 the *Freeman's Journal* published a letter upbraiding the merchants of Dublin for failing to take steps to oppose an embargo described as 'a remnant of the arbitrary and illegal precedents endeavoured to be established by the detestable race of Stuarts'.[261] Greater exertion was shown by the merchants of Cork, the principal centre of the export trade in provisions, and a very outspoken petition from the 'freemen, freeholders, citizens, merchants, traders, and Protestant inhabitants' of the city was signed by 488 persons and presented to the king by Lord Midleton:

In the pursuit of an inexpedient, unnecessary, and perhaps illegal power of taxation over a bold, numerous, experienced, free and distant people, we have seen our armies defeated, our fame tarnished, our American trade totally destroyed ... our national honour lowered to the dust, by an introduction of foreign mercenaries to fight our domestic quarrels ... and [we] now most humbly supplicate your Majesty to remove those evils of which we complain. To direct the sword may be sheathed. That our commerce may be restored, and that oeconomy, union, peace and liberty may be permanently established thro' all parts of the empire.[262]

Sweeping though this critique was, much of the support for the petition was grounded on the commercial interests of the Cork merchants. In November of the same year Lord Harcourt forwarded a second petition from the 'mayor, sheriffs, merchants and traders of the city of Cork' which complained that 'the embargo on butter and cheese is universally distressing to this kingdom, and particularly to the southern parts thereof'.[263] Opposition to the embargo from the southern port was persistent. In June 1777 Lord Buckinghamshire forwarded a third petition calling for its removal or suspension and in October of the same year he informed the secretary of state that 'there has been a further meeting of the merchants and traders of the city of Cork, who have sent up to their representatives in parliament a petition addressed to the House of Commons, stating the

[260] *Ibid.*, 24 February 1776.   [261] *Ibid.*, 9 May 1776.   [262] *Ibid.*, 4 June 1776.
[263] Harcourt to Weymouth, 15 November 1776, PRO SP 63/455, fo. 182.

general distress as they term it, arising from the embargo and praying the interposition of the House therein'.[264] The viceroy added that 'a similar petition is preparing from the merchants of the city of Dublin and will perhaps be followed from other places'; by this time he was sufficiently concerned by the prospect of a widespread agitation to advise that 'if some relaxation of the embargo could be allowed it would tend greatly to quiet the minds of the people in general'.[265] John Fitzgibbon, the future Earl of Clare, was the author of a pamphlet which placed the embargo in the context of acts of the British parliament that had 'wrested from Ireland an old and an established [woollen] manufacture' and left 'three of her provinces, to subsist as they may, without the advantage, of any considerable manufacture' – a linkage that threatened to bring British mercantilist legislation into question.[266]

There is some evidence that opinion outside parliament was influenced by opposition arguments. When, in December 1777, the students of the Trinity College Historical Society – a body whose members can be safely assumed to have had no direct involvement in the provisions trade – debated 'Whether it is for the advantage of the state, that the king should have it in his power to prohibit the free export of the commodities of the country?' they replied in the negative by a margin of two to one.[267] Within parliament, however, repeated efforts to use the embargo to shake the government's majority failed. Although Denis Daly, an opposition-inclined independent representing County Galway, succeeded in having a committee established to enquire into the export trade in provisions, supporters of government were able to have the committee dissolved before it could report by the comfortable margin of 137 to 80.[268] The opposition took the question of the embargo from the committee onto the floor of the whole House, where the arguments employed on both sides showed that attitudes had scarcely developed since the first debate on the American crisis two and a half years earlier. James Wilson, the opposition member for County Antrim, claimed that the question at issue was whether Ireland would 'be governed by the authority of the English cabinet or the consent of the Irish parliament' and reminded his listeners that 'it has been the in-solent, and repeated boast of the English ministers, that they have a right to tax us'.[269] Sir Henry Cavendish, responding for government, argued

---

[264] Buckinghamshire to Weymouth, 26 June 1777 and Buckinghamshire to Weymouth, 30 October 1777, PRO SP 63/457, fo. 142 and PRO SP 63/458, fo. 154 respectively.

[265] Buckinghamshire to Weymouth, 30 October 1777, PRO SP 63/458, fo. 154v.

[266] [John Fitzgibbon], *Commerce not a Fit Subject for an Embargo* (Dublin and Limerick, 1777), p. 7.

[267] Historical Society minutes, 3 December 1777, TCD Mun. Soc./Hist. 2, pp. 138–9.

[268] *FJ*, 11 December 1777.

[269] Cavendish debates, IV, 16 December 1777, pp. 116–18. NLI Pos. 7,003.

that 'there is but one minister [Lord North], and I will venture to say he never said so', and concluded with a rhetorical appeal to the pro-British sentiments of the members: 'when Great Britain is in distress, shall we take that opportunity to raise the people in opposition? rather let us unite throughout the whole kingdom to assist, and nourish her in the hour of distress.'[270] Another supporter of the administration, Charles Sheridan, who represented the pocket borough of Belturbet, developed Cavendish's argument against inciting unrest out of doors in a revealing direction:

> the major part of the lower rank of our people [are] not well affected to us. It is not the wish of any gentleman to aim at increasing this disaffection, to furnish the people with arguments to justify their disaffection. Supposing in case of an invasion, the standards of the enemies were erected in this country, would it tend to prevent the discontented from arranging themselves under them to have placed government in a most unfavourable light, to have told the people, that the distresses they may have suffered from the present embargo, do not proceed from necessity, but that this measure has been adopted from the basest motives . . . ?[271]

It was a telling point. The opposition could not, in practice, confine an agitation on an economic issue such as the provisions embargo to the Protestant community alone, however much they might wish to do so, and the implications of an agitation encompassing sections of the Catholic population were, at this point in time, still too alarming to contemplate.

Although even such a shrewd and disinterested observer as Arthur Young believed that the embargo had sacrificed 'the interests of a whole people to a few monopolizing individuals in another country',[272] the failure of the opposition's smouldering anti-embargo campaign to ignite must ultimately be attributed to the fact that, while profits were transferred from the pockets of Irish merchants to those of British commissaries with military contracts, the impact upon agricultural producers was comparatively slight because the damage inflicted on the continental export trade was largely offset by the increased demand for provisions to supply the army in North America. By February 1778, even such a committed organ of patriotic opinion as the *Hibernian Journal* was forced to acknowledge as much: 'The embargo laid by government on the exportation of provisions, is thought by many of the most sensible men in this kingdom, to be an unconstitutional coercion; yet if its consequences are minutely looked into, it will be found not to have operated much, if any thing, to the general disadvantage of Ireland.'[273] This conclusion was based on the continuing high prices of foodstuffs and it has been

---

[270] *Ibid.*, pp. 118–21.   [271] Ibid., pp. 125–6.
[272] Arthur Young, *Tour in Ireland (1776–1779)*, II (London, 1892), p. 246.
[273] *HJ*, 16 February 1778.

confirmed by modern research.[274] In conditions of continued market buoyancy, the opposition's hopes of using the embargo as a stick to beat the ministry could not be realised.

Saratoga

When the new parliament opened for its first session in October 1777 Lord Buckinghamshire made no reference to America in the speech from the throne – a failure for which he was criticised by Whitehall and which he justified by referring to the 'unusual circumstance of meeting a new House of Commons in which there are ninety untried members'.[275] This cautious approach contrasts with Harcourt's boldness in 1775 and has been interpreted as a sign of increased patriot strength in the new House of Commons.[276] In view of the comfortable majorities enjoyed by government throughout the session, however, the contrast can more plausibly be attributed to the different tempers of the two viceroys. The decision of Walter Hussey Burgh, formerly an outspoken supporter of America, to accept the position of prime sergeant is a truer indication of the strength of the administration and the weakness of opposition at this time. Buckinghamshire advised the secretary of state for America, with no obvious sign of irony, that Hussey Burgh now believed he would deserve 'to lose his head if, in the present situation, he did not zealously support his Majesty's measures for the reduction of the Americans'.[277] The scale of the parliamentary majority enjoyed by the ministry is evident from the division on a motion for financial retrenchment moved by the rising star of the patriot party, Henry Grattan, which was crushed by 131 votes to 62 on 17 November; those voting with government included Alexander Montgomery, brother of the deceased American hero General Richard Montgomery.[278]

On 11 December the *Freeman's Journal* carried reports of the surrender of General Burgoyne's northern army at Saratoga. Paradoxically, the news of a British military disaster in America may have strengthened the position of administration in the Irish parliament. When, two days later, Sir Edward Newenham rose to propose a motion calling on the House of Commons to address the king for the removal of 'those ministers who

---

[274] See T.M. O'Connor, 'The embargo on the export of Irish provisions', *IHS* 2 (1940).
[275] Buckinghamshire to Lord George Germain, 31 October 1777, HMC Stopford-Sackville Mss., I (1904), p. 246.
[276] See, for example, Lammey, 'The growth of the "patriot opposition"', pp. 273–4.
[277] Buckinghamshire to Germain, 4 November 1777, HMC Stopford-Sackville Mss., I (1904), p. 247.
[278] *FJ*, 20 November 1777.

advised this destructive war' other patriot members displayed more caution. Another prominent member of the opposition, Barry Barry, announced that 'he was against agitating any subject relative to America' while a third, George Ogle, requested that consideration of the motion be deferred as the matter was under consideration in the British parliament, a suggestion to which Newenham was induced to yield. This behaviour suggests an awareness in opposition ranks that the 'silent majority' of the Anglo-Irish community would disapprove of attempts to embarrass the ministry at such a critical juncture. News of the American victory was greeted with near-incredulity by supporters of government, and *Faulkner's Dublin Journal* initially deprecated what it termed 'fabricated paragraphs' about the surrender of General Burgoyne's army.[279] When the scale of the defeat became apparent the same paper argued that the reverse would only serve to harden the anti-American (and anti-patriot) resolve of the population: 'The Americans by their ingratitude, and their abettors here, have at length roused the spirit of the nation; to which the latter have not a little contributed, by their exultation at the surrender of Gen. Burgoyne.'[280] The above statement appears to have been reprinted from a British source, but there are indications that Saratoga also stimulated loyalist sentiment among the Anglo-Irish population. Thus the Trinity College Historical Society answered the question 'Whether gentle terms of capitulation are more honourable for a surrendering general, than such as are severe?' (a veiled reference to the convention under which General Burgoyne had surrendered his army) in the affirmative by the emphatic margin of 17 votes to 8.[281]

The strong position of government in the House of Commons was confirmed in February 1778 when Henry Grattan again raised the question of public finances and the bloated civil list, an issue which aroused such strong interest among the inhabitants of Dublin that members complained of the 'mob' which had gathered outside the doors of parliament. The sergeant-at-arms interrupted the debate at one point to inform the speaker that 'the people were ready to break in' and that the assistance of the municipal authorities had been requested.[282] Not only did opposition to the civil list and the high level of taxation required to maintain it enjoy popular support, it was also an issue which might have been expected to appeal to independent-minded members who would not normally have espoused patriot causes, but Grattan's moderately worded resolution that offices 'created or revived or endowed with great additional salaries are

---

[279] *FDJ*, 13 December 1777; this would appear to have been reprinted from a British source.
[280] *Ibid.*, 24 January 1778.
[281] Historical Society minutes, 1 April 1778, TCD Mun. Soc./Hist. 2, p. 201.
[282] Cavendish debates, VI, 6 February 1778, pp. 30–3; NLI Pos. 7,003.

become a heavy charge upon his Majesty's faithful subjects, unnecessary
to the dignity of his crown, and under a prince of less virtue dangerous
to the constitution' was brushed aside by 143 votes to 66 – an even larger
margin than had been recorded in November, before news of Burgoyne's
defeat arrived.[283] The members of the Anglo-Irish political nation, real-
ising the imminence of a larger war involving old and familiar enemies,
were beginning to rally around the throne.

Presbyterian Ulster may have been an exception, however, and there
is some evidence that the news of Saratoga gave a fresh stimulus to anti-
war sentiment which had declined following the British successes of 1776.
Within days of the arrival of the news, James Wilson, the patriot member
for County Antrim, deplored the circumstances in which the British army
found itself in North America and claimed that 'the earth was teeming
with the blood of our glorious countrymen who have become a prey to the
carnage of a hopeless war'.[284] A memo prepared by the lord lieutenant
for the chief secretary prior to the latter's visit to London in December
1777 mentioned the 'inclination to favour the Americans which appears
in the north of Ireland'. A marginal note in the same document reads:
'Illumination at Belfast upon the news of Genl. Burgoyne's misfortune?'
The question mark probably reflected uncertainty about whether such
an event had occurred, but it seems likely that some houses, if not the
town as a whole, were illuminated.[285] The *Londonderry Journal* published
a verse which gleefully contrasted the joy expressed by supporters of the
war when news arrived that General Howe had captured Philadelphia,
the seat of Congress, with their shock on learning of the Saratoga disaster
only a day or two later:

> While yet the full-swollen tide of passion flowed,
> and haughty triumph in each bosom glowed,
> O just reverse, the next day's packet shows
> a captive army, and victorious foes! –
> Now, sad and solemn, strike each muffled bell!
> Ring, justly ring, 'tis conquered Burgoyne's knell![286]

Yet even in the north, and even after Saratoga, opponents of Lord North's
administration held back from endorsing the idea of American independence. In January 1778 Lord Chatham's speech of 20 November 1777 to
the British House of Lords was published in pamphlet form. The speech
rehearsed Chatham's well-known view that 'without peace, without an

---

[283] Buckingham to Weymouth, 7 February 1778, PRO SP 63/459, fo. 59v.
[284] Cavendish debates, IV, 16 December 1777, p. 118; NLI Pos. 7,003.
[285] Memo by Buckinghamshire for Sir Richard Heron, 26 December 1777, NLI Ms.
13,035 (16).
[286] *LJ*, 19 December 1777. The poem was published under the heading 'For the London-
Derry Journal' and appears to have been a local composition.

immediate restoration of tranquillity, this nation is ruined and undone'
but also rejected the idea of American independence in the most emphatic
terms: 'as to America and its views of independency, I must own, I always
looked upon that country to be as much a part of Great Britain, to every
purpose but that of taxation, as Devonshire, Surrey, or Middlesex'.[287] An
advertisement in the *Belfast News-Letter* stated that the pamphlet was 'to
be sold by the booksellers in Belfast, Londonderry, Newry, and Armagh,
and the carriers of this news paper', while a notice in the *Londonderry
Journal* advised readers that it was 'now selling by the printer hereof'.[288]
It seems likely that Chatham's views still reflected those of many Irish
Protestants on the eve of war with France.

But for a minority of radical patriots in all parts of the country, Saratoga
represented a welcome opportunity to arraign the ministry for incompe-
tence, to argue for the recognition of American independence, and to
indulge in the self-righteous satisfaction that is natural to prophets of
doom who have been vindicated by the course of events. Pre-publication
advertisements for the *Dublin Evening Journal*, a new and strongly patriotic newspaper which began publication in February, referred to Saratoga
in terms that were less than funereal: 'Our armies defeated, and capit-
ulating to those whom our sagacious ministers termed cowards, and
to whom, deeming them too feeble to resist, they had arrogantly proposed the galling yoke of slavery.'[289] Some Dublin patriots reacted to the
official day of fasting held on 27 February 1778 by meeting in taverns
to 'celebrate the fast over a plentiful table' and by drinking toasts which
included the following: 'May those who fast for the purpose of supporting despotism, be never better supplied with provisions than General
Burgoyne was at Saratoga.'[290] On the same day William Steel Dickson,
minister of the Presbyterian congregation at Ballyhalbert, County Down,
who had previously attributed blame to both British ministers and American rebels in a sermon of December 1776, preached a much more partisan
text to the same congregation. Comparing the present 'civil war' between
'kindred blood' with that which Israel had unsuccessfully waged against
the breakaway kingdom of Judea, he praised Abner, an Israelite who,

As he perceived that the public interest would be more effectually served by
a friendly accommodation than the ravages of the desolating sword, he chose to
acquiesce in the determination of the revolted tribe, and suffer them to enjoy their
new-born independence, rather than push his claims of unlimited submission, and
thereby protract a war, the end of which, he foresaw, must have been bitterness.[291]

---

[287] *Ibid.*, 2 December 1777.   [288] *BNL*, 13 January 1778 and *LJ*, 16 January 1778.
[289] *FLJ*, 31 January 1778.   [290] *Dublin Evening Journal*, 28 February 1778.
[291] William Steel Dickson, 'On the ruinous effects of civil war' in Clifford, *Scripture Politics*,
   p. 51.

Dickson did not base his appeal for the recognition of American Independence on moral considerations alone but pointed to the threat posed by France, a threat which grew each year as Britain dissipated its strength in the American conflict: 'America may continue her resistance a few campaigns longer; and if it does so, France may continue to talk of peace, while she prepares for war . . . our enemies cannot, probably, effect to day, what a few years may render easy, or even accomplish to their hands.'[292] Dickson's fears of a French war were realised more quickly than he anticipated.

Within a few weeks, news arrived of the Franco-American alliance and the recall of the British ambassador from the French court. On 23 March the occasional patriot Denis Daly proposed a loyal address which was adopted unanimously by both houses. It assured the king that 'your Majesty may rely with the greatest confidence, on the entire affection of your faithful subjects of Ireland; and depend on their co-operating cheerfully with your Majesty to the utmost of their ability, in asserting the honour of your Majesty's government, and establishing the security of your dominions'.[293] Less than six months previously Daly had been scathing in his condemnation of the embargo on the export of provisions, had accused the British ministry of 'sacrificing us, only that America might be distressed by it', and claimed that 'enslaving that country [was] being made a pretence of plundering Ireland'.[294] But now, moving the loyal address to the king, he stressed the community of interest that bound the Irish political nation to its mother country:

I do not think this a time to expose any of our weaknesses to our enemies. The fate of Great Britain, and Ireland are embarked in the same bottom. Nothing but a spirit of unanimity can have success. This period is not proper for disputes upon domestic mismanagement. It would be improper to debate upon a part when the whole is at stake.[295]

Luke Gardiner, confirming his reliability as a political weather vane, commended the patriot opposition for the support it had extended to government at a critical juncture: 'whatever obstructions they may occasionally make to the measure of administration yet they still have those great objects in view, an attention to the public weal, and an alacrity to support the dignity, and the power of the empire'.[296] Several patriot members representing open county seats followed Daly's example. John Beresford was able to inform a member who normally resided in England that George Ogle of County Wexford, Barry Barry of County Cavan,

[292] *Ibid.*, p. 48.   [293] PRO SP 63/459, fo. 187.   [294] *HJ*, 1 November 1777.
[295] Cavendish debates, IX, 23 March 1778, pp. 44–5; NLI Pos. 7,004.
[296] Cavendish debates, IX, 23 March 1778, p. 49.

William Brownlow of County Armagh, Sir Edward Newenham of County
Dublin and 'Black Alexander Montgomery' of County Donegal had all
supported the address.[297] George Ogle ventured to express the view that
'the policy of England with regard to Ireland for some years past has been
narrow, and confined' but was quick to add an appeal for unity in the face
of the common enemy: 'this is no season for complaint, this is no time
to show any discontent. The fate of England and Ireland are inseparably
united. The threads are interwoven, indissolubly interwoven. He can't
be a friend of his country who would wish to cut that knot asunder.'[298]
Nearly two years after the American declaration of independence, emulation of the American example in Ireland remained inconceivable to
members of the Anglo-Irish patriot opposition.

The shadow of France

Reports that reserve officers from Irish regiments in the French service –
'some of the best disciplined officers in Europe' as the *Hibernian Journal*
described them – were crossing the Atlantic to enter the American service may have aroused mixed feelings among pro-American patriots but
can only have strengthened their belief in the inveterate hostility of Irish
Catholics to the interests of Great Britain.[299] What other motive could
have inspired men to transfer their allegiance from his Most Christian
Majesty to the Continental Congress? State papers indicate that secret
recruitment for the French service was still continuing in Ireland, although its scale was much reduced since the period before the Seven Years
War.[300] Another report concerning the Irish regiments which appeared
in the pro-government *Saunders' News-Letter* in January 1778 must have
excited very different sentiments among the various sections of the population: 'By actual accounts lately received from Paris we are assured, that
the Irish brigade, consisting of six battalions of 950 men each, which were
quartered at Aire, Bethune, Doway, and Cambray, have been ordered to
the sea side, to Calais, Gravelines, Bergues and Dunkirk.'[301] A Wexford-
born naval chaplain made no attempt to disguise his pro-American sentiments in a letter that he forwarded from his ship in Brest harbour to a
fellow priest in his native county in late December 1777: 'What an epoch
for after ages, the ever remarkable year 1777 for the independence as well

---

[297] John Beresford to Thomas Allan, 25 March 1778, in William Beresford (ed.), *The
Correspondence of the Right Hon. John Beresford* (London, 1854), I, pp. 25–6.
[298] Cavendish debates, IX, 23 March 1778, p. 49; NLI Pos. 7,004.
[299] *HJ*, 18 September 1776.   [300] See, for example, PRO SP 63/457, fo. 116.
[301] *SNL*, 8 January 1778.

as bravery of the Americans in the field of Mars', he enthused.[302] The anti-British sentiment of the Irish émigrés is again shown by a question which John MacMahon, head of the medical service at the *école militaire* in Paris, put to Benjamin Franklin, the American minister: 'Whatever the issue of it may be with regard to France America's independence is assured for ever. When will poor oppressed Ireland's turn come?'[303]

Against this background, claims by O'Conor, Curry, O'Leary and other Catholic apologists that the loyalty of their coreligionists had been abundantly demonstrated by their peaceful behaviour since 1691 were easily refuted by sceptical patriot commentators:

Are we to think they [Catholics] are endued with less precaution than the rest of mankind, that they must endanger life and property, without any alas, any prospect, however distant of success? No! no! they are more wary than that – several circumstances must occur to stir up any flame of rebellion among them – they must have leaders of capacity and some influence; they must have arms, and disciplined forces, to prevent the English from assisting us; and they must have help from some foreign maritime power, under whose yoke they may amply enjoy the benefits of popery and bondage of both mind and body.[304]

By the spring of 1778, as France extended diplomatic recognition to the United States and moved towards open war with Great Britain, an invasion of Ireland became a real possibility for the first time since 1759. Protestant Ireland closed ranks in the face of old enemies, domestic as well as foreign. Among those who spoke in favour of Denis Daly's loyal address from a patriot perspective was Edmond Butler, a member for County Kilkenny, who linked the twin dangers of foreign invasion and Catholic insurrection. Butler acknowledged that the 'practice and principles of Whiteboyism' had been driven underground for the moment but added the following rider: 'how readily they might be brought again into action is very well known to every man who has observed the deportment of persons suspected of such notions'. The prospect of foreign invasion, in Butler's view, could only provide a new stimulus for disaffection and unrest among the Catholic population:

What an air of joy and expectation has been observed upon their countenances upon such expectations . . . Instead of that moderation we enjoy they would look for a despotic government under which their religion would be established; and

---

[302] Fr H. Ennis to Fr John Kavenagh, 29 December 1777, Passionists' archive, NLI Pos. 7,654, p. 159.
[303] MacMahon to Franklin, 22 March 1778, in W.B. Willcox (ed.), *The Papers of Benjamin Franklin*, XXVI (New Haven and London, 1987), p. 153.
[304] *HJ*, 14 May 1777.

they allowed the common benefits of subjects was preferable to, and less ignomin-
ious than living under a government where they were cut off from the possibility
of acquiring honours, or riches, where they were marked men. Instead of this language in whispers, it will be loudly avowed; and after all, are not such sentiments
natural and reasonable?[305]

Henry Flood, a once and future patriot but for the moment an office-
holder, expressed similar views from the opposite side of the House a
few days later. 'In this divided country', he declared, 'where one party
must be at the mercy of the other, it was better that the papists should be
at the mercy of the Protestants, than the Protestants at theirs.'[306] That
which alarmed the political and religious establishment was, of course, a
source of renewed hope for the Catholic masses. Speaking of lower-class
Catholics, Sir Edward Newenham informed the lord privy seal that 'their
insolence rises upon every French mail' and proposed that 'the remains
of General Burgoyne's army should be landed here'.[307] Having visited
Kilkenny in April 1778 he was able to provide his correspondent with
a first-hand account of popular sentiment there: 'The tunes their pipes
played and the toasts they gave, were as good evidence as if given under
their hands. The declarations of the younger females, who have not as
yet learned political hypocrisy, were as bold as in former times.'[308] This
assessment was shared by Henry Flood who, in a letter to the lord lieutenant from the same county, described how 'the idea of invasion, when
thought certain' affected the 'countenances of many of the lower order
who have come within my observation'.[309] Whatever conceptual problems the novel phenomenon of a civil war fought between the *Gaill* of
America and those of Great Britain may have posed for the traditional
Jacobite ideology of the Catholic populace in 1775, the familiar prospect
of war between Britain and the Bourbon powers presented no such difficulties in 1778.

Conclusion

The outbreak of hostilities between Britain and America was widely deplored by Irish Protestants, many of whom feared that taxation of the
colonies might be invoked as a precedent for the taxation of Ireland.
Opposition to the war was strongest among the Presbyterian community,

[305] Cavendish debates, IX, 23 March 1778, pp. 56–7; NLI Pos. 7,004. I have normalised
the punctuation.
[306] *HJ*, 1 April 1778.
[307] Newenham to Lord Dartmouth, 5 March 1778, in HMC Dartmouth Mss. (1896),
p. 239.
[308] Newenham to Dartmouth, 21 April 1775, in *ibid.*, p. 240.
[309] Flood to Buckinghamshire, 14 June 1779, in NLI Ms. 13,038(3).

reflecting the close personal ties of many Presbyterians with the colonies. Ministerial arguments that colonial demands threatened the unity of the empire were disputed by patriots but persuaded a section of Anglican opinion. After the declaration of independence and the British military successes of 1776 a decline in pro-American sentiment became apparent in the Irish press, members of the Anglo-Irish community who had formerly been ambivalent in their views rallied to support the unity of the empire while others – Presbyterians included – who had favoured the American cause lapsed into neutrality. The humiliating surrender of a British field army at Saratoga had contradictory effects, both inspiring loyalists with a new determination to restore the reputation of British arms and providing opponents of the war with persuasive evidence that it could not be won. Finally, the importance of the American conflict receded as the drift towards war with France focused attention on the balance of forces in Europe and encouraged all Protestants to unite in the face of an external threat.

If the Catholic élite gave uncritical support to the ministry's American policies throughout this period, lower-class Catholics were equally unrestrained in celebrating British defeats. Yet although political song in Irish provides clear evidence of popular admiration for American military commanders, the Bourbon powers continued to be the principal focus of attention for those who hoped for the restoration of a Catholic political nation and the overthrow of the Revolution settlement in Ireland. Accordingly, the spirits of the Catholic masses rose as those of the Protestant political nation fell in the spring of 1778.

3   International war, 1778–1781

Irish Protestants appeared to have found a new sense of unity in the early months of 1778 – a feeling inspired not only by the reappearance of a historic and 'natural' enemy in the form of Catholic France, but also by the belated adoption of conciliatory policies towards the American colonies by Lord North's ministry. The effective dropping of the British parliament's claim to tax the colonies resolved a central issue on which most members of the Irish political nation had sympathised to some extent with the Americans, even as the threat of a European war increasingly overshadowed the distant conflict in America. But divisions of opinion on America persisted in a less acute form. If some Protestants felt that British concessions on the taxation issue provided a realistic basis for reconciliation with the colonies, others believed that American independence was a *fait accompli* which should be recognised as soon as possible in order to release resources for the critical struggle against France.

The French war also had some potential to narrow the political gulf that had opened up between élite and popular strata of Catholic society since the 1760s. For the latter, war with France raised expectations that the long-predicted liberation of Ireland was finally at hand and consolidated pro-American sympathies which were already apparent. For Catholics of property, however, the Franco-American alliance represented something of a dilemma. To support the crown in its efforts to suppress a rebellion which could be viewed as a recrudescence of the levelling, anti-monarchical and anti-Catholic Puritanism of the 1640s required a comparatively small adjustment of their traditional political outlook – the fact that an American privateer which captured a number of Cork-owned vessels in 1777 was named the *Oliver Cromwell* may have seemed entirely appropriate to Catholic merchants in the port.[1] But to support Britain in a war against France, a country where many of the clergy had studied, where many merchants traded, and where relatives of many of the Catholic gentry were pursuing military careers, was quite a different

[1] PRO SP 63/458, fo. 45.

170

matter. Reticence, equivocation and neutralism might have been expected, but the Catholic élite showed few signs of wavering in its policy of support for the constitutional status quo.

Anglican opinion and war with France

The co-operation promised by both houses of parliament to the crown following the breach between Britain and France was echoed by a series of loyal addresses from the regions. The address of the 'mayor, sheriffs, Common Council, freemen, and citizens of Cork' – groups which had previously protested vigorously against the embargo on the export of provisions – was accompanied by a voluntary contribution of more than £4,000 which the citizens donated with a view to 'raising recruits for your Majesty's service to be applied in such a manner as you in your great wisdom shall be pleased to direct'.[2] The 'lord mayor, sheriffs, commons and citizens of the city of Dublin', less generous with their money but equally lavish with their sentiments, expressed their 'firm confidence' in the king's wisdom and justice and declared their readiness 'to promote every measure that shall be necessary to secure the honour and dignity of your throne and advance the safety and happiness of your people'.[3] Several addresses contained implied criticism of the Americans. For example, the grand jury and gentlemen of County Westmeath accused the French of having 'insidiously fomented an unnatural civil war' for their own purposes; the high sheriff, grand jury and inhabitants of County Clare asserted that the court of France had concluded an alliance with the Americans 'in order to render abortive those ample terms of reconciliation which your Majesty's most gracious disposition induced you to propose'; while the grand jury and gentlemen of County Longford expressed 'the greatest resentment and indignation' at the 'treacherous schemes of our natural enemy the French to prevent a reconciliation with America'.[4]

The formation of independent 'volunteer' companies to suppress the Whiteboy agitation in the south-east was noted in the previous chapter and the example was now imitated throughout the country as the realisation spread that units of the army would have to be concentrated if they were to provide a credible defence against invasion. As early as March 1778 Lord Buckinghamshire informed the secretary of state with complete equanimity that 'many gentlemen propose at their own expense to levy independent companies to preserve the tranquillity of the country

---

[2] PRO SP 63/459, fo. 141. [3] *Ibid.*, fo. 233.
[4] See respectively *ibid.*, fo. 234 and PRO SP 63/462, fos. 18 and 26.

when the regular troops may be withdrawn from their cantonments'.[5] Far from being viewed as a challenge to government, such initiatives were regarded as commendable efforts by loyal and well-disposed individuals to fill the vacuum created by government's financial inability to embody a national militia. Around the same time, John Beresford, a commissioner of the revenue, advised a member of parliament who resided in England that the 'zeal and spirit of this country is up, and, if proper measures are adopted, great support may be had' – adding that such measures should include a relaxation of the restrictions on Irish trade.[6] This warning reflected a deepening economic depression that not only posed a potential threat to public order but also represented a serious financial problem for the Irish administration as the decline in trade began to affect customs receipts.

Support for the American cause among Irish Protestants was weakened not only by the conclusion of the Franco-American alliance but also by the conciliation proposals brought forward by Lord North in early 1778. He informed the British House of Commons in February that the Americans 'must be certain of something fixed and decided' if they were to drop their demand for independence and proceeded to offer them an unconditional 'cessation of the exercise of taxation'.[7] In effect, the ministry belatedly adopted the policy that had long been advocated by Lord Chatham and gave way on the constitutional principle that had precipitated the rebellion – the British parliament's right to tax the colonies. The despatch of the Carlisle peace commission was extensively reported in the Irish press, as were the commissioners' unavailing efforts to engage the Continental Congress in dialogue. The Americans' refusal to negotiate with the commissioners must have disillusioned many Irish Protestants who sympathised with their argument that taxation without representation was unconstitutional and who had hitherto hoped that the declaration of independence was either a negotiating gambit or a pragmatic measure dictated by the necessity to maintain discipline in the armies raised by Congress. Once the failure of Lord Carlisle's mission became known in Ireland in the autumn of 1778 it was no longer possible to doubt that the point at issue was the integrity of the empire or the independence of the united colonies. By January 1779, Lord Buckinghamshire could assure Lord George Germain that 'the outrageous and illiberal conduct of the American Congress has greatly cooled the ardour of many of their reputed friends in Ireland, and upon the fullest enquiry I am really

[5] Buckinghamshire to Weymouth, 29 March 1778, in PRO SP 63/459, fo. 218.
[6] John Beresford to Thomas Allan, 21 March 1778, in Beresford (ed.), *Correspondence of the Right Hon. John Beresford*, I, p. 22.
[7] *BNL*, 3 March 1778.

of opinion that the country has at no period been in general better disposed'.[8]

But if sympathy for the American cause had been undermined, initially by the colonies' declaration of independence, then by their conclusion of a French alliance, and finally by Congress's contemptuous rejection of peace proposals that were widely regarded as reasonable, this process was to some extent counteracted by an increased war-weariness and by a belief that Britain could not simultaneously wage a successful war against both the Americans and the French. Lack of military success in North America, together with the threat posed by France closer to home, led some members of the political nation to conclude that the American war should be terminated forthwith in order to concentrate resources for the struggle against France. Even before the formal breach in relations between Britain and France was announced a patriot journal used the imminence of a French war to argue that Britain should bow to the inevitable and accept the reality of American independence: 'If the colonies be independent in fact, and in a capacity to remain so, without the permission and good pleasure of any nation upon earth, will it not be intrinsic wisdom and sound policy, at a crisis so awful and alarming as the present, for parliament to subscribe to the decree of nature, and to say, *be it so?*'[9] Some months later *Faulkner's Dublin Journal*, perhaps the most pro-government of the Irish newspapers, acknowledged the likelihood that royal authority would never be restored in the rebel colonies: 'Divide and conquer is an old axiom, and is now beyond a doubt the policy of the natural enemies of Great Britain, the French: in which they have unhappily too well succeeded, by fomenting secretly divisions between England and its American colonies, until a breach is opened that in all human probability will never be closed.'[10] In late 1778 the *Londonderry Journal* predicted the despatch of further reinforcements to America in the spring and deplored the diversion of forces urgently needed at home: 'One would imagine that it was merely for the purpose of slaughtering our troops, and leaving us prey to the French, that this wicked war with America is continued.'[11] In such circumstances, with the anti-French sentiment of the Protestant population thoroughly aroused, patriot commentators were faced with the problematic task of opposing a war against America which was unnecessary, unwinnable and, arguably, reprehensible, on the one hand, while supporting an unavoidable and truly patriotic war against America's ally, France, on the other. On the principle that the best form of defence is attack, opposition authors even insinuated that supporters of the ministry

[8] Buckinghamshire to Germain, 14 January 1779, in HMC Lothian Mss. (1905), p. 343.
[9] *Dublin Evening Journal*, 14 March 1778.   [10] *FDJ*, 6 October 1778.
[11] *LJ*, 11 December 1778.

harboured pro-French sympathies: 'It is remarkable, that none are so much alarmed at the thoughts of an invasion, as those who are most attached to the American interests. Our loyalists appear quite unconcerned on that score. Perhaps, they imagine, they have nothing to apprehend from their old friends.'[12] Such strained arguments may have comforted radical patriots but cannot have persuaded many of those who were politically uncommitted; the general tenor of the press in 1778 suggests that the war effort in both the American and European theatres now enjoyed the support of the great majority of Irish Protestants.

The *Hibernian Magazine* treated its readers in successive months to portraits and biographical sketches of 'that gallant officer' General Sir Henry Clinton, commander-in-chief of British land forces in America, and of Vice-Admiral John Byron, commander-in-chief of British naval forces in America, before giving further flattering details of Clinton's American career in a third issue.[13] Irishmen who were serving in America were particular objects of interest. The *Londonderry Journal* reported on Lord Rawdon, eldest son of the Earl of Moira, who was wounded at the battle of Germantown,[14] while *Finn's Leinster Journal* informed its readers that:

The Earl of Drogheda, who is now with his regiment of light dragoons in America, published in September last a kind of proclamation, inviting his countrymen to come over to the royal standard, offering his Majesty's pardon, and promising to embody them, and head them himself against the rebels, by whom they had been so long deluded. In consequence thereof 400 came in from Washington's army, which his lordship immediately clothed in a new green uniform.[15]

The texts of sermons preached on 10 February 1779, an official day of 'fast and humiliation', illustrate the support of the established church for the war effort in America. A number of these sermons were published and, although the attitudes expressed towards the American conflict differed in emphasis, all gave unambiguous backing to the British ministry's current policy. Rev. Thomas Paul, who preached at St Thomas's church, Dublin, took as his main theme the argument that 'great national calamities are generally inflicted by God, for the punishment of sin'. On examining the condition of the body politic he found that 'Liberty once the protection of the state and glorious birth-right of a British subject is now degenerated into a shameful and dangerous licentiousness' and that opposition to the ministry was 'exerted more for private than public

---

[12] *Dublin Evening Journal*, 7 April 1778.
[13] *HM*, October 1778, 537; November 1778, 593–4; and December 1778, 657–60.
[14] *LJ*, 29 May 1778.   [15] *FLJ*, 19 December 1778.

benefit'.[16] As a divine punishment for the sinfulness of its people, Britain had been obliged to 'supplicate peace from her own revolted children' and had found 'even that peace refused, except upon terms dishonourable to the mother-country and injurious to her commercial interests', while the colonists had concluded 'an alliance with the rival power of these kingdoms, with the inveterate enemy of the peace of mankind, and thereby involved us farther in the calamities of war'.[17] The only solution was moral regeneration and a turning away from sinfulness; then, it might be hoped, God would 'bless our enterprises, defeat the designs of every foreign and domestic enemy, heal all our unhappy divisions, and render us once more a glorious, prosperous and a united people'.[18] It is evident from his use of the first person in passages such as this that Paul regarded the Anglo-Irish community as a constituent part of the British people. Rev. J. Walsh, who preached on the text 'Let every soul be subject unto the higher powers. For there is no power but of God: the powers that be are ordained of God', was more outspoken still in his support of government. 'If our brethren in America', he declaimed, 'now in arms against our gracious sovereign, and joined in an unnatural alliance with our treacherous enemies, can persuade themselves of the legality, and justness of their cause, they should bow before the papal chair, to obtain a sanction for this delusion; for the sacred scriptures will afford them none.'[19] He posed a rhetorical question which might equally well have been addressed either to the rebellious colonists or to the patriot opposition in Ireland: 'Shall the extreme members of an empire repine, or upbraid the ruling power, because they are more limited in trade, the source of wealth, than the very seat of government, whence issue the vital streams, which animate the whole?'[20] For the speaker and, it must be assumed, for the bulk of his congregation, the only reasonable answer to the question was an unequivocal 'no'. A third sermon, delivered by the historian Thomas Leland in St Anne's church, Dublin, was more balanced than the others and acknowledged that a share of the blame for the outbreak of hostilities could be laid at the door of 'Great Britain' – a term which, for Leland, comprehended the members of his congregation: 'We called them [the Americans] weak; we felt them powerful: we talked of subduing; we found resistance and defiance. In our pride we dictated submission; with equal and perhaps no less dangerous pride, they renounced all

---

[16] Rev. Thomas Paul, *A Sermon, Preached at St. Thomas's Church, Dublin, on Wednesday the 10th of February, M DCC LXX IX* (Dublin, n.d.), pp. 9, 19 and 20.
[17] *Ibid.*, p. 19.   [18] *Ibid.*, p. 22.
[19] Rev. J. Walsh, *A Sermon Preached at the Parish Church of Tawney, on Wednesday the 10th of February, M,DC,LXXIX* (Dublin, 1779), p. 9.
[20] *Ibid.*, p. 12.

connection.'[21] But Leland was satisfied that official attitudes had since changed for the better – 'disappointment and distress have been our instructors' – and that the policy of ministers was now 'to restore and conciliate, and to re-establish peace on terms of concession and compliance'. Quoting from the book of Isaiah, he detected a new willingness on the part of government to 'undo the heavy burdens, and to let the oppressed go free'. Ireland, as well as America, stood to gain from this welcome change in policy:

It seems to be acknowledged, that equity and policy call loudly, to invigorate this part of the empire, whose vigour hath been miserably exhausted, by the present quarrel; and by a reasonable and necessary extension of our commerce, to reward our attachment, and enable us to indulge our affection to the parent-state, by an effectual assistance in time of need.[22]

On the day following the fast the patriotic *Dublin Evening Post* claimed that: 'Many honest citizens are said to have been at a loss how to behave themselves in church. For if we have been aggressors in the war, to pray for success to our arms, were impious.'[23] This statement implicitly acknowledges that the fast was widely observed. In contrast to previous occasions, the opposition press refrained from disparaging comments about either the size or the composition of the congregations, and I have found no mention of patriotic feasts being organised in opposition to the fast on this occasion.

None the less, patriots remained as willing as ever to challenge the British and Irish administrations when this could be done without appearing to oppose the war effort. The opposition was presented with an ideal opportunity to give vent to both its anti-ministerial and its anti-French fervour when Admiral Augustus Keppel, a political associate of Lord Rockingham's, was court-martialled for allegedly mishandling the British fleet in the naval battle fought off Ushant in July 1778. The charges against the admiral were portrayed in the patriot press as a politically inspired prosecution of a gallant Whig seaman by a corrupt Tory administration and his acquittal was the signal for opposition celebrations throughout Britain and Ireland. In Dublin, the news was greeted with the ringing of bells and illuminations which 'drew out astonishing multitudes of persons to admire the beautiful effect of the lights'. Dublin corporation followed the example of London by unanimously voting the freedom of the city to the admiral. Volunteer companies paraded in Belfast and fired

---

[21] Thomas Leland, *A Sermon Preached in the Church of St Anne's, Dublin, on Wednesday the 10th of February, 1779* (Dublin, 1779), pp. 14–15.
[22] *Ibid.*, pp. 17–18.   [23] *DEP*, 11 February 1779.

feux de joie in Cork and Derry. In the latter place, the volleys were accompanied by 'the loud and repeated huzzahs of a prodigious concourse of people'.[24] It was an early sign of the politicisation of the Volunteer movement and a clear indication that the support which the great majority of the political nation gave to the war effort could not be equated with support for Lord North's ministry.

The Catholic masses and war with France

The sense of optimism which the renewal of hostilities between Britain and France engendered among lower class Catholics is vividly conveyed in a song composed by Eoghan Rua Ó Súilleabháin in the summer of 1778:

> Tá an cruatan ar Sheoirse
>   cé mór a neart ar farraige,
> ní réidhfidh Éire an gnó dhó
>   a shlóite cé tréan,
> tá an Impireacht go fórsach
>   'na chomhair is rince fada acu
> fúigfidh é go ró-lag
>   's a gcomhairle go tréith;
> Francaigh Spáinnigh i neart atáid
>   gan fabhar gan bháidh gan taise dhó
> cuirfid sin an rógaire oilc
>   ón gcoróin 'na rith le gleo claimh.[25]

(George [III] is in distress, though great is his strength at sea, Ireland won't solve his problem, though his forces are strong, the [Holy Roman] Empire is forcefully coming for him while doing the *rince fada* [a popular dance], and will leave him enfeebled and their parliament exhausted; the French and Spaniards are powerful and have no sympathy, affection or pity for him, they are the ones who'll put the evil rogue to flight from the crown with armed combat.)

S.J. Connolly, relying chiefly on Ó Súilleabháin's inclusion of Austria among the enemies threatening Britain, has described this song as 'a web of confused and inconsistent images' and argued that it should be regarded as a manifestation of popular folklore rather than popular politics.[26] This assessment could hardly be more mistaken. In reality, the composition is a coherent and well-informed expression of a rational

---

[24] *FLJ*, 24 and 27 February 1779; *LJ*, 23 February 1779.
[25] 'Tá an cruatan ar Sheoirse' in RIA Ms. 24 P 20, p. 90; edited in Ó Foghludha (ed.), *Eoghan Ruadh Ó Súilleabháin*. '*Comhairle*' literally means 'council' but was also used in the sense of 'parliament'.
[26] Connolly, *Religion, Law and Power*, p. 248.

political outlook. Its identification of Austria as an enemy of George III
reflects not only the Franco-Austrian alliance that had existed since the
diplomatic revolution of 1756 but, more immediately, the anti-Austrian
stance adopted by George III as elector of Hanover in the crisis that
would shortly pit Austria against Prussia in the War of Bavarian Succession (1778–79).[27] Ó Súilleabháin envisaged the restoration of the Stuart
pretender as a result of a successful invasion of both Britain and Ireland
by the united Bourbon powers:

> Go gcloiseamna mar scéalta
> nach bréagach le n-aithris
> gur neartmhar teacht invasion
> fá scléip go Fionntrá:
> in Albain, in Éirinn
> in éineacht 's i Sasana.[28]

(May we hear as news which will not be false to report, that an *invasion* is coming
in might and gaiety to Ventry [County Kerry]: in Scotland, in Ireland together
and in England.)

Ó Súilleabháin was a master of both language and metre and his choice
of the English term 'invasion' is unlikely to have been based on metri-
cal considerations alone: it is a reasonable inference that the word had
acquired such currency by mid-1778 as to be generally understood even
by monoglot Irish speakers. Significantly, the poet made no reference to
the transatlantic dimension of the war. The importance of the conflict for
his intended audience lay in the fresh possibility of a violent reversal of
power relations in Ireland – a reversal that would result in the expulsion
of the Anglo-Irish élite and the restoration of a native ruling class:

> gach allúrach coimhtheach
> tá 'na shuí i mbroghaibh Banba
> beidh scaipeadh orthusan timpeall
> is díbirt i gcéin.[29]

(every alien foreigner, who is installed in the mansions of Ireland, will be scattered
all around and driven far away.)

Several topical references illustrate the role of vernacular song in dissem-
inating a knowledge of contemporary military and diplomatic developments among the general population:

[27] I have discussed this song at greater length in ' "*Tá an cruatan ar Sheoirse*" – folklore or
politics?', *Eighteenth-Century Ireland* 13 (1998).
[28] RIA Ms. 24 P 20, p. 91. Ventry was the site of a legendary invasion of Ireland in the
Fiannaíocht cycle of tales.
[29] *Ibid.* The word '*allúrach*', literally a person from overseas, has pejorative connotations.
See p. 13 above for use of the phrase '*allúrach coimhtheach*' by an Ulster author.

*Count d'Estaing is namhaid dó
's é i bhfábhar le Cormac;
d'iompaigh* Russia *lámh ris
's ní ghráfadh go héag.*[30]

(Count d'Estaing is his [George III's] enemy, and he [Count d'Estaing] is in favour with Carlos [III of Spain]; *Russia* has turned its back on him [George III] and would never be friendly until death.)

These lines reflect inaccurate press reports that a French naval squadron commanded by the Comte d'Estaing was about to commence joint operations with the Spanish fleet, as well as better-founded reports that British overtures to Russia had been rebuffed.[31]

Well-informed political verse such as the above demonstrates the fallacy of the common representation of the Catholic majority as an ignorant and apolitical mass by historians who discount the evidence of sources in Irish. The assumption that illiteracy or ignorance of English necessarily implied a lack of knowledge of contemporary politics is unsustainable. Indeed, Eoghan Rua Ó Súilleabháin himself noted the lively interest taken by the *menu peuple* in the European conflict:

*Atá scéalta maithe nó ag rith
i gcóigíbh na Banban
go bhfuil gach táin 'san Eoraip
's a bhfórsaí go tréan
ag tabhairt iarrachtaí fá Sheoirse
's a sheolta amuigh ar farraige.*[32]

(There are excellent new reports circulating in the provinces of Ireland, that all the hosts of Europe and their powerful forces, are making attacks on George and his shipping out at sea.)

Newspapers were published not only in Dublin but also in such provincial centres as Newry, Belfast, Derry, Strabane, Sligo, Galway, Limerick, Cork, Clonmel, Waterford, Kilkenny, Wexford and Drogheda. While most people were too poor to buy newspapers, the practice of reading the news aloud and, when necessary, of translating it into Irish, was common. A verse entitled 'What's news from America? Or, Paddy's Reply' which appeared in the Kilkenny-published *Finn's Leinster Journal* in 1780 illustrates both this practice of public reading and the extent of popular interest in the war. The work takes the form of a conversation on the subject of the American war between two national stereotypes, 'English

---

[30] *Ibid.*, p. 90. 'Cormac' is identified as Carlos III in RIA Ms. 24 C 56, p. 818.
[31] See, for example, *FLJ*, 9 May, 3 June, 11 and 22 July 1778.
[32] RIA Ms. 24 P 20, p. 90.

John' and 'Irish Pat', in which John applies as follows to the illiterate Pat for details of the latest war news:

> All that you know come tell us pray,
> since you heard read the news to day.[33]

It may be concluded that the obstacles posed by illiteracy and ignorance of English were easily surmounted by those who were eager for information about the war.

The belief that war between Britain and France raised the possibility of a renewed effort to restore the house of Stuart was not confined to lower-class Catholics. In May 1778 the *Dublin Evening Journal* reported from Paris that Jacobite exiles were arriving in France from Italy and added that 'the enthusiasm of these gentlemen for the Stuart family prompts them to believe that the Toulon fleet is to take the Chevalier de St. George [Prince Charles Edward] on board, and land him once more in his faithful country of Scotland'.[34] In the same month, Frederick Hervey, Anglican bishop of Derry, wrote to Edmund Sexten Pery, speaker of the House of Commons, from Rome, warning him that Ireland was certain to be the first target of French military preparations, that the Catholic population was 'ripe for an almost general revolt', and that they were 'stimulated and encouraged' in this intention by persons in Rome. The purpose of the planned invasion and rising would be 'to render Ireland independent, and to establish, as in the Swiss cantons, a reciprocal toleration of religions, to abolish all tithes except such as are to be paid by the Roman Catholics to their own clergy, and to throw themselves under the protection of France and if possible of Spain'.[35] As if this were not enough, Hervey added that he had just received intelligence that 'overtures had been made to the Chevalier to persuade him to go on board the Toulon fleet, which is to join that at Brest'. Far from being a paranoid anti-Catholic, the bishop was an early advocate of Catholic relief and it is likely that his warning reflected the boastful optimism of members of Rome's Irish community. The expression of such militant and optimistic views by members of the lower clergy based outside of Ireland is attested elsewhere. Thus a certain Fr Ennis, a Wexford-born priest who was chaplain on board the *Bretagne*, a French ship of the line, sent an enthusiastic eye-witness account of the indecisive naval battle fought off Ushant in July 1778 to a fellow priest still resident in his native county: 'The French performed wonders! the *Bretagne* sustained the shock of every ship in the English line, one after another, and made them all sheer off with torn sides and tattered

---

[33] *FLJ*, 1 January 1780.   [34] *Dublin Evening Journal*, 21 May 1778.
[35] Hervey to Pery, 15 May 1778, in HMC Emly Mss., 8th report, appendix I (1881) p. 197.

riggings.'[36] Fr Ennis expressed the hope that his next letter would contain news of 'something more decisive'.

Signs of popular unrest became increasingly obvious as the economic depression, caused in the first instance by the interruption of both legal and illicit transatlantic commerce, worsened as a result of the disruption of trade with mainland Europe which followed France's entry to the war. As early as 16 March 1778 warehouses were looted and two persons killed in rioting in Cork city sparked by rumours of intended large-scale exportation of potatoes and oats, the staple foodstuffs of the poor.[37] A similar provisions riot took place at the Drogheda meal market on 13 May, when an attempt to transport large quantities of oats to the north was prevented.[38] In the same month Sir Edward Newenham warned of imminent disorder and laid the blame at the door of James Reynolds, a prominent Dublin merchant and the treasurer of the Catholic Committee, whose 'power and influence among the lower order' he described as 'amazing'.[39] In fact, Reynolds was in failing health; he tendered his resignation as treasurer of the Catholic Committee in June and died in October 1778.[40] But whatever the truth of his involvement, it is reasonable to see Newenham's allegations as a reflection of the Catholic background of most of those involved in agitating economic questions. Serious disorder spread to the capital on 21 July when a 'riotous and armed mob in number between four and five hundred persons' destroyed woollen goods imported from England, prompting the lord lieutenant and Privy Council to issue a proclamation offering rewards totalling £500 for information leading to the apprehension of those involved.[41]

Incidents of economically motivated violence, while a source of concern to the administration and a harbinger of more serious unrest in the following year, remained sporadic during 1778. From the beginning of 1779, however, there was a fresh upsurge of attacks on members of the military – a phenomenon which appears to have abated since the previous high point of such attacks at the end of 1777. The reasons for the lull in the violence directed against army personnel can only be guessed at, but it would appear that attacks were always more frequent during the winter months – perhaps because of the greater protection afforded to assailants by dark winter evenings. An incident in Clonmel on

---

[36] Fr H. Ennis to Fr John Kavanagh, 1 August 1779. Passionists' archive, NLI Pos. 7,654, p. 168.
[37] *BNL*, 24 March 1778.   [38] *Ibid.*, 19 June 1778.
[39] Newenham to the Earl of Dartmouth, 19 May 1778, HMC Dartmouth Mss., 15th report, appendix I (1896), p. 242.
[40] McGeehin, 'The activities and personnel of the General Committee of the Catholics', p. 110.
[41] *FJ*, 24 July 1778.

4 January 1779 in which a soldier was houghed provides some information on the background of those engaged in the attacks. One of the assailants was identified as Thomas Ferrol, an eighteen-year-old shoemaker, who appears to have made good his escape.[42] Before the end of the month a second member of the Clonmel garrison was attacked and houghed.[43] On this occasion, one of the alleged attackers was committed to gaol within a few days. He was John Brien, described as a 'broguemaker', who was subsequently convicted and was hanged on 31 July, having been 'conducted to the place of execution by the battalion [the army unit stationed locally] and light infantry companies of the Clonmel Independents [the local Volunteer corps]' – a precaution which indicates that the condemned man enjoyed the support of a sizable section of the local community.[44] This show of force prevented any attempt to rescue the prisoner but retaliation was swift: only three days after Brien's execution another member of the Clonmel garrison was attacked by five men who 'knocked him down, and after trampling on his body and otherwise abusing him much, tied a handkerchief round his neck, to which they fastened a large stone, and threw him into the river'.[45] Similar incidents were reported from other garrison towns in the three southern provinces. Dublin was the scene of a particularly concentrated series of attacks which began in December 1778 when a private in the 9th regiment of dragoons was houghed in the Coomb.[46] The attacks intensified in January:

Sunday evening, about five o'clock, as one of the 4th, or Ligonier's horse, was going home to the barracks, he was houghed in Pill lane, and his head cut in a shocking manner. On the same evening, a grenadier of the 68th foot, was houghed in Barrack-street, and now languishes in the hospital without hope of recovery. And on last Wednesday night, corporal Brooke, of the 13th dragoons, was seized upon and held by two of these wretches in Smithfield, while a third came up and cut the sinews of his leg above the ankle.[47]

In April, a soldier on sentry duty was houghed in Galway city, while in November another sentry was houghed while standing guard at the north gaol in Cork city.[48] The above list of attacks, even if complete, would suggest the existence of widespread disaffection. It must be borne in mind, however, that the list is unlikely to be complete, as is suggested by the following report of an incident which took place in Waterford city in March 1779:

[42] *FLJ*, 9 January 1779.   [43] *Ibid.*, 3 February 1779.
[44] *Ibid.*, 6 February, 31 July and 4 August 1779.   [45] *Ibid.*, 7 August 1779.
[46] *BNL*, 18 December 1778.   [47] *FLJ*, 27 January 1779.
[48] *Ibid.*, 14 April and 4 December 1779.

On Saturday night, a sentinel at the county jail, was attacked by seven despera-
does, on their nocturnal rambles, who, for a considerable time, pelted him with
stones . . . he, stimulated by the first law of nature, and knowing that one of the
same corps was lately houghed, while in the execution of his duty, shot one of
them dead on the spot.[49]

I have failed to find any report of a member of the Waterford garrison
being houghed in the previous year, although the possibility that the attack
took place in a different locality cannot be excluded.

Apart from these concerted attacks on military personnel, the contemporary press also furnishes frequent reports of more casual and spontaneous clashes between military parties and the populace which are,
none the less, indicative of strained relations between the army and the
Catholic community in the southern provinces – the absence of similar
reports from Ulster is striking. Thus, one reads that a soldier lost an ear in
a clash at Kilcullen, County Kildare, between local people and a party of
artillery which was passing through *en route* from Cork to Dublin.[50] The
cause of the Kilcullen riot was not reported, but another clash between
a group of soldiers and local people at the Cashel races appears to have
been triggered when one of the former pushed a child out of his way.[51] In
another incident, a party of soldiers escorting five deserters to Kilkenny
was attacked at Timolin, County Kildare, by a 'riotous mob' which attempted to rescue the prisoners; one civilian was killed and a soldier was
seriously injured in the resulting fracas.[52] Such attempts to rescue captured deserters or unwilling recruits were a recurring cause of clashes between civilians and military personnel, as was the activity of press gangs.
A pitched battle erupted on the quayside in Dublin when an attempt was
made to impress a group of forty agricultural labourers who were trav-
elling to England to work in the harvest. The 'Irish gallowglasses', as a
sympathetic report in the patriot-inclined *Hibernian Magazine* described
them, repulsed their adversaries 'with pitchforks, reaping-hooks, &c. and
cut the lieutenant across the throat and cheek with a reaping-hook'.[53] A
subsequent attempt to impress two sedan-chair men caused a large crowd
to congregate. The crowd threatened to pull down a building used by the
press gang and dispersed only when the sheriff arrived and promised that
the chairmen would be set at liberty.[54]

An *aisling* by the County Cork poet Éamonn Ó Flaitheartaigh, which
appears to have been composed sometime between Spain's entry into
the war in June 1779 and Admiral Rodney's relief of the Gibraltar garrison in the following January, reveals that an element of ambivalence

---

[49] *SNL*, 11 March 1779.   [50] *Ibid.*, 4 January 1779.   [51] *FLJ*, 13 March 1779.
[52] *Ibid.*, 5 June 1779.   [53] *HM*, June 1779, 374.   [54] *Ibid.*, July 1779, p. 431.

persisted in popular attitudes towards the Americans for some time after their conclusion of an alliance with France. On the one hand, he counted them along with the Irish, French and Spaniards among those who were fighting against Britain, and extolled George Washington's prowess as a military leader; on the other hand, he recognised their British ethnicity and portrayed the war in North America as a civil war among the traditional enemies of Ireland – in brief, as a '*cogadh an dá Ghall*', although Ó Flaitheartaigh did not employ that phrase. A personification of Ireland addressed the poet:

> *Ba chiúin tais cneasta a bréithre líofa gasta léirghlic*
> *ag maíomh na startha léifid san saothar so romham,*
> *ar sí tá an aicme chraosach d'fhúig Gaeil le seal fá daorbhroid*
> *ag cloí 's ag creachadh a chéile is ní réidhfid go fóill;*
> *atá an taoiseach fear go fraochta idir namhaid ba thaca déanach*
> *i gcoimheascar catha is éirligh mar aon lena shlóigh*
> *Washington 'sa laochra is nach tím i dtaisteal taobh leo,*
> *is cúinse ar bith ní méin leis go ngéillfid dá ndeoin.*[55]

(Quiet, tender and kindly were her fluent, quick and perceptive words, relating the accounts that will be read in this work below, she said the voracious class that kept the Gaels in bondage for a time, are destroying and plundering each other and won't settle yet; the leader of men is ferocious among enemies who were recent allies, in a violent and deadly struggle along with his army [are] Washington and his heroes, and he's not slow to march at their side, and he's unwilling that they should concede any terms voluntarily.)

A less equivocal but also a less realistic and less well-informed image of Washington and the Americans was presented in an updated version of the well-known Jacobite song '*Síle Ní Ghadhra*' composed by Séamus Ó Dálaigh, a tailor from Mungret, near Limerick city. In this work, the eponymous personification of Ireland lauded Washington in the prophetic message she imparted to the poet:

> '*Ós cantar', ar sí, 'leatsa díogras mo scéala,*
> *is aithris mór-thimpeall do chloinn Scoit na saor-bheart,*
> *go bhfuil fáistine fíora na ndraoithe is na n-éigse,*
> *de dhearbhthoil Íosa á síorchur ar mhéirligh.*
> *Súd Washington calma treallúsach thiar,*
> *mar Hannibal Carthage i dtreasaibh ba dhian,*
> *ag leagadh 's ag leadradh na nDanar sa ngliadh,*
> *is tré loscadh 'na gceallaibh beidh daltaí an phoic adharcaigh*
> *is a maireann dá gcaraid gan fearann, gan feadhmas.*'[56]

[55] '*Ar mo leaba aréir go déanach*' in RIA Ms. 23 D 42, p. 30.
[56] '*Ag Sionainn na slim-bhárc cois Inse go déarach*' in RIA Ms. 23 D 12, p. 26. 'Scot' was a mythical ancestor of Milesius; 'Dane' alludes to the Norse raiders of the Viking period and is a common term of abuse in Irish literature.

('Since', she said, 'the import of my story is being recited to you, spread it around among the children of Scot of the noble feats, that the true prophecy of the druids and of the poets, by the settled will of Jesus is being continually enacted on the villains. There in the west is brave daring Washington, like Hannibal of Carthage in fierce battles, felling and thrashing the Danes in combat, and having been scorched in their churches the disciples of the horned buck [Satan?] and their surviving friends will be without property and power.')

This work, too, would appear to date from after Spain's entry to the war, but the fact that the Spanish monarch was anachronistically named 'Philip' is indicative of the rhetorical rather than topical nature of the piece.[57] None the less, the song provides further evidence of the popularity that Washington and the American cause had come to enjoy among the native population.

The alliance between France and America can only have helped to consolidate the pro-American sympathies of the common people. For example, the Catholic services held in Philadelphia to mark the third anniversary of the declaration of independence did not pass unnoticed in the Irish press:

On Sunday, the 4th July, being the anniversary of the day which gave freedom to the vast republic of America, the Congress, the president and councils of the state, with other the civil and military officers, and a number of principal gentlemen and ladies, at 12 o'clock attended at the Roman chapel, agreeable to invitation received from the minister plenipotentiary of his most Christian Majesty. A *Te Deum* was performed on the occasion, to the great satisfaction of all present.[58]

This was, in a much overused phrase, a 'defining moment' – the point at which the new American state broke with the anti-Catholicism that had featured prominently in colonial propaganda during the agitation against the Quebec act and which would remain a central element of British political discourse for another two or three generations. The importance of the development was not lost on Irish Catholics. Even such an outspoken supporter of the constitutional status quo as Fr Arthur O'Leary was happy to use the American example as a stick with which to beat anti-Catholic patriots in Ireland. When, towards the end of 1779, it was rumoured that a bill to banish the regular clergy would be introduced in the next session of parliament, O'Leary played the American card: how, he asked, could 'banishment and proscription, on account of religious systems' possibly be contemplated in Ireland at a time when

---

[57] The error was not uncommon; for a newspaper article in which the Spanish monarch is twice referred to as 'Philip', see *LJ*, 6 April 1781.
[58] *Ibid.*, 16 November 1779; *HM*, November 1799, 650.

'the Presbyterians and Catholics chant the *Te Deum* in the same chapel in America'?[59]

The Catholic élite and war with France

The reaction of Catholics of higher social standing to the news of the rupture between Britain and France was very different from that of their less affluent coreligionists. An early indication of their outlook was provided by a 'humble address' to George III from the Catholics of County Fermanagh, signed by twenty-four persons headed by Denis Maguire, bishop of Kilmore. The address assured the king of the signatories' support for all measures to 'disappoint the designs, and punish the perfidy of your enemies'.[60] Further loyal addresses followed. One, on behalf of the Catholics of Ireland, was dated 13 April 1778 and signed by 301 persons who represented a cross-section of the lay and clerical élites. Included among the signatories were Lords Fingal, Gormanstown, Dillon, Trimbleston, Cahir and Kenmare; James Butler, archbishop of Cashel, and four other Munster bishops; Anthony Dermot and John Curry – both prominent members of the Catholic Committee; and several parish priests. The signatories promised to 'offer up our most earnest and fervent supplications for the success of your Majesty's arms against all your enemies' and, more practically, to use the 'utmost exertion' of their influence in order to 'confirm the lower class of people in a steady adherence to that duty, fidelity and allegiance'.[61] Most impressive, perhaps, in view of the 311 signatures it attracted and the manner of its adoption was a 'humble address' from the Catholics of Newry, County Down, which was endorsed at a public meeting on 8 April 1778. The Newry address made explicit the condemnation of the American rebellion that was only implicit in the Fermanagh and the national addresses:

We humbly beg leave to assure your Majesty that the undutiful, obstinate and ungenerous perseverance of America gives us heart-felt grief: We feel for the distresses of the parent-state like afflicted sons, and weep, that tears are the only arms allowed us to prove our attachment to your royal person, and to support the rights and dignity of the crown and constitution of Great Britain.[62]

Both the national and Newry addresses were considered sufficiently important by administration to be published in the *London Gazette*.[63] Where they were invited to do so, members of the Catholic élite were also willing to sign addresses prepared by members of the established church. For example, when the lord lieutenant forwarded a loyal address from

[59] *FJ*, 20 November 1779.   [60] PRO SP 63/460, fo. 56.   [61] PRO SP 63/462, fo. 20.
[62] *Ibid.*, fo. 24.   [63] *HM*, June 1788, 363.

the 'high sheriff, nobility, representatives, clergy, freeholders and gentlemen of the County of Waterford' he was able to assure the secretary
of state that 'the gentlemen of the Roman Catholic persuasion in that
county joined in this address, and showed great zeal and loyalty upon
this occasion'.[64] As was to be expected, the higher clergy continued to
counsel their flocks to remain peaceful and obedient to the established
government. In September 1778 a pastoral letter from John Carpenter,
Catholic archbishop of Dublin, quoted Romans 13:1 ('Let every one be
subject to higher powers, for there is no power but from God') and urged
the faithful of his archdiocese to 'an uninterrupted continuance of your
fidelity and allegiance to his most sacred Majesty King George the Third'.
In an unmistakable allusion to Luke Gardiner's Catholic relief act which
had received the royal assent in August, Carpenter advised his flock that
'you ought indeed at this juncture to be impressed with the deepest sense
of gratitude for the eminent favours already conferred upon you'.[65]

Gardiner's act was of symbolic importance as it represented the first
relaxation of the Penal code and could thus be seen as the first tangible
benefit of the policy of support for the existing political order pursued by
the Catholic Committee since the early 1760s. But while its provisions
permitting Catholics to take long-term leases and to inherit property on
the same basis as Protestants were of undoubted benefit to Catholics of
higher social status, they made no material difference to the great majority of the population. It has been suggested that the origins of the
Catholic relief act lay in the desire of administration to promote recruitment among Catholics – and even that its promoter, Luke Gardiner, was
a stalking-horse acting on behalf of Lord North.[66] But the evidence of a
military motivation for the first measures of Catholic relief, while persuasive in the British – and more especially the Scottish – contexts, is lacking
in relation to Ireland. Certainly, there was no obvious mechanism by
which the small class of existing and potential Catholic landowners who
were the sole beneficiaries of the 1778 act could have easily translated
their goodwill towards government into a substantial flow of military
recruits. Luke Gardiner was, moreover, a man of independent means
who had a sincere commitment to Catholic relief. Less than two weeks
before the heads of the bill were introduced, Buckinghamshire appealed
to the secretary of state for urgent guidance on the policy to be followed
and was advised that, while it would be desirable to put Irish Catholics

---

[64] Buckinghamshire to Weymouth, 23 May 1778, in PRO SP 63/460, fo. 139.
[65] *FLJ*, 2 September 1778.
[66] See R. Kent Donovan, 'The military origins of the Roman Catholic relief programme
of 1778', *Hist. Jn.* 28 (1985); Thomas Bartlett, *The Fall and Rise of the Irish Nation: The
Catholic Question 1690–1830* (Dublin, 1992), pp. 83–6.

'as nearly as circumstances will permit, on the same footing as is doing here [in Britain]', the lord lieutenant, as the man on the spot, was in the best position to adopt 'the most advisable and prudential plan on this delicate subject'.[67] It seems safer, therefore, to regard the measure as the result of a range of concurrent factors: an official desire to harmonise Irish and British legislation, the natural partiality of an assembly of landowners towards a measure likely to stimulate the market for land, and – perhaps most importantly – concern on all sides that a refusal to extend the British precedent to Ireland might throw the loyalty of the Catholic élite into question at a time when a French invasion appeared imminent.

In the event, administration gave Gardiner's bill its discrete support while the measure was vigorously opposed by most of the leading members of the parliamentary opposition and by the patriot press out of doors.[68] George Ogle, a prominent critic of the bill, conceded that 'perhaps the better sort of people [among the Catholics] are well affected' but immediately added 'the common people are not so'.[69] When the certified bill was returned from England the *Freeman's Journal* commented that it proved the partiality of administration towards those 'whose religious and political principles are favourable to despotism' and declared that the 'ominous' bill ought to make 'all but the tools of government to unite to defeat the arbitrary intentions of our rulers'.[70] Henry Grattan compared the measure with the hated Quebec act. In Canada, he asserted, government had sought 'to make the papists a balance against the Protestants, and having carried that point there, the same was to be attempted in Ireland.'[71] Barry Yelverton was the only prominent patriot to support the measure, arguing that 'by the present state of our statutes we became two nations inhabiting the same country' and that passage of the bill would induce Catholic landowners to 'look up to parliament for protection – this will weaken regal power, and be one means of preserving the great balance of the constitution, the equilibre of the three estates'.[72] Such sophistication was premature and the debates on Gardiner's bill illustrate the nearly unanimous opposition which existed among Anglo-Irish patriots to even a modest measure of Catholic relief at this point. Members of the Catholic élite were not slow to draw the obvious conclusion. Sylvester O'Halloran, a prominent surgeon and antiquary, informed Edmund Burke that 'though threatened with war and invasion, yet the sons of despotism and tyranny – for surely such may the pretended

---

[67] Buckinghamshire to Weymouth, 24 May 1778 and Weymouth to Buckinghamshire, 31 May 1778, in PRO SP 63/460, fos. 143 and 160 respectively.
[68] For the attitude of the patriot press, see Day, 'The Catholic question', p. 138.
[69] *FLJ*, 24 June 1778.   [70] *FJ*, 28 July 1778.   [71] *HM*, December 1779, 701.
[72] *Ibid.*

sons of liberty, in Ireland be called! – seem as anxious to prevent a firm coalition of all parties for their mutual defence as ever'.[73] The difference in attitude between the government and opposition was further highlighted by Buckinghamshire's speech to both houses of parliament at the end of the session. The Catholic relief act, he argued, would 'by rendering us more united at home, make us more formidable to our enemies abroad'.[74] Once the act became law, those Catholics who owned, expected to inherit or intended to lease land rushed to testify their loyalty to George III on oath before 1 January 1779 – a legal requirement for those who wished to benefit from the act's provisions.[75] In such circumstances, it is hardly possible to regard the large numbers taking the oath as a true reflection of political opinion.

Presbyterian opinion and war with France

While the evidence suggests that news of the American victory at Saratoga revived anti-war sentiment among Presbyterians in Ulster, it is equally clear that America's alliance with Catholic France silenced all but the most committed supporters of the rebel colonies. As early as April 1778 General Irwin, commander-in-chief of the army in Ireland, drafted a memo in which he proposed to concentrate his forces in Munster as he believed the French were most likely to 'transport troops &c and arms to distribute among the inhabitants there who are by far the greater part papists'. Ulster, he felt, could be left relatively undefended, partly because of its distance from mainland Europe, but also because 'the disposition of the inhabitants of the north (with regard to a foreign enemy) will in all probability prevent an attempt being made on the east or north coast'.[76] The phrase in parentheses suggests that the general was less sanguine about northern attitudes towards the colonies, but events later in the month suggested that he had little to fear on that score either. On 28 April 1778 the war came uncomfortably close to the predominantly Presbyterian counties of Antrim and Down when an American ship, the *Ranger,* commanded by John Paul Jones, captured a British ship, the *Drake,* after a battle at the mouth of Belfast Lough. The engagement was observed by thousands of spectators on the shores of both counties and evidence of popular sentiment is provided by memorials presented to

---

[73] Sylvester O'Halloran to Edmund Burke, 1 August 1778, in J.B. Lyons (ed.), 'The letters of Sylvester O'Halloran', *North Munster Antiquarian Journal* 9 (1962–63), 39.
[74] *HM,* September 1778, 534.
[75] It has been estimated that 85 per cent of those who took the oath in Dublin between 1778 and 1782 did so in the short period between October and December 1778 – precisely the period required by the act; see Fagan, *Divided Loyalties,* p. 162.
[76] An unaddressed memo by General Irwin dated 3 April 1778, in PRO SP 63/460, fo. 82.

government shortly afterwards by the 'sovereign, burgesses and principal inhabitants' of Belfast and the 'principal inhabitants' of Lisburn. Both memorials drew attention to the gallantry of Lieutenant William Dobbs, a locally born officer who, though not a member of the *Drake*'s crew, had voluntarily gone on board the ship after it was under way and sustained serious wounds in the subsequent action.[77] Similarly, on 12 May, the 'mayor, aldermen, sheriffs and commonality' of Carrickfergus, from whose harbour the *Drake* had emerged to challenge the *Ranger*, adopted a humble address to the throne in which they expressed the belief that 'in a time of common danger it is the duty of every subject of the empire to offer his assistance for the defence of its just rights'.[78] The address was signed by several hundred citizens of Carrickfergus, an open borough represented in parliament by Barry Yelverton.

Ulster took an early lead in the formation of independent Volunteer companies to fill the role that would have been played either by a militia or by government-sponsored independent companies had the state of the public finances permitted. In April 1778 the *Belfast News-Letter* reported that there were already 'two companies of Volunteers in this town training; one consists of about 90, the other 60; and the numbers of both daily increasing'.[79] A sermon preached by Rev. James Crombie before the First Company of Belfast Volunteers in July 1778 constituted a paean of praise for the balanced and mixed nature of the British constitution which was designed to guard against 'the turbulence of the people, the ambition of the nobles, and usurpations of the crown'.[80] It was a constitution which 'if maintained inviolate, would render us happy at home, and respectable abroad' and was justly 'the most important object of patriotism and public spirit'.[81] The absence of any references to either the transatlantic conflict or domestic Irish concerns is striking and may have reflected differences of opinion in the ranks of the Volunteers themselves – Crombie avoided potentially divisive issues and delivered a sermon that might have been heard from a Presbyterian pulpit at any time during the eighteenth century.

Evidence of such differences is found in other sources. When the independent electors of County Antrim dined together to mark the second anniversary of James Wilson's election the toasts, in contrast to the previous year when the colonial rebellion had seemed to be on the brink of collapse, included 'Peace with America, and a sound drubbing to the French' and 'May the wretched statesmen who have wantonly lost America, never

[77] *Ibid.*, fo. 52.   [78] PRO SP 63/462, fo. 5.   [79] *BNL*, 21 April 1778.
[80] James Crombie, *A Sermon on the Love of Country. Preached before the First Company of Belfast Volunteers, on Sunday, the 19th of July, 1778* (n.p., 1778), p. 16.
[81] *Ibid.*, p. 17.

be trusted with the difficult task of recovering it' – expressions which
reveal both a belief that the colonists could not be defeated militarily
and that reconciliation with them was still possible, although not while
Lord North's ministry remained in office.[82] On the other hand, when
the Newtownards Volunteer company dined together two weeks later to
commemorate the battle of the Boyne the toasts included not only 'James
Wilson' and 'John Wilkes' – unambiguous evidence of patriot sympathies
in both the Irish and British contexts – but also 'Gen. Howe' and 'Admiral
Howe', as well as 'Reunion to the British empire, and disgrace to them
who oppose it' – equally unambiguous evidence of support for the British
war effort in America. In the light of these sentiments a further toast of
'Speedy peace with America, and war with France' suggests nothing more
than support for the efforts of the Carlisle peace commission.[83] When
the Londonderry Independent Volunteers dined together in June they
drank 'Success to the commissioners, and peace with America.'[84] Likewise, when all the Volunteer companies of the city assembled on 1 August
1778 to commemorate the relief of Derry in 1689 the toasts included 'A
speedy and constitutional peace with America' as well as 'The representatives of Derry, and success to them in their opposition to the popery
bill.'[85]

Anti-Catholicism retained its potency and was often coupled with outspoken patriotism. For example, the editor of the *Londonderry Journal*
gave the following humorous summary of a letter submitted by a 'sad
rebel' which was deemed unsuitable for publication: 'he talks, heaven
bless us! little less than downright treason – of America – the *Queback* bill –
the papistry bill – the Jacobite infernal crew of *ministration*, &c. and, in
the climax of his passion, even wishes for another O[liver] C[romwell]'.[86]
The Franco-American alliance had, however, made anti-Catholicism a
double-edged weapon for the opponents of government as the colonists
were henceforth tainted by association with a Catholic power. Thus the
Londonderry Journal quoted an anonymous gentlemen who, on hearing
of the passage of Gardiner's Catholic relief bill, burst out 'D[am]n my
eyes, what a pack of scoundrels – they have sold America to the French,
and are now giving Ireland to the pope' – a view which equated the efforts
of the Carlisle peace commission to conciliate the colonists with those of
the Irish administration to consolidate the loyalty of the Catholic élite.[87]
The same newspaper reprinted, from an American loyalist source, the
manifest of a cargo supposedly captured on a French vessel bound for
America:

---

[82] *BNL*, 26 June 1778.   [83] *Ibid.*, 7 July 1778.   [84] *LJ*, 19 June 1778.
[85] *Ibid.*, 4 August 1778.   [86] *Ibid.*, 2 October 1778.   [87] *Ibid.*, 8 August 1778.

Mass-books, 50,000 – Racks and wheels, 200 – Consecrated wafers, 3,000,000 – Crucifixes, 15,000 – Rosaries, 70,000 – Wooden shoes, 200,000 – Paint for the ladies faces, five chests. – Pills for the cure of the French disease, 10,000 boxes. We also learn that the passengers on board were all priests, in the disguise of hair dressers, tooth drawers, fiddlers, and dancing masters.[88]

Not only had overt support for the colonists become unattractive to most sections of Protestant opinion, but the transatlantic conflict was also increasingly overshadowed by political and military difficulties closer to home.

Irish privateers

The entry of France into the war and the consequent availability of a large volume of enemy shipping in European waters provided a new opportunity for Irishmen to involve themselves in the conflict by fitting out or serving on Irish-based privateers. In early 1779 a privateer named the *Amazon* set out on its maiden voyage from Belfast with a crew of eighty. This was the first privateer ever fitted out in the town and it had a short career, being wrecked in March 1780.[89] As early as March 1778, before the formal commencement of hostilities between Britain and France, it was reported that a privateer with thirty guns and a crew of 200 called the *Dublin* was being built for a group of Dublin merchants at Ringsend.[90] The *Dublin* returned from its first cruise in February 1779 having failed to take a prize, a fact which was said to have 'struck a damp on the spirit of enterprise' of the Dublin merchants.[91] However it was reported at the same time that 'the little fishing village of Rush [County Dublin] has already fitted out four vessels, one of them is now at Rogerson's Quay, ready to sail, being completely armed and manned, carrying 14 carriage guns and 60 of as brave hands as any in Europe'.[92] The ship that was ready to sail may have been the *Fame*, a Dublin-based privateer which was reported to have taken a French prize a month later and continued to operate in the Mediterranean until 1782 when it put into Naples in an unseaworthy condition.[93] I have found no evidence to suggest that the other vessels said to have been fitted out at Rush ever saw service as privateers – at least under British colours – and it is likely that some of those preparations were in reality directed *against* British shipping. In January 1782 it was reported that a native of Rush named John Kelly 'about three years ago got three chests of arms from the city, under pretence of commanding a letter of marque to New York, and as a cruiser against our

---

[88] *Ibid.*, 4 December 1778.   [89] Joy, *Historical Collections*, p. 142.
[90] *FJ*, 24 March 1778.   [91] *HM*, February 1779, 127.   [92] *Ibid.*
[93] *FJ*, 13 March 1779; *FLJ*, 6 February and 14 December 1782.

combined enemies' but had instead sailed to Dunkirk where he obtained a commission to command a privateer in the French interest.[94] At least one privateer was also fitted out at Cork, a port that was more conveniently situated for attacks on French shipping than either Dublin or Belfast: it was reported in February 1779 that an unnamed Cork privateer mounting six guns and with a crew of sixty had taken a French prize into the southern port.[95] Britain's declaration of war against the United Provinces in December 1780 and the prospect of easy pickings from a power with a large merchant marine and a comparatively small navy gave a fresh impetus to a form of enterprise that had languished since earlier expectations were disappointed at the start of the French war. By January 1781 Belfast merchants were reported to be fitting out a schooner to 'cruise against the Dutch'.[96] Later in the same month no fewer than three privateers were said to be fitting out at Cork, together with a fourth at Castletownshend, 'to cruise against the Dutch and other enemies'.[97] In March it was reported from Limerick that 'a number of ladies' were fitting out an eighteen-gun privateer with a crew of 100 'to cruise against the French, Spaniards, and Dutch'.[98] Despite this late effort, officially sanctioned privateering from Irish ports remained small in scale. In March 1781 the *Freeman's Journal* placed Irish privateering in context and saw it as symptomatic of a more general lack of enterprise: 'The little town of Dartmouth, in England, sends out more privateers than the whole kingdom of Ireland. If our merchants show as much torpidness in extending their commerce, the liberty of a free trade will be of little consequence to the general welfare of Ireland.'[99] There was, however, a second Irish privateering effort, opposite in direction and at least equal in magnitude, which showed no lack of enterprise. If some saw war with France as an opportunity to attack French shipping, for others it was an opportunity to use French ports as a base for operations against British shipping.

The first commissions granted to Irish privateers in France were issued by the American minister Benjamin Franklin, a fact which may surprise but is easily explained: the captains of the Irish privateers calculated that they and their crews would have a greater chance of passing as Americans than as Frenchmen if captured, a consideration which might make the difference between being treated as prisoners of war and being executed as traitors.[100] Franklin was reluctant at first to grant commissions to non-Americans and he refused an application from Christopher Farran of Rush, County Dublin, an experienced smuggler who commanded a cutter

---

[94] *DEP*, 8 January 1782.   [95] *Ibid.*, 6 February 1779.   [96] *FLJ*, 6 January 1781.
[97] *Ibid.*, 20 January 1781.   [98] *Ibid.*, 3 March 1781.   [99] *FJ*, 13 March 1781.
[100] William Bell Clark, *Ben Franklin's Privateers* (Baton Rouge, 1956), p. 24.

of twelve guns and who was represented to him as 'an attached friend to the American cause'.[101] But in May 1779 Franklin was prevailed upon to issue a commission to another smuggling cutter from Rush, formerly called the *Friendship* but now renamed the *Black Prince*, which at first was nominally commanded by an American but had an Irish crew. Having cruised successfully in the English channel the *Black Prince* appeared off the Irish coast in its new role in September of the same year. A contemporary press report describes what happened when the captain of a revenue cutter gave chase to what he mistook for a smuggling vessel:

coming alongside, he hailed the crew with his trumpet, in answer to which the cutter hoisted the thirteen stripes and poured a broadside into the *Townshend* which very much damaged her rigging. The enemy, which now appeared to be the *Black Prince* privateer, then sheered off... The *Black Prince* was so near the *Townshend*, that her people knew the faces of two of the rebel crew to be men of Rush, with whom they were acquainted.[102]

The *Black Prince* then anchored off the north Dublin coast and one of its boats put into Rush in search of new hands, returning with nine additional crewmen.[103] Command of the *Black Prince* was assumed by Patrick Dowling in October 1779 and in the same month a commission was issued to Edward Macatter for a second Irish-crewed privateer, the *Black Princess*. In February 1780 Franklin issued a third commission to Luke Ryan, captain of the *Fearnot*.[104] The exploits of this small Irish-crewed navy, sailing under American colours and operating out of Dunkirk and other French ports, were regularly reported in the Irish press and excited great indignation among loyalists. The *Londonderry Journal*, reporting the capture by the *Black Prince* and the *Black Princess* of two passenger vessels on the Dublin to Holyhead route, denounced their crews as 'renegade pirates'.[105] The Volunteer corps of Dublin city mustered and marched to Rush on the same occasion, in the mistaken belief that the 'pirates' would again put in there.[106] But hostility to the privateers was far from universal, as is clear from the content of a petition submitted to government by the merchants and traders of Dublin. The merchants asked that measures be taken to curb privateering in the Irish Sea and claimed:

That the undisturbed success of those privateers has unhappily afforded too much encouragement to a new and most dangerous species of enemy. Persons who long accustomed to violate the law as smugglers have traitorously taken up arms against

[101] *Ibid.*   [102] *FLJ*, 15 September 1779.   [103] *Ibid.*, 22 September 1779.
[104] Clark, *Ben Franklin's Privateers*, pp. 165–6.   [105] *LJ*, 17 March 1780.
[106] *Ibid.*, 21 March 1780.

their country, and who from the sort of vessels they navigate, as well as from the accurate knowledge of the coast and harbours of this kingdom, are peculiarly alarming to your petitioners.[107]

This account agrees with the findings of the historian of the privateers commissioned by Benjamin Franklin, who wrote that 'many Irish sailors, lured by the success of the *Black Prince* ... flocked to Dunkirk, intending to ship in her or in other privateers'.[108] But Franklin stopped issuing such commissions and Irish privateers began to appear under French colours during 1780. One such ship, commanded by the Wexford-born Chevalier de Clonard, captured several vessels off the south coast before itself being taken in an engagement.[109] State papers indicate that another French privateer, the *Furet*, which preyed on shipping between Cork and Bristol in December 1780, had 'many Irish on board'.[110]

There was no decline in the activity of Irish privateers during 1781. The year opened with reports in early January of the exploits of the *Tartar*, a privateer commanded by Luke Ryan – formerly a Rush-based smuggler – which succeeded in capturing a British frigate off Cork.[111] *Finn's Leinster Journal* informed its readers that Ryan's ship was crewed by 'near 200 men, most of them Irish and Americans'.[112] In May, the lord lieutenant apprised the secretary of state that two new privateers were being fitted out at Dunkirk, one of which was to be commanded by Patrick Dowling.[113] By August, the two vessels had arrived off the Wexford coast and both Dowling's ship, the *Nancy*, and the unnamed second privateer commanded by an Irishman named Conoran, had taken prizes; a report in the state papers says that 'there were but six French men' on board Conoran's privateer and that 'the rest of the crew were all Irish'.[114] In the same month, the collector of Waterford reported the presence off the Waterford coast of a French privateer called the *Princesse de Norrice* which was commanded by a Captain McCarthy and had a crew of 250 men, of whom 'not more than five or six' were French.[115] At the same time, yet another Dunkirk-based privateer – the *Dreadnought*, commanded by the John Kelly previously mentioned – was operating off

---

[107] PRO SP 63/468, fo. 408. The petition is undated but was received by the lord lieutenant on 6 March 1780.
[108] Clark, *Ben Franklin's Privateers*, p. 60.   [109] *HM*, October 1780, 549.
[110] Edward Roche to Thomas Winder, secretary to the Revenue Commissioners, 15 December 1780, PRO SP 63/471, fo. 479.
[111] *FLJ*, 6 January 1781.
[112] *Ibid.*, 3 January 1781. For an account of Luke Ryan's career, see Eden to Sir Stanier Porten, 2 May 1781, in PRO SP 63/474, fo. 299.
[113] Carlisle to Hillsborough, 31 May 1781, PRO SP 63/475, fo. 7.
[114] William Eden to Porten, 3 August 1781, *ibid.*, fo. 145.
[115] Lieutenant Francis May to [Eden?], 8 August 1781, *ibid.*, fo. 178.

the coast of Wicklow.[116] A month later, the presence of a French cutter called the *Phoenix*, George Ryan commander, was reported off the Wexford coast.[117] Later in September, the collector of Belfast reported the capture of a ship bound from Bristol to Belfast 'by the *Fantasie* of Dunkirque, Patrick Dowling commander, mounting fourteen 3 and 4 pounders and manned with, from 40 to 60 men, supposed to be mostly Irish'.[118] It may be doubted whether Patrick Dowling was really as ubiquitous as the state papers suggest, but it is clear that many Irishmen were serving on board French privateers by 1781. It must be asked what, if anything, this tells us about popular political attitudes?

Privateering can be viewed as a purely commercial operation of no political significance, and this view may be adopted all the more readily when the previous careers of several of the most prominent privateer captains as smugglers are noted. None the less, it must be recognised that any Irishman taking up arms against the British crown ran the risk of being charged with treason if captured – a risk that would not have existed had he chosen to serve on board a British privateer. This was the fate of Luke Ryan when he was captured while in command of the *Calonne*, a French privateer taken off the English coast. The Irish administration was also requested to collect evidence to establish that a second prisoner taken on board the *Calonne*, one John Coppinger, was a native of Cork.[119] A similar request was made for information about two natives of the Fingal area named Sweetman and Knight, who were serving as lieutenant and pilot respectively on board a French privateer, the *Count de Guichen*, when that ship was taken by the Royal Navy.[120] The report by Nicholas Morrisson, state solicitor, of the subsequent investigation which he conducted in Rush sheds some light on attitudes in the locality. One loyalist who was acquainted with Matthew Knight told the state solicitor that he would gladly have travelled to London to identify the prisoner, but 'being apprehensive that if the inhabitants of Rush would hear he made such discovery they would take away his life therefore hath declined to be examined or go to London'. This experience was repeated with respect to James Sweetman in the neighbouring town of Lusk where those who could identify him refused to testify, 'being under apprehensions and in dread of the inhabitants'. Clearly, the anti-British privateers

[116] Eden to Porten, 4 August 1781, *ibid.*, fo. 211.
[117] Collector of Ross (signature illegible) to Eden, 8 September 1781, *ibid.*, fo. 88.
[118] George Macartney Portis, collector of Belfast, to Eden, 17 September 1781, *ibid.*, fo. 156.
[119] Porten to Eden, 20 August 1781, *ibid.*, fo. 203; for correspondence relating to the prosecution of Luke Ryan, see fos. 58, 76, 78, 201, 205 and 207.
[120] Porten to Eden, 1 September 1781, PRO SP 63/476, fo. 1.

enjoyed widespread support among the Catholic population of Fingal. This might still be interpreted as the apolitical solidarity of a closely knit and clannish community where smuggling had long been a way of life – a community characterised in Morrisson's report as being 'of a very riotous disposition and not amenable to the law'.[121] But evidence exists that the crews of Irish privateers regarded their activities as acts of war rather than piracy. In January 1780, when Benjamin Franklin was asked to intercede with the French authorities to obtain the release of Irish prisoners who had been taken on board British ships and who now wished to serve under Luke Ryan, Franklin's correspondent assured him that 'Mr. Ryan is very sure these eight people will be faithful to him and to their oath of allegiance to the United States'.[122] When Ryan himself was captured, reports in the Irish press indicated that he was awaiting his trial in London with – as events were to prove – justified complacency: 'Luke Ryan appears as perfectly at ease in his confinement in the New Goal, as if none of those *outré* circumstances which attend his case hung over him; he asserts his having no doubt that an officer of his rank is now detained at Philadelphia, to await his fate.'[123] Such sang-froid can only have increased the respect with which Ryan and his colleagues were viewed by many of his compatriots.

The *aisling* by Éamonn Ó Flaitheartaigh, a County Cork author, which was referred to previously establishes that the successes of the Irish privateers were applauded far from their north Dublin heartland. In Ó Flaitheartaigh's work, the traditional figure of a beautiful woman personifying Ireland cheered the poet with a rousing description of his countrymen's exploits at sea:

> '*Atá buíon againn is éachtach ar taoide anois le tréimhse*
> *ag tógaint loingis laochra idir éadach is lón,*
> *atá an* fleet *amuigh ar Thetis chum díoltais agus léirscrios*
> *is ní ar bith ní léigfid 'na ngaorsan i ngleo;*
> *tá na* Americans *'s an Spáinneach 's an Francach cliste páirteach*
> *is mórán eile i bpáirt leis ná háirmhim im sceol,*
> *tá an mhuir acu gan spleáchas is Rí na Cruinne lámh leo*
> *is ní stadfaidh siad den stáir sin go gcáiblid an choróin.*'[124]

('There is a band of ours that has been powerful at sea for some time now, capturing the warships with both sails and stores, the *fleet* is out on the sea seeking revenge and destruction, and they'll let nothing come close to them in battle; the

[121] Morrisson to Eden, 27 October 1781, PRO SP 63/477, fo. 7.
[122] John Torris to Benjamin Franklin, 18 January 1780, in William B. Wilcox (ed.), *The Papers of Benjamin Franklin*, XXXI (New Haven and London, 1995), p. 392.
[123] *FLJ*, 1 December 1781.
[124] '*Ar mo leaba aréir go déanach*' in RIA Ms. 23 D 42, p. 30.

Americans and the Spaniard and the wily Frenchman are involved, and many others are also engaged whom I won't mention in my account, they control the sea regardless and the King of the Universe [God] is at their side, and they'll not pause in their dash until they topple the crown.')

There is, moreover, independent evidence that support for anti-British privateers existed in County Cork. In March 1779 the captain of a Bristol brig taken by an American privateer while sailing from Cork to Galway deposed that the American vessel had been guided by a hooker from the port of Kinsale and claimed that 'the said privateer could not possibly with safety [have taken] this deponent in the course in which he ran without the assistance and direction of the said hooker'.[125]

The invasion alert of 1779

Britain's strategic position was further weakened in June 1779 when Spain entered the war after a period of military preparation. Almost immediately Ireland and Britain were threatened with invasion as a joint Franco-Spanish fleet assembled in the Bay of Biscay. Protestant Ireland was galvanised into action by the threat and thousands rushed to join their local Volunteer companies and to form new corps in districts where none existed. According to one estimate the strength of the Volunteers grew from around 15,000 in April 1779, to almost 30,000 in September, to more than 40,000 in December, and to 60,000 by the middle of the following year.[126] The administration had few misgivings about the loyalty of this rapidly expanding unofficial militia and as late as May 1779 Buckinghamshire advised the secretary of state that the total number of Volunteers did not exceed 'eight thousand men, some without arms, and in the whole very few who are liable to a suspicion of disaffection'.[127] In the same month the commander of the garrison at Belfast, one of the areas where the Volunteers were strongest, informed the acting commander in chief of a visit he had received from the captains of the local Volunteer companies:

The three captains of the associating companies paid me a visit this morning, with a tender of their services offering to march at any time, or to any place I should please to direct...I am well assured they lost entirely, or, at least, in a great measure, their penchant to the American cause; – they are disgusted with the Americans for their alliance with France, and rejecting the late offers

125 Deposition by John Whiting, 30 March 1779, PRO SP 63/464, fo. 227. The words in brackets are illegible because of tight binding.
126 David Smyth, 'The Volunteer movement', p. 70.
127 Buckinghamshire to Weymouth, 23 May 1779, in PRO SP 63/464, fo. 362.

of government [i.e. the Carlisle peace commission]: I believe the American flag would cause as great an alarm as the French.[128]

This assessment was shared at the highest levels and in July 1779, as fears of a Franco-Spanish landing mounted, the lord lieutenant ordered the governors of each county to be issued with arms for distribution among the local Volunteer corps.[129] Within a short time the force was playing an important role in assisting the civil magistrates in their law-enforcement activities, thereby allowing the army to concentrate on its military duties.[130]

If Catholic support for the Americans had grown during the course of the war, the Bourbon powers remained the primary focus of attention in vernacular political literature and it was to them, rather than to George Washington, that the crucial role in the liberation of Ireland was invariably assigned. Séamus Ó Dálaigh's version of '*Síle Ní Ghadhra*' attributed the following description of the climactic struggle to the eponymous Síle:

> '*Tá Rí na Sardinia, is Laoiseach go laochta,*
> *Philib 's an tImpire taoiseach Bhohémia*
> *go barcach, go buíonmhar, go fiochmhar, go fraochta,*
> *ag tarraingt tar taoide le Stíobhart dom éileamh;*
> *gabhadh gach galach d'fhuil Chaisil na dtriath*
> *is fearchoin leath Choinn chathaigh na gcliar*
> *go lonnach lannaibh chum troda mar iad,*
> *'s le gníomh goil is gaisce anois cartaidh gach cladhaire,*
> *do dhiúltfadh reacht Pheadair i bhfearann ceart Feidhlim.*' [131]

('The king of Sardinia, and Louis heroically, Philip and the Emperor, the ruler of Bohemia, with ships and hosts are fiercely and furiously, coming over the sea with a Stuart to claim me; let every champion of the blood of Cashel of the kings [Munster] and the warriors of battling *leath Choinn* [Ulster, Connacht and Meath] of the clergy angrily seize blades to fight like them, and with deeds of valour and heroism now drive out every rogue who would reject the rule of Peter [the pope] in the true land of Feidhlim [Ireland].')

Whatever may be thought of his inaccurate references to Sardinia, Austria and 'Philip', the prospect outlined by Ó Dálaigh was not unlike that which many Protestants feared when the combined fleets of the Bourbon powers massed in the summer of 1779. In July of that year the *Hibernian*

---

[128] Major General Maxwell to Lieutenant General Cunningham, 24 May 1779, in PRO SP 63/465, fo. 9.
[129] Buckinghamshire to Weymouth, 23 July 1779, *ibid.*, fo. 441.
[130] See Pádraig Ó Snodaigh, 'Some police and military aspects of the Irish Volunteers', *Irish Sword* 13 (1977–79).
[131] RIA 23 D 12, p. 26; however the final line, illegible in this manuscript, is taken from a later copy in RIA Ms. 23 E 12, p. 238.

Magazine published a poem about the crucial role played by the Irish brigade in the French service in the defeat of the Austrians at Cremona in 1702. One thought borrowed another and the writer posed the following question: 'These brave men were drove from their country by the late Revolution; and if in our days, by a succession of political blunders, an open[ing] should be left for the return of their descendants, by over-draining this kingdom of its forces, what desperate acts of retaliation may not be expected?'[132] Although the proportion of Irishmen in the ranks of the Irish regiments had declined sharply since the end of the Seven Years War, their officer corps remained largely Irish and the recruitment of private soldiers continued on a small scale. Even after France had entered the war, Lord Buckinghamshire received an intelligence report that officers of Dillon's regiment were recruiting in Connacht and Clare.[133] The Catholic population at home maintained their interest in the exploits of the Irish regiments – for example, in the part played by the Régiment de Dillon in the French capture of Grenada in July 1779.[134]

Fr Arthur O'Leary, although himself a former chaplain in the French service, exerted himself to combat the Francophile sympathies of the populace. In August 1779, at the height of the invasion scare, an *Address to the Common People of the Roman Catholic Religion* which cautioned against placing any reliance on French promises appeared under his name. Revealingly, the *Address* cited the French court's shabby treatment of Prince Charles Edward after his escape from Scotland in 1746 as an illustration of Gallic perfidy – a choice of example which provides further evidence of the prevalence of Jacobite sentiment among the masses. For good measure, it was falsely claimed that the Stuart pretender had recently died:

He died about two months since without issue, and by his death has rid the kingdom of all fears arising from the pretensions of a family that commenced our destruction and completed our ruin. Of this I think fit to inform you, as in all likelihood, if the French landed here, some might give out that he might be in their camp, in order to deceive you by an imposture that would end in your destruction.[135]

Such a dishonest tactic would have done little credit to O'Leary were he the author, but he may not have been responsible for the passage in question. In a letter published three months later he denied authorship

---

[132] *HM*, July 1779, 423.
[133] Weymouth to Buckinghamshire, 26 June 1779, PRO SP 63/465, fo. 155.
[134] See Fr H. Ennis to Fr John Kavanagh, 14 September 1779, Passionists' archive, NLI Pos. 7,654, p. 184.
[135] Arthur O'Leary, *An Address to the Common People of the Roman Catholic Religion, concerning the Apprehended French Invasion* (Cork, 1779), p. 8; the address also appeared in *HM*, August 1779, 473.

of sections of the *Address* without disowning any specific passage.[136] On
the other hand, it is possible that his qualified denial may have been a
damage limitation exercise – the pro-British *Address* had, as will be seen,
made him an object of hatred in vernacular song. However one argument
in the pamphlet bears all the hallmarks of O'Leary's authorship. Advising
Catholics to stand aloof from the conflict in the event of a French invasion,
he argued that 'the common people are never interested in the change
of government. They may change their masters, but they will not change
their burden. The rich will still be rich. The poor will be poor.'[137] It was
a telling point, but was answered by Tomás Ó Míocháin in a song which
reveals the hostility felt towards the priest by those Catholics who hoped
for the overthrow of British power in Ireland.

Ó Míocháin's song, perhaps more clearly than any other work of the
period, illustrates the ability of vernacular song to convey a coherent
political message to the rural populace while countering the propaganda
of a pro-government author. It will be quoted in full:

> *A uaisle Inis Éilge de chnuascheap na nGael*
> *atá luascaithe i mbuaireamh is suaite ag an saol*
> *do chaill le camdlí is le hachtannaibh daoir*
> *gach paiste de thalamh bhur sinsear,*
> *gach paiste de thalamh bhur sinsear;*
> *músclaidh go lúth-chliste feasta chum éacht,*
> *is lúbaidh go hurlainn bhur lannaibh go léir*
> *i gcoinne gach dream d'fhág sibhse go fann*
> *le fada gan sealbh gan saoirse,*
> *le fada gan sealbh gan saoirse.*
>
> *Níl suairceas i scéal, i nduanta ná i ndréacht,*
> *ná greann ar chomhluadar na n-uasal atá faon,*
> *muna mbeadh giolla an óir do shíolraigh ó Mhóir*
> *ina pheata ar gach baiste agus pósadh,*
> *ina pheata ar gach baiste agus pósadh;*
> *féach Bráthair Ó Laoghaire, cidh claon linn a rá*
> *mar chruann an coiléar leis an té bhíos ar lár;*
> *do bheirim do siúd mór-thairbhe an úird,*
> *is cead raide don aicme atá scólta,*
> *is cead raide don aicme atá scólta.*
>
> *Do bheirim an chraobh do Washington saor,*
> *is do Jones atá ar farraige 'greadadh piléar,*
> *is iad siúd an bhuíon a throideas go binn*

---

[136] *FJ*, 20 November 1779. The claim concerning Prince Charles's death was reprinted
in a subsequent anthology of O'Leary's pamphlets: see Arthur O'Leary, *Miscellaneous
Tracts* (Dublin, 1781), p. 96.

[137] O'Leary, *An Address to the Common People*, p. 13.

ag seasamh i ngradam 's i nglóire,
ag seasamh i ngradam 's i nglóire;
is tríothu siúd fleet *mara Laoisigh do shiúil*
is pé lonradh beag lascaine gheallaid na búir,
ní bhfaighdís ceart léas ar bhothán na ngé
   gur leathain an eagla ar Sheoirse,
   gur leathain an eagla ar Sheoirse.

Nach léir díbh an tan bhí clann Iácob na ngíomh
i bhfad aige Pharoah faoi cháin agus chuing,
trí urnaithe síor is clúchleasaibh claímh
   go rángadar slán as an Éigipt,
   go rángadar slán as an Éigipt;
an sómpla so leanaidh re meanmain ard
ós dócha nach maireann lucht fearaibh is fearr
le faobhar is fíoch gan staonadh gan scíth,
   lomchartaidh bhur namhaid thar Thetis,
   lomchartaidh bhur namhaid thar Thetis.[138]

(O worthies of Inis Éilge [Ireland] of the fruitful stock of the Gaels, who are rocked by trouble and shaken by life, who through a perverse law and oppressive acts lost every patch of your ancestors' land; rouse yourselves nimbly for killing henceforth, and flex all your blades up to their hafts against every group which kept you enfeebled, for long without property or freedom.

There is no merriment in tales, in songs or in poems, nor gaiety in the company of the enfeebled gentry, except for the golden lackey [Arthur O'Leary] descended from Mór [a reference to O'Leary's obscure background], who is a pet at every baptism and wedding. Behold Friar O'Leary, though I hate to say it, how the collar tightens on the one who strays; I bestow on him the great benefit of clergy, and freedom of action on the class that is tormented.

I bestow the laurels on noble Washington, and on [John Paul] Jones who's at sea firing bullets, they are the band that's fighting brilliantly, standing forth in esteem and glory; through them the sea *fleet* of Louis [XVI] has come, and whatever glimmer of respite the boors have promised, they'd never have obtained permission to lease [even] a goose-shed until fear took hold of George [III].

Don't you know of the time when the children of active Jacob, were for long by Pharoah kept under tribute and a yoke, until by continual prayer and famous feats of arms they came safely out of Egypt; follow this example with a high spirit, since it's likely that no better body of men exists, with the blade and ferocity, without pause or rest, expel all your enemies over the sea.)

In a song of only four verses Ó Míocháin appealed to the ethnic solidarity of his listeners and their sense of dispossession and oppression, portrayed O'Leary as the pampered pet and fêted favourite of the Anglo-Irish ruling class, attributed to the Americans and the French all the credit for

---

[138] '*A uaisle Inis Éilge de chnuascheap na nGael*' in Maynooth Ms. C 18, pp. 25–7; edited in Ó Muirithe, *Tomás Ó Míocháin.*

whatever changes had recently been made to Penal legislation, and concluded with a call for rebellion and the expulsion of the English colony. Songs such as this confirm the accuracy – in so far as it relates to the Catholic masses – of an anonymous assessment of Irish political attitudes which appeared in print in 1779:

the expectation of a great part of the nation leads them to believe they will be offered national independence by foreign assistance. And, in this idea, whatever addresses or reports on the other side of the water may say, all persuasions are united; the Roman Catholics, from the similitude of religious sentiments; the Protestants, from the conduct of the French with regard to America; and all sects and denominations, from the decay of their trade, and the continuance of every check to it.[139]

Catholic disaffection was no novelty, but the above report also records the sudden emergence of a new and unprecedented phenomenon: during the early months of 1779 the policy or – more accurately – the lack of policy of the British ministry succeeded in alienating the majority of the Irish political nation.

The alienation of the political nation

Ireland's deteriorating economic situation was obvious to all by early 1778 and the British ministry responded sympathetically in April of that year when Lord Nugent, an Irish peer who was also a member of the British House of Commons, proposed a series of measures to relax the restrictions on Irish trade. In particular, Nugent proposed that Ireland should be allowed to trade freely with the British colonies, except for a few specified products of which woollens and tobacco were the most important; that the prohibition on the export of Irish glass should be repealed; and that duties on the import of Irish cottons to Britain should be abolished. The prime minister indicated his support for Nugent's proposals, arguing that 'to relax the trade laws would benefit the Irish, and ultimately enrich ourselves'.[140] The proposals initially aroused little opposition on either side of the house. Edmund Burke did criticise them, but only on the grounds that they did not go far enough: 'How widely', he declaimed, 'did the unlimited terms offered to the Americans differ from those now held out to Ireland!'[141] Opinion in Ireland was favourably impressed and believed that a useful start had been made. The *Londonderry Journal*, for example, assured its readers that 'there seemed great unanimity in the

---

[139] *The Alarm; or, the Irish Spy. In a Series of Letters on the Present State of Affairs in Ireland, to a Lord High in the Opposition. Written by an Ex-Jesuit, Employed by his Lordship for the Purpose* (Dublin, 1779), p. 19.
[140] *FJ*, 16 April 1778.   [141] *Ibid.*

House, and a strong desire to do much good for Ireland'.[142] But within weeks a flood of petitions against the proposed measures began to pour into Westminster from Glasgow, Liverpool, Bristol, Manchester and other commercial centres where the effects of Irish competition were feared. Nugent's original proposals were diluted and, although the right to export to the colonies (some specified products excepted) was conceded, it was a right that Irish merchants could not exercise in practice in the absence of a corresponding freedom to import colonial produce on the return voyage.

Reaction in Ireland to this set-back was muted. The relaxation and, by the end of 1778, the complete lifting of the embargo on the export of provisions helped to mollify both the parliamentary opposition and Irish commercial interests. None the less, the message that, as Sir Samuel Bradstreet, patriot member for Dublin city, put it, 'beggarly Glasgow and the *loyal* town of Manchester had more weight in the scale than the interest of this kingdom'[143] was not lost on the members of the political nation and the slogan 'free trade to Ireland' began to feature among the toasts drunk by Volunteer corps.[144] Reports filtering back from America about the inducements that the Carlisle peace commission was holding out to the colonies in return for little more than a nominal acknowledgement of British sovereignty gave grounds to hope that a similar flexibility would be shown in relation to Ireland. It was reported that the peace commissioners were 'authorised and desirous ... to extend every freedom to trade' to the colonies and that they acknowledged 'the entire privilege of the people of North America to dispose of their property, and to govern themselves without any reference to Great Britain, beyond what is necessary to preserve that union of force, in which our mutual safety and advantage consist' – terms which Irishmen, of whatever political hue, could only regard with envy.[145] A correspondent writing in *Finn's Leinster Journal*, by no means an organ of opposition opinion, complained that the Irish had been 'treated with ineffable contempt, from the proud peer at St. James's, to the pert, ignorant, and conceited shop-keeper of Cheapside', but argued that military defeat in America had obliged Britain to adopt a more liberal policy from which Ireland would shortly benefit:

England is brought to reason! After begging, and begging in vain, her revolted colonies in America to treat with her, she turns her dejected eyes to Ireland as her only hope; and, we hear, is willing to give us freedom of trade, if we give her

---

[142] *LJ*, 17 April 1778.
[143] *HJ*, 8 June 1778. Bradstreet's description of Manchester as 'loyal' was an ironic allusion to the regiment raised there by Prince Charles Edward in 1745.
[144] *LJ*, 19 June and 4 August 1778.
[145] *FDJ*, 24 October 1778 and *HM*, November 1778, 628 respectively.

assistance. Bills for this purpose are to be brought into the British parliament immediately after their meeting.[146]

It was impossible for administration to view Ireland's deteriorating economy with complacency, if only because of the precipitate fall in revenue that resulted. In the summer of 1778 it was necessary to obtain a loan from the Bank of England before the Irish garrison could be encamped; in 1779 the British treasury took over the payment of regiments from the Irish establishment that were serving overseas; and in the summer of the same year a direct subvention from the British treasury was needed before the army could again be encamped. Such financial expedients fostered the belief that further economic concessions were inevitable.

None the less, calls for the non-consumption of British produce appeared in the patriot press with increasing frequency from early 1779. At the beginning of February, an article in the *Dublin Evening Post* urged parliament to take a lead in organising such a movement:

There is nothing more certain, than that our parliament could relieve this oppressed country, from the burthens and oppressions we labour under, by setting on foot, under their own sanction and authority, a general association, against the importation of English manufactures.[147]

As parliament was not expected to be summoned before the autumn, this approach betrayed a certain lack of urgency and may have been designed more to concentrate the minds of ministers than to rouse the political nation. A similar call which appeared in the *Freeman's Journal* before the end of February also lacked any practical programme of action, but it shows that Britain's strategic weakness was perceived by Anglo-Irish patriots as a factor increasing their leverage:

The glory of Old England has compelled the people of America, under every disadvantage, to depend upon themselves. England has lost America – she cannot bear the loss of Ireland. Continue to live upon the produce of your own country; consume *nothing British*; and, without the necessity of taking up arms, (to which we are not equal) you will compel these haughty tyrants to do you justice.[148]

Given the parlous state of the economy in general, and of the public finances in particular, it was easy to believe that a substantial relaxation of the restrictions on Irish trade would be introduced sooner rather than later, but when Lord Newhaven, an Irish peer who held a seat in the British House of Commons, raised the question in February and again in March 1779, his efforts were opposed by a ministry anxious not to antagonise British commercial interests again, as had happened in 1778.

[146] *FLJ*, 28 November 1778.   [147] *DEP*, 4 February 1779.
[148] *FJ*, 27 February 1779.

Lord North argued on 12 March that it would be wiser to wait until the effects of the previous year's measures had become apparent before making any major change to the legislation governing Irish trade. Even before reports of the prime minister's speech reached Ireland proposals to give immediate but limited effect to the idea of a non-importation agreement appeared in the patriot press:

> As the assizes in the adjacent counties will speedily commence, a friend to the trade and prosperity of this kingdom sincerely recommends, to the gentlemen who may compose the different grand juries to enter into associations and pledge themselves to each other, that they will not buy for themselves or their domestics, any kind of woollen cloth that is not of Irish manufacture.[149]

The only measures in favour of Irish trade to be actually approved by the British parliament were a bounty on Irish hemp imported into Britain and the abolition of a seventeenth-century prohibition on the importation of Irish tobacco into Britain. *Faulkner's Dublin Journal*, a resolutely pro-government newspaper, attempted to portray the latter measure as a significant concession: 'The British parliament, having come to the resolution of encouraging the growth of tobacco in this kingdom, it is to be hoped that every advantage will be pursued by the inhabitants of this country. That tobacco can be raised here in perfection, is evident from the restrictions formerly imposed.'[150] But it required no great agricultural expertise to realise that Ireland's frosty springs and damp autumns would prevent it from rivalling Virginia as a producer of tobacco. The opposition press was quick to capitalise on an egregious blunder:

> Now that Great Britain has lost America for ever, nothing, to be sure, can exceed the benevolence of the British nation, in suffering us to enrich ourselves by the cultivation of tobacco. When it shall be discovered in a century hence … that no revenue will accrue by this commodity, they will, perhaps, extend to us the favour of cultivating grapes exclusively, and amuse us with the advantages we shall obtain by the produce of wine.[151] … the British ministry, touched with a sense of our sufferings, have resolved to let us raise rice and vines, as both the French and American commerce may thus be affected! – Also to cultivate cloves, cinnamon, nutmegs and pepper, in order to mortify the Dutch.[152]

The British parliament was perceived to have added insult to injury and the Irish political nation responded with furious indignation.

A week after the last item above appeared, *Saunders' News-Letter* and the *Freeman's Journal*, papers which normally occupied opposite ends of the political spectrum, both published an article welcoming 'the patriotic

---

[149] *Ibid.*, 13 March 1779.   [150] *FDJ*, 1 April 1779.   [151] *FJ*, 1 April 1779.
[152] *DEP*, 8 April 1779.

ardour of encouraging Irish manufactures, adopted by all ranks of any fashion or consequence'.[153] By then, resolutions in favour of using Irish manufactures, or opposing the consumption of British imports, were being adopted by the county grand juries at their spring assizes, beginning with a non-importation resolution adopted by the County Galway jury on 27 March. Within days the County Tyrone jury adopted a similar resolution and the grand juries of Meath and Mayo resolved to use Irish manufactures. On 5 April, the grand jury of the large and influential county of Cork followed suit and resolved not to wear any cloth of foreign manufacture for a period of seven years.[154] More importantly still, the Common Council of Dublin Corporation adopted a resolution against the importation of British goods on 16 April.[155] Ten days later a non-importation resolution drafted by a committee of seven which included James Napper Tandy was adopted by a meeting of the 'aggregate body of the citizens of Dublin' convened by the city's sheriffs.[156] Lord Buckinghamshire considered the latter resolution to be of such a 'dangerous tendency' that he forwarded a newspaper report of the aggregate body's proceedings to the secretary of state and summoned the lord chancellor, prime serjeant and attorney general to consider the most appropriate response. The law officers concurred in advising that no sign of official disapproval should be shown, as such a course of action 'would have no other effect than making this disagreeable disposition worse'.[157]

Studied inaction may have been the most prudent policy in the circumstances, but the non-importation movement continued to gather momentum. In late May the lord lieutenant had to advise the secretary of state that the names of merchants who continued to import English goods were now being published in the press, a tactic intended 'for the abominable purpose of drawing the indignation of the mob upon individuals'; the tactic would appear to have been effective, for within a few days he informed Lord George Germain that shops in Dublin had been attacked by a gang of butchers who were dispersed by the military – further evidence of the politicised nature of that trade in the capital.[158] In May also, opposition-sponsored resolutions calling for an investigation into the 'causes of discontent' in Ireland were adopted by both houses of the British parliament but no concrete proposals for further relief

---

[153] *SNL* and the *FJ*, 15 April 1779.
[154] These resolutions were widely reported. See, for example, *LJ*, 13 and 16 April 1779; and *FLJ*, 14 April 1779.
[155] *SNL*, 17 April 1779.   [156] *HJ*, 28 April 1779.
[157] Buckinghamshire to Weymouth, 29 April 1779, in PRO SP 63/464, fo. 315.
[158] Buckinghamshire to Weymouth, 29 May 1779, in PRO SP 63/465, fo. 32; Buckinghamshire to Germain, 2 June 1779, in HMC Stopford-Sackville Mss., I (1904), pp. 255–6.

emerged before the summer recess. The *Dublin Evening Post* lamented that 'notwithstanding all the lullaby promises, nothing has been done for the relief of poor Ireland. *Live horse and you shall have grass*, is the only consolation that oppressed country hath given it.'[159] Use of an Irish proverb – even in translation – by an organ of patriotic opinion was an early augury of changing attitudes. By September there were indications that the non-importation strategy was beginning to have an effect. The manufacturers of Halifax, Yorkshire, who 'at first affected proudly to laugh' at the Irish resolutions, were by then reported to have 'altered their tone, and are become as crest fallen and dejected as they were absurdly vain and arrogant'.[160] If the agitation was helping to transform attitudes in England's manufacturing districts, its effects on the political climate in Ireland itself were still more profound.

The campaign for the relaxation or removal of the restrictions on Irish trade almost doubled the number of pamphlets on political and economic issues published in 1779.[161] More remarkable still was the unprecedented tone adopted by some of the pamphleteers. It is indicative of the support the agitation received from all sections of the population that by far the most substantial work in favour of free trade came from the pen of John Hely Hutchinson, a member of parliament for Cork city who was normally a supporter of government. His pamphlet on the 'commercial restraints of Ireland' was careful to acknowledge 'the superintending protection of Great Britain, necessary to the existence of Ireland', but none the less claimed that the 'power of regulating trade in a great empire is perverted, when exercised for the destruction of trade in any part of it'.[162] Hely Hutchinson's criticism was mild in comparison with that of other authors. An anonymous pamphlet which has been attributed to both Henry Grattan and Henry Flood denounced the dominion 'usurped' by Britain over other parts of the empire ('Such was the power exercised against America, and denounced against Ireland – the resistance of the former has saved the latter') and argued that Britain, in its weakened condition, had no effective means of resisting the non-importation associations. In a gesture towards the Catholic population, the author predicted that the non-importation movement would 'enrol us

---

[159] A translation of the saying '*mair a chapaill agus gheobhair féar*'; see *DEP*, 3 July 1779.
[160] *FLJ*, 11 September 1779.
[161] R.D. Collison Black, *A Catalogue of Pamphlets on Economic Subject Published between 1750 and 1900 and now Housed in Irish Libraries* (New York, 1969), lists thirteen original Irish-published titles in 1777 and fifteen in 1778, compared with twenty-eight in 1779.
[162] [John Hely Hutchinson], *The Commercial Restraints of Ireland Considered* (Dublin, 1779), pp. 113 and 187.

as a people' by uniting all sections of the population in a common cause and, alluding to Gardiner's Catholic relief act, he argued that 'The law has made the Roman Catholic our fellow citizen, the association [against importing British goods] will give him an opportunity of signing himself a fellow citizen.'[163] This inclusive rhetoric in its turn paled in comparison with that of 'Guatimozin' – the pen-name of Frederick Jebb, a Dublin surgeon. Setting the dispute about restrictions on Irish trade in a wider constitutional context, Jebb drove home his central contention that the 'parliament of Ireland is as complete in its own jurisdiction, as is the parliament of England' in a series of trenchantly argued letters.[164] This view had been argued by Charles Lucas a generation before; but unlike Lucas, Jebb held out an olive branch to the Catholic populace, arguing that 'if men of all denominations in the kingdom shall unite against the common oppressor, no doubt can be entertained of success'.[165] Most remarkable and original, however, was his tentative advocacy of complete separation from Britain:

We run infinitely more risk of being invaded by the enemies of Great Britain, in the time of her wars, from which we derive perpetual loss but no advantage, than we should do upon our own account, if we led peaceably a separate life. Were we removed from English influence, we should grow rich as Holland has done, and we should be as much secured from the effects of general malice, as the inhabitants of that country were, when they shook off the Spanish yoke.[166]

The articulation of such a separatist perspective by an Anglo-Irish author sharply distinguishes the more extreme polemics associated with the free-trade agitation from ideas that had been common currency among Anglo-Irish patriots for the previous thirty years. While patriot pamphleteers had frequently repudiated the right of the British parliament to legislate for Ireland, and some had gone so far as to assert the constitutional equality of the two kingdoms, the new writers who appeared in 1779 were the first to question the value of maintaining any constitutional link with Great Britain.

It is impossible to quantify the contribution made by the example of America to this development, but it is difficult to avoid the conclusion

---

[163] *A Letter to the People of Ireland on the Expediency and Necessity of the Present Associations in Ireland, in Favour of our own Manufactures* (Dublin, 1779), pp. 7 and 53. For plausible arguments against the pamphlet's attribution to Grattan see James Kelly, *Henry Flood: Patriots and Politics in Eighteenth-Century Ireland* (Dublin, 1998), p. 258 (footnote). The sympathetic attitude taken towards Catholics makes the attribution of the work to Flood unlikely.

[164] [Frederick Jebb], *The Letters of Guatimozin, on the Affairs of Ireland* (Dublin, 1779), p. 8. The first letter in the series appeared in *FJ*, 17 April 1779.

[165] *Ibid.*, p. 16.   [166] *Ibid.*, pp. 18–19.

that the colonies' declaration of independence, together with the changing strategic balance, was a significant factor. Certainly, there can be
no doubt about the source of Frederick Jebb's inspiration. 'I confess', he
wrote, 'that, as an Irish man, I feel considerable gratification in the checks,
which the progress of England's usurpations hath received in America.'
In another passage he boasted that 'those armies, which you [the British]
could not beat in America, consisted chiefly of Irish emigrants'.[167] On
the other hand, it must be acknowledged that the concept of an Irish
non-importation campaign was not original. Jonathan Swift's *Proposal
for the Universal Use of Irish Manufacture*, with its memorable advocacy
of a law for 'burning every thing that came from England, except their
people and their coals', had appeared almost sixty years previously,[168]
and Samuel Madden had urged the use of 'no sort of clothes and
furniture, which are not manufactured in Ireland' in 1738.[169] Earlier
still, the House of Commons had passed resolutions in favour of the
exclusive use of Irish clothing and furniture on two occasions during
the reign of Queen Anne.[170] But the most recent examples of such a
tactic, and the precedents with which the members of the Irish political
nation would have been most familiar in 1779, were undoubtedly the
successive non-importation agreements entered into by the American
colonies in opposition to the stamp act in 1765–66, the Townshend duties in 1767–70 and the 'coercive acts' in 1775–76. The conclusion that
the use of non-importation as a weapon in the campaign for free trade
must – to some extent – have been inspired by the American example is
inescapable.

The evolution of Presbyterian opinion

While the non-importation movement commanded the enthusiasm of
both the Anglican and the Catholic communities it was much less popular in Presbyterian Ulster – a fact which has been plausibly attributed
to the fear of provoking a retaliatory boycott of Irish linens in Britain.[171]
Conversely, the rapid expansion of the Volunteer movement during the
course of 1779 was particularly marked in the northern province because of its large Protestant population. A number of sermons preached
by Presbyterian ministers to Volunteer corps during the year were published. It seems reasonable to suppose that sermons addressed to societies

---

[167] *Ibid.*, pp. 19 and 53.   [168] McMinn (ed.), *Swift's Irish Pamphlets*, p. 50.
[169] Madden, *Reflections and Resolutions*, p. 59.
[170] Buckinghamshire to Weymouth, 18 October 1779, in PRO SP 63/467, fo. 44.
[171] See, for example, Smyth, 'The Volunteer movement in Ulster', pp. 93–4 and David
Lammey, 'A study of Anglo-Irish relations between 1772 and 1782 with particular
reference to the "free trade" movement' (PhD thesis, QUB, 1984), p. 167.

whose members held a range of political and religious views, and which were written with an eye to subsequent publication, would have tended to avoid divisive controversies and to have emphasised matters on which a consensus existed. If this assumption is correct, published Volunteer sermons can be regarded as sensitive barometers of the state of mainstream Protestant opinion in Ulster during the turbulent year of 1779.

One of the earliest such sermons was delivered in March by Rev. William Steel Dickson to the Echlinville Volunteers in the Ards peninsula of County Down. In a discourse combining elements of 'real Whig' rhetoric with Christian moralising he contrasted 'luxury's accursed influence' which induced people to rely on the protection afforded by a standing army with the 'generous spirit' that had formerly 'diffused itself through the inhabitants of the British Isles, covered our ancestors with glory, laid the foundations of our liberties in blood, and rendered the name of Britain illustrious',[172] but acknowledged that the emergence of the Volunteers in the hour of danger showed the present generation was not entirely bereft of their ancestors' virtues.[173] Fear of Catholicism loomed large in the minds of Presbyterians and Dickson painted a grim picture of the spiritual slavery that would follow a successful French invasion: 'Could we renounce the privileges of Protestants which our fathers have handed down to us sealed with their blood, and, devoutly kneeling, at the shrine of infallibility, receive with thankfulness our spiritual chains! Surely no. The thought is too humiliating. Religion revolts, and the spirit of man rises in arms against it.'[174] The divisive issue of the colonial conflict was avoided except for a passing reference to the absence of a substantial proportion of the British army in America: 'Those arms which lately spread terror through the nations of the earth, are employed in a ruinous war, three thousand miles distant.'[175] If the constitutional dispute that had precipitated the American war was too controversial to be broached, the pragmatic assessment that the army currently serving in North America might be more usefully deployed closer to home commanded wider agreement.

An unusual pamphlet entitled *The Alarm; or, the Irish Spy* which appeared in the summer of 1779 claimed that separatist ideas were being propagated in Belfast and summarised the arguments of local patriots in the following terms:

---

[172] William Steel Dickson, *A Sermon, on the Propriety and Advantages of Acquiring the Knowledge and Use of Arms, in Times of Public Danger* (Belfast, 1779), p. 15.

[173] *Ibid.*, p. 18.

[174] *Ibid.*, p. 20. Dickson later claimed that the sermon as preached advocated the admission of Catholics to membership of the Volunteers but that the relevant passage was omitted from the published version because of a public outcry against the proposal. See McBride, *Scripture Politics*, p. 154.

[175] *Ibid.*, p. 21.

That empire is now taking its progress westward, and that Europe will dwindle into that inferior situation, with regard to America, that the African and Asiatic provinces now bear to her; that it is, therefore, at this time, the interest of Irishmen to look to the advantages of their posterity, and endeavour to establish themselves independent of England as a key of commerce between Europe and America.[176]

In July 1779 John Hay, a Belfast correspondent of Benjamin Franklin's, who was trying to arrange a passage to America for a party which included himself and thirty-three others, treated the possibility of an Irish rebellion seriously but believed that its course and outcome would be very different from that of the conflict in America: 'Discord sowed in deep rooted prejudices civil and religious must prevent that happy unanimity which has crowned America with success – The contest in that case would partake much more of the nature of civil war than even your country has experienced.'[177] The most optimistic future for Ireland that this supporter of the American revolution could envisage was the achievement of equality with Great Britain within the British empire by means of an agitation similar to that which was already being directed against restrictions on Irish trade:

By a continuation of that spirit Ireland may arrive at that stage when she will rather be considered as the ally than the subject and perhaps the ruling power taught by the conduct of America and its consequence an awful lesson how dangerous it is to trample on the rights of mankind will avoid future strides towards unjust authority.[178]

A sermon preached by Rev. James Crombie to the Volunteer companies of Belfast on 1 August 1779 confirms the existence of a body of separatist opinion in the Belfast area but the vigorous attack which Crombie made on the concept of Irish independence indicates that the idea was not entertained by the bulk of the politically active population – even among those who, like John Hay, were supporters of the American cause. The aim of the French, Crombie declared, had always been the 'establishment of universal despotic monarchy' and the hope that they would confer freedom on Ireland was a delusion: 'We have heard that their design is not to destroy the liberties of *this kingdom*, but to enlarge them. What, freedom from slaves! Can they give what they do not themselves possess? Give, no, it is the glorious privilege, of which they are eagerly ambitious to deprive you.'[179] In other respects, the ideas expressed in Crombie's

---

[176] *The Alarm; or, the Irish Spy*, letter III, Belfast, 18 June 1779, p. 18.
[177] John Hay to Franklin, 6 July 1779, in W.B. Wilcox (ed.), *The Papers of Benjamin Franklin*, XXX (New Haven and London, 1993), p. 63.
[178] *Ibid.*, pp. 63–4.
[179] James Crombie, *The Expedience and Utility of Volunteer Associations for National Defence and Security in the Present Critical Situation of Public Affairs Considered* (Belfast, 1779), p. 22.

sermon closely resembled those in Dickson's. A 'general apostasy from patriotic principles' had undermined the once powerful British nation, of which Irish Protestants formed part: 'We have fallen with a rapidity almost unexampled in the history of the world.'[180] As Dickson had done, Crombie also invoked the spectre of a Catholic church which continued 'to wage impious war against the common rights of mankind'.[181] Unlike Dickson, Crombie did not restrict his attention to the threat posed by the Bourbon powers but urged his congregation to be vigilant in guarding against the Catholic threat at home:

It is true we have not only open enemies to contend with, but also, the peculiar misfortune, of having within our own bosom suspected citizens to watch over. Your associations free your country from all apprehensions of danger from these last. While they are calculated to intimidate foreign enemies, they will serve as an effectual check upon the insolence of popish faction.[182]

The American conflict was not mentioned and, although the demand for trade concessions was being vigorously pressed in the country at this time, only a glancing allusion was made to the restrictions on Irish trade. Having mentioned the need to protect commerce from the hazards of war, Crombie exclaimed: 'Alas! Let us not think of it now. – The generous concern you discover for the sinking interests of a kingdom [Great Britain], whose contracted policy, has always dealt severely with you, does honour to your feelings. I drop this subject.'[183] Unsuccessful efforts had been made to secure agreement on a non-importation resolution in Belfast, and the diffidence of the above comment suggests that the issue remained a divisive one among local Volunteers.[184]

The ideas expressed in a third Volunteer sermon, preached by Rev. William Crawford before the Strabane Rangers in September, were consistent with the foregoing, although a greater emphasis was placed on 'real Whig' ideas. The people of the Swiss cantons and the Dutch provinces who revolted against Austria and Spain were held up as exemplars of citizen-soldiers to be emulated, as was the patriotism of 'Hampden, Sydney, Russell, and those incorruptible Britons who appeared with so conspicuous a lustre, at the Glorious Revolution'. Closer to home, the 'noble resistance' of Irish Protestants to James II, 'that political tyrant and votary of popish superstition', was recalled.[185] But the heroic virtue that had once distinguished the British people – including the Protestants of Ireland – was no more: 'Where is the genius of the empire', asked

---

[180] *Ibid.*, p. 8.   [181] *Ibid.*, pp. 24–5.   [182] *Ibid.*, p. 32.   [183] *Ibid.*, p. 23.
[184] See *LJ*, 30 April and 7 May 1779 respectively; as noted in Smyth, 'The Volunteer movement in Ulster', p. 94.
[185] William Crawford, *The Connection betwixt Courage and the Moral Virtues Considered* (Strabane, 1779), pp. 16–18.

Crawford, 'which encircled the heads of our valiant countrymen with such splendid laurels at Agincourt, at Crecy, at Malplaquet, Ramillies and Blenheim...?'[186] As William Steel Dickson had done, Crawford attributed the blame for Britain's latter-day decadence to the growth of luxury which had 'corrupted our morals, and destroyed our public spirit', as a result of which 'our possessions in America, a principal source of our grandeur and our opulence, have, it is more than probable, been cut off from us forever'.[187] As James Crombie had also done, Crawford drew attention to the internal Catholic threat with a pointed hint that must have been intended to remind those who heard and read his sermon of the 1641 rebellion. Volunteering, he declared, was not only useful against foreign enemies, 'it will also, by the divine blessing, be an effectual security of our internal peace...We know what happened once; there was a time – but I drop the disagreeable idea.'[188] A single brief reference was made to Irish grievances: 'There are, it is true, certain restrictions imposed upon us, inconsistent with rights to which we have an undoubted claim; but we *now* feel them like men, and, in this respect, comfort ourselves with the pleasing expectation of better days.'[189] This was a formulation that minimised the importance of restrictions on Irish trade while suggesting that relief could not be withheld for much longer.

Only a month later the members of the Strabane Rangers heard Rev. Andrew Alexander preach a sermon on *The Advantage of a General Knowledge of the Use of Arms*. As might be expected in a sermon on such a theme, Alexander stressed the importance of an armed citizenry as the 'best security against domestic tyranny, and foreign invasion or conquest' while condemning 'mercenary troops' as 'destructive to the liberty of the subject'.[190] Yet again, the Swiss cantons, the United Provinces, and the citizens of Derry who had resisted James II were praised as examples of soldier-patriots who had frustrated the designs of tyrants. But Alexander went much further than the preachers who have been considered above. Speaking in an atmosphere of heightened political interest just two days before the opening of a new session of parliament, he noted another, more contemporary, example of heroic patriotism – one that had escaped the notice of his fellow ministers: 'To those examples it is scarcely to be doubted, but the present time will enable posterity to add another of the same kind on the other side of the Atlantic, as illustrious and memorable as any that history can afford.'[191] Given the

---

[186] *Ibid.*, p. 18.   [187] *Ibid.*, p. 19.   [188] *Ibid.*, p. 20.   [189] *Ibid.*, p. 23.
[190] Andrew Alexander, *The Advantage of a General Knowledge of the Use of Arms* (Strabane, 1779), pp. 11–12.
[191] *Ibid.*, p. 20.

constraints on a preacher's freedom of expression, this is a significant comment and strongly suggests the existence at this time of a sizable body of pro-American opinion among the members of the Volunteer corps concerned. In November, the same corps was preached to by Rev. Hugh Delap who addressed the question 'whether, and how far, magistracy is of a divine appointment'. As would be expected from a Presbyterian minister, Delap argued that, while magistracy itself was of divine appointment, 'the particular forms of government, and the persons entrusted in the administration of them . . . God has left entirely free to the choice and appointment of men'.[192] He reiterated long-standing Presbyterian views on the right of subjects to resist unconstitutional innovations, claiming that if rulers 'act in open violation of the laws of the constitution; to resist, is, not only commendable, but an indispensable duty'.[193] There was no suggestion, however, that George III's administration of Ireland was in any way unconstitutional. On the contrary, Delap painted a frightening picture of the fate awaiting Protestants in the event of an invasion by France or Spain, powers whose invariable aim had always been to 'wreath about our necks the yoke of popery and slavery, and their inseparable attendant arbitrary power'. Delap's anti-Catholicism was unrestrained. Not only were the Volunteers reminded of the massacre of Protestants in 1641 but Catholic teachings and devotional practices were condemned – including transubstantiation, prayers for the dead, the use of relics, and 'many other abominable superstitions too gross to mention'.[194] Concluding with a ringing call to his congregation to remember the conduct of their ancestors at the Boyne and the siege of Derry, Delap expressed his conviction that 'you will think nothing too difficult to do, nor dangerous to undertake, for the interest of your king and country, laws and constitution'.[195]

The sermon preached by Rev. Samuel Barber, a 'new light' minister, to two Volunteer corps in County Down in October was very different in its outlook. Referring to the Catholic population, Barber noted that 'the present generation have behaved peaceably and quietly, though as a religious society they have been subjected to penal laws, shocking to enumerate' and he hoped that the time would soon arrive 'when religion in every part of the globe, shall be as free as the sun that shineth'.[196] While expressing no opinion on the causes of the American war, Barber observed that 'flourishing colonies, equal in extent and fertility to kingdoms,

---

[192] Hugh Delap, *A Sermon, Preached in the Old-Bridge Meeting-House near Omagh, the 14th, of November 1779: before the Omagh and Cappagh Volunteers* (Strabane, 1779), p. 9.
[193] *Ibid.*, pp. 13–14. [194] *Ibid.*, p. 18. [195] *Ibid.*, p. 21.
[196] Samuel Barber, *A Sermon, Delivered in the Meeting-House of Rathfriland, October 24, 1779, to the Castlewellan Rangers, and Rathfriland Volunteers* (Newry, 1779), p. 9.

have separated, (I fear) for ever, from the British government, and leagued with our enemies'.[197] In relation to the prospect of a French landing, however, his views were in complete accord with those of his fellow ministers:

I shudder at the very thought! All our liberties gone! The word of a tyrant our law! Our parliaments and juries annihilated, our tongues tied from even complaining, and every generous, and noble sentiment stifled in the birth! Our toleration as a religious society revoked, and this very house, which ye have built and adorned at such great expense, employed to purposes ye never intended! We indeed labour under oppressions, but the little finger of a French or Spanish government, would be thicker than the loins of the British.[198]

Taken together, the Presbyterian sermons of 1779 suggest that the political outlook of most Volunteers in Ulster remained conventionally Whiggish. France, Spain, popery, arbitrary government, standing armies and the enfeebling effects of luxury were excoriated; while Protestantism, the British constitution, patriotic citizen-soldiers and the heroism of earlier generations of Britons were extolled. Various comments scattered through the sermons suggest that a substantial body of Volunteer opinion wished to terminate the American war and indicate that a small minority of Ulster patriots had begun to contemplate the possibility of a French alliance and the severing of links with Britain.

The sudden upsurge in the popularity of Volunteering, the opening of a new session of parliament, a unanimous resolution of the Commons in favour of 'free trade', and a patriot-organised campaign for a short money bill of six months' duration, all helped to raise the political temperature by November 1779. It is notable that several addresses either 'instructing' or urging members of parliament to vote against any money bill of longer duration than six months were adopted in Ulster – in marked contrast with the caution that prevailed in the northern province when non-importation resolutions were under discussion only six months previously. The county of Down and the borough of Belfast, both of which had refused to commit themselves on the earlier occasion, now sent strongly worded instructions to their members, with the former attracting 1,633 signatures. The address of the 'sovereign, burgesses, and other principal inhabitants' of Belfast declared:

That nothing can relieve us from impending ruin but the enjoyment of a free and unrestrained trade; – a right to which we are entitled by the laws of nature, by the principles of our constitution, and by the interest which the empire at large must ever have in our strength and happiness.[199]

[197] *Ibid.*, p. 3.   [198] *Ibid.*, p. 4.
[199] *BNL*, 16 November 1779. For County Down, see *DEP*, 25 November 1779.

Similar instructions were adopted by meetings of freeholders in the Ulster counties of Cavan, Armagh, Tyrone and Antrim, as well as in Derry city and the boroughs of Carrickfergus and Downpatrick.[200] It is difficult to avoid the conclusion that the popular mood had altered considerably in the space of six months.

The publication, probably in October, of an extraordinary tract entitled *Letters of Owen Roe O'Nial* by Joseph Pollock, a Presbyterian lawyer from Newry, County Down, establishes that separatist sentiment was not confined to Belfast and provides the first clear articulation of the pro-independence viewpoint described in the *Irish Spy* and attacked by James Crombie.[201] The title of the pamphlet – a reference to the commander of the Ulster Catholic army in the 1640s – would itself have been remarkable enough, but the ideas contained in the work were unprecedented. The pamphlet was nothing less than an open appeal for the establishment of Ireland as an independent state with the support and protection of France. The Americans, Pollock explained, had spurned the proposals of the Carlisle peace commission because they 'had procured *friends*, and they preferred them to *masters*'.[202] He then posed the following question: 'Will they [the French] *choose* to visit us as enemies, or as friends? For visit us they probably will. – Will they attempt a conquest to which they are probably unequal; or will they choose the easier road, and offer an *alliance* . . . ?'[203] Pollock had no doubts about the answer. The aim of the French was to weaken Britain and, as a means to that end, they would be happy to assist Ireland in achieving 'emancipation from the authority of an usurping English parliament' just as they were already doing in the case of the American colonies. Anticipating the objection that Ireland's proximity to Britain made it impossible for her to imitate the example of the colonies, he argued that 'The Atlantic rolls not between us and England; but neither does it roll between us and *her* enemies. These enemies are on the way. Before the wind changes they are here.'[204] If Pollock's attitude towards France differed completely from that of the Presbyterian ministers who were quoted above, the same can be said of his attitude towards the Catholic population. Unity among the people of Ireland was, he argued, an essential precondition for independence. Unless the people could 'entertain for each other a mutual and general confidence' and 'lay aside all rancour of prejudice on account of distinctions either political or religious' the attempt to secure independence would merely lead to chaos

---

[200] *DEP*, 30 October, 13, 25 and 30 November 1779; *FDJ*, 16 November 1779; *BNL*, 26 November 1779.

[201] [Joseph Pollock], *Letters of Owen Roe O'Nial* (n.p., 1779). Pollock quotes (p. 25) a letter of Arthur O'Leary's which was published in late August and serialisation of the *Letters*, which had previously appeared as a pamphlet, begun in the *Freeman's Journal* of 6 November 1779.

[202] *Ibid.*, p. 19.   [203] *Ibid.*, p. 21.   [204] *Ibid.*, p. 22.

and confusion.[205] Religious toleration would be essential in an independent Ireland, and Pollock pointed to Switzerland, the United Provinces and Pennsylvania as examples of states where such toleration had already been put into practice – noting that in Switzerland 'the greater number of the Roman Catholic cantons are democratical, that of the Protestant cantons aristocratical in their government'. Ireland's putative allies, the French, were themselves 'in religion, as liberal a nation as any in Europe'.[206] He did not, however, envisage complete equality for the Catholic population from the start; instead, the changes made in their favour would be 'gentle, gradual, and rather the effect of an insensible alteration of opinion and removal of prejudice, than an act of force or power in the state'.[207] The Volunteers were identified as the force which, with French assistance, would throw off the British yoke. They were men 'who may yet teach England that the soil of their own country benumbs not their courage; that it is not on the plains of Flanders or America alone that Irishmen can conquer!' – the reference to Flanders was almost certainly an allusion to the part played by Irish regiments in the French service at the battle of Fontenoy.[208] The American inspiration for Pollock's separatist ideas is evident in several passages, but the following is perhaps the most explicit: 'the sun of England, in whose meridian beams our feebler light was lost, is now set, – perhaps for ever: and the Hesperian star of America, which set with England, for a time, is now risen, a Lucifer to light us into day. It has moved, 'till it is vertical in glory, and points to our political salvation!'[209] In his conclusion, Pollock dismissed the idea of a legislative union with Britain as a means of securing free trade; Britain would still discriminate against Ireland because even such a union 'could not make her feel for Ireland as she does for her own most insignificant village'.[210] Its hostility towards Britain, enthusiasm for America, goodwill towards Catholics, and – most surprising of all – its welcome for the prospect of a French invasion, sets the *Letters of Owen Roe O'Nial* apart from all previous patriot polemics. One is tempted to dismiss it as the production of an unrepresentative ideologue, but Pollock's subsequent prominence in the Volunteer movement leaves little doubt that his views, while certainly not typical of the majority of the Presbyterian community, none the less came to be shared by a radical minority of his coreligionists.

The loyalist reaction

The groundswell of support in the political nation for the free-trade campaign is evident from the resolutions of the county grand juries – at least

---

[205] *Ibid.*, p. 24.   [206] *Ibid.*, pp. 24–5.   [207] *Ibid.*, pp. 26–7.   [208] *Ibid.*, p. 28.
[209] *Ibid.*, p. 29.   [210] *Ibid.*, p. 36.

fifteen of which adopted non-importation resolutions[211] – but it did not prevent the expression of more conservative opinions by those who were shocked and alarmed by the sudden appearance of an articulate separatist constituency. A sense of outrage and betrayal is palpable in the claim of one anonymous pamphleteer that Britain had 'spent her treasure, and her blood more than once to prevent the bloody banners of Rome from flying triumphant in this kingdom, in return for which, in the time of her greatest need, we associate with her natural foes, the avowed enemies of our religion'.[212] To create difficulties for Britain at the present critical moment would not only be dishonourable, it would also damage Ireland's own longer-term interests, 'for should you by your dissensions, so far humble your parent state as to oblige her to grant independence to America, she will then have nothing [by way of trade] left to grant worthy your acceptance' – a view which presumed that commercial concessions would continue to be dispensed by the grace and favour of the British parliament and that such concessions would be less generous if Britain found itself in straitened circumstances.[213] The growth of separatist sentiment is evident from the fact that the same author felt obliged to attack the 'absurd' and 'ridiculous' notion of an independent Ireland, and its inspiration is equally apparent from the nature of his attack. Carefully distinguishing between the circumstances of America and Ireland, he argued that the former was 'a vast (I had almost said a boundless) continental empire' while 'we are shut up in the limits of a small island'.[214] Ireland, because of its geographic position, must inevitably be either a British or a French dependency. In the latter event, 'Though we should not be slaves in appearance, we must actually be so in reality, and could enjoy our freedom on no better tenure than the *durante bene placeto* of the French king.'[215] A second loyalist pamphlet accused the patriot opposition of using what the author accepted was a 'plausible popular call, for an association to wear our own manufactures' in order to 'spread disaffection through the nation, imitate the American non-importation agreement, and in the end like them, accept of freedom from the house of Bourbon'.[216] This pamphlet too conveys the sense of astonishment felt by its anonymous author at the abrupt change in the outlook of some members of the extra-parliamentary opposition. It was, he wrote, 'really amazing to hear, with what seeming sincerity, ease, and unconcern, they talk over those plans of their future grandeur, which a few months ago,

---

[211] O'Connell, *Irish Politics and Social Conflict*, p. 135.
[212] 'A Grazier', *Thoughts on the Present Alarming Crisis of Affairs: Humbly Submitted to the Serious Consideration of the People of Ireland* (Dublin, 1779), pp. 12–13.
[213] *Ibid.*, p. 9.   [214] *Ibid.*, pp. 13–14.   [215] *Ibid.*, p. 16.
[216] *A Defence of Great Britain, against a Charge of Tyranny in the Government of Ireland, by an Irishman* (Dublin, 1779), p. 5.

the hardiest of them would have startled at'.[217] In an aside, this writer attributed the American rebellion to 'republican sects, who had a long and deep-rooted malignance to kingly government, and the Church of England' and detected similar forces at work in Ireland where 'a spirit of republicanism under the specious name of liberty, has long pervaded every part of our constitution' and fostered opposition to the American war.[218]

Other writers preferred to counter patriot demands by proposing alternative remedies of their own. A pamphlet which first appeared in London and which may have been the work of an English author showed some astuteness and an element of foresight in arguing that Ireland should be allowed to trade on exactly the same terms as Great Britain, a measure which would not only remove all grounds for discontent between the two countries but also ensure that Ireland would fully support the prosecution of the American war in order to maintain 'her own rights and interests in that part of the world'.[219] Such a policy, it was argued, would transform Ireland from an imperial liability into an asset. The author of a pamphlet with the ominous title *Renovation without Violence yet Possible* attempted to reconcile his desire to maintain the unity of the empire with Whig principles by proposing that Ireland, the American colonies, and even the possessions of the East India Company, should all send representatives to 'the great common parliament of the empire, at London', there to 'adjust the quota of supplies to be furnished by each part to the common-fund, the treasury of the empire; whilst every province should retain its own distinct parliament, to regulate its interior police, and the proper means of raising its proportion of the general supply'. A further proviso that all parts of the empire would enjoy full freedom of trade in return for their contribution to the imperial exchequer was designed to win opposition support for a scheme which was so clearly impractical that it appears to have met with general indifference.[220]

This was not the case with an alternative proposal for bridging the gap between Whig principles and the practicalities of governing Ireland as a British dependency. As early as the autumn of 1778 Buckinghamshire advised Lord George Germain that a 'union with England and the opening the ports of Ireland' had been suggested by a number of unnamed persons as the 'only method of parrying the impending evils', but the

---

[217] *Ibid.*, p. 6.   [218] *Ibid.*, p. 7.

[219] *A Comparative View of the Public Burdens of Great Britain and Ireland. With a Proposal for Putting both Islands on an Equality, in Regard to the Freedom of Foreign Trade* (London printed and Dublin reprinted, 1779), p. 41.

[220] *Renovation without Violence yet Possible* (Dublin, 1779), p. 10.

lord lieutenant had thought it wiser 'not to risk any opinion upon so nice a subject'.[221] By the spring of 1779 similar reports were appearing in the press. In April, *Finn's Leinster Journal* told its readers that 'it is absolutely resolved on, as the only method to prevent what they [the ministry] term the growing obstinacy of this kingdom, to make a bold push for a union'.[222] The next issue of the same paper carried letters from London and Dublin which respectively confirmed and denied the report – it may not be coincidental that the project was favoured by British ministers and viewed with extreme caution by Buckinghamshire.[223] A union between Britain and Ireland was a solution that met the demand of patriots for full constitutional equality with the inhabitants of Britain and it would once have been greeted with general enthusiasm by the Anglo-Irish population, but attitudes had evolved since the 1740s. The author of the anonymous pamphlet attributed to both Grattan and Flood noted that the position of England in the world had completely altered since the Anglo-Scottish union of 1707, pointing out that while England 'gave to Scotland her colonies – she would give to you her debts'.[224] Worse than that, Ireland's nominal representatives at Westminster would lack either the knowledge or the incentive to represent their constituents' interests: 'we should have a few individuals, insignificant in England, engrossing the powers of Ireland, jobbing away her interest, never residing with her people, and of course, ignorant of her condition, and unawed by her resentment'.[225] These objections were largely practical and might have been overcome by improvements in communication and transport, but arguments of a more subjective nature were invoked by Sir James Caldwell in the introduction to a pamphlet which aimed to prove that existing restraints on Irish trade were damaging the economy of Great Britain itself:

all ranks of people, and in particular the parliament, are so very jealous of their own importance, of the liberty of disposing of their own money, and of an independent and separate constitution, that they would rise in one body, with the greatest vigour, to oppose any measure that would for ever deprive them of these advantages which they consider as the supreme blessing of life.[226]

---

[221] Buckinghamshire to Germain, 23 August 1778, in HMC Stopford-Sackville Mss., I (1904), pp. 251–2.

[222] *FLJ*, 17 April 1779.

[223] For the reports, see *FLJ*, 21 April 1779. For the differing approaches of the British and Irish administrations, see James Kelly, 'The origins of the act of union: an examination of unionist opinion in Britain and Ireland, 1650–1800', *IHS* 25 (1987), 251–2.

[224] *A Letter to the People of Ireland*, p. 63.   [225] *Ibid.*, p. 65.

[226] Sir James Caldwell, *An Enquiry how far the Restrictions Laid upon the Trade of Ireland, by British Acts of Parliament, are a Benefit or a Disadvantage to the British Dominions in General, and to England in Particular* (Dublin, 1779), p. x.

These views represented the spirit of the moment, but support for a union – or a less than whole-hearted opposition to the idea – was also evident in some quarters. Even 'Guatimozin', whose separatist tendencies were noted above, had mixed feelings on the question and excluded the option for reasons of pragmatism rather than principle:

As to an union now with England, I confess I am doubtful of its expediency. Time was that it would have been a glorious proposition to Ireland – but to unite ourselves to the vices and the decay of England, when her prosperity has taken flight with her virtues, is an experiment of which no man can promise good consequences.[227]

Similarly, when the Trinity College Historical Society debated the question 'Whether an union with Great Britain would be of advantage to Ireland' in January 1779, the question was negatived by the narrow margin of eight votes to six.[228] Rumours of an imminent union were revived in October 1779 as a new session of the Irish parliament opened. Reports in the press informed the public that the 'favourite measure [of government] in respect to the fate of this kingdom, is most certainly a union'.[229] The response to the prospect was not uniformly hostile. Having referred to reports from London that 'this kingdom will be united for ever to the fate of Great Britain', a Dublin correspondent of *Finn's Leinster Journal* commented that he would 'at present forbear making any restrictions on this important project'.[230] The fine line separating support for, and opposition to, the principle of a union in the minds of some is nowhere more apparent than in a pamphlet entitled *The First Lines of Ireland's Interest* which was published in early November. The anonymous author was described as 'a very respectable and truly patriotic writer' in one newspaper[231] and he took a broadly patriotic stance – opposing the war in America and condemning the British parliament's 'usurped claim of binding the people and kingdom of Ireland' – before concluding that 'the sooner this union takes place, it will be so much the better for both countries'.[232] But if the author was hostile to the new separatist ideas he was also far from being a committed advocate of a union. While he denounced those 'enthusiasts in politics' who were prepared to wade 'through currents of blood, to an independence, which, in the end, can yield no greater advantages, than a union', he also conceded that 'If we can get a free trade, without paying a fine, it would, perhaps, be better for us to continue as we are.'[233]

[227] [Jebb], *The Letters of Guatimozin*, p. 56.
[228] Historical Society minutes, 6 January 1779, TCD Mun. Soc./Hist. 3, pp. 297–8.
[229] *FLJ*, 9 October 1779.   [230] *Ibid.*, 30 October 1779.
[231] *Magee's Weekly Packet*, 18 December 1779.
[232] *The First Lines of Ireland's Interest in the Year One Thousand Seven Hundred and Eighty* (Dublin, 1779), pp. 6 and 56 respectively.
[233] *Ibid.*, pp. 56–7.

The free-trade crisis

The campaign for free trade had been sustained by the widespread observance of non-importation resolutions and it entered its final critical phase with the start of a new session of parliament in October 1779. Lord Buckinghamshire was able to provide an accurate prediction of events to Lord George Germain two weeks before the session opened: 'The desire of unlimited commerce will be the unanimous language of this House of Commons. The few moderate men will either be awed by national clamour into silence or their voice will be lost amidst the general cry.'[234] On the first day of the session Henry Grattan moved an amendment to the address to the throne which advised George III that 'the only means left to support the expiring trade of this miserable part of your Majesty's dominions, is to open a free trade and let your Irish subjects enjoy their natural birthright'. Some patriot speakers raised wider constitutional issues. Samuel Bradstreet rejected the British parliament's 'authority and right of interference in the affairs of this kingdom' while Sir Edward Newenham took this argument to its logical conclusion by questioning the need for Grattan's amendment: 'we are an independent nation: we have a separate and distinct parliament, and separate courts of judicature, – why then should we solicit favour from another country?' A close associate of Grattan's, John Forbes, went some way towards endorsing separatist ideas by arguing that since 'every wind wafts the disagreeable intelligence of some loppage from the empire, it is time for us to look to ourselves, and avoid being swallowed in the same ruin'.[235] The defection of two office-holders – the prime sergeant, Walter Hussey Burgh, and the vice-treasurer, Henry Flood, both of whom had once been prominent members of the opposition – precipitated a general loss of nerve on the government benches, and an amended resolution calling for 'a free and unlimited trade' was carried unanimously.

The address to the throne was a serious embarrassment but not a critical defeat for government and a non-committal answer was returned in due course; however, extra-parliamentary pressure continued to mount. On 8 October, four days before the opening of the parliamentary session, a meeting of the freeholders of County Galway adopted an address to the county's members of parliament which 'strongly recommended' that they should refuse to vote for a money bill of longer than six months' duration until a free trade was granted. The address was said to have been signed by more than 700 freeholders but it was far from being a spontaneous

---

[234] Buckinghamshire to Germain, 30 September 1779, in HMC Stopford-Sackville Mss., I (1904), p. 258.
[235] Report of the debate of 12 October 1779, in *HM*, January 1780, 44–5.

initiative. Evidence emerged a year later that the address had been organised by Denis Daly, who was anxious to appear to be acting under pressure from his constituents.[236] Lord Charlemont, likewise, arranged for the freeholders of County Armagh to 'instruct' their representatives.[237] On 22 October the aggregate body of the freeholders and citizens of Dublin city adopted comparable instructions on the proposal of James Napper Tandy.[238] On the same day, a similar resolution was adopted by the 'sovereign, burgesses, and other principal inhabitants of Belfast'.[239] Within weeks, resolutions variously 'instructing' and 'recommending' members of parliament to support a short money bill had been adopted by some twenty counties, with Ulster well to the fore.[240] Orchestrated though the campaign to exert pressure on members undoubtedly was, it could not have been so successful had it not reflected a sense of anger and frustration at British inaction that was widely shared by the members of the political nation. Indeed, the addresses appear to have been welcomed even by some office-holders, who were thus able to cite pressure from their constituents in mitigation of their failure to support government on the issue.[241] The necessity for a short money bill was also urged from the pulpit of the established church in a published sermon preached before the goldsmiths' corps of Volunteers in Dublin, with the Rev. Samuel Butler condemning those 'drones' who lacked the civic virtue to join the Volunteers and enthusiastically endorsing the non-importation movement.[242]

With the support of even the established clergy in doubt, pressure on government was further increased on 4 November when the Volunteer corps of Dublin assembled and paraded to mark the anniversary of William III's birth. As they discharged a *feu de joie* around the statue of King William in College Green, immediately outside the doors of parliament, a placard bearing the legend 'A short money bill – A free trade – Or else!!!' was affixed to its pedestal.[243] The thinly veiled threat must have been readily intelligible but the *Dublin Evening Post* spelt out its implications:

---

[236] For the address see *DEP*, 12 October 1779, where it was published with sixty-eight signatures and a statement that it was signed 'by the above, and seven hundred and thirty-one other freeholders'. The background to the address was revealed in a letter published in the same paper on 8 April 1780.
[237] Samuel Maxwell to Charlemont, 30 October 1779, in HMC Charlemont Mss., 12th report, appendix X, p. 364.
[238] *DEP*, 23 October 1779.   [239] *BNL*, 16 November 1779.
[240] O'Connell, *Irish Politics and Social Conflict*, p. 178.
[241] A.P.W. Malcomson, *John Foster: The Politics of Anglo-Irish Ascendancy* (Oxford, 1978), pp. 226–7.
[242] Rev. Samuel Butler, *A Sermon Preached in the Parish Church of St Michan, Dublin, on Sunday the 17th Day of October, 1779* (Dublin, 1779), p. 13.
[243] *HM*, November 1779, 654–5.

The slighting of one petition, in an hour of insolence, plunged us into the horrors of war with those who ought to have been heard and protected in their freedom and properties. – The words which appeared on the pedestal of King William's statue, spoke the most intelligible language; they were suitable hieroglyphics, for a year, big with the fate of Ireland![244]

The allusion to the American 'olive branch' petition of 1775 was unmistakable, as was the message that similar ministerial 'insolence' on this occasion would plunge Britain into war with another of its dependencies. By this stage, emotions were running so high and the progress of events had acquired such momentum that the possibility of a clash between the Volunteers and the regular army – an event which would have been inconceivable only a short time before – could no longer be discounted. Already confronted with commercial and parliamentary opposition, and now with the threat of armed rebellion to be considered, the ministry was challenged on yet another front when James Horan, a Dublin alderman and merchant, announced his intention of exporting woollen goods to Rotterdam in violation of the prohibition placed on such exports by British legislation. Although prominent members of the parliamentary opposition intervened to persuade Horan to defer taking this step, it was clear that government had only been granted a stay of execution. An alarmed John Beresford informed an English correspondent that no jury in Ireland would be willing to uphold the English act and that, whatever the legal position might be, existing restrictions on Irish trade were unenforceable in practice: 'In case that they do not get an export of woollen goods', he wrote, 'the consequence will be, that they will recover damages, they will export, and no officers will be able to prevent it.'[245]

The Catholic masses and free trade

An eye-witness account of the Volunteers' parade in College Green, Dublin, on 4 November leaves no doubt that the demand for free trade enjoyed the support of the population as a whole. The fourth of November was the birthday of William III and the day's celebrations would normally have been shunned by Catholics but they made an exception in 1779:

The respect and veneration which appeared in the mob on this occasion were conspicuous. They yielded with unusual temperance and condescension to every arrangement, a smile of congenial affection appeared on the countenance of the

---

[244] *DEP*, 6 November 1779.
[245] Beresford to Robinson, 22 November 1779, in Beresford (ed.), *The Correspondence of the Right Hon. John Beresford*, I, pp. 86–7.

people . . . In the evening, a thing never done on the 4th of November, the whole city was illuminated; and it was observable that all distinction of religion and prejudice were suspended. The antient Jacobite, who found heretofore in William's partiality towards England with regard to this country, a patriotic mask for his political antipathy, was content to yield to the occasion, comforting himself that the king, upon this day, was made to recant.[246]

The enthusiasm shown by the 'ancient Jacobites' of Dublin for a Volunteer movement which, though Protestant in composition and Williamite in sympathy, had begun to champion Irish economic interests, was not extended to the members of the army who paraded on the same day, as the author of the above account noted with regret:

Happy should we be if we were able to close the scene without censure; but candour must confess that the rude disapprobation shown by the people to the procession of the garrison, after that of the Volunteers was over, did not correspond with other transactions of the day. The unfortunate soldiery are not blamable for the faults of administration.[247]

Another newspaper referred approvingly to 'those generous elevated ideas of our country's rights, which at present happily seem to animate all degrees and denominations among us' – a consensus which was both welcome and novel.[248]

On the day of the Volunteers' display in Dublin the *Freeman's Journal* printed a letter signed by 'A Revolutionist, but no Williamite' which criticised the commemoration of King William in view of that monarch's 'manifest partiality for England' in agreeing to prohibit the export of Irish woollen goods. The editor justified the arrangements on the grounds that they 'might be more properly supposed to be in honour of the Volunteers, to whom we owe every constitutional compliment, than to the memory of King William, whose partiality has undone this country'.[249] Catholics were thus reassured that they could safely support the Volunteers and the demand for a free trade without betraying their political principles. This was not an isolated instance. Two days later the same paper began to republish 'by particular desire' the letters of 'Owen Roe O'Nial' – one of the historical personages whose memory was most esteemed by the Catholic masses.[250] Only one other figure from Irish history enjoyed a comparable place in popular affection: namely, Patrick Sarsfield, Jacobite hero of the

---

[246] *LJ*, 12 November 1779.   [247] *Ibid.*   [248] *FLJ*, 10 November 1779.
[249] *FJ*, 4 November 1779.
[250] *Ibid.*, 6 November 1779. For Eoghan Rua Ó Néill see Cecile O'Rahilly (ed.), *Five Seventeenth-Century Political Poems* (Dublin, 1952), pp. 23–7; Ó Muirgheasa (ed.), *Céad de Cheoltaibh Uladh*, pp. 17–24; Seosamh Mag Uidhir (ed.), *Pádraig Mac a Liondain: Dánta* (Dublin, 1977), p. 5; Ó Fiaich (ed.), *Art Mac Cumhaigh*, p. 81; Ciarán Ó Coigligh (ed.), *Raiftearaí: Amhráin agus Dánta* (Dublin, 1987), p. 147.

siege of Limerick.[251] Within days, a letter appeared in the press urging every county to let its members of parliament know that 'the Irish nation expects one glorious and unanimous effort from those who represent them, to rescue a suffering people from the hands of despots' and the author's pseudonym on this occasion was 'Sarsfield'.[252] Not only were the historical heroes of the masses mobilised in support of the demand for free trade but the popular Jacobite air '*Síle Ní Ghadhra*' was also commandeered for use in the patriot cause. The language used in the latest version was English rather than Irish but the message was almost as militant as that of earlier compositions:

> And now, my brave boys, is the crisis of fate;
> if we miss this good time we shall ever be late.
> our cries and petitions will ever hereafter
> be only the subjects of jibes and of laughter.
> The Manchester chaps will put spokes in your wheels,
> and Scottish complaints follow close at their heels.
> Hibernians their best blood should cheerfully spill,
> before they are duped by a long money bill.[253]

Some weeks later a patriot correspondent who signed himself 'Hibernicus' warned against the threat of a union under which Irish members at Westminster, isolated from their constituents, would form 'as the Scots members do at present, part of the prime-minister's phalanx'. He added a plea for national unity which illustrates the rapid evolution that had taken place in the thinking of some patriots during the short period since the passage of Gardiner's relief act: 'Let not the enemies of Ireland sow dissension amongst us by talking of Protestant or popish interest, as if they were distinct, when it is clear that they are the same. We are all embarked in one and the same bottom, and must sink or swim together.'[254]

The Dublin mob was not content to play the part of passive spectators, relegated to the role of applauding the efforts of their social superiors in parliament and the various Volunteer corps. Instead, the populace acted directly, both to prevent the importation of British goods and to pressure members of parliament to vote for a short money bill. On the night of 1 November, for example, a 'well armed' crowd attacked a shop and,

---

[251] For Patrick Sarsfield see Mícheál Ó Máille and Tomás Ó Máille (eds.), *Amhráin Chlainne Gaedheal* (Dublin, 1905), p. 94; J.C. MacErlean (ed.), *Duanaire Dháibhidh Uí Bhruadair*, III (London, 1917), pp. 142–56; Breandán Ó Buachalla (ed.), *Nua-Dhuanaire*, II (Dublin, 1976), p. 4; Tomás Ó Concheanainn (ed.), *Nua-Dhuanaire*, III (Dublin, 1981), pp. 2–3 and 84; Ó Coigligh (ed.), *Raiftearaí*, p. 148.
[252] *FLJ*, 10 November 1779.
[253] A song to the tune of 'Sheelah na Girah' in *Magee's Weekly Packet*, 13 November 1779.
[254] *Magee's Weekly Packet*, 18 December 1779.

having broken the windows and damaged the stock, they dispersed with shouts of 'a free trade or death, and confusion to all importers'.[255] The most spectacular intervention happened on 15 November 1779 when, in an action reminiscent of the eruptions of December 1759, February 1771 and February 1778, a large and unruly crowd assembled outside parliament. The lord lieutenant reported to Whitehall that:

> a drum was beat throughout that part of this city which is called the Liberties which is inhabited by great numbers of the lower classes of the people, viz. weavers, dyers, tanners, skinners and such like who thereupon gathered in a very large body, many of them armed with bludgeons, cutlasses and pistols... as the members came thither they made them get out of their chairs and coaches, and administered an oath to them to vote for the good of Ireland, for a free trade and a short money bill.[256]

The *Hibernian Magazine* estimated the number of those involved at 'about eight thousand working manufacturers, mostly armed with swords and pistols' and noted that a serious clash with the military was only narrowly averted:

> a party of Highlanders came to disperse the mob, but the latter remaining resolutely determined to keep their ground, the lord mayor perceiving that any forcible attempts to disperse them must be attended with fatal consequences, very prudently discharged the military, and mildly addressing the populace, remonstrated on the impropriety of their proceedings, and enjoined them to depart peaceably, as a more effectual mode to attain the end universally wished for. Several patriotic members of parliament, and other gentlemen, harangued them to the same effect, upon which they dispersed quietly.[257]

The high level of politicisation of the populace is apparent from a handbill distributed by the lawyers' corps of Volunteers on the same evening. It advised the crowd that a short money bill was likely to be voted but that 'nothing is so likely to prevent the success of it as your assembling again about the parliament house as you did this day'.[258] A badly shaken John Scott, the attorney general and one of those principally targeted for abuse by the mob, sent an understandably alarmist account of the situation to an English correspondent in which he laid particular emphasis on the disaffection of the Catholic population: 'here is a people mixed with republicans, French and American emissaries, most of them of the religion of France, and the principles of America'.[259] On the following Sunday, 21 November, a pastoral letter was read at every Mass in the

[255] *Ibid.*, 6 November 1779.
[256] Buckinghamshire to Weymouth, 15 November 1779, PRO SP 63/467, fo. 106.
[257] *HM*, November 1779, 655.   [258] *SNL*, 16 November 1779.
[259] Scott to Robinson, 21 November 1779, in Beresford (ed.), *The Correspondence of the Right Hon. John Beresford*, I, p. 82.

city exhorting congregations 'to avoid mixing with any tumultuous or riotous meetings, which cannot but be highly offensive to magistracy and government'.[260] But attacks on importers continued despite this clerical intervention. On 22 November the premises of a woollen-draper were broken open 'by a numerous mob, armed with swords and pistols, who, under pretence of his goods being English, took and carried away every article [of] linen and woollen goods out of his shop'; while on 10 December 'a riotous mob attacked the house of Messrs Nicholson and Kerr, linen-drapers, in St Andrew's-street, under pretence (as is supposed) of their having English goods'.[261]

The popular support shown for the Volunteers in Dublin on 4 November was not confined to the capital. As the demands of Anglo-Irish patriots became more radical and their rhetoric more populist and anti-British in tone it became increasingly easy for plebeian Catholics, accustomed as they were to Jacobite propaganda in which the oppression of Ireland by England formed a central theme, to give their support to the opposition. In a novel development, prominent members of the parliamentary opposition were lauded in vernacular verse. Tomás Ó Míocháin, the County Clare poet who had previously celebrated the British evacuation of Boston and vilified Arthur O'Leary for his pro-British stance at the time of the invasion scare, now composed another song in praise of the Volunteers and of Henry Grattan, Walter Hussey Burgh and Barry Yelverton. The song was written, as Ó Míocháin put it, 'ar bhfuascailt na nÉireannach ó dhaorchuing na Sacsan le saorarm gáirmhianach na Banban, dá ngoirtear Volunteers' – that is, 'on the liberation of the Irish from England's oppressive yoke by the glory-seeking free army of Ireland, called Volunteers'. Opposition leaders were extolled in extravagant terms:

> Ar Ghrattan ba náir gan trácht go taitneamhach,
> cáidhfhear ceanamhail, cáilmhear, ceannasach,
>   seol scóip is trealamh gan tím;
> is ba dheacair dá bhfágfainn bláth-Bhurgh beachtaithe,
> ráib le'r tagaradh cás na Banba,
>   i nglór beoil ba bheannaithe binn.
> Ligeam 'na ndiaidh go dian gan dearmad
> Yelverton fial ag fiach na bhfealladh-chon,
> sciath gheal-tseasamhach, íodhan acmhainneach,
> rialach, rabairneach, triathach, teanga-chlis,
>   lann óir is luiseag na nGaoidheal.[262]

---

[260] *FLJ*, 24 November 1779.
[261] *Ibid.*, 27 November 1779 and *HM*, December 1779, 710.
[262] 'A ghasra ghrámhar, gháireach, ghreannmhar' in RIA Ms. 23 H 39, p. 13; edited in Ó Muirithe (ed.), *Tomás Ó Míocháin*.

(Grattan it would be shameful not to mention with affection, an excellent ami-
able man, reputable and commanding, a spirited well-equipped guide without
timidity; and harsh would it be were I to omit polished and precise Burgh, a
champion by whom Ireland's case was asserted, in diction that was blessed and
sweet. Let us admit quickly after them without fail, generous Yelverton hunting the treacherous dogs, a bright and steadfast shield, a sturdy spear, regular,
unstinting, lordly, quick-tongued, the golden blade and the knife-point of the
Gaels.)

Such extravagant and novel praise for members of a Hanoverian parliament by a Jacobite writer represented a frank recognition of the equally
unrestrained and unprecedented nature of the rhetoric employed by opposition leaders during the critical month of November 1779 when the
short money bill and the demand for free trade were in agitation. Grattan
had explicitly appealed 'out of doors' when, speaking in support of a
short money bill, he declared that 'our constituents looked for other measures, and it was dangerous, at this time, to exasperate the people'.[263]
Hussey Burgh made the most memorable contribution of all to the same
debate when he observed that 'the English sowed their laws like ser-
pents' teeth, and they sprung up in armed men'; a contemporary report
states that the House 'broke out in a burst of applause, which was echoed
by the gallery'.[264] It is not too fanciful to hear in Ó Míocháin's song a
more distant echo of the same burst of applause. Barry Yelverton distinguished himself by his defence of the mob that surrounded parliament on
15 November when the matter was debated the following day. The House
of Commons, he declared, should not 'interpose on every occasion where
the people expressed their resentment against any person they might
suppose an enemy to their interests in parliament'. John Scott, the effective leader of government business, had been the principal target of
the mob's fury and was incensed at Yelverton's justification of their conduct, branding him 'the seneschal of sedition' – a description that can
only have enhanced his reputation with the Catholic masses.[265] The tone
of the present composition is strikingly different from that of the songs
by Ó Míocháin noted previously but in all cases the underlying principles are those that animate Irish political verse of the period generally: a
desire for the overthrow of British power in Ireland and the restoration
of the Catholic nation to the rights of which it had been stripped by the
Williamite Revolution.

---

[263] Debate of 23 November 1779, quoted in *HM*, June 1780, 333.
[264] Debate of 25 November 1779, quoted in *ibid.*, August 1780, 452.
[265] Debate of 16 November 1779, quoted in *ibid.*, April 1780, 223–4.

The political nation placated

The various pressures for removal of the restrictions on Irish trade that have already been described would probably have overcome the resistance of British ministers before much longer in any event, but the free-trade campaign reached a symbolic climax on 24 November, when Grattan's motion against granting new taxes was carried in the Commons by a landslide vote of 170 votes to 47, with committed patriots being joined, not only by independents such as Luke Gardiner, but also by many normally loyal supporters of government who were overawed by the unanimity which prevailed on the question among almost all sections of Irish opinion. The contribution made by American events to the alienation of the political nation is apparent from some of the contributions. Sir John Parnell, who sat for the pocket borough of Inistioge and was a habitual supporter of government, bitterly contrasted 'the proceedings of the English towards us' with their conciliation of the Americans 'when disloyalty drew from them what loyalty could not' – an obvious reference to the terms offered by the Carlisle peace commission – and urged his fellow members of parliament to 'negotiate with the English, as friends upon an equal footing, and not as dependants; not under the name of a despicable union, but with the union and dignity consistent with our separate legislature'.[266] The policy of refusing concessions could not be maintained for long when even the friends of government were speaking in such terms, and Buckinghamshire advised Lord Hillsborough, recently appointed secretary of state and a major landowner in County Down, that 'an effectual extension of trade is essential to restore tranquillity and relieve the distresses of this kingdom'.[267] General Irwin, the commander-in-chief, informed Lord George Germain that he had approved the short money bills in his capacity as a privy counsellor 'because I am of opinion that should they be rejected there will be a rebellion in this country', adding that it was 'not possible to conceive a parliament more under the subjection of the people than this is'.[268] In such circumstances, and given the weakness of Britain's international position, major concessions to Irish opinion could no longer be avoided. On 9 December Lord North bowed to the inevitable and proposed resolutions in the British House of Commons to permit the export of Irish glass and woollens, and to give Ireland full access to the colonial trade, provided duties equal to those in force in Britain were imposed by the Irish parliament.

---

[266] Debate of 23 November 1779, in *ibid.*, June 1780, 333.
[267] Buckinghamshire to Hillsborough, 9 December 1779, in PRO SP 63/467, fo. 216.
[268] Irwin to Germain, 8 December 1779, in HMC Stopford-Sackville Mss., I (1904), p. 263.

The success of the new policy was soon apparent. As early as 13 December Thomas Waite, the under-secretary at Dublin Castle, informed Lord George Germain that news of the trade concessions had 'spread a general joy through the city'.[269] A week later, Buckinghamshire advised the same minister that the response of the House of Commons to the measures had 'exceeded my most sanguine expectations, and fully met my wishes'.[270] Thomas Conolly, who represented County Londonderry and normally supported the government, went so far as to declare that the freedom to trade with the British colonies was a 'free gift' and that 'it is now doubly our interest to assist them [the British] in securing the colonies'.[271] The patriot members also vied with one another in the effusiveness of their praise for the trade concessions. This was inspired, in part, by a desire to discourage popular unrest that was showing some signs of running out of control. For Denis Daly, the independent member for County Galway who had engineered the first address for a short money bill, it was now essential 'to declare to the world we are satisfied, not so much to England as to Ireland, to silence those clamours some people seem ready to make use of'.[272] George Ogle echoed this view, stating that it was the duty of the members to express their approval of Lord North's proposals 'in as ample and explicit a manner as possible' since the 'expectations of the people have been raised to a very high degree'.[273] Barry Yelverton, representing the open borough of Carrickfergus and himself one of the most outspoken members during the free-trade crisis, now believed that the 'unanimity of the House on this occasion would quiet the apprehensions of the multitude and disappoint the views of wicked incendiaries'.[274] Grattan discouraged those who may have hoped to continue with extra-parliamentary agitation by pronouncing that Ireland now had its 'constitution restored, or certainly very near a full restoration'.[275] With the claims of the British parliament to legislate for Ireland in mind, Hussey Burgh cautioned against a concern 'with mere points of speculation, with dormant claims that may never be revived'; the remaining constitutional issues would be resolved by the passage of time and, as Ireland grew 'in strength and opulence', the 'chimerical idea of binding us by foreign laws' would be quietly discarded.[276] A resolution stating that free trade would 'give new vigour to the zeal of his Majesty's brave and loyal people of Ireland, to stand forward in support

[269] Thomas Waite to Germain, 13 December 1779, in *ibid.*, p. 263.
[270] Buckinghamshire to Germain, 21 December 1779, in *ibid.*, p. 264.
[271] Debate of 14 December 1779, in *HM*, November 1780, 622.
[272] *Some Authentic Minutes of the Proceedings of a Very Respectable Assembly, on the 20th of December, 1779* (Dublin, 1780), p. 10.
[273] *Ibid.*, p. 11.   [274] *Ibid.*, p. 33.   [275] *Ibid.*, p. 41.   [276] *Ibid.*, p. 46.

of his Majesty's person and government, and the interest, the honour, and the dignity of the British empire' was unanimously adopted by the House of Commons.[277] Outside of parliament, a brief hesitancy on the part of the press when the first reports of Lord North's resolutions were received gave way to enthusiasm as the favourable reaction of the political nation became apparent. The illumination of Limerick city was reported to be so brilliant that it 'brought thousands of the country folks to town, thinking it was on fire'.[278] In Cork city a Volunteer corps unanimously addressed the lord lieutenant and pledged 'every effort to contribute to the safety, honour and prosperity of these free kingdoms'.[279] Volunteer corps also paraded and celebrated in Armagh city and in Banbridge, County Down.[280]

The loyalty of the Catholic élite

The Franco-Spanish invasion attempt of 1779 inspired songs in Irish predicting the imminent liberation of the Gael, but it also produced a very different reaction among Catholics of higher social rank. Government was inundated with addresses of loyalty from all four provinces, beginning in late June with an address from the Catholics of Waterford city and county which was subscribed by about 130 individuals.[281] This was followed in early July by another address signed by 147 persons which expressed the willingness of the Catholics of Wexford town and county 'to risk their lives and fortunes in defence of his Majesty's crown and the safety of this kingdom' – an address presented by the strongly anti-Catholic patriot George Ogle.[282] During August, further addresses followed from the 'Roman Catholics of Ireland' (represented by three peers, three members of the gentry and three merchants)[283] and from 101 Catholics in Kilkenny city – the latter group declaring that 'where the honour and glory of these kingdoms are at stake, we know no distinction of religion, but unite as British subjects in defence of his Majesty's person and government'.[284] In September the Catholics of the town and county of Galway declared themselves to be 'impressed with the warmest sentiments of loyalty, and the most grateful sense of the indulgences we have received, from the benignity of majesty, and the benevolence of an

---

[277] Debate of 20 December 1779, in *HM*, December 1780, 676.
[278] *FLJ*, 29 December 1779 (supplement).
[279] Address dated 26 December 1779, in PRO SP 63/468, fo. 40.
[280] *BNL*, 4 January 1780.   [281] PRO SP 63/465, fo. 178.
[282] *Ibid.*, fo. 363. See also *LJ*, 13 August 1779.   [283] *LJ*, 13 August 1779.
[284] For a covering letter, see Buckinghamshire to Weymouth, 3 August 1779, PRO SP 63/466, fo. 25; for the text of the address, see Brady (ed.), *Catholics and Catholicism*, pp. 201–2.

enlightened age'.[285] In October, 124 of the Catholics of County Roscommon, headed by Dominic O'Conor Don and Charles O'Conor, signed an address which stated that they were 'firmly united... for the defence of his Majesty's person and government'.[286] In November, a loyal address was submitted by the 'Roman Catholic inhabitants of the city and county of Londonderry' which was signed by 'Doctor Philip McDavitt, t[itular] b[ishop] of Derry followed by his clergy, and many hundreds of their respectable hearers', who expressed their willingness to 'boldly stand forth in defence of our king and country, and oppose with all our might any foreign enemy, who shall dare to invade his Majesty's realms'.[287] The bishop of Derry also wrote a pastoral letter which admonished the faithful to 'guard against the illusions, and idle suggestions of designing enemies; who, by engaging you in the pursuit of any measures contrary to the interest of the present government, would only lead you to your ruin'.[288] In this, McDavitt was following the lead given by the archbishop of Dublin in a pastoral letter read to congregations in his archdiocese on 19 September 1779 that exhorted them to 'observe that faithful and loyal line of conduct, which will render you pleasing to government, and worthy of its benign attention towards you'.[289]

Such addresses and letters might easily be dismissed as risk-free and self-serving verbiage designed to ingratiate their authors with the authorities. However, some Catholics were prepared to render practical assistance in the hour of danger. In June, the Anglican bishop of Cork informed the commander in chief that a few Catholics had volunteered and been accepted into the local Volunteer corps when rumours spread that the French fleet had been sighted off Bantry.[290] On 30 July, a body of forty-six Catholics in Drogheda offered their assistance to the local Volunteer corps.[291] During the month of August a number of prominent Catholics in Limerick city opened a subscription to provide an additional bounty for recruits enlisting in the army, 'upon condition of their not being taken out of the kingdom', and more than a hundred persons contributed sums ranging from one to fifty guineas.[292] A similar subscription was established at a meeting of the Catholic gentlemen of County Limerick who, in addition, resolved to encourage recruiting, to make

[285] PRO SP 63/463, fo. 10. About 600 names are appended to the address but, strangely, they are nearly all written in the same hand.
[286] PRO SP 63/467, fo. 5.   [287] Ibid., fo. 161.   [288] LJ, 16 November 1779.
[289] FLJ, 25 September 1779.
[290] Isaac Mann, bishop of Cork, to Lieutenant-General Cunningham, 5 June 1779, PRO SP 63/465, fo. 85.
[291] Brady, Catholics and Catholicism, p. 200.
[292] HJ, 18 August 1779 and Munster Journal, 23 August 1779 (a copy of which is preserved in PRO SP 63/466, following fo. 126).

efforts to capture deserters, and to provide assistance when called upon by government or by 'any of the armed societies in our different baronies'– a reference to the local Volunteer corps.[293]

The loyal disposition shown by prominent members of both the Catholic laity and clergy during the invasion alert of 1779, when a Franco-Spanish landing seemed imminent, was naturally maintained during the course of 1780 when the fortunes of war turned in Britain's favour. In June 1780 hand-bills were distributed in Dublin 'by the direction of the Roman Catholic ecclesiastical superiors' which counselled the population against participation in 'irregular meetings' and urged them to prove themselves 'deserving of the favour of a mild and generous government' – injunctions that were probably inspired by an agitation directed against the heads of an anti-combination bill then before parliament.[294] When news arrived later in June of the British victory at Charleston, the bishop of Limerick ordered a public thanksgiving to God 'for having been pleased to hear their constant prayers, by blessing his Majesty's arms with the late signal success'.[295] In August, Philip McDavitt, bishop of Derry, displayed his own zeal for the war effort when he presented the Strabane battalion of Volunteers with a contribution of £39-16-3 from the clergy of his diocese,[296] a gift welcomed by the *Freeman's Journal* as evidence that the 'apathy and coolness which formerly subsisted between the Protestants and Roman Catholics of this kingdom' were at last giving way to 'the greatest cordiality and strictest friendship'.[297]

It was indeed true that Catholics were being openly enrolled in certain Volunteer corps by 1780, although the practice was itself a source of controversy. When the Sligo Volunteers criticised neighbouring corps for accepting Catholic members they were informed by an anonymous 'Carrick Volunteer' that the 'tide of good sense, moderation, and liberal sentiment is rushing in strongly on the public, and Sligo is too little to resist the torrent'.[298] So far as Catholic involvement in the Volunteers was concerned, this assessment proved to be correct and by 1781 the principal point of controversy was no longer the inclusion of individual Catholics in predominantly Protestant corps, but rather the emergence of largely Catholic units in some localities. A self-styled 'True Blue' who was alarmed by this development recommended the blending of Catholic Volunteers with predominantly Protestant corps as the best solution to the problem. The same author drew his readers' attention to the enormous gulf in political attitudes that divided the Catholic élite, whom he was willing to welcome into the ranks of the Volunteers, from the mass

---

[293] *Ibid.* [294] *FLJ*, 17 June 1780 and *HM*, June 1780, 351.
[295] *DEP*, 1 July 1780 and *HJ*, 3 July 1780. [296] *LJ*, 15 August 1780.
[297] *FJ*, 26 August 1780. [298] *FLJ*, 23 September 1780.

of their coreligionists – those who professed 'that form of religious persuasion which, assisted by idle traditional notions of heritage, &c. necessarily weds the unlettered and unenlightened part of the people (I would not be so disingenuous as to involve the other class in so harsh a charge) to our natural enemies, and supplants the present dominating interest from holding a share in their favour'.[299] This important distinction was frequently drawn. When the students of the Trinity College Historical Society debated 'Whether the Roman Catholics should be admitted into our armed associations?' in May 1780 the question was negatived by nine votes to six, but a year later the same body answered the question 'Whether papists *of property* should enter into Volunteer associations?' in the affirmative by the large margin of fourteen to four.[300] The continuing complaisance of the self-styled Catholic leadership towards the authorities was shown by the humble address presented by the Catholic Committee to Lord Buckinghamshire on his departure from Ireland in December 1780 – an address which did not, however, make any reference to the American war;[301] and by the bishop of Meath's decision to endorse a general fast called by government in February 1781 for the purpose of 'imploring a special blessing on his Majesty's arms both by sea and land'.[302]

The anxiety of the Catholic élite to ensure that no dissonant voices from within their community would reach the ears of those in authority was shown in November 1781 when an advertisement for a newly published pamphlet entitled *The Urgent Necessity of an Immediate Repeal of the Whole Penal Code Candidly Considered* appeared in the press. Unlike earlier productions on the same subject, this work was primarily intended for a Catholic audience and had the declared aim of 'exciting them to a just sense of their civil and religious rights as citizens of a free nation'.[303] The advertisement insinuated that a failure to repeal repressive legislation would inevitably lead to rebellion:

> Beware ye senators! look round in time,
> rebellion is not fixed to any clime.
> In trade, religion, every way oppressed,
> you'll find, too late, such wrongs must be redressed.
> Seize quick the time – for now, consider well,
> whole quarters of the world at once rebel.[304]

[299] *The Volunteer*, IX, 3 July 1781, pp. 33–4.
[300] Minutes of the Historical Society, 10 May 1780 and 6 June 1781, in TCD Mun. Soc./Hist. 3, pp. 492 and 654 respectively. The emphasis is mine.
[301] *HM*, December 1780, 686.
[302] The bishop's pastoral letter on the subject has been published in Brady, *Catholics and Catholicism*, pp. 212–16.
[303] *DEP*, 10 November 1781.   [304] *Ibid*.

The rebellion of Britain's North American colonies was an obvious case in point, but it may not have been the only one in the author's mind as reports of the native rebellion against Spanish rule in Peru led by Tupac Amaru were also appearing in the Irish press at this time.[305] The newspaper advertisement was followed by an even more outspoken hand-bill which opened with the assertion that 'America by a desperate effort has nearly emancipated herself from slavery', and concluded by saying that the creation in Ireland of 'a real, durable peace, unattainable be-tween tyrants and slaves' was the sole object of the author.[306] The pam-phlet was the production of Matthew Carey, the young son of a Dublin baker, and the prospect of its publication so alarmed the members of the Catholic Committee that a meeting was held on the day after the advertisement appeared in the press at which a resolution expressing 'detestation and abhorrence of the disloyal and seditious tendency' of the advertisements was adopted. The resolution was signed by more than fifty of the capital's leading Catholics headed by Lords Fingal and Kenmare.[307] A sub-committee was establish at a subsequent meeting to investigate the possibility of prosecuting Carey. This vigorous and prompt intervention succeeded in preventing the publication of a work that might have seriously tarnished the image of loyalty projected by the élite mem-bership of the Catholic Committee.[308] Carey's failure to publish a pam-phlet which, however outspoken or abrasive his language may have been, was none the less advocating reform rather than revolution, underlines the importance of vernacular song as an uncensored source of information on the outlook of the Catholic masses.

The political nation divided

If the spring assizes of 1779 were notable for the adoption of non-importation resolutions, those of 1780 were marked by the adoption of 'humble addresses' expressing gratitude for George III's 'paternal care in alleviating the distresses' of Ireland. Addresses along such lines were com-municated by the grand juries of counties Dublin, Monaghan, Cavan, Tyrone, Mayo, Londonderry, Cork, Clare, and Tipperary, as well as by that of Cork city.[309] Further 'humble addresses' containing effusive

---

[305] *Ibid.*, 8 November 1781.
[306] R.D. Edwards (ed.), 'The minute book of the Catholic Committee, 1773–92', *Archiv. Hib.* 9 (1942), 61–2.
[307] *Ibid.*, pp. 62–3.
[308] For a summary account of the affair, see Eamonn O'Flaherty, 'The Catholic question in Ireland, 1774–93' (MA thesis, UCD, 1981), pp. 54–5.
[309] PRO SP 63/468, fo. 71; PRO SP 63/469, fo. 91; PRO SP 63/463, fos. 25, 36, 39, 41, 44, 46, 48 and 42 respectively. In addition, a humble address from the grand jury of County Westmeath is reported in *FJ*, 21 March 1780.

expressions of gratitude were received from the 'mayor, sheriffs, and citizens of the city of Limerick'; from the freeholders of counties Longford, Kildare and Kilkenny; from the 'mayor and citizens' of Kilkenny borough; and from 'the sovereign, burgesses and principal inhabitants' of Belfast'.[310] The last of these assumed that economic growth would follow the removal of commercial restraints and predicted that such 'happy effects' would demonstrate to all the 'indisputable truth, that Britain and Ireland must rise or fall together'. In March Belfast was 'elegantly illuminated' when the act giving Ireland free access to the colonial trade was passed.[311] The feeling that Irish demands had been fully conceded was widespread. In Derry city, when the last of the British acts giving effect to the commercial concessions was passed, the local Volunteer corps 'appeared under arms, and fired three volleys; the bells were rung; and, at night, the city was brilliantly illuminated'.[312] In contrast, news of the return from Britain of a bill to repeal the sacramental test for officeholders – a measure necessary to maintain the superior status of Protestant Dissenters vis-à-vis Catholics following passage of Gardiner's relief act – appears to have been received without any obvious enthusiasm in April, but it can only have contributed to the emerging mood of satisfaction with government. When news of the removal of the last restrictions on Irish trade reached Dublin,

The whole city was illuminated on account of the liberty granted by England to this kingdom, to trade with the colonies. The castle, the exchange, post-office, college, and other public edifices were all lighted up in the grandest manner. Artillery were discharged from several ships in the river, and other demonstrations of joy evinced for so happy an event to the trade of this kingdom.[313]

John Hely Hutchinson, member of parliament for Cork city, advised the secretary of state that the 'citizens of Cork are, as they certainly ought to be, thoroughly contented and highly sensible of the advantages and favours they have obtained'.[314] In Ulster, however, it would appear that satisfaction may have been stronger among Anglicans than among Presbyterians. A Presbyterian correspondent from County Armagh informed Francis Dobbs, a patriot pamphleteer and prominent member of the Volunteers, that ' "We have got all we want; We have got everything" – is the cry, industriously circulated by those who think themselves of first authority and consequence here, and are the most humble, obsequious

---

[310] PRO SP 63/468, fo. 308; PRO SP 63/463, fos. 28, 30, 32, 33 and 24 respectively.
[311] BNL, 10 March 1780.   [312] LJ, 7 March 1780.   [313] HM, March 1780, 175.
[314] Hely Hutchinson to Hillsborough, September 1780, in HMC Donoughmore Mss., 12th report, appendix IX (1891), p. 299.

retainers to the [primate].'[315] The Duke of Leinster, who commanded the Dublin Volunteer corps which had played such a prominent part in the campaign for free trade, proposed a motion of thanks for the trade concessions in the House of Lords. The motion also promised that peers would 'use their endeavours to promote peace and order among the people, who might by misguided men be diverted from the pursuit of the advantages the extension of trade afforded us'.[316] But to committed patriots, the prospect of on-going agitation seemed all too unlikely. A member of the Volunteers in Belfast complained in March that a 'languor prevails; and too many, through influence or inattention, seem not to be alive in the public cause'.[317] In the same month a writer in the *Freeman's Journal* lamented that 'a political stupor prevails over the faculties of Irishmen'.[318]

Clearly, the political climate of 1780 was very different from that of the previous year. Discussing the change in mood that followed the trade concessions of December 1779, Maurice O'Connell attributed what he described as the 'collapse of radicalism' to 'one great cause – the consciousness among landlords that the free trade agitation was developing into a demand by the middle classes for a real share in political power'.[319] In addition, he argued that the support given by parliamentary patriots to the combinations act of 1780, and their lack of unity in relation to the tenantry act of the same year, lost them the support of the urban artisanate and rural leaseholders respectively.[320] These explanations are implausible. Proposals for parliamentary reform had scarcely been voiced during the campaign for free trade. In any event, the agitation owed little to the direction of parliamentary leaders, having arisen at a time when parliament was in recess. Furthermore, the combinations act would scarcely have been noticed outside the major cities and the first parliamentary division on the tenantry act, a measure sponsored by Henry Grattan, did not take place until June – some two or three months after the 'humble addresses' noted above had signalled the return of a substantial section of the political nation to its customary loyalty. O'Connell's explanations are also quite unnecessary. The free-trade campaign in all its manifestations (non-importation resolutions, assaults on importers, intimidation of parliamentarians, Volunteer sabre-rattling, freeholders' instructions, etc.) reflected support for the repeal of restrictions on Irish trade rather than an undefined ideology of 'radicalism'. British mercantilist legislation

---

[315] William Campbell to Francis Dobbs, 15 January 1780, in NLI Ms. 2,251, p. 24. The word in brackets is represented by a stroke in the original but the meaning is clear from the context.
[316] Debate of 2 March 1780, reported in *HM*, February 1781, 99.
[317] *DEP*, 14 March 1780.   [318] *FJ*, 30 March 1780–.
[319] O'Connell, *Irish Politics and Social Conflict*, pp. 258–9.   [320] *Ibid.*, pp. 281–2.

had long been viewed as a grievance by all sections of Irish opinion and this feeling was exacerbated by an economic depression, by the concessions held out to America by the Carlisle peace commission, by the success of British manufacturers in emasculating the proposed concessions of 1778, and by the derisory nature of the relief granted by the British parliament in the spring of 1779. It was entirely predictable that the agitation would subside once it attained its objective and there is no need to invoke any other factors to account for the more relaxed mood that prevailed in 1780. This is not to deny that the general ferment associated with the free-trade campaign created favourable conditions for the propagation of other long-standing patriot ideas in relation to the powers of the Irish parliament *vis-à-vis* both the executive and the British parliament. Furthermore, the ideas expressed by authors such as 'Guatimozin' and 'Owen Roe O'Nial' broke new ground and represented the first engagement with separatist ideas by members of the Anglican and Presbyterian communities. None the less, such ideas were confined to a small minority and the bulk of the Protestant population happily reverted to its customary loyalty once the restraints on Irish trade were removed.

Constitutional demands

Although the trade concessions of December 1779 triggered a revival of loyalist sentiment, support for the patriot opposition in the wider political nation did not immediately decline to the level that had prevailed in the period before the free-trade agitation commenced. In the early months of 1780, opposition papers and pamphleteers continued vigorously to criticise the trade concessions as being either inadequate in themselves, or, if adequate, as being insecure for as long as the British parliament maintained its claim to legislate for Ireland. Writing in the *Hibernian Journal,* 'Sarsfield' lamented that the 'very parliament which spoke in the language of *unlimited* freedom one day, returned thanks for receiving it by *halves* in the next'.[321] An opposition pamphlet dated 25 January attacked those who suggested that Ireland's demands had been met with the granting of free trade: nothing, the author argued, could give them 'permanence and stability, or effectually consolidate that union of affection and interests between the sister kingdoms, so devoutly to be wished, but a solemn renunciation of the absurd and ensnaring doctrine of the supremacy and omnipotence of the British legislature'.[322] The author of a pamphlet entitled *Moderation Unmasked* ridiculed the freedom to trade with the British colonies that the ministry had purported to grant and claimed that they

---

[321] *HJ*, 5 January 1780.
[322] *Thoughts on News-Papers and a Free Trade* (Dublin, 1780), p. 28.

'would do us just as essential a service by giving us a trade with the Spanish settlements in South America; with the Spice Islands of the Dutch; or with the territories of his serene highness of Japan! – The colonies are gone forever.'[323] The same author stressed the need for unity among all religious denominations if Ireland's rights were to be restored and did so in words that have a familiar ring to the modern reader: 'Why should we recollect that we have different appellations – Protestants, Roman Catholics, Dissenters? Let them be forgotten, and they are forgotten – We remember only that we have the common one of Irishmen.'[324] The threat that would be posed to the religious establishment by Catholicism if Ireland's constitutional links with Britain were broken had become a common theme of loyalist propaganda; but as patriot apologists appealed for Catholic support they increasingly urged Protestants to set aside 'the remembrance of past hostilities'.[325] The close connection between Anglo-Irish patriotism and anti-Catholicism, which had been evident as recently as 1778 when patriot members of parliament led the opposition to Luke Gardiner's Catholic relief bill, was breaking down. The patriots' need to mobilise Catholic support for the non-importation campaign in 1779 – and their success in doing so – was a domestic factor influencing this ideological *renversement*, but the Franco-American alliance may also have assisted the process. When the patriotic *Dublin Evening Post* published a list of 'discoveries extraordinary' for the year 1779 the first item on the list was 'Catholics and Presbyterians chanting *Te Deum* together in America!'[326]

In January 1780, the Common Council of Dublin city debated a pair of 'humble addresses' to the king and lord lieutenant which expressed the Council's gratitude for the trade concessions received; the addresses were 'after much debate, and by a very small majority of voices, carried' – a disappointing outcome for the opposition in one of its traditional strongholds.[327] Only a month later, however, a meeting of the freeholders of the city unanimously agreed to instruct the city's members of parliament to use their 'best endeavours to procure such a declaratory act as will entirely secure the constitutional rights of this free and independent nation against all foreign legislation whatsoever', as well as to support a modification of Poynings' law. Two weeks later similar instructions were adopted by a meeting of the freeholders of County Dublin with only one dissenting voice.[328] Further evidence of patriot resilience in the

---

[323] *Moderation Unmasked; or, the Conduct of the Majority Impartially Considered* (Dublin, 1780), pp. 44–5.
[324] *Ibid.*, p. 68; cf. Marianne Elliott, *Wolfe Tone: Prophet of Irish Independence* (New Haven and London, 1989), p. 312.
[325] *Moderation Unmasked*, p. 67.   [326] *DEP*, 25 November 1779.
[327] *HM*, January 1780, 63.   [328] *Ibid.*, March 1780, pp. 174–5.

capital was provided in April when the influential guild of merchants discussed a proposal to grant the freedom of the guild to Lord North and Lord Hillsborough in recognition of their roles in securing free trade. Only twenty-nine merchants supported the proposal while sixty-nine opposed; one unnamed member commented that 'General Washington, as he was more instrumental in this affair, might with greater propriety be complimented with such freedom.'[329] More striking still, in view of the normally conservative outlook of the Board of Aldermen, is a unanimous resolution dated 31 May 1780 that the Board would give no 'force or countenance, within their jurisdiction, to any law or statute, but such as have been enacted by the King, Lords and Commons of Ireland'.[330]

In Ulster also a substantial body of patriot opinion viewed Lord North's commercial concessions as inadequate from the first. One of the earliest notes of caution was sounded by the Volunteers of Newry, County Down, who warned that privileges conferred by the British parliament could be revoked by the same body at a future date.[331] The same point was made by Francis Dobbs, a member of the established church and a Volunteer major in County Armagh, in an open letter to Lord North dated 1 January 1780. Dobbs emphasised that the trade concessions had been granted as 'a matter of *expediency*, not of right'. Having queried whether Ireland was to be considered a 'conquered nation' or a 'free kingdom' he added that, even if the former were the case, 'there is one right that I apprehend cannot be taken from us: It is a right I almost blush to mention; it is the right of the vanquished; the right of regaining our freedom, whenever we are able to throw off your yoke'.[332] While pamphleteers such as 'Guatimozin' and 'Owen Roe O'Nial' had expressed similar views, language bordering on sedition had not previously been used in a work published over the author's name. Dobbs's views were not those of the majority of his coreligionists but neither was he an isolated individual. His *Letter* was of sufficient general interest to be reprinted in the *Belfast News-Letter*, then also publishing a series of letters from an anonymous 'Miller' who appears to have been Rev. William Bruce, a Presbyterian minister.[333] The 'Miller's Letters', written in a simple colloquial style, reiterated the view that 'Ireland isn't dependant on England at all' and argued that free trade had been extorted from the British ministry by the threat of force:

---

[329] *FLJ*, 8 April 1780.   [330] *Ibid.*, 31 May 1780.   [331] *BNL*, 31 December 1779.
[332] Francis Dobbs, *A Letter to the Right Honourable Lord North, on his Propositions in Favour of Ireland* (Dublin, 1780), pp. 7 and 9–10.
[333] For Dobbs's *Letter*, see *BNL*, 25 January 1780. Serialisation of the 'Miller's Letters' continued from 11 January to 17 March 1780. For their attribution to Bruce, see Colin Hill, 'William Drennan and the radical movement for Irish reform, 1779–1794' (MLitt thesis, TCD, 1967), pp. 29–30.

Has England given us a free trade? She has lately *allowed* us to export woollens, and glass, and several other things; but she has not given us every thing we have a right to ask. And if she had, we have no reason to thank her for our own, which she kept from us as long as she could, and 'till we were able to take it.[334]

The existence of a considerable body of patriot opinion in east Ulster is shown by the unanimous adoption of a resolution by the True Blue Volunteers of Lisburn, County Antrim, on 2 February in which they congratulated Dobbs for supporting 'the dignity of his country, by asserting its right to constitutional independent legislation; without which, the liberty of trading would indeed be but a temporary expedient'.[335] Similarly, the sovereign, burgesses, and inhabitants of Belfast adopted an address to the town's members of parliament which declared that they could not 'be persuaded that the freedom of our trade will be secure, or the emancipation of our country complete, unless our legislature be restored to its ancient dignity and independence' and instructed the members to support both a modification of Poynings' law and an act declaring the exclusive right of the Irish parliament to legislate for Ireland.[336] When the grand jury of County Down adopted a 'humble address' thanking the king, the lord lieutenant and Lord Hillsborough for free trade on the casting vote of its chairman, the continued opposition of the minority to an 'idle and unnecessary' measure induced the proposer of the address to 'thrust the grateful sentiments into the fire'.[337] Shortly thereafter, more than 2,000 County Down freeholders signed instructions directing their members of parliament to work for the repeal of Poynings' law and for a declaration of legislative independence.[338] Similar instructions were adopted by the freeholders of Lisburn.[339]

These addresses were not spontaneous expressions of opinion. As early as 6 February the lord lieutenant advised Lord Hillsborough that 'great pains are taken by mischievous emissaries to procure instructions from county meetings' but assured the secretary of state that 'endeavours will, on the other hand be exerted to baffle them'.[340] If Dublin and east Ulster were the principal centres of the opposition's strength, the number of counties which instructed their members in relation to Poynings' law and a declaration of legislative independence discloses the presence of sizable bodies of patriots in all four provinces. A model address suitable for adoption 'by all the grand and petty juries of this kingdom' was published in the opposition press at the end of February; however, the gentry-based grand juries were more inclined to adopt 'humble addresses' expressing

[334] *BNL*, 17 March 1780.   [335] *Ibid.*, 8 February 1780.   [336] *Ibid.*, 14 March 1780.
[337] *LJ*, 28 March 1780.   [338] *Ibid.*, 11 April 1780.   [339] *Ibid.*
[340] Buckinghamshire to Hillsborough, 6 February 1780, in PRO SP 63/468, fos. 180–1.

their gratitude for free trade than to engage in constitutional agitation – the grand jury of County Wicklow being a rare exception.[341]

A second avenue remained open to local patriots, and opposition-inspired addresses which variously 'instructed', 'called upon', 'entreated' or 'advised' members of parliament to support efforts to modify Poynings' law and to assert the Irish parliament's exclusive right to enact legislation were adopted at a series of county meetings. In addition to those already mentioned above, such addresses were adopted by meetings of freeholders in counties Donegal, Leitrim, Antrim, Galway, Meath, Wexford, Mayo, Roscommon and Armagh.[342] Contentions arose in some areas. In County Cork, where the patriotic instructions were adopted by an opposition caucus convened for the purpose of selecting a candidate for the next general election and chaired by the aspiring candidate, Lord Kingsborough, the instructions were indignantly rejected by Richard Townsend, the sitting member whose seat was threatened.[343] In Kerry, two conflicting sets of instructions, both apparently validated by the sheriff, were presented to the members.[344] The loyalist address was signed by 340 persons who declared that they considered themselves 'as connected with our sister kingdom by the strongest ties of blood, name, language, religion and laws' and that they consequently rejected the suggestion that 'those ties which now bind the one kingdom to the other should be loosened'. The patriot address, in contrast, attracted 412 signatures and contained the standard instructions on the issues of Poynings' law and a declaration of legislative independence. In his reply, one of the members for the county (who eventually voted with the opposition) expressed his respect for the many 'very intelligent and independent freeholders' who 'differed from each other, by signing addresses of a very opposite nature' – an indication that the lists of names appended to both addresses were substantially genuine.[345] In Tipperary, where the sheriff ignored a request to convene a meeting of freeholders, instructions proposed by Sir Edward Newenham were adopted at a meeting chaired by Lord Kingsborough, who also performed a similar function at the unofficial meeting of patriotic freeholders held in County Cork.[346] In Fermanagh

---

[341] For the draft address, see *DEP*, 29 February 1780. For the address of the Wicklow grand jury, see *DEP*, 13 April 1780.

[342] *Ibid.*, 29 February; 16 March; 1, 6, 8, 11 and 13 April 1780; and *FJ*, 18 April 1780.

[343] *FJ*, 11 April 1780. Kingsborough's title was a courtesy one which he used as the son of a peer, Lord Kingston. He was allied with James Bernard, the second member for Cork, and was elected to represent the county at the next election.

[344] *Ibid.*, 8 and 13 April 1780. While Arthur Blennerhasset, a member for the county, stated that neither address had been authenticated in his reply to the loyalist address, he stated that they had both been authenticated when responding to the patriot address.

[345] *Ibid.*, 13 April 1780.   [346] *DEP*, 1 April 1780.

the freeholders simply thanked the members for the 'uprightness' of their past conduct and stated that it was 'unnecessary' to give them instructions; while in Tyrone the county meeting did endorse the modification of Poynings' law and a declaration of legislative independence, but declined to instruct the county's members as this would 'imply doubts' about their future conduct.[347] In both cases this suggests a mildly patriotic stance – given that the members for both counties tended to oppose administration – but such lukewarm resolutions were not calculated to raise the political temperature throughout the country and must have disappointed more militant patriots.[348] Thomas Conolly, the influential member for County Londonderry, bluntly informed the freeholders who addressed him that all constitutional demands should be deferred until 'such time as our sister kingdom is at leisure to canvass that important subject, and to meet the question with a calmness and moderation, which nothing but a time of peace can admit of'.[349] A prominent independent member, Denis Daly, objected to the instructions he received from his County Galway constituents on the grounds that many of the freeholders who signed them were Catholics. A letter which subsequently appeared in an opposition paper provided some embarrassing details about Daly's manœuvrings in the autumn of the previous year: at that time he had sent instructions to his constituency for an address in favour of a short money bill to be drawn up and presented to him – an address that he was pleased to receive 'with a cordial politeness, though signed but by fourteen Protestants, the rest being all Catholics'.[350]

The 'instructions' adopted by county meetings of freeholders, together with the 'humble addresses' expressing gratitude for free trade presented to the crown by many grand juries, indicate that the consensus within the political nation which had successfully borne down British resistance on the question of free trade no longer existed. In the absence of such a consensus, normal methods of parliamentary management were able to prevail in 1780 and a declaration of Ireland's legislative independence proposed by Henry Grattan, and an amendment to Poynings' law introduced by Barry Yelverton, both fell well short of a majority. A detailed discussion of these debates would lie outside the scope of this work, but two aspects are of relevance here: namely, a number of revealing references to America made by some of the speakers, and the light which the voting figures shed on the views of the electorate.

[347] *Ibid.*, 25 March and 4 April 1780.
[348] For the records of the members concerned, see Sayles, 'Contemporary sketches'.
[349] *LJ*, 28 April 1780.
[350] *DEP*, 8 April 1780. For the address concerned, see *DEP*, 12 October 1779.

In moving his motion for a declaration of rights Henry Grattan made two notable references to America. In the first, he argued that the American war had weakened Britain's ability to resist Irish demands. An ideal opportunity therefore existed to assert the legislative independence of the Irish parliament: 'It is not in the power of England to resist. Can she war against ten millions of French, eight millions of Spaniards, three millions of Americans, three millions of Irish? England cannot withstand accumulated millions with her ten millions.'[351] In his second reference to America, Grattan drew attention to the contrast between the sweeping concessions offered to the colonies by the Carlisle peace commission and Britain's less generous attitude towards Ireland. This line of argument had previously been used during the campaign for free trade and it was now employed in the constitutional sphere also: 'She offered America the entire cession of her parliamentary power, and can she refuse the Irish the freedom of fellow-subjects? Every thing short of total independence was offered to the Americans – and will she yield that to their arms, and refuse it to your loyalty?'[352] It is a reasonable inference that the contrast between Britain's willingness to negotiate with rebels in arms and her reluctance to make concessions to the loyal Anglo-Irish community continued to rankle in the minds of the latter. Sir John Blaquiere, a former chief secretary, accepted the principle that the British parliament had no legislative authority in Ireland – as did the great majority of those who opposed Grattan's motion – but argued that it was 'inexpedient' and 'ungracious' to draw attention to a moribund claim which it was not intended to revive. Blaquiere appealed to an unlikely authority in support of his view:

He begged leave to apply the opinion of Doctor Franklin, that first philosopher and politician with respect to America. When the doctor was informed that though the parliament of England had repealed the stamp act, they had declared their right to bind America, the doctor replied, 'let them make laws against our lives, enchain our liberties, or plunder our property, so long as they proceed no farther than the journals or records of their house, we shall rest satisfied, and suffer them to enjoy their innocent, ineffectual, and unoffending vanity'.[353]

If this argument suggests the existence of a body of patriot opinion which might be swayed by the views of Benjamin Franklin, another pro-government speaker appealed to a very different constituency – those who were frightened by the prospect that Irish patriots might follow the example of their American counterparts. 'Let us grow wise by the contest of America', urged John Toler, 'and let us not breed groundless jealousies' between Britain and Ireland. He added the warning that social revolution

<hr/>

[351] Debate of 19 April 1780, in *HM*, May 1781, 266.   [352] *Ibid.*   [353] *Ibid.*, 268.

might follow if Grattan's resolution were passed: 'we cannot tell where it may end, we shall not want Levellers'.[354]

Debate on Grattan's motion was adjourned *sine die* by a vote of 136 to 97 while Yelverton's motion was defeated by 130 to 105; the fact that it was not necessary to vote against Grattan's motion may account for the slightly larger government majority on the former occasion. Gross figures that include members who owned or who had purchased seats in boroughs are a very insensitive gauge of opinion in the electorate, but even when county members alone are considered the impression of a divided political nation persists. The voting list for Yelverton's motion to amend Poynings' law reveals that only a slight majority of the county members, thirty-five out of sixty-four, supported the motion. Regional variations were not great, as the thirty-five who voted with the opposition included eleven out of eighteen county members in Ulster, six out of twelve in Munster, fifteen out of twenty-four in Leinster, and three out of ten in Connacht.[355] In subsequent divisions the opposition obtained leave to bring in the heads of a mutiny bill, despite government opposition, by the enormous majority of 140 to 18 – a victory which reflected the concern of members that the courts might refuse to recognise the validity of the British mutiny act, thus leaving the Irish garrison without any system of military discipline. When the bill returned from England with an amendment that made it perpetual most members turned a deaf ear to opposition warnings about the creation of a standing army and the amended bill was accepted by an emphatic 114 votes to 62.

These parliamentary divisions reflected divisions in the political nation at large. In April Buckinghamshire was able to share some good news about a split in the ranks of the capital's Volunteer corps with the secretary of state: 'The Dublin politicians are sensibly affected with an event of this morning, the expulsion of Mr Napper Tandy from the corps of the Dublin Volunteers. His disgrace was occasioned by his proposing to expel the Duke of Leinster for the conduct of himself and his friends in parliament.'[356] Tension between parliament and sections of the Volunteer movement increased in August following the enactment of the perpetual mutiny act and a sugar tariff that the opposition believed to be inadequate to protect Irish sugar refiners from British competition. The Merchants' corps of Volunteers in Dublin condemned the votes of the Commons on the two questions as 'destructive in our opinion, to the constitutional

---

[354] *Debates of the House of Commons of Ireland, on a Motion whether the Kings Most Excellent Majesty, and the Lords and Commons of Ireland, are the Only Power Competent to Bind or Enact Laws in this Kingdom* (Dublin, 1780), pp. 14 and 15.

[355] For a list of members voting for and against Yelverton's motion, see *FJ*, 9 May 1780.

[356] Buckingham to Hillsborough, 24 April 1780, in PRO SP 63/469, fo. 120.

rights, and injurious to the commercial interests of this kingdom' – provoking an indignant House of Commons in its turn to address the lord lieutenant for the prosecution of those opposition journals in which the resolution of the Merchants' corps had appeared.[357] The controversy spread outside the capital with, for example, the officers of the Coleraine battalion of Volunteers resolving that 'any particular body of men publicly condemning or vilifying the legislature of this kingdom, particularly during the sitting of parliament, is unconstitutional'; while the Belfast battalion supported their Dublin counterparts by resolving that 'what the voice of the Irish nation, our dear and much respected country, declares to be true; is not false, scandalous, seditious, or libellous'.[358]

Yet the clear impression throughout the latter half of 1780 is one of gradually declining support for the patriot opposition and growing confidence on the part of government and its supporters. On the eve of the parliamentary debate on the perpetual mutiny bill a patriotic correspondent writing from Dublin deplored the public's lack of concern in relation to the issue:

All ranks of men, Protestants and Roman Catholics, are equally interested in the debates on this day, Friday and Wednesday next; when Irish honour is to be established, or lost for ever. Sorry we are to observe such an apathy among the citizens of Dublin, when their all is at stake. Where are those virtuous aldermen and commons, who used to support the freedom and honour of Ireland?[359]

Similarly, an opposition pamphleteer who advocated the formation of a 'constitutional association' – a national organisation with a patriotic programme, a proposal clearly inspired by the Association movement in England – tried to find glimmers of hope despite the appearance of widespread public apathy: 'The ardour of the people has been smothered, though not extinguished. The idea of instructing the representatives through the kingdom, has not been embraced as warmly, as one might have expected, from the seasonable juncture, and the obvious utility of such a measure.'[360] In September 1780 the Dublin patriots again resorted to this familiar tactic by calling on the city's sheriffs to convene an aggregate meeting of the freemen to 'take into consideration the expediency of a non-importation agreement – an address to his Majesty to dissolve the parliament of Ireland – and a resolution of thanks to the Volunteer corps

[357] See PRO SP 63/470, fos. 304–15 for material relating to this episode, including copies of the *Freeman's Journal* of 19 August, the *Hibernian Journal* of 18 August, and the *Dublin Evening Post* of 19 August 1780.

[358] *LJ*, 5 and 8 September 1780 respectively.   [359] *FLJ*, 12 August 1780.

[360] *A Scheme for a Constitutional Association: with some Obvious Reasons for Adopting such a Measure* (Dublin, 1780), p. 13.

of this city'. Such resolutions were duly approved by the freeholders on
6 September, but although their meeting was described as 'very numerous' in the patriot press, state papers recorded that the attendance consisted 'of inferior citizens and of the most factious spirits' and described
the resolution calling for a dissolution of parliament as 'ridiculous'.[361]
The failure to mount a new non-importation campaign (conceived as a
retaliatory measure against the low duty on refined sugar imported from
Britain) reveals the extent to which the extra-parliamentary opposition
had declined in strength since the beginning of 1780. This decline, and
the simultaneous revival of loyalist sentiment, was encouraged – if it was
not inspired – by a series of British victories that appeared to have transformed the course of the war.

The loyalist revival

British forces had recovered Georgia as early as December 1778 and in
October of the following year a Franco-American attack on Savannah was
repulsed with heavy losses. When news of this victory reached Ireland
in December 1779 it was celebrated in several localities in Ulster. In
Magherafelt, County Derry, the local Volunteer corps fired a *feu de joie*,
the town was illuminated and loyal toasts were drunk; in Lurgan, County
Armagh, the Volunteers celebrated the British success 'against the House
of Bourbon' by drinking toasts to 'the British fleet' and 'the land forces
of the Anglo realms'; in County Antrim, the Cullybackey company of
Volunteers paraded and 'fired three volleys in honour of the successes
by his Majesty's arms'.[362] These celebrations took place shortly after the
British ministry had announced its intention of repealing the restrictions
on Irish trade and this factor is likely to have influenced the manner
in which the news from Georgia was received. Further evidence of the
Protestant population's swing back towards traditional attitudes is provided by the results of debates at the Trinity College Historical Society.
When the question 'Whether America was justifiable in her secession
from Great Britain?' was discussed in November 1779, at the height of
the free-trade crisis, it passed in the affirmative *nemine contradicente* with
twenty-two members present – a remarkable result which reflects the
alienation of the political nation at that time.[363] But when substantially
the same question ('Whether America was justifiable in declaring herself independent on the mother country?') was debated only two months

---

[361] *HJ*, 6 September 1780; Sir Richard Heron to Sir Stanier Porten, 6 September 1780, in
PRO SP 63/471, fo. 55.
[362] *BNL*, 4 January 1780 and *HJ*, 5 January 1780.
[363] Historical Society minutes, 3 November 1779, in TCD Mun. Soc./Hist. 3, pp. 410–11.

later there were fourteen ayes and seven noes – suggesting that loyalist sentiment was already reviving.[364] The celebrations following Admiral Rodney's victory over a Spanish squadron and his success in resupplying the besieged garrison of Gibraltar were more widespread than those that had followed the victory at Savannah. In Dublin the Volunteers fired three volleys in St Stephen's Green; in Derry city the volleys of the garrison were answered by those of the local Volunteer corps and the bells of the churches were rung; and in Belfast the local Volunteer battalion fired three volleys and the evening concluded 'with illuminations, and every mark of unfeigned joy'.[365] The popular enthusiasm aroused by this victory is confirmed by the choice of Rodney's portrait and a drawing of his defeat of the Spanish fleet as frontispieces in the *Hibernian Magazine* in March and April 1780 respectively.

A still more significant indication of the mood of Protestant Ireland is provided by the intensity of the celebrations which marked the surrender of the American garrison at Charleston, South Carolina, to General Clinton, news of which reached Ireland in June 1780. This was the most serious defeat suffered by American arms during the entire course of the war and it resulted in the restoration of royal authority in a second southern colony. Rodney's victory had been against Spain, a historic foe of Protestant Britain, and the enemy force defeated at Savannah was as much French as American, but the event celebrated on this occasion was a successful British offensive against the capital of one of the rebel colonies. In Belfast, the *News-Letter* reported that 'on account of the success of his Majesty's arms in the reduction of Charles Town, there were great rejoicings here. – In the evening the troops fired a *feu de joye*; and at night the town was finely illuminated', although the local Volunteers appear not to have taken part in the celebrations.[366] The Volunteer battalion in Derry city showed no such reticence: 'On Friday last, on account of the taking of Charlestown by his Majesty's troops, that part of the 36th regiment now here on garrison duty... paraded in the Diamond at 12 o'clock, and fired three volleys; the Derry Battalion also fired three volleys; in the evening the market house was illuminated, the bells were rung, &c.'[367] In Cork, the Volunteer corps of the city 'proceeded to the Mall, where they fired three volleys, for joy of the success of his Majesty's arms at Charlestown'.[368] In Kilkenny, it was reported that 'the different Volunteer associations of this city' each fired 'three volleys, with the greatest exactness, to testify their joy on the success of his

[364] Historical Society minutes, 5 January 1780, in *ibid.*, p. 434.
[365] *LJ*, 14 March 1780 and *BNL*, 10 March 1780.   [366] *BNL*, 27 June 1780.
[367] *LJ*, 27 June 1780.   [368] *DEP*, 1 July 1780.

Majesty's arms in Carolina'; the evening concluded with 'illuminations and general festivity'.[369] In Limerick city, the news of 'General Clinton's signal victory over the United States of America' was greeted with 'a scene of rejoicings for three days, not to be excelled in his Majesty's dominions' and the Volunteers fired a *feu de joie* on the South Mall.[370]

The exploits of Lieutenant-Colonel Banastre Tarleton and his British Legion – a force largely composed of American loyalists – provided supporters of the war effort with a suitably dashing hero, while the prominent part played by Lord Rawdon, eldest son of Lord Moira, and the significantly named 'Volunteers of Ireland' – a regiment recruited from among Irish immigrants in the American colonies – in the Carolinas campaign was a particular source of satisfaction for Irish loyalists. The role of this regiment was emphasised in press reports of the battle of Camden at which Lord Cornwallis routed a much larger American force commanded by Horatio Gates, the victor of Saratoga. A letter from one of the regiment's officers detailed the important part played by the Volunteers of Ireland in the battle and described it as 'the most glorious day for Britain that ever happened in America'.[371] Another officer in the army wrote that 'the Irish Volunteers behaved with the steadiness and bravery of veterans, although it was the first action they were ever in as a military body, and the enemy made a more obstinate resistance than usual'.[372] At home, their namesakes responded appropriately. In Derry city, 'the bells were rung, at night the market house was illuminated, and Capt. Bennet's company [the 'Apprentice Boys' company of Volunteers] fired three volleys'.[373] In Limerick, the Volunteers also fired volleys to celebrate the victory at Camden and 'the evening concluded with every demonstration of joy'.[374] A portrait of Lord Cornwallis, 'that very active and successful commander', provided the frontispiece of the October issue of the *Hibernian Magazine*. The 'Volunteers of Ireland' were merely the most obvious manifestation of Irish loyalism in the American theatre: when several locally recruited 'provincial' regiments consisting mostly of American loyalists were disbanded at the end of the war their 585 officers included seventy-eight Irishmen – a figure which pales in comparison with the eighty-eight who were born in Scotland but comfortably exceeds the fifty-six who were natives of England.[375]

---

[369] *FLJ*, 24 June 1780.   [370] *HM*, June 1780, 350.   [371] *FLJ*, 1 November 1778.
[372] *SNL*, 18 October 1780.
[373] *LJ*, 20 October 1780. For Bennet's company, see *ibid.*, 13 October 1780.
[374] *FLJ*, 23 October 1780.
[375] The disbanded regiments did not include either the Volunteers of Ireland, a unit transferred to the Irish establishment, or the Royal Highland Immigrants, a unit transferred to the British establishment. See K.G. Davies (ed.), *Documents of the American Revolution 1770–1783 (Colonial Office Series)*, XXI (Dublin, 1981), pp. 20, 227–50.

A further boost for loyalist morale came in late November when news of Benedict Arnold's defection reached Ireland; a letter in which he denounced America's alliance with France and promised to 'devote my life to the re-union of the British empire' was published in the Irish press.[376] The *Hibernian Magazine*'s frontispiece in December was a portrait of Major André, the British officer who arranged Arnold's defection and was executed by the Americans in controversial circumstances. The impact of this unbroken series of British successes on Irish perceptions of the war was considerable. The surrender of Charleston, in particular, was widely seen as a turning point. The pro-government *Faulkner's Dublin Journal* was unrestrained in its optimism:

The great and good news from Charles Town comes so opportunely, that it is doubly welcome. What could possibly operate more effectually to ease the minds of all who have been distressed on account of the late alarming insurrections in England [the Gordon riots], than the knowing just at this moment, (when quiet is substantially restored at home) that the most important enterprise which has been undertaken in the course of the whole unhappy war with America has been successful, and that a variety of strong circumstances concur to prove that peace across the Atlantic is at no great distance, and that Great Britain has reasonable grounds to hope for a speedy recovery of her colonies?[377]

Significantly, even the strongly patriotic *Hibernian Journal* assured its readers that Ireland stood to benefit economically from a British victory in America:

It is thought that the entire submission of the two Carolinas will follow the reduction of Charlestown; should so desirable an event take place, it will be of singular advantage to this kingdom by opening an immediate trade with those provinces. The northern parts of Ireland will be particularly benefitted, as the Carolinas are the chief market for linens, plain and stamped.[378]

Within a week, the same paper published a plan for a compromise peace settlement whereby Britain would have retained New York, New Jersey, South Carolina and Georgia while recognising the independence of the other nine colonies.[379] The advocacy of such ideas by supporters of the opposition was not simply a product of war-weariness, pessimism or neutralism, though all of these existed; it also reflected the existence among the Protestant population of a current of imperial patriotism in the tradition of Lord Chatham. This was a patriotism that celebrated the success of the free-trade agitation, applauded the Volunteers, and asserted the prerogatives of the Irish parliament; but also valued the strength and unity

---

[376] *FLJ*, 25 November 1780.   [377] *FDJ*, 24 June 1780.
[378] *HJ*, 23 June 1780. This article had previously appeared in *SNL*, 21 June 1780.
[379] *Ibid.*, 25 June 1780.

of the British empire as a defence against domestic and foreign 'popery' and arbitrary government. This perspective was concisely expressed in a poem composed in honour of the Galway Volunteers:

> Not far the time, when trade shall crowd our shore,
> and Poynings' shameful fetters be no more;
> when laurelled Rodney shall o'erthrow the dons,
> and smiling peace re-visit Georgia's sons;
> when gallant Parker shall our hopes complete,
> and fleets united make a quick retreat;
> when western shores shall boast of Clinton's fame,
> and future ages shall record his name:
> then shall our ships to foreign ports repair,
> in other climes shall Irish bales appear;
> our quays once more with merchandize abound,
> and trade extend to every nation round.[380]

A pamphlet which appeared towards the end of 1780 expressed similar sentiments in more prosaic language:

The black clouds which lately hung over the British empire now seem to be dispersing on all sides, and its ascendancy over its united enemies is already assumed: an honourable peace with all its ancient dependencies seems to be an event at no great distance. The dawn of Ireland's happiness and future greatness is come, the day of it is at hand; the glorious conduct of her own sons has opened the flattering prospect before her eyes, and nothing but their intemperate zeal can fatally cloud the scene.[381]

By the end of the year, reports were circulating that Virginia had acknowledged royal authority, that 'the rebel governor [Thomas Jefferson] had been confirmed in his station by General Clinton', and that 'preliminaries for a pacification had been transmitted from Congress to New York'.[382] These rumours were unfounded, but the fact that they were regarded as credible confirms the existence of a widespread belief that Britain had finally gained the upper hand and that the American rebellion was about to collapse after a five-year struggle.

During 1780, loyalist writers stressed that Ireland's commercial grievances had been fully redressed and that Britain's claim to legislate for the country, while not formally renounced, would 'lie dormant for the future, like her claim to the crown of France'.[383] British arms, it was claimed, were on the brink of total victory in America and the resulting peace

---

[380] *HJ*, 17 July 1780.
[381] *Seasonable Advice to the People of Ireland during the Present Recess of Parliament* (Dublin, 1780), p. 31. The parliamentary recess began on 2 September 1780.
[382] *FLJ*, 13 December 1780.   [383] *Seasonable Advice*, p. 24.

would be a 'constitutional' one with the colonies enjoying the exclusive
right of taxing themselves: it was wrong, as one author put it, 'that the
Americans should dwell eternally upon a stretch of power, which has been
confessed, and promised to be rectified; whilst they themselves practice
daily a much greater stretch of power, in carrying on their revolt'.[384] In
addition to such positive arguments, the separatist sentiments expressed
by some patriotic authors during 1779 provided ample material for a
loyalist reaction which stressed the horrors that would inevitably ensue
if an attempt were made to separate from Britain. This argument was
employed at the highest level. Lord Buckinghamshire himself advised
'independent gentlemen' in parliament that 'however distressing a quarrel
between the two kingdoms might be to England, it would necessarily
in its consequences be subversive of the Protestant interest here, and
completely ruinous to Ireland'.[385] A pro-government pamphleteer asked
rhetorically 'Whether the British declaratory act has not become a mere
shadow of that substance which is already transferred to us...?' and
wondered how, in the event of a separation, Ireland would be able to 'push
a foreign trade without that [naval] protection we must look to England
for?'[386] Likewise, the students of the Trinity College Historical Society
gave a negative answer to the question 'Whether Ireland could possibly
subsist independent of any other nation?'[387] One clerical author, having
inveighed against 'all the trumpery mysteries, and errors broached by the
mother of harlots' (the Catholic church), pointedly advised the Volunteers
that:

There have been ambitious and designing men in every age and nation, who
under pretence of redressing grievances, or rescuing their country from slavery,
so cajoled the people, as to persuade them to submit their necks to a heavier yoke,
and did, in the end, become more tyrannical and overbearing than those, against
whom they had spirited up the people.[388]

Religious arguments were widely employed. An anonymous letter 'to
the Volunteers of Ireland' warned that, in the event of separation from
England, their strength would be insufficient to save the country from
'Gallic slavery' because, if a French army landed 'thousands, nay, millions, of your fellow-subjects, through inclination, or a thirst of spoil,

---

[384] *A Candid Display, of the Reciprocal Conduct of Great Britain and her Colonies* (Dublin,
n.d. – 1780?).
[385] Buckingham to Weymouth, 9 February 1780, in PRO SP 63/468, fo. 205.
[386] *A Volunteer's Queries, in Spring, 1780* (Dublin, 1780), pp. 8 and 9.
[387] Historical Society minutes, 19 January 1780 in TCD Mun. Soc./Hist. 3, p. 438. There
were nine ayes and fourteen noes.
[388] Rev. James Creighton, *The Christian Soldier: A Sermon Addressed to the Volunteers of
Ireland* (Dublin, 1780), pp. 27 and 30.

would join her standard; the superstitious devotees of Rome throughout the kingdom would be armed against you; the horrible carnage of 1641 would be renewed; and you would soon fall a prey to famine, the sword, or popish tyranny'.[389] Another loyalist author supported the view that independence from Britain was incompatible with continued Protestant supremacy with arguments that were less lurid but all the more plausible for the temperate tone in which they were expressed. Ireland, he argued, would not long remain a Protestant state without the continued 'protection or dominion' of Great Britain:

It is a notorious truth, that in all countries not under the protection or dominion of a foreign power, the religion professed by the majority of the people must finally prevail, and become the religion of the state ... the Protestant cause, having lost the protection of that power who planted it in this island, but will then look upon its distress with unconcern, perhaps with complacency, after a few vain struggles must yield, and be glad to accept of a toleration, if its rivals are so generous as to grant it.[390]

At the same time as opposition writers were articulating a new and more tolerant attitude towards the Catholic population, loyalist authors were increasingly employing anti-Catholic rhetoric.

Popular disaffection

Although 1780 was punctuated with reports of British victories and witnessed a gradual reduction of political tension within Ireland, attacks on military personnel continued unabated. In January alone, two soldiers were houghed in Dublin (one of whom was identified as the commander-in-chief's orderly sergeant), as well as one each in Kilkenny and Cork.[391] In February, a second soldier was houghed in Kilkenny while a third was stabbed and killed with his own bayonet.[392] Arrests followed and the four men charged with the Kilkenny attacks were identified in press reports as Martin Delaney, a shoemaker, Francis Ryan, a hatter, and George and Daniel Cummins, both carriers.[393] Members of the garrison retaliated indiscriminately against the townspeople – a strong indication that the attacks were only an extreme manifestation of a more general hostility towards the military:

Thursday evening a number of soldiers, armed with swords, bayonets, &c, went through the streets of this city in a most riotous and alarming manner, stabbing and abusing every person who came in their way, killing pigs, horses, etc.

---

[389] *HM*, October 1780, 560.   [390] *Seasonable Advice*, pp. 19–20.
[391] *SNL*, 19 January 1780; *FLJ*, 12 and 22 January 1780.
[392] *FLJ*, 9 and 12 February 1780.   [393] *Ibid.*, 16 and 26 February 1780.

and breaking windows as they passed. – Though we cannot but allow that the wanton acts of violence committed lately on three soldiers were very irritating, yet, when we reflect on the abhorrence expressed by all ranks of people against these acts...we must be astonished at their having taken this method of re-venging, upon the innocent, the injuries committed by villains, who are as ob-noxious to the peaceable inhabitants of this city, as they can possibly be to the army.[394]

Similar scenes were enacted in Galway where a member of the garrison was houghed on 18 June.[395] A man named James Blood was charged with the attack and tried but, following his acquittal in September, the Galway garrison rioted and attacked the gaol; order was restored but it was considered necessary to withdraw the regiment involved from the town.[396] An even more serious clash between the military and civilians took place in Drogheda on 12 May 1780 when a party of soldiers that had been stoned by a crowd opened fire, killing five people.[397] In Cashel, County Tipperary, the local Volunteer corps offered a reward of fifty guineas for information leading to the apprehension of 'one or more of the villains' who houghed a soldier whose regiment was encamped near the town.[398] At the end of August a soldier was houghed in Dublin after an apparent lull of some months.[399] A suspect was arrested within days and was described in newspaper reports as a hackney chaiseman – a fact which indicates that butchers were not the only group involved in such attacks in the capital but confirms the impression that the houghers were not drawn from the lowest levels of society.[400] Within a week of the last houghing a party of soldiers that had just escorted marine deserters to a tender in Dublin port were attacked by a group of carmen:

who assaulted them in such a terrible manner, that the soldiers were compelled to fire on them, upon which a considerable body of the carmen fell upon the party, cut them in a most dreadful manner and broke their firelocks to pieces. One of the men had his arm broke and is now dressing at the castle guard, the others are taken to the infirmary.[401]

Hostility to the military was common in Dublin. When the city's garrison paraded and fired a *feu de joie* to celebrate the British victory at Charleston the large crowd of onlookers maintained what a patriotic author described as a 'melancholy silence':

---

[394] *SNL*, 15 February 1780.   [395] *FLJ*, 28 June 1780.
[396] PRO SP 63/471, fos. 102–4.   [397] PRO SP 63/469, fos. 217–20.
[398] Pádraig Ó Snodaigh, 'Some police and military aspects of the Irish Volunteers', *Irish Sword* 13 (1977–79), p. 223.
[399] *FLJ*, 6 September 1780.   [400] *Ibid.*, 9 September 1780.
[401] William Hall, deputy town major of Dublin, to General Irwin, 6 September 1780, PRO SP 63/471, fo. 69.

Numerous crowds attended, but it was to be lamented that victory could not command acclamations by the defeat of our natural enemies, as all was melancholy silence, from a reflection, that it was triumphing over the misfortunes of our unhappy brethren, and a deeper incision in the wounds of the empire.[402]

Given that Catholics constituted a clear majority of the Dublin population by 1780, the attribution of the crowd's silence to a concern for the unity of the British empire is entirely unconvincing. In any event, the surrender of Charleston, coming within months of the successful defence of Savannah against a Franco-American force which included the Dillon regiment of the Irish brigade, suggested to most contemporaries – Jacobite, loyalist and patriot alike – that the southern colonies, at least, were in the process of being restored to the empire.

Attacks on the military continued in Dublin during 1781. In one incident a party of sixty recruits raised in the Midlands by a Lieutenant Ryan was lodged in a house near the barracks. Lord Carlisle, who succeeded Buckinghamshire as lord lieutenant in December 1780, described what happened during the officer's absence in a letter to the secretary of state dated 3 May: 'a violent mob assembled, broke into the house where his men were lodged, threatened to kill the non-commissioned officer in whose care they were, set the recruits at liberty, and carried off some clothing &c.'[403] Those responsible were described as manufacturers from the Liberties who had had previous 'disputes' with recruiting parties; however, their success in dispersing such a large body of men suggests that some of the recruits may have been detained against their will. Popular sympathy for deserters was manifested in another incident in August 1781, when a party of soldiers arrested a weaver suspected of desertion and was promptly attacked by 'a mob of men, women and children, to the amount of upwards of two thousand' who released the prisoner, continued to pursue the soldiers and killed one of them.[404]

A popular Jacobite song entitled '*An Buachaill Bán*' ('The White Boy') composed by Seán Ó Coileáin, a west Cork schoolmaster, sometime after the start of hostilities between Britain and the United Provinces in December 1780, confirms both the continuity of popular support for Britain's military enemies and the changing attitude of the Catholic masses towards the opposition in Ireland. Not only were the French, Spanish, Dutch and Americans praised, but so also were Anglo-Irish patriots:

---

[402] *FJ*, 22 June 1780.
[403] Carlisle to Hillsborough, 3 May 1781, PRO SP 63/472, fo. 278.
[404] *FLJ*, 29 August 1781.

> *Atáid Francaigh aosta, agus Spáinnigh gléasta*
> *agus cinn na bPléimeann mór ar sáil*
> *fá bhrataibh aonta i longaibh caola*
> *mar aon re laochra* Americá;
> *táid dronga tréan-fhear anso agus faobhair ghlas*
> *de bhuíon na hÉireann is claíomh 'na lámh*
> *ag iarraidh téarma is saoirse céirde*
> *is do bhéarfaid géilleadh dod Bhuachaill Bhán.*[405]

(The olden French and the well-equipped Spaniards, and the leaders of the great Flemings are on the sea, under united banners in sleek ships, along with the heroes of *America*; here are bands of strong men with shining weapons, from among Ireland's host, with swords in their hands, seeking a time-limit and a free trade, and they'll give allegiance to your White Boy [Prince Charles Edward].)

The '*téarma*' or time-limit probably refers to patriot demands for a limited rather than a perpetual mutiny act, while the reference to freedom of trade reflects continuing opposition claims that the low duty on imports of refined sugar, by making the refining of raw sugar in Ireland uneconomic, would effectively prevent the development of Irish trade with the West Indies. It may be noted that the phrase '*saoirse céirde*' is a calque on the English 'free trade' and would have been misunderstood by anyone who was unfamiliar with the latter – an indication that the slogan had diffused through all levels of Irish society.[406] But if the song shows an acute awareness of opposition demands in some respects, its assumption that Anglo-Irish patriots would welcome a Stuart restoration points to a profound ignorance of patriot ideology among sections of the Catholic masses, as well as the inability of many Catholics to conceive of any restoration of Ireland's rights that did not have the overthrow of the house of Hanover as an essential concomitant. At another level, the song signals the potential that was emerging for an alliance between the opposite extremes of the political spectrum. This song, as much as Joseph Pollock's *Letters of Owen Roe O'Nial*, represents an early stage in the evolution of opinion that would lay the basis for a coalition between Defenders and United Irishmen in the 1790s.

Recruitment after Saratoga

The difficulties encountered in meeting recruitment targets, and in retaining men once recruited, in the period before Saratoga have been

---

[405] '*Maidin lae ghil fá dhuille géag-glais*' in RIA Ms. 24 C 26, pp. 399–400.
[406] '*Ceird*' means 'trade' in the sense of 'craft' or 'occupation' but not in the sense of 'commerce' or 'exchange'. The song was still current in the early years of the twentieth century but '*saoirse ceirde*', its meaning forgotten, had by then been replaced with the meaningless '*saorghus caor dó*'; see Peadar Ó hAnnracháin, 'Filidhe ó Chairbre', *Irisleabhar na Gaedhilge* 18 (1908), 265.

discussed above. These problems became more acute after the start of hostilities with France. Whereas troops had been transferred from Ireland to America during the earlier period, it now became necessary to reinforce the Irish garrison (which had fallen below 9,000 men) as a matter of urgency. Two additional regiments were despatched from Britain but it was also hoped to raise 2,500 recruits locally to strengthen the depleted regiments already stationed in Ireland.[407] The commander-in-chief was soon complaining of the high rate of desertion and emphasising the need for additional measures 'to fill up the augmentation, which I do not find as successful as I could wish'.[408] The pressure to complete the ranks and the difficulty in procuring recruits led to the enlistment of many men who were unfit for service, as General Irwin informed the lord lieutenant following his review of the army during its encampment in the summer of 1778:

With regard to numbers who join, I had but too strong a proof of it the other day, when I drew out this army here to perform some manoeuvres, and I found the number of fighting men infinitely short of the numbers in my returns; that is, the men were present, but forced to be turned out of the ranks when we began to fire, &c.[409]

By September, some 1,800 new recruits had been enrolled but no fewer than 450 of them had already absconded.[410] The high rate of desertion was attributed to the 'ready protection and shelter given to deserters' by the general population, the indifference of many magistrates, and the high bounties offered to recruits – a factor which induced many to enlist with the intention of deserting at the first opportunity.[411] By January 1779 the number of recruits had reached 1,884 (presumably exclusive of deserters) but they were becoming 'every day more difficult to be got'.[412] In March it was finally agreed that new officers who had succeeded in raising more than half their quota of recruits would be allowed to pay seven guineas per man to cover the shortfall – thereby providing funds to defray the cost of finding replacements in other parts of George III's dominions.[413] The traditional expedient of offering an amnesty to deserters who returned

---

[407] For a summary of the Irish military establishment at the outbreak of the French war, see O'Connell, *Irish Politics and Social Conflict*, p. 71.
[408] Irwin to Buckinghamshire, 2 August 1778, in HMC Lothian Mss. (1905), p. 334.
[409] Irwin to Buckinghamshire, 15 August 1778, in *ibid.*, p. 336.
[410] Irwin to Buckinghamshire, 16 September 1778, in PRO SP 63/461, fos. 128–9.
[411] Irwin to Buckinghamshire, 30 September 1778, *ibid.*, fo. 149.
[412] Buckinghamshire to Weymouth, 3 January 1779, enclosing tables provided by General Irwin, PRO SP 63/464, fos. 4 and 7–10.
[413] Weymouth to Buckinghamshire, 3 March 1779, *ibid.*, fos. 114–15. Ensigns and lieutenants were expected to recruit eighteen and twenty-five men each respectively.

to their regiments was resorted to in August 1779 and again in February 1781.[414]

Little appeared to have changed in relation to rates of desertion by the autumn of 1780 when Buckinghamshire advised Lord George Germain of the problem this presented for the recruiting service in Ireland:

> Upon the 30th of January, 1779, this establishment wanted 1,967 men; at the end of August 1780 (nineteen months afterwards), the deficiency was 1,274. Permit me also to observe that a considerable proportion of the recruits has been raised in Scotland for the Highland regiments. In the last two months the desertion, &c., has exceeded the recruits by 27.[415]

In the intervening period, however, opposition attacks on the use of British legislation in Ireland had presented the recruiting service with an additional obstacle. The growing reluctance of magistrates to be seen to act under the authority of the British mutiny act had serious implications both for the maintenance of military discipline and for the recruitment effort. In May 1780 it was reported from Dublin that 'Since Mr. Bushe's mutiny and desertion bill has been seriously mentioned in parliament, the drums of the several recruiting parties in this city, six in number, have been silenced, as no magistrate can be found hardy enough to attest soldiers under an English act of parliament.'[416] The problem was not confined to the capital. Some months later the chief secretary forwarded the text of an advertisement which had been posted up in Lisburn, County Antrim, to Whitehall; the advertisement offered to provided legal assistance to soldiers who 'by the usual mode of bribes or intoxication may be induced to enlist and who on cool reflection – may repent of the same' in the event of their being court-martialled under the provisions of British legislation.[417] This was a daring initiative which had the potential considerably to weaken the strength of the army in Ireland given its chronically high rate of desertion. Fortunately for government, parliament enacted a perpetual mutiny bill within a week, thereby placing the military code of discipline beyond legal challenge.

The usual difficulty of raising recruits remained. In October 1780 Buckinghamshire counselled the secretary of state against a proposal to withdraw three regiments for service overseas and to replace them with newly raised regiments on the grounds that 'it may take a very long time indeed to complete them'. The lord lieutenant also questioned the loyalty

---

[414] Weymouth to Buckingham, 28 August 1779, in PRO SP 63/466, fo. 105 and a printed proclamation dated 7 February 1781 in PRO SP 63/472, fos. 100–1.
[415] Buckinghamshire to Germain, 20 October 1780, in HMC Stopford-Sackville Mss., I (1904), p. 277.
[416] *FLJ*, 31 May 1780.
[417] Heron to Porten, 12 August 1780, in PRO SP 63/470, fos. 248–50.

of such Irish recruits as might be induced to enlist in the new corps: 'nor will they from obvious reasons be composed of men upon whom the same dependence may be had in the unfortunate chance of any civil commotion, as upon those who are to be withdrawn'.[418] Surprisingly, however, a new recruitment drive organised by Lord Carlisle early in 1781 was unusually successful. This campaign differed from previous efforts in having as its aim, not the completion of under-strength British regiments with Irish recruits, but rather the raising of forty independent companies. As early as 5 April, Carlisle transmitted details of 1,300 recruits to the secretary of state, adding that a further 200–300 men had been raised since the list was compiled.[419] The contrast between the relative ease with which these recruits were found and the great difficulties that had been encountered previously requires explanation. Certainly, the effect of the loyalist revival, together with the improved prospects of a British victory in America, cannot be wholly discounted, especially as the units were mainly recruited in 'the northern parts of the kingdom'.[420] However, it is likely that the principal factor contributing to success on this occasion lay in the nature of the formations being raised – detached companies intended for garrison duty in England rather than battalions intended for active service in America.[421] In 1779 Lord Buckinghamshire had suggested that recruits could be raised much more readily if it were specified that they would be retained in Europe, 'as the idea of being sent to America is disagreeable to many'.[422] The greater readiness of men to enlist in 1781 may therefore be more apparent than real.

Carlisle took a more optimistic view and the success in recruiting the independent companies prompted him to revive the proposal that three new regiments should be raised in Ireland, thereby allowing an equal number of existing regiments to be deployed elsewhere. The secretary of state informed Carlisle that the king regarded his proposal with scepticism in view of the 'constant desertion of the troops raised in Ireland' but was none the less willing to sanction the recruitment of one regiment to test the water.[423] On 24 November, two weeks before news of Cornwallis's surrender at Yorktown arrived in Ireland, Carlisle reported that recruitment of the new corps was so far advanced that it would be possible to withdraw one of the old regiments for foreign service

---

[418] Buckinghamshire to Hillsborough, 7 October 1780, in PRO SP 63/471, fo. 184.
[419] Carlisle to Hillsborough, 5 April 1781, in PRO SP 63/472, fo. 200.
[420] Carlisle to Hillsborough, 8 April 1781, ibid., fo. 208.
[421] For the background, see Piers Mackesy, The War for America 1775–1783 (London, 1964), p. 371.
[422] Buckinghamshire to Hillsborough, 17 December 1779, in PRO SP 63/467, fo. 255.
[423] Hillsborough to Carlisle, 8 September 1781, in PRO SP 63/473, fo. 161.

'very soon'.[424] In this case also, an awareness that it was intended to retain the new corps on garrison duty in Ireland is likely to have contributed to the relative ease with which recruits were raised.

The practice of impressing seamen into the navy, which had been viewed as a grievance by members of the patriot opposition during the early years of the war, seems to have attracted much less criticism once France replaced the American colonists as the principal enemy. When the students of the Trinity College Historical Society debated the question 'Whether it would be for the advantage of a free state, that the king should have a power of impressing seamen?' in December 1778 they answered in the affirmative by a majority of seventeen votes to three.[425] In the middle of the following year the generally patriotic *Hibernian Magazine* noted the 'great success which the press-gang meets with every night' in Dublin, and commented that this contributed 'no less to safety and peace in our streets, than it does to the public service in general'.[426] By 1780, however, in the wake of the free-trade agitation and at a time when the opposition was actively pressing constitutional demands in relation to Poynings' law and British parliament's power to legislate for Ireland, the university debating society reversed its earlier position by voting twelve to five against the question 'Whether the power of impressing seamen ought to be allowed in a free country?'[427] A year later, with a loyalist revival underway, the student debaters reversed themselves once again and affirmed their belief that 'impressing men for the sea service, ought to be allowed in a free country' by the comfortable margin of sixteen votes to seven.[428]

The decline of patriotism

There was an early indication that 1781 was unlikely to see an improvement in the fortunes of the opposition when Dublin's Common Council voted to confer the freedom of the city on Lord Carlisle, having first rejected a motion by James Napper Tandy that the question be deferred until more was known about Carlisle's disposition.[429] None the less, the extra-parliamentary opposition continued to press for the constitutional changes they had failed to obtain in 1780 – a declaration of legislative independence and the modification of Poynings' law – although these were increasingly presented as part of a more traditional patriot agenda rather

---

[424] Hillsborough to Carlisle, 22 November 1781, *ibid.*, fo. 341.
[425] Historical Society minutes, 2 December 1778, in TCD Mun. Soc./Hist. 3, pp. 284–5.
[426] *HM*, July 1779, 430.
[427] Historical Society minutes, 17 May 1780, in TCD Mun. Soc./Hist. 3, p. 495.
[428] Historical Society minutes, 7 March 1781, *ibid.*, p. 614.   [429] *FLJ*, 24 January 1781.

than as measures necessary for the protection of free trade. The tactics used were those that had failed in 1780: propaganda among the general population, convening county meetings and 'instructing' members of parliament. A handbill distributed among a crowd that was waiting outside Dublin's Rotunda in February 1781 to catch a glimpse of members of high society as they arrived for a masked ball included the following:

> Advice to *Irishmen* of every rank ... Meet in constitutional aggregate bodies and instruct your representatives to demand (and not to grant *any* supplies to the crown until the demand is granted) a full, clear and explicit declaration of Ireland's uncontrovertible *independence* – a repeal of Poynings' law – the obtaining the *Judges* Bill, an *Habeas Corpus* Act – and a curtailing of all useless employments and unmerited pensions ... Let the city and county of Dublin begin; and the glorious flame will spread from Derry to Dingle.[430]

Around the same time, Lord Charlemont advised Dr Alexander Haliday of Belfast of his 'fixed opinion' that the 'firm though moderate interference of the people by instructing their representatives' would be necessary if the parliamentary opposition was to succeed in the forthcoming session of parliament.[431] Revealingly, Charlemont focused on repeal of the perpetual clause of the mutiny bill and a modification of Poynings' law as the two measures that should be included in the instructions to members. Instead of demanding a declaration of the exclusive right of the Irish parliament to legislate for Ireland, as the opposition-inspired instructions of the previous year had done, he suggested closing the addresses with a request for members to support 'whatever measures their wisdom may deem most effectual towards the farther securing to the legislature of this kingdom that independency which their virtuous efforts have already asserted and gained'. This was a tacit acceptance that a declaration of legislative independence was no longer a realistic goal. Instead, the parliamentary opposition would challenge pro-government members to behave in accordance with their own claim that legislative independence had already been achieved. In keeping with this strategy, the Dublin Lawyers' corps of Volunteers formally resolved that 'our countrymen, roused to a sense of their own importance, and demanding restitution of their rights, have opened a glorious prospect of commercial and constitutional freedom'.[432]

The opposition campaign of 1781 failed to rekindle the enthusiasm of 1779. In January, only a month after arriving in the country, Lord Carlisle felt able to advise the secretary of state that 'wild notions of

---

[430] *Ibid.*, 3 March 1781.
[431] Charlemont to Haliday, 3 March 1781, in HMC Charlemont Mss., 12th report, appendix X (1894), pp. 379–80.
[432] *DEP*, 9 June 1781.

republicism [*sic*] become every day more the objects of contempt and derision' and that 'the national fever is subsiding', while sounding a note of caution about the possibility of a relapse.[433] In the middle of the year he reassured an English correspondent that 'our political stupor continues, owing to the general dispersion of those [members of parliament] who ... are seldom long together without doing some mischief'.[434] The contrast between the public mood in the autumn of 1781 and that which had prevailed two years previously was equally obvious to supporters of the opposition: 'Notwithstanding parliament must meet in a week', lamented one writer, 'such is the apathy of public spirit, that it is no more the subject of conversation, than if no question of consequence was to be agitated. How unlike the commencement of the last session, when every eye was animated with freedom, and every mouth breathed the spirit of patriotism!'[435] The campaign to instruct members was a failure and 'instructions' appear to have been adopted only in the opposition strongholds of Dublin (by the mayor and both houses of Dublin Corporation and by a meeting of freeholders in the county) and east Ulster (by the freeholders of County Down and the borough of Belfast).[436] In addition, the freeholders of County Leitrim resolved that their existing members of parliament had forfeited their support 'for not complying with the instructions of their constituents, on a late important occasion'.[437] These, at least, are the only addresses for which I have found reports in the contemporary press. While it is possible that the freeholders of other counties may have adopted such addresses, the following exhortation by an opposition writer suggests that it is unlikely: 'May the county of Louth be recorded for its singularity, and may every other county, city, and independent borough in Ireland, immediately follow up the example of Down, Leitrim and Dublin, by instructing their respective delegates in all constitutional points necessary for discussion in the grand assembly of the nation.'[438] The freeholders of County Louth had resolved that 'our present representatives have behaved as true friends to Ireland, and therefore we do not think it necessary to instruct them as to their conduct in parliament' – a resolution which was tantamount to a repudiation of the parliamentary opposition since the county's members were both consistent supporters of government.[439] The range of issues covered by the patriotic addresses is also revealing. The Dublin city address mentioned a declaration of legislative independence, modification of Poynings' law, a habeas corpus act, tenure of judges, a reduction of

---

[433] Carlisle to Hillsborough, 29 January 1781, in PRO SP 63/474, fo. 20.
[434] Lord Carlisle to Lord Gower, 30 June 1781, in HMC Carlisle Mss., 15th report, appendix VI (1897), p. 509.
[435] *FLJ*, 6 October 1781.   [436] *DEP*, 23, 25 and 30 October 1781.
[437] *Ibid.*, 27 October 1781.   [438] *FLJ*, 24 October 1781.   [439] *DEP*, 11 October 1781.

places and pensions, a limited mutiny bill, and a revision of the sugar duty – a patriotic wish-list which, by encompassing everything, emphasised nothing. The other addresses showed local variations but were equally wide-ranging: the County Down address omitted the reference to a declaration of right, as Charlemont had recommended, and that of Belfast omitted the reference to places and pensions but added a proposal for the establishment of an Irish navy to protect the country's trade. The constitutional demands that had preoccupied the opposition a year before had, by the autumn of 1781, been relegated to the position of two points among several in a broader programme.

The outcome of the Volunteer reviews was also disappointing for the opposition. In early June a correspondent of the *Dublin Evening Post* predicted that the Volunteer review due to be held at Belfast in a few weeks would be characterised by 'the irresistible languages of truth and freedom', the resolution of the Dublin Lawyers' corps having 'conspicuously led the way'.[440] In the event, the resolution adopted at the Belfast review entirely avoided political questions and merely thanked Lord Charlemont, the reviewing general, 'for the trouble you have taken in communicating to us the sentiments of the gentlemen of the Lawyers' Corps' – a politely worded rebuff.[441] The review held at Derry was more satisfactory from an opposition point of view, the resolution expressing confidence that Ireland would 'be emancipated from every bond, and fully reinstated in all the privileges necessary to the entire freedom and independence of the Irish constitution'.[442] None the less, it was clear that many Volunteer corps were anxious to avoid becoming embroiled in political controversy. Francis Dobbs, a Volunteer major and prominent patriot, later recalled that the 'addresses and resolutions after the reviews in 1781, were greatly diversified – some contained politics, and spoke the boldest truths; whilst others avoided all political discussion'.[443] The failure of the Volunteer rank and file to endorse the opposition's demands was not lost on waverers among the political élite. On the resumption of parliament Edward Tighe, member for the pocket borough of Athboy, informed Lord Buckinghamshire, the former lord lieutenant, that the 'cold water thrown in the north upon the resolutions framed by the Lawyers' Corps, and carried down in August by Lord C[harlemont]. &c. added to the loyal spirit exhibited upon a rumour of invasion has been of the greatest service to government'.[444] In the absence of popular pressure, many members who had opposed government in 1779 returned to their allegiance in 1781.

---

[440] *Ibid.*, 14 July 1781.   [441] *Ibid.*, 28 July 1781.   [442] *Ibid.*, 2 August 1781.
[443] Francis Dobbs, *A History of Irish Affairs, from the 12th of October, 1779, to the 15th September, 1782, the Day of Lord Temple's Arrival* (Dublin, 1782), p. 44.
[444] Tighe to Buckinghamshire, 23 November 1781, in HMC Lothian Mss. (1905), p. 403.

The year was also characterised by a noticeable increase in the content of pro-government material in the newspapers and in the output of loyalist pamphlets. Indeed, in December 1780 the attorney general recommended that opposition newspapers should not be prosecuted for publishing a resolution of the Merchants' corps of Volunteers critical of parliament – as the Commons had requested in August – on the grounds that 'the language of those offensive publications and the spirit which suggested them seemed gradually to slacken or alter' after the recess of parliament.[445] None the less, the new and more moderate tone of the press cannot be viewed simply as a reflection of changing public attitudes. An anonymous patriot put a pointed question to William Eden, Lord Carlisle's chief secretary: 'You say, the people of Ireland are perfectly satisfied with our present commercial and political condition: Why then was Guatimozin pensioned? Why were editors of news-papers bribed?'[446] It was true that the talents of Frederick Jebb ('Guatimozin') had been turned against the opposition, and the *Freeman's Journal*, once the principal patriot organ, became increasingly pro-government during the course of 1781. A pamphlet co-authored by Jebb struck a few well-aimed blows at the extra-parliamentary opposition. His targets included the role played by Presbyterian ministers in political agitation:

The inhabitants of a district, obscure and remote, are not likely to increase their respect for the ancient laws and constitution of the land, when they behold their gospel-minister, clad in uniform, and at the head of a body of armed citizens, drawing up resolutions for the reformation of those very laws and constitution, and publishing them in all the news-papers for the purpose not only of directing the conduct of the legislature therein, but likewise of supplying a neighbour's aid of seditious support to the wavering, or weak of spirit, all around the country.[447]

The practice of Volunteer corps adopting political resolutions was condemned as unconstitutional ('a body of citizens meeting in arms, and professing to be so, have no more right *constitutionally* to influence the legislature, than the 5th regiment of dragoons has')[448] – a view with which the members of the Trinity College Historical Society concurred.[449] Jebb also provided an unflattering, but probably all too accurate, account of the

---

[445] John Scott to Lord Buckinghamshire, 11 December 1780, in PRO SP 63/471, fo. 418.
[446] *A Letter to William Eden, Esq. Occasioned by a Pamphlet Commonly Attributed to Him* (Dublin, 1781), p. 49.
[447] [Frederick Jebb and Robert Johnson], *Thoughts on the Discontents of the People Last Year, respecting the Sugar Duties* (Dublin, 1781), p. 5.
[448] *Ibid.*, p. 6.
[449] Historical Society minutes, 15 November 1780, in TCD Mun. Soc./Hist. 3, p. 560. The question 'Ought Volunteer associations to interfere in parliamentary measures?' was answered in the negative by nineteen votes to five.

methods by which the extra-parliamentary opposition procured patriotic 'instructions' from unrepresentative meetings of politically committed freeholders:

Some hours are employed in eloquent abuse of administration, or of the parliament, and when all the oratory of the assembly hath been expended, a string of resolutions comes forth from some gentleman's pocket, where they had been previously magazined, they are *unanimously* agreed to, and then published in all the news-papers in town, with the speeches of the various orators upon the occasion and comments.[450]

Another pro-government author cited Sir William Blackstone's *Commentaries* in support of the view that the practice of instructing members of parliament was itself unconstitutional as the members were elected 'in order to consult for the nation at large, but not, weather-cock-like, to veer with the vocal blast of any one set of men, or place in particular'.[451] The same author went so far as to defend Poynings' law as a positive feature of the Irish constitution: by using its power to amend the heads of bills before they were transmitted, the Privy Council actually reduced the risk of such measures being entirely suppressed in Britain.[452] The use of such arguments confirms that supporters of the constitutional status quo had recovered their self-confidence and that the patriotic tide had ebbed since the high-water mark of 1779. By 1781 it was again possible to portray patriots as seditious conspirators plotting an American-style rebellion, or as cynical demagogues anxious to be bought off with a place or a pension:

I am sorry to perceive that most of the demands among us, similar to those among former unhappy governments [the American colonies], arise but from men who are leaders and stimulators of sedition, who become clamorous in order to grow conspicuous, to make themselves the idols of the people, hoping that their silence may afterward be sought through the potent peace-offerings of gaped-for gold.[453]

Charles Francis Sheridan, a member of parliament who two years previously had written a pamphlet to controvert the doctrine of Sir William Blackstone that the 'power and jurisdiction of [the British] parliament is so transcendent and absolute, that it cannot be confined either for causes or persons, within any bounds', now returned to print with a tract attacking the patriot position on 'the three great national questions' – a declaration of legislative independence, Poynings' law and the perpetual

---

450 [Jebb and Johnson], *Thoughts on the Discontents of the People Last Year*, pp. 33–4.
451 *An Essay on the Act of Poynings, and the Present Mode of Appeal. Addressed to the Right Honourable William Eden, previous to his Becoming a Member of the Parliament of Ireland* (Dublin, 1781), pp. 9–10.
452 *Ibid.*, p. 12.   453 *Ibid.*, p. 23.

mutiny bill.[454] Condemning the opposition for trying to whip up popular unrest in relation to issues of little or no practical importance, Sheridan urged patriots to allow their enthusiasm 'to be regulated by the evident utility of the objects contended for' and repeated the assurance frequently given by government supporters that the 'exclusive authority of our own parliament was, if not in *theory*, at least in *fact* restored to us' by the repeal of the restrictions on Irish trade.[455] Another pro-government pamphlet even argued that a perpetual mutiny act was, paradoxically, preferable to the biennial measure advocated by the opposition since, if a new act were required in every session of parliament, it would be 'hereafter in the power of the crown to refuse the royal assent to it, in order to reduce us once more to be under the bondage of an English act'.[456]

British military successes had helped to stimulate loyalist sentiment during 1780 and news favourable to government continued to arrive well into the following year. It might be supposed that Britain's declaration of war against the United Provinces in December 1780 would have been unpopular with the Irish political nation, given the central position occupied by William of Orange in the Protestant pantheon, the frequency with which patriot orators invoked the Dutch revolt against Spanish rule as an example of successful resistance against tyranny, and the Calvinist religious establishment of the United Provinces. This was not the case. Rather, since Britain declared war on a state that was willing to remain neutral, the Dutch war bolstered loyalist feeling by underlining the confidence with which government now viewed the war. As early as December 1780 the merchants of Belfast were reported to be fitting out a schooner called the *Harlequin* 'as a letter of marque to cruise against the Dutch'.[457] In March 1781 Belfast was the scene of 'great rejoicings' and the local Volunteer battalion paraded and fired a *feu de joie* when news arrived that Admiral Rodney had captured the Dutch trading station of St Eustatius; in the evening 'there were bonfires, town was elegantly illuminated, and other demonstrations of joy were shown on the occasion'.[458] The news was greeted with similar enthusiasm in Dublin, where the 'illuminations were general and superb; the different volunteer corps assembled . . . and fired a *feu de joye*, amidst the acclamations of an innumerable concourse of spectators'.[459] Press reports concerning the course

[454] Charles Francis Sheridan, *Observations on the Doctrine Laid Down by Sir William Blackstone, respecting the Extent of the Power of the British Parliament, particularly with relation to Ireland* (London and Dublin, 1779).
[455] [Charles Francis Sheridan], *A Review of the Three Great National Questions relative to a Declaration of Right, Poynings' Law, and the Mutiny Bill* (Dublin, 1781), pp. 22 and 27.
[456] *An Answer to a Pamphlet, Entitled, Observations on the Mutiny Bill by a Member of the House of Commons* (Dublin, 1781), p. 39.
[457] Joy, *Historical Collections*, p. 164.   [458] *Ibid.*   [459] *FLJ*, 24 March 1781.

of the struggle on the American continent remained optimistic during the first half of 1781. It was predicted in January that 'Lord Cornwallis and General Leslie would be masters of North Carolina and Virginia, before the end of March'.[460] Good news from the south continued in February when it was reported that 'near 3000 of the inhabitants of North Carolina have set up the royal standard under a Mr. Johnstone; and numbers are daily flocking in, resolved no longer to submit to the tyranny of their provincial governments, the horrors of war, and, as they say, the unnatural alliance with their former allies the French'.[461] In the same month a newspaper in Cork – often the first European port to receive news from America – reviewed the latest reports from New York and concluded that 'there now appears a real prospect of America being reduced to obedience in two or three months at farthest'.[462] The author of this piece referred contemptuously to General Nathanael Greene, the American commander in the Carolinas, as 'mister' Greene, but Irish assessments of the balance of forces changed as the campaigns in the south and Virginia progressed. Another paper showed a better appreciation of military realities in October when it referred to 'the brave, persevering and gallant officer, Major General Greene' in its account of the latest developments in South Carolina.[463] None the less, the general perception during most of 1781 that the war was going well for Britain kept the morale of Irish loyalists buoyant and provided the extra-parliamentary opposition with no issues on which it could capitalise. Just as prospects for Britain began to appear less favourable – the French having seized Tobago in June – the sudden reappearance of an external threat precipitated a further intense outburst of loyalty among the Protestant population.

The invasion alert of 1781

The scant support which existed in Protestant Ireland for the Francophile attitudes of extreme patriot propaganda was evident from the reaction of the Volunteer movement when reports arrived in early September that a combined Franco-Spanish fleet with an army of 15,000 men on board was *en route* for Munster. Volunteer corps vied with each other in their eagerness to place themselves at the disposal of government. William Eden, the chief secretary, lost no time in informing the prime minister of what he termed an 'extraordinary turn in the disposition of the volunteer corps through every part of this kingdom', as a result of which government had 'already received addresses from near two-thirds of the

---

[460] *Cork Evening Post*, 29 January 1781 and *LJ*, 9 February 1781.
[461] *FLJ*, 21 February 1781.   [462] *Cork Evening Post*, 26 February 1781.
[463] *FLJ*, 10 October 1781.

whole number, expressing the utmost zeal and loyalty, and desiring, if any danger should happen or be apprehended, to be employed in whatever manner his Excellency shall please to command'.[464] Volunteer units in areas where support for the patriot opposition had been strongest were just as eager to offer their services as those in less politicised regions. On 7 September the assembled delegates of the Dublin Volunteer corps unanimously addressed the lord lieutenant to 'offer their assistance to act in such manner as shall be thought necessary for the safety and protection of this kingdom'.[465] Similar addresses were adopted by Volunteer corps in such areas of patriot strength as County Antrim, Newry and Belfast.[466] Lists of those corps placing themselves at the disposal of government were published in the press and indicate that eagerness to cooperate with the authorities was general in all parts of the country.[467] Lord Carlisle, on his part, was so confident of the Volunteers' loyalty that he decided to employ them in 'detached services' and for the maintenance of public order in districts from which the army had been withdrawn to meet the threat of invasion in Munster – districts which 'might otherwise be left exposed to the ravages of the lower class of the people'.[468]

If the Protestant population was united in the face of an external threat, Catholics continued to be divided largely along class lines. Invasion-threatened Cork displayed in microcosm the range of attitudes which existed. On the one hand, a striking example of the loyalty of the Catholic élite was seen during the invasion alert when a Catholic merchant in the city named George Goold advanced a loan of £600 to General Irwin, the commander-in-chief, for use in paying the expanded local garrison.[469] General Irwin wrote to the chief secretary from Cork as follows:

Mr Goold a considerable Roman Catholic merchant here, professing in his own name and in that of all his acquaintances of that profession the utmost loyalty to His Majesty and zeal for the service, has been with me offering in his own name and theirs any service in their power, and assuring me (to use his own expression) that even to his last guinea shall be at the king's disposal and that if I want money I have only to call on him for it; every thing is perfectly quiet here, no run on the bank as was apprehended, and the people showing much less fear than I should have thought.[470]

Goold's action was applauded alike by supporters of government, the patriot opposition and the Catholic Committee – which body voted him

---

[464] William Eden to Lord North, 13 September 1781, in Beresford (ed.), *Correspondence of the Right Hon. John Beresford*, I, p. 172.

[465] PRO SP 63/476, fo. 67.   [466] *Ibid.*, fo. 116; *BNL*, 18 September 1781.

[467] See, for example, *FLJ*, 19 September 1781.

[468] Carlisle to Hillsborough, 8 September 1781, in PRO SP 63/476, fo. 62.

[469] For a fuller account of this episode, see McGeehin, 'The activities and personnel of the General Committee of the Catholics of Ireland', pp. 131–4.

[470] Irwin to William Eden, 10 September 1781, PRO SP 63/473, fos. 236–7.

its thanks. But the loyalty exhibited by Goold was far from universal and the commander-in-chief's report of the calm prevailing in Cork was less than candid. On 8 September, two days before the above report was written, a soldier was stabbed and killed by three men. On the following night, a military party descended on the street where the killing took place and destroyed two houses before engaging in a general retaliation against the populace reminiscent of an earlier episode in Kilkenny:

> Last night [9 September] a great number of riotous soldiers assembled together and ran tumultuously through the city, marking their progress by the most wanton outrages upon the persons and houses of the inhabitants. Many were severely wounded, others were obliged to leave their houses to the mercy of that lawless mob and an universal consternation was spread throughout the town.[471]

Such collective punishment would have no rationale, and would scarcely have been ignored by the commander-in-chief, had the attacks on soldiers been random acts of criminal violence. The action of the military makes sense only if the attacks are seen as a manifestation of the attitudes of the wider community, a community of which the attackers formed part and whose political assumptions they shared. It may be noted that a member of the Cork garrison had also been houghed in May 1781,[472] and in 1782 American prisoners confined at Kinsale were transferred to England because of the large numbers who were escaping 'by the support of evil minded people which abound at Cork'.[473] The prevalence of disaffection in Cork is confirmed by an exhortation read at all Catholic churches in the city on 16 September 1781, the Sunday following the military riot described above:

> The Roman Catholics of this city, are earnestly exhorted to maintain, at all times, but particularly now, when we are threatened by foreign enemies, a peaceable behaviour, and to show their zeal and loyalty to his present Majesty and government. They are to consider the military that has been sent here for our defence, as their best friends and protectors; and so far from quarreling with them, we strenuously exhort you, to cherish and use them with every civility in your power, that by this and every other demonstration, all our enemies may see that one only interest unites us, and that we are ready to sacrifice our lives and fortunes in support of this common cause.[474]

This was a forthright expression of a perspective shared by many members of the upper strata of Catholic society, both clerical and lay, but the fact that it was considered necessary to deliver such a message to the inhabitants of Ireland's second city indicates the prevalence of very

---

[471] *FLJ*, 15 September 1781.   [472] *FDJ*, 17 May 1781.
[473] Captain William Bennett, Royal Navy, to Mr Stephens, 25 May 1782, PRO HO 28/2, fo. 142.
[474] *Cork Evening Post*, 17 September 1781.

different attitudes among lower-class Catholics. Descriptions were published in the press of three men who were wanted for killing the soldier. They were named as Maurice Twomey, a 19-year-old cooper; John Nevill, a 24-year-old carpenter; and Thomas Nevill, an 18-year-old carpenter – an artisan background that is consistent with the information available on houghers in other urban centres.[475] At the end of the year the 'mayor and inhabitants' of Galway offered a reward of one hundred guineas, in addition to fifty guineas offered by the local Volunteer corps, for information leading to the apprehension of houghers in that city.[476]

While it would be unsafe to regard those engaged in attacks on military personnel as representative of the general Catholic population, it would be equally unwarranted to view George Goold as a typical Cork merchant. There is, in fact, ample evidence that the loyalties of the Cork merchant class were more equivocal than the Catholic Committee would have been happy to admit. State papers described a Cork merchant named Hayes as having 'the character of a most rancoured Yankee' and as talking 'in Cork houses in a most impudent and seditious manner' in 1779.[477] When, in January 1780, Lord Buckinghamshire reported to Lord Hillsborough that provisions being exported by Cork merchants and ostensibly intended for the United Provinces were in fact going to France he also advised the secretary of state that 'any measure to be taken by me, or the Privy Council, to stop the sailing of these provisions would be immediately productive of dangerous violence' – a view which Hillsborough characterised as being 'little short of a declaration that all government in Ireland is dissolved'.[478] In March of the same year the governor of the Leeward Islands informed the British Treasury that ships cleared from Cork were conducting a clandestine trade with the enemy at the Dutch island of St Eustatius.[479] A year later, during the administration of Lord Carlisle, nothing had changed in the southern port except that provisions which had previously been consigned to Dutch ports were now being cleared for Ostend in the Austrian Netherlands because of the British declaration of war against the United Provinces. The chief secretary frankly admitted that he could think of no means of countering this tactic except 'the most precarious one of giving notice to the king's cruisers in the Channel to detain the vessel if they shall find her stretching for the coast of

[475] *Ibid.*   [476] *HJ*, 12 December 1781.

[477] H. Davis, a customs officer at Cork, to the Commissioners of the Revenue, 16 February 1779, in PRO SP 63/464, fo. 103v.

[478] Buckinghamshire to Hillsborough, 30 January 1780, and Hillsborough to Buckinghamshire, 6 February 1780 in SP 63/468, fos. 120 and 132 respectively.

[479] Governor William Burt to John Robinson, 15 March 1780, in K.G. Davies (ed.), *Documents of the American Revolution 1770–1783 (Colonial Office Series)*, XVI (Dublin, 1977), p. 328.

France'.[480] Cork merchants were not alone in engaging in such practices. An intelligence report received by the Irish administration from the Royal Navy stated that a vessel owned by a Dublin merchant named Connor and captained by Christopher Sheridan, a native of Howth, had sailed from the city with dry goods consigned to British-held New York, but 'instead of going there, they carried the goods into James's or York River in Virginia and sold there to the rebels'.[481] Nor was this an isolated incident. In September 1780 James Madison, a future president of the United States, was informed by a correspondent at Richmond, Virginia, that 'several vessels have lately come in cleared from different ports, but the men and cargoes the produce of Ireland'.[482] The religious background of the merchants who were involved in the above activities is unknown, and they may well have been motivated by nothing more profound than a desire to sell to the highest bidder, but their conduct detracts from the image of universal loyalty which the addresses of the Catholic Committee sought to convey.

Yorktown

A new session of parliament opened on 9 October 1781 – by coincidence, the day on which the Franco-American bombardment of British positions at Yorktown commenced. Administration contemplated the new session with complacency. In his report on the first day's proceedings Lord Carlisle advised the secretary of state that the session 'gave a prospect of much good temper and favourable disposition to his Majesty's government',[483] views echoed by the chief secretary who informed Lord North that the members had shown 'a disposition towards Great Britain less suspicious than was ever known'.[484] The address returned by the Commons in reply to the speech from the throne was fulsome in its expressions of loyalty:

We behold with a spirit animated by just resentment the unnatural and dangerous combination of enemies to which his Majesty's dominions are exposed and we entreat your excellency to assure his Majesty of our loyal and earnest disposition to give him every assistance compatible with our means and circumstances.[485]

[480] Eden to Porten, 26 March 1781, PRO SP 63/474, fo. 227.
[481] PRO SP 63/475, fo. 233.
[482] David Jameson to James Madison, 20 September 1780, in W.T. Hutchinson and W.M.E. Rachal (eds.), *The Papers of James Madison*, II (Chicago, 1962), p. 94.
[483] Carlisle to Hillsborough, 10 October 1781, in PRO SP 63/476, fo. 228.
[484] William Eden to North, 13 October 1781, in Beresford (ed.), *Correspondence of the Right Hon. John Beresford*, I, p. 174.
[485] PRO SP 63/476, fo. 251.

William Eden expressed his confidence in the strength of government, not only in parliament but in the country as a whole, in a letter to Lord North: 'I do not think that the declamations of our opponents will have any effect among the people. Government stands high in the opinion of the day.'[486] On 3 November, Grattan proposed an amendment to the mutiny act to make it biennial rather than perpetual. As he had done in different circumstances in the previous session, he again highlighted the contrast between Britain's policy towards Ireland and America:

Commissioners have been sent to America, to offer a branch of the British empire in arms against the parent state, unconditional terms to tax themselves, and regulate their own army. Two of the commissioners have been sent over to govern this kingdom – Will his excellency [Lord Carlisle], or the right hon. gentleman his secretary [William Eden], say, that Ireland is not entitled to the terms offered America? – That the loyal and affectionate sister of England is not entitled to the indulgence held out to the enemy of England – to the ally of France?[487]

This rhetoric had no discernible effect on pro-government members and the motion was defeated by the convincing margin of 133 to 77. Later in the month Edward Tighe informed Lord Buckinghamshire that 'the complexion of parliament is very fair, and the accounts from the country good and promising'.[488] Carlisle was equally sanguine, advising an English correspondent that 'our troops [are] as steady as possible, and our last division [was] 144 to 63 upon the popular business of the sugar trade, I think you may congratulate me upon having turned one corner if not more of this session of parliament'.[489] In a letter to the secretary of state dated 22 November 1781 the viceroy stressed the importance of returning bills from England promptly so that the session could be concluded before the spring assizes – a manœuvre which would 'deprive the opposition of their most favourite opportunity to raise ferments in the kingdom'. None the less, Carlisle was happy to state that 'popular ferments' were 'much allayed' since his assumption of office.[490] The patriot opposition, both in parliament and the country, had lost the momentum and sense of purpose which had characterised it in 1779 and early 1780 but, unknown to the lord lieutenant, Irish politics were about to be 'turned upside down' by a factor entirely outside his control.

The critical situation in which the army under Lord Cornwallis found itself in September 1781 took the Irish public as much by surprise as it

---

[486] Eden to North, 14 November 1781, in Beresford (ed.), *Correspondence of the Right Hon. John Beresford*, I, p. 189.
[487] Debate of 13 November 1781 in *HM*, November 1782, 597.
[488] Edward Tighe to Buckinghamshire, 23 November 1781, in HMC Lothian Mss. (1905) p. 403.
[489] Carlisle to Lord Gower, 23 November 1781, in HMC Carlisle Mss., p. 534.
[490] Carlisle to Hillsborough, 22 November 1781, in PRO SP 63/477, fo. 109.

did the British commanders in North America. As late as 22 November the consistently loyalist *Faulkner's Dublin Journal* was still insisting that 'Lord Cornwallis is by no means so desperately situated as may be imagined; for it is very possible for Sir Henry Clinton to join him.'[491] A week later the same paper claimed that Admiral Digby had attacked the French fleet blockading Yorktown 'and taken five ships of the line, and destroyed several others, which threw the leaders at Boston to such despair as to declare openly their wish for peace and reconciliation'.[492] But by this date even the *Dublin Journal* had come to doubt the likelihood of ultimate British victory and the paper closed its implausible report with the despairing comment 'we wish it may be true'. On 4 December the Irish press reported the surrender of the Yorktown garrison.

Conclusion

The four years between the surrender of General Burgoyne at Saratoga and that of Lord Cornwallis at Yorktown witnessed large fluctuations in the mood of the Anglo-Irish community. An early revival of anti-war sentiment in the immediate aftermath of Saratoga gave way to traditional feelings of loyalty once France entered the war as America's ally. At the same time, British efforts to negotiate with the colonies through the Carlisle peace commission had the dual effect of convincing many that government was willing to redress legitimate American grievances while simultaneously raising expectations that similar concessions would be made to Ireland. The disappointment of these hopes transformed 'free trade' from a slogan of the patriot opposition into a demand supported by all sections of Irish society. By late 1779 an outbreak of hostilities between elements of the Volunteers and the army was a real danger and a small group of radical patriots was briefly driven to toy with the 'American option' of separation from Britain in alliance with France. Lord North's propositions on Irish trade successfully defused this crisis and loyalist sentiment quickly reasserted itself among the Protestant community – a process facilitated by British victories in both Europe and America. The political ferment which accompanied the free-trade agitation had, however, given patriots an opportunity to popularise the principle of Ireland's constitutional parity with Great Britain, although a majority of the political nation accepted quasi-official assurances that no further attempts would be made to legislate for Ireland at Westminster. Many patriots appreciated that the cross-community consensus which had brought success in the non-importation campaign would be equally essential in the event of any future conflict with Great Britain and this realisation contributed to

<hr />

[491] *FDJ*, 22 November 1781.   [492] *Ibid.*, 1 December 1781.

the emergence of a body of opinion that was favourably disposed towards further measures of Catholic relief.

The contrast which had long been apparent in the Catholic community between the political loyalty of many members of the social élite and the unrestrained disaffection of the masses continued unchanged throughout this period. The likely behaviour of the Irish population in general, and of Catholics in particular, in the event of a French landing was a matter of great practical importance to French military planners, and a modern student of that country's strategy towards Ireland has summarised the evidence of the French archives as follows:

> There was considerable disagreement amongst the Irish in France as to whether the Catholic nobility and gentry as well as the expanding merchant class would assist in the event of a landing, for fear of losing their possessions and position in the event of defeat. However strategists were generally agreed that the mass of Irish Catholics, with little to lose, would support a landing by a substantial army whose objective was to secure the permanent withdrawal of the English from Ireland.[493]

This assessment is corroborated by the extant sources which express contemporary opinion within Ireland. The gentry and sections of the urban élite, pursuing a policy of *rapprochement* with the house of Hanover in the hope of securing a gradual reduction of their legal disabilities, were happy to condemn both the American colonists and their European allies; but plebeian Catholics, imbued with a Jacobite world-view and with little to gain from a relaxation of Penal legislation, celebrated American victories in song and, at times, gave violent expression to their anti-British sentiments. None the less, a crucial change had taken place in the political outlook of the populace. In response to the increasingly anti-British rhetoric of Anglo-Irish patriots and to the reassessment of attitudes towards the Catholic population taking place in their ranks, a new solidarity with the patriot opposition and its demands had developed among lower-class Catholics. By 1781, convergence on such issues as Irish independence, a French alliance and Catholic relief meant that cooperation between the conventional extremes of the political spectrum was no longer inconceivable.

---

[493] Marcus de la Poer Beresford, 'Ireland in French strategy during the American War of Independence 1776–83', *Irish Sword* 12 (1975–76), 23.

4 Britain defeated, 1781–1783

As had previously happened after General Burgoyne's defeat at Saratoga, the instinctive reaction of leading patriots in the immediate aftermath of Lord Cornwallis's surrender at Yorktown was to rally around the throne. Barry Yelverton had intended to move a resolution calling for the amendment of Poynings' law on 4 December but instead proposed an address effusive in its expression of loyalty to the crown, the British connection and the empire. In his speech on the occasion he declared that:

> We are called upon to testify our affection and unalterable attachment to that country, and to convince foreign nations *we do not despair of the commonwealth* but that the British empire still has power and resources to render her formidable to her numerous enemies, and to convince them that the dismemberment she has suffered has only served to draw the remaining parts into closer union and interest.[1]

The address was opposed by a minority of opposition members on the grounds that it might encourage government to persist with the American war, but was adopted by the overwhelming margin of 167 votes to 37.

The debate in the House of Commons on the loyal address proposed by Barry Yelverton testifies to the profoundly pro-British outlook of the Anglo-Irish political élite. The address was seconded by Samuel Bradstreet, one of the members for Dublin city and a regular opponent of government measures, who pledged that the Irish opposition would 'act in a very different manner from what is called the opposition in England' and called on his fellow patriots to 'demonstrate by our unanimity in the hour of trial, that in our opposition we have only the good of the empire at heart'. While not repudiating his earlier opposition to the war in America, he expressed a resentment at American actions which must have been shared by many of his constituents: 'I have always reprobated the American war, yet I think that this country has no great obligation to America, except it be for sending her privateers into our channels and

---

[1] Debate of 4 December 1781 in *DEP*, 6 December 1781.

destroying our trade.'[2] The loyal response of these prominent patriots in Britain's hour of distress may have owed something to the importance both men attached to domestic reform. Bradstreet had introduced the heads of a habeas corpus bill which went through the House of Commons with the support of administration earlier in the session but the bill had not yet returned from England. Yelverton, similarly, was hopeful of securing official support for his efforts to amend Poynings' law by abolishing the Privy Council's power to suppress or to alter the heads of bills. These measures had long been central planks in the patriot platform and one should not be surprised to find that some members of the opposition behaved with greater discretion than usual while their fate hung in the balance.

The thirty-seven members who opposed Yelverton's address took a different view and argued that Britain's difficulties presented an opportunity for extracting sweeping constitutional concessions that might never recur. 'The British minister's dream of subduing America is vanished', declared John Forbes in the debate on Yelverton's address, quickly drawing the conclusion that this was 'the time to shew that it is unwise to oppress any country'.[3] Two sharply contrasting strategies thus competed for support in parliament and in the wider political nation. An extravagant display of loyalty to the mother country might help to preserve what remained of the empire and to discourage a Franco-Spanish descent on Ireland. It might also, in the words of Thomas Conolly, member for County Londonderry, 'speak so home to the feelings of Great Britain, that her gratitude will grant whatever this nation can want'.[4] On the other hand, a vigorous campaign by the patriot opposition might succeed in wresting from a weakened British ministry those constitutional concessions that had been refused when the balance of power between the two kingdoms was more unfavourable to Ireland.

The political nation and British defeat

Outside of parliament, some patriot writers did not attempt to hide their pleasure at the humiliating defeat suffered by British arms. The *Hibernian Journal* expressed the hope that Irish members of the Yorktown garrison would put their time as prisoners of war in Virginia to good use by studying the management of tobacco plantations so as to have 'an opportunity of embarking in the cultivation of that valuable plant' on their eventual return to Ireland – a comment apparently inspired by the commercial relief granted by the British parliament when it permitted the export of Irish

[2] Debate of 4 December 1781 in *HM*, January 1783, 45.   [3] *Ibid.*, p. 46.   [4] *Ibid.*

tobacco in March 1779.[5] That the episode should be resurrected more than two years later and long after free trade had been conceded is telling evidence of the depth of the indignation it had excited. None the less, early reactions suggested that the instinctive loyalty of the Protestant political nation would prevail on this occasion, as it had in 1775 at the start of the American war and again in 1778 when France entered the conflict. The *Freeman's Journal* assured its readers that the defeat at Yorktown was merely a temporary setback and that Britain would quickly regain its former military dominance: 'Let her admirals and generals rouse into a true spirit of action, her people be united, and lay by, at the present alarming crisis, all party animosities, and act with one heart and with one arm, and there is no doubt but the ensign of Albion will again wave to victory, to fame and to honour.'[6] By 1782 the *Freeman* was no longer the opposition organ it had once been, but the still patriotic *Hibernian Journal* expressed a similar confidence in Britain's powers of recuperation, while stressing the significant role that Ireland would play in the process. The following verses were intended to be sung to the air of *Rule Britannia*:

> See now Britannia flies dismayed
>   bereft of empire and of spoil.
> Behold her daughters claim thy aid,
>   and promise to reward the toil.
> All hail, Hibernia! Immortal shalt thou reign
> great empress of the earth and main.
>
> Britannia shall no victor own,
>   her flag shall still command the main,
> 'tis thine to guard her sacred throne,
>   and give her empire once again.
> All hail, Hibernia! Immortal shalt thou reign
> great empress of the earth and main.[7]

Anglo-Irish patriots evidently had no difficulty in combining ambitious – not to say grandiose – ideas of Ireland's future importance with a commitment to the unity of what remained of the British empire. But the mood of embattled loyalty generated by the first reports of Cornwallis's surrender dissipated in the following weeks and it was the strategy of opposition advocated by Grattan and Forbes rather than the appeals for loyalty and unanimity made by Yelverton and Bradstreet which began to win support out of doors. This outcome seemed unlikely in early December; but it was, paradoxically, a reflection of the colonial nature of the Irish political nation.

---

[5] *HJ*, 12 December 1781.   [6] *FJ*, 29 December 1781.   [7] *HJ*, 17 December 1781.

The changing political mood in Ireland closely paralleled and imitated that in England, where Cornwallis's surrender, far from infusing the population with a new spirit of national unity, served to revive extra-parliamentary protests against the American war, to invigorate the parliamentary opposition and to deal an ultimately fatal blow to Lord North's administration. In London, news of the Yorktown débâcle produced what a student of political opinion in that city has described as a 'resurgence of articulated popular opposition to the American war'.[8] As early as 6 December 1781 the lord mayor, aldermen and livery of the city of London adopted a sternly worded 'humble address, remonstrance and petition' which was presented to George III at a levee on 14 December. It bluntly informed the king that 'Your Majesty's fleets have lost their wonted superiority: Your armies have been captured: Your dominions have been lost.'[9] The London address demanded an immediate termination of the American war in a tone far removed from humility. At Westminster too, pressure on the ministry was increasing steadily as usually reliable members made clear their distaste for a continuation of the transatlantic conflict. On 14 December, Lord North felt obliged publicly to disavow the idea of waging an offensive war on the American continent and informed the House of Commons that the British army would not 'march and countermarch as formerly'.[10] The ministry's intention was to stand on the defensive in those areas around New York and Charleston that were still in British hands – a strategy which would tie down forces urgently needed for the war against France and Spain while serving no readily identifiable purpose, apart from the political one of disguising the reality of American independence. Government had backed into an untenable position and the patriot opposition in Ireland, reading the writing on the wall, renewed its efforts to secure the endorsement of the Volunteer movement for its programme of constitutional reform.

On 28 December, a meeting representative of the Armagh Regiment's southern battalion called on delegates from all the Volunteer corps in Ulster to assemble at Dungannon on 15 February 1782. The Armagh resolution was expressed in a militant tone that had scarcely been heard since the height of the free-trade agitation in late 1779:

Resolved, that to avert the impending danger from the nation, and to restore the constitution to its original purity, the most vigorous and effectual methods must be pursued, to root corruption and court influence from the legislative body.[11]

---

[8] Sainsbury, *Disaffected Patriots*, p. 160.   [9] *DEP* and *FDJ*, 20 December 1781.
[10] *DEP*, 22 December 1781.   [11] *LJ*, 4 February 1782.

This extreme language was deplored by government supporters and it seemed possible that it might alienate many of the Volunteers throughout the northern province to whom the Armagh regiment's invitation was addressed, but the same sentiments were being voiced by respectable citizens in the first city of the empire. On 31 January the livery of London adopted a resolution which might have been modelled on that of the Armagh Volunteers:

Resolved, that the unequal representation of the people, the corrupt state of parliament, and the perversion thereof from its primitive institution, have been the principal causes of the unjust war with America, of the consequent dismemberment of the British empire, and of every grievance of which we complain.[12]

It was difficult to charge Anglo-Irish patriots with disloyalty when their views coincided so closely with those of the constitutional representatives of the city of London. Moreover, their debt to the English opposition may have been organisational as well as ideological: it has been plausibly suggested that the meeting of the Volunteers at Dungannon was modelled on the delegate meetings of the Association movement in England.[13]

Catholic opinion and British defeat

If the surrender of the Yorktown garrison was regretted by the great majority in parliament and by most members of the political nation, the vernacular literature leaves no doubt that the reaction of the Catholic population was very different. Washington's victory was celebrated in Irish verse both as a welcome event in itself and also as confirmation that the long-predicted end of British rule was finally at hand. In an *aisling* to the air of '*Síle Ní Ghadhra*' composed by Uilliam Ó Lionnáin, a Kerry-born tailor who lived at Six-mile-bridge, County Clare, the *spéirbhean* (spirit-woman) personifying Ireland rejoiced at the downfall of her oppressors and lauded the hero of the hour, George Washington:

> *Do labhair 'na dhéidh sin go béasach i nGaoilge*
> *is d'aithris dom scéala do mhéadaigh mo chroíse:*
> *go rabhadar béaraibh an Bhéarla go cloíte,*
> *gan arm, gan éadach, go traochta, gan tíortha.*
> *Atáid cartaithe i gcarcair 'na ndreamaibh gan treoir,*
> *faoi atuirse i nglasaibh ag Washington beo,*
> *gan ghradam, i mairg, gan charaid ná lón;*
> *'na ngrathain ag screadach le heaspa na feola*
> *do chleachtaigh na bathlaigh do chaitheamh gan teora.*[14]

---

[12] *FLJ*, 13 February 1782.   [13] Smyth, 'The Volunteer movement in Ulster', p. 118.
[14] '*Sealad im aonar cois féile do bhiosa*' in RIA Ms. 23 I 48, pp. 29–30.

(She thereupon spoke politely in Irish, and told me news that swelled my heart: that the English-speaking tyrants were defeated, without weapons or clothing, subdued and without territory. They've been flung into prison in dispirited groups, dejected and in fetters, by vigorous Washington, without status, in sorrow, without a friend or provisions; the starvelings are screaming for want of the meat, that the louts were accustomed to consume without limit.)

For Ó Lionnáin, the importance of Washington's victory lay in the fact that the power which had vanquished Catholic Ireland in 1691 and triumphed over the Catholic states of Europe in 1763 had at last been defeated. He recognised that one of the British empire's most important possessions had seceded and anticipated a repetition of the process closer to home. But if Ó Lionnáin's *aisling* was inspired by the sudden transformation of the military balance of power, with the benefit of hindsight it is impossible not to see it also as an expression of a second important *renversement* – one which belonged to the ideological rather than the military sphere. By 1782, English-speaking republican Dissenters were being lauded in Irish political song – a development that would have been utterly inconceivable only ten years before. For the Catholic masses, hostility to England excused a multitude of failings.

Britain's defeat was also celebrated in an *aisling* by Seán Ó Muláin, a County Cork poet, who represented the American victory as the prelude to an allied invasion of Britain:

> Tá Hannover séidte le tréimhse ag Washington
> is na méirligh mhallaithe dá dtraochadh ar feo,
> tá Holónt gan ghéill go fraochmhar feargach
> 's is taomach treascartha atá Liospóin;
> is dearbh dubh-chúinsí go bhfúigfear Sacsana
> ina mhúrthaibh lasrach gan géilleadh don chóip,
> beidh scriosadh ceart ar champaí an chamdhlí chealgaigh
> 'na gcamluí ar machaire ag téacht don fhómhar.[15]

(Hanover has been finished off by Washington for some time, and the accursed plunderers are subdued and decaying, Holland hasn't yielded and is furious and angry, and Lisbon is moody and prostrate; certain is the grim prospect that England will be left in a sea of flame unless it surrenders to the band, the camps of the crooked treacherous régime will be completely destroyed and lie twisted on the battlefield with the coming of autumn.)

Ó Muláin saw the conquest of Britain as leading to the restoration of the Catholic nation in Ireland (*'beidh clanna Mhílesius go féastach fleadhúil'* – 'the descendents of Milesius will be festive and jovial') and the overthrow

---

[15] *'Sealad dem shaol aerach iontach'* in RIA Ms. 23 M 14, pp. 244–5. Pressure from France and Spain forced the court of Lisbon to prohibit British warships and privateers from bringing their prizes into Portuguese ports: see *LJ*, 24 November 1780.

of the Anglo-Irish colony (*'beidh an aicme so do bhrúigh sinn dúbhach faoi atuirse'* – 'this class that oppressed us will be sorrowful and dejected'). Inevitably, the *aisling* envisaged a political settlement involving the restoration of the Stuart pretender:

> *'S is carthanach caonmhar caomh glan ceannasach*
> *ár Séarlas calma faoi réim i gcoróin.*[16]

(Kind, tender, gentle, sincere and noble will be our gallant Charles [Stuart] ruling and crowned.)

A drinking song composed by Tomás Ó Míocháin was also inspired by Britain's military collapse in North America. Ó Míocháin recounted *'mar cloíodh sa ghleo seo slógh na Breatan'* ('how the British host was vanquished in this fight') and celebrated British reverses in India and the Caribbean as well as in North America:

> *Táid thiar dá séideadh ag Wade is ag Greene,*
> *soir dá sníomh ag Hyder Ali;*
> *ní díon do Chlinton cnoc ná coill,*
> *beidh ruathar poill is péiste ar Arnold.*
>
> *I mbarcaibh gliadh sa ngrianoileán*
> *sin cíortha carntha eastát na Sacsan,*
> *Washington gan chiach gan chás*
> *is an diabhal go brách ar Chornwallis.*[17]

(They're being blasted in the west by Wade [recte 'Wayne'] and Greene, and eastwards being wrung by Hyder Ali, Clinton has no shelter from hill or wood, Arnold will be riddled with holes and maggots.
 In battleships in the sunny isle [Tobago], English possessions have been raked and pounded, Washington is without sorrow or worry, and damned forever is Cornwallis.)

Like Ó Muláin, Ó Míocháin welcomed these British defeats not merely as severe blows to British power and prestige but also as harbingers of the imminent liberation of Ireland – a liberation that would be social and economic as well as political and religious:

> *Cé docht bhur gcéim ag plé le cíos,*
> *gan réim ag ríomh le maoraibh measta,*
> *is feas i ngaobhar dhaoibh séan is síth,*
> *saorgacht, saoirse féir is fearainn.*

[16] *Ibid.*, p. 245.
[17] *'A ghéagaibh gníomha Choinn is Eoghain'* in RIA Ms. 23 K 10, p. 70; edited in Ó Muirithe (ed.), *Tomás Ó Míocháin.* Hyder Ali defeated a British army in September 1780 and the French captured Tobago in June 1781. I would agree with Ó Muirithe that 'Wade' is an error and that 'Wayne' was intended: Benedict Arnold led a British foray into Virginia in early 1781 and Anthony Wayne was an American general in the same theatre.

Gach gleidhire Gaoileach bríomhar buan
is gach groífhear suairc gan séad gan taisce,
faigheadh a chlaíomh go líofa luath:
seo an chaoi is an uair chum caortha cogaidh.[18]

(Though harsh is your condition in bargaining over rent, powerlessly compounding with calculating agents, we know that prosperity and peace are close at hand, liberty, freedom of grazing and of land.

Every lively steadfast Gaelic warrior, and every sturdy cheerful man of no property or wealth, let him take his sword keenly and swiftly: here's the chance and moment for a blazing war.)

Unlike many of Ó Míocháin's earlier compositions, this song contains no expression of Jacobite sentiment. Were it not for the specific references to the American war it might be mistaken for a composition of the 1790s.

At the end of January 1782 news arrived of a further British reverse that was of particular interest to Irish Catholics. In late November 1781 the French recaptured the Dutch island of St Eustatius from a more numerous British garrison after a surprise descent in which elements of the Irish regiments of Dillon and Walsh played a vital role. The account of the operation transmitted by the French commander, the Marquis de Bouillé, was reprinted in the Irish press:

The Comte de Dillon arrived at the [British] barracks at six o'clock, and found part of the garrison performing their exercise on the parade. Deceived by the dress of the Irish, they were only made sensible of their danger by a discharge of muskets close to their breasts, by which most of them fell. Governor Cockburn, as he came to the place where they were exercising, was instantly taken by the chevalier O'Connor, captain of the chasseurs of Walsh.[19]

The element of surprise had been achieved because of the red uniforms worn by the Irish regiments, a legacy of their origin as part of James II's Irish army. Count Arthur Dillon, colonel of the eponymous regiment, later claimed that more than 350 Irishmen who were among the prisoners taken at St Eustatius enlisted in the regiments of Dillon and Walsh.[20]

Such episodes must have been viewed with a degree of ambivalence by members of the Catholic élite – Charles O'Conor's grandson, for example, seems to have relished his namesake's exploit in capturing the governor of St Eustatius[21] – but an attitude of complete loyalty to the established constitution was maintained in public. When an official fast was proclaimed for 8 February 1782 a pastoral letter read at all Catholic

---

[18] *Ibid.*
[19] *FLJ*, 23 January 1782. A paraphrase of this report appeared in *HM*, February 1782, 86.
[20] J.C. O'Callaghan, *History of the Irish Brigades in the Service of France* (Glasgow, 1870), p. 628.
[21] *Ibid.*, p. 627.

churches in Dublin on the previous Sunday urged the faithful to observe the fast and to pray that God might 'bless the councils, and direct
the measures, of our most gracious sovereign King George the 3d'.[22]
Catholics of higher social status had good reason to pursue such a policy
since the question of Catholic relief had again appeared on the political
agenda. As in 1778, the initiative came from neither the patriot opposition nor the administration. Rather, as Lord Carlisle reported to the
secretary of state, the members of parliament who 'take the lead in this
are chiefly independent gentlemen, though some of them are disposed
to shew a degree of deference to the sentiments of government'.[23] Lord
Hillsborough, in his turn, gave the viceroy no encouragement to support
the measure, informing him that 'in the present delicate state of public
affairs it would be perhaps advisable not to stir any questions relative to
religion'.[24] But the decision did not lie with government, and the prime
mover of the 1778 relief act, Luke Gardiner, gave notice of his intention to bring forward a further measure of Catholic relief at the end of
January. George Ogle, a prominent patriot and one of the most vocal
opponents of Gardiner's first relief act, provided an early indication that
the thinking of opposition members had evolved during the four years
since the subject was last considered when he announced that he would
'go every length in support of the bill, consistent with the interest of the
Protestant religion'.[25] This evolution, in its turn, would oblige the members of the Catholic élite to review their previous assumption that they
could hope to receive a sympathetic hearing only from the supporters of
government.

Patriotism triumphant

When, in January 1782, the Historical Society of Trinity College debated
'Whether the late bad success of the British arms in America should be
matter of lamentation to the people of Ireland?' the opinion of the students was finely balanced and the question was decided by the minimum
margin, with twelve voting against and eleven in favour – a close result
which reflects the divided and ambivalent nature of the response of the
Anglo-Irish community to events in America.[26] Loyalist sentiment was
more evident at the Historical Society's next meeting when it was decided

---

[22] *DEP*, 5 February 1782.
[23] Carlisle to Hillsborough, 29 December 1781, in PRO SP 63/480, fo. 12.
[24] Hillsborough to Carlisle, 24 January 1782, *ibid.*, fo. 85.
[25] *FLJ*, 6 February 1782.
[26] Historical Society minutes, 2 January 1782, TCD Mun. Soc./Hist. 4 (the pages in this
volume are not numbered).

by thirteen votes to eight that Ireland could not 'exist as a free state, independent of any other nation'.[27] Further evidence of the continuing strength of imperial loyalty was provided later in January when the quarter assembly of the lord mayor, aldermen, sheriffs and commons of Dublin conferred the freedom of the city on Lord Rawdon, eldest son of Lord Moira and the officer on whom command of British forces in the Carolinas had devolved when Cornwallis marched into Virginia.[28] Rawdon's military successes during 1781 included a victory over Nathanael Greene at Hobkirk's Hill and the relief of the besieged British garrison at Ninety-Six. A month previously, the Volunteer corps of his native Moira had celebrated his birthday by parading and firing three volleys; the day concluded with 'illuminations, bonefires, and every other demonstration of joy' as the County Armagh town honoured its famous son *in absentia*.[29] The decision of the Dublin commons, normally a stronghold of patriot sentiment, to honour Rawdon 'in consideration of his intrepid and gallant behaviour as a soldier and commander in defence of his country' is particularly striking in view of the very different attitude towards events in America that was being expressed by the livery of London at this time. In February, the Anglo-Irish community was again reminded of the involvement of some of its most prominent members in the American conflict when news arrived that Lord Edward Fitzgerald, son of the duke of Leinster, had been wounded at the battle of Eutaw Springs, the last major engagement of the war in North America.[30]

Given the divided state of opinion in the political nation, it is not surprising that the call for a meeting of Ulster Volunteer delegates to consider measures to 'root corruption and court influence from the legislative body' met with a muted reception. The meeting's opponents again urged an argument that had been used to some effect against earlier patriot-inspired attempts to involve the Volunteers in political questions – the argument that it was unconstitutional for armed associations to attempt to influence government policy.[31] A letter from a County Tyrone correspondent which appeared in the *Belfast News-Letter* and was deemed sufficiently important to be reprinted in the *Londonderry Journal* argued that the proposed meeting was 'useless, absurd and unconstitutional' and informed the Volunteers bluntly that 'you have no legal right to discuss political questions, in your armed collective capacity'; rather, meetings of freeholders summoned by sheriffs for the purpose of addressing members of parliament were the proper constitutional means by

---

[27] *Ibid.*, 9 January 1782.   [28] *FLJ*, 23 January 1782.
[29] *BNL*, 14 December 1781. Rawdon did not return to Ireland until 14 January 1782, see *FLJ*, 19 January 1782.
[30] *FLJ*, 13 February 1782.   [31] See p. 266 above.

which voters might make their views known to their representatives.[32] Another anonymous letter, purporting to be from a Volunteer officer, claimed that: 'This nation enjoys at this moment in profound peace, its constitutional rights, religion, liberty and property, in its utmost extent, under English protection; and any revolution that disturbs such tranquillity must be very ill timed and very ill applied.'[33] The same author dismissed the constitutional concerns outlined in the Armagh Regiment's resolution as 'the phantoms of an imaginary, patriotic, enthusiastic imagination'.

On the other hand, the frustration of British ambitions in North America and the increasing fragility of Lord North's administration convinced many patriots that the moment for resolute action had arrived. 'England is now in a state of imminent danger and distraction, racked and tortured to the very heart', wrote a correspondent under the pseudonym 'Naboclish' (*'ná bac leis'* or 'don't worry about it') in the *Dublin Evening Post*, before telling his readers 'Now is the time, now is the day of salvation. Grasp it!'[34] This sense of urgency was shared by many in Ulster, and the promoters of the Dungannon meeting were quick to defend the propriety of a delegate meeting of Volunteers. A correspondent of the *Belfast News-Letter* countered the argument that it would be unconstitutional for the Volunteers to express a view on political questions by asserting that 'the citizen and Volunteer are not different characters, but one and the same character under different titles', and by pointing out that the meeting would be much more representative of opinion in the province than the small caucuses of political activists which constituted the typical attendance at county meetings: 'Instead of a few freeholders shivering in the corner of a county hall, there will I hope be a full and fair representation of a great part of the freemen and free-soldiers of Ulster. The *people* are to meet on the business of the people.'[35] It is clear, however, that the extreme language of the invitation issued by the Armagh Regiment was something of an embarrassment for many advocates of the Dungannon meeting, one of whom was reduced to arguing that the objectionable terms used in the invitation made it all the more essential to secure a good attendance of delegates:

It is objected, that the resolutions of the assembly which appointed this meeting, are intemperate and rash, and that the purpose of the meeting is to adopt violent and unconstitutional measures ... if such is the intention of those who have called the meeting, the sure method to defeat them, is to send deputies better disposed, with proper instructions.[36]

---

[32] *BNL*, 5 February 1782, and *LJ*, 12 February 1782.   [33] *FDJ*, 16 February 1781.
[34] *DEP*, 5 February 1782.   [35] *BNL*, 7 February 1782.   [36] *LJ*, 4 February 1782.

In the event, the Dungannon meeting was attended by delegates from some 140 Volunteer corps, a figure that represented somewhat less than half the total number of units in Ulster at the time.[37]

The resolutions adopted at Dungannon did not emerge spontaneously from debate among the delegates but had been drafted in advance, several of them at a meeting in Dublin attended by Francis Dobbs, major of the southern battalion of the Armagh Regiment of Volunteers, and such prominent members of the parliamentary opposition as Lord Charlemont, Henry Grattan and Henry Flood.[38] The Dungannon resolutions opened with a defensive assertion that 'a citizen by learning the use of arms, does not abandon any of his civil rights'. This was a rhetorical sleight of hand since the right of Volunteer freeholders to instruct their members in their capacity *as freeholders* had not been questioned. The right of those who did not enjoy the parliamentary franchise to enter into political resolutions was more problematic but it is unclear whether the term 'citizen' as used in the Dungannon resolutions was intended to encompass such persons. Other resolutions declared that the 'claim of any body of men other than the king, lords, and commons of Ireland, to make laws to bind this kingdom' and the 'powers exercised by the Privy Council of both kingdoms, under, or under colour, or pretence of, the law of Poynings' were unconstitutional; rejected trade embargoes and the unlimited mutiny act; asserted the independence of the judiciary; and – in a brief but revealing flash of loyalism – called for a boycott of Portuguese wine 'until such time as our exports shall be received in the kingdom of Portugal, as the manufactures of part of the British empire'.[39] Arguably the most memorable resolution, that which welcomed the relaxation of Penal legislation 'against our Roman Catholic fellow subjects', was proposed by Joseph Pollock ('Owen Roe O'Nial') and seconded by Rev. Robert Black, Presbyterian minister of Dromore, who reassured any doubters who may have been present that the contemporary Catholic community had 'eradicated from amongst them those bigoted and superstitious notions by which their ancestors were governed'.[40]

Although the delegates at Dungannon adopted the resolutions presented to them with near unanimity, this cannot be taken as an accurate

---

[37] See Smyth, 'The Volunteer movement in Ulster', p. 119; and Pádraig Ó Snodaigh, 'The "Volunteers of '82": a citizen army or armed citizens – a bicentennial retrospect', *Irish Sword* 15 (1983), 184.

[38] Dobbs, *A History of Irish Affairs, from the 12th of October, 1779, to the 15th September, 1782*, p. 52.

[39] The resolutions were widely published in the Irish press. See, for example, *HM*, February 1782, 110–11.

[40] *FLJ*, 27 February 1782.

reflection of Volunteer opinion as a whole. David Smyth, the historian of the movement in Ulster, has pointed out that the patriotic orientation of the attendance was assured in advance because those corps that had a principled objection to political involvement declined to send delegates.[41] What remained in doubt until the last moment was the number of units that would accept the Armagh Regiment's invitation. The actual result, an attendance of perhaps 40–50 per cent of what might have been expected in less contentious circumstances, was a respectable but by no means an overwhelming display of opposition strength.[42] Certainly, the meeting at Dungannon was not an immediate cause of concern to government. Lord Carlisle informed the secretary of state, Lord Hillsborough, that the 'violent expressions' in the resolutions of the Armagh Regiment had given 'so much disgust that the meeting was not above half so numerous as it otherwise would have been'. Having noted the moderate wording of the resolutions adopted and the presence of several aspiring members of parliament among the delegates, he concluded that 'in all probability no such meeting would have been held if an idea had not gone about that a general election is likely soon to take place'.[43] Likewise, Roger Bristow, the port surveyor of Newry and a reluctant delegate at Dungannon, forwarded a complacent account of the proceedings there to government:

Upon the whole I think the result of the meeting has been nothing more than this, some measures have been resolved (not unanimously) to be necessary, but no mode of obtaining them proposed, or even hinted at, except the return of proper members to a future parliament – how far this is to be dreaded, is not I believe very alarming.[44]

This was true as far as it went and Bristow's assessment appeared to be confirmed on 22 February when the House of Commons postponed consideration of a declaration of legislative independence proposed by Grattan until 1 August – a date when the House would be in recess – thereby effectively killing the measure without formally rejecting it.

It is noteworthy that Grattan threw the entire responsibility for his motion onto the ministry by opening his speech with a reference to some recent acts of the British parliament in which Ireland had been named:

[41] Smyth, 'The Volunteer movement in Ulster', p. 120.
[42] The 143 units represented at Dungannon on 15 February may be compared with the 306 units that attended a second meeting at the same venue on 21 June 1782; see Ó Snodaigh, 'The "Volunteers of '82"', p. 184.
[43] Carlisle to Hillsbrough, 18 February 1782, in PRO SP 63/480, fo. 224.
[44] Roger Bristow to Robert Ross, 17 February 1782, ibid., fo. 230.

After the ample discussion in this house, of the great question of right, the 19th of April, 1780, and the universal reprobation of the assumption of the British parliament, to bind this kingdom, then received, I had been silent on the subject, if that parliament had not since that time continued its tyrannical and unconstitutional assumption, by enacting several laws to bind Ireland, which I have in my hand.[45]

This apologetic approach shows a consciousness on Grattan's part that most of the political nation rejected the power of the British parliament to legislate for Ireland in principle, but also his awareness of the widespread assumption that the practice was falling into disuse and that de facto legislative independence would be achieved without the need for a dangerous and divisive confrontation with the mother country. The vote of 137 to 68 on Grattan's motion – an increase of thirty in the government's majority since Grattan had previously moved such a resolution in April 1780 – indicates that many were still unwilling to run the risk of such a confrontation in February 1782. The portents among the electorate were no more favourable to the opposition. At the end of the month a by-election in Dublin city was won by the opposition candidate, Travers Hartley, by the quite narrow margin of 270 votes in a total poll of 2,674.[46] The constituency had not been contested in the general election of 1776, but the result of this by-election differed little from those that had been held during the life of the previous parliament.[47] If the opposition could not secure a more emphatic endorsement than this in the most open constituency in the country it had little chance of making major gains in the approaching general election. None the less, it must also be acknowledged that the Dungannon meeting had served its immediate purpose by providing a basis on which a national campaign of addressing members of parliament during the spring assizes could be built.

Already, on 21 January, the freeholders of County Sligo had addressed their members and 'most earnestly' required them to support a modification of Poynings' law, repeal of the perpetual mutiny act, and a 'just equalization' of the sugar duty, but the Sligo address made no mention of the declaratory act of 1720 (6 George I).[48] Leading patriots now took steps to ensure that the resolutions of the Dungannon meeting would be echoed by a chorus of addresses from all parts of the country. Lord Carlisle kept Whitehall informed of the progress of the campaign which was being orchestrated by the opposition:

---

[45] Debate of 21 February 1782 in *HM*, July 1783, 380.   [46] *FLJ*, 2 March 1782.
[47] For the results of by-elections in 1767, 1771 and 1773, see p. 76 above.
[48] *DEP*, 16 February 1782.

I have since been informed, and have good reason to believe that Mr Flood and Mr Grattan not only by their conversation but by letters to the country, are exerting themselves with many others to obtain addresses from the Volunteer corps and from the grand juries at the ensuing assizes, as well as instructions from the counties to their representatives strongly insisting upon the exclusive right of the parliament of Ireland, to enact laws binding upon this kingdom, and I think that such proceedings are likely to be conducted with all the heat and violence that may be expected from intemperate zeal.[49]

A few days later the lord lieutenant provided British ministers with the text of the draft resolution which was being circulated in the counties and which pledged its signatories to maintain 'the constitutional right of this kingdom to be governed by such laws only as are enacted by the king, lords and commons of Ireland'.[50] By 5 March, at least twenty Volunteer corps had individually endorsed the Dungannon resolutions.[51] While some of these were Ulster corps that were merely ratifying the action of their delegates at Dungannon, and others – such as the Lawyers' corps, the Liberty Volunteers of Dublin, and the Independent Dublin Volunteers – had long been identified with the patriot opposition, there was also a sprinkling of addresses from units that might not have been expected to be so forward in adopting a political position. These included the Loyal Limerick Volunteers, the Clonmel Independents, the Cork Union and the Tipperary Light Dragoons. More importantly, the Dungannon resolutions were also endorsed by delegate meetings of the Volunteers corps of Dublin (1 March) and Waterford (3 March). None the less, it would appear that it was not until 4 March that the first non-Volunteer body, the grand jury of County Westmeath, adopted the substance of the Dungannon resolutions. The opposition campaign was gathering some momentum, but there was still little to suggest that the developing agitation of 1782 would prove to be any more effective than that of 1780 which had generated an impressive series of addresses from county meetings but ended without achieving anything.

On 5 March, however, reports of the success of General Conway's resolution in the British parliament against 'the further prosecution of offensive warfare' in America appeared in the Irish press. 'In consequence of this important decision', the *Dublin Evening Post* informed its readers, 'the nation are at last within the prospect of enjoying the blessing of a

---

[49] Carlisle to Hillsborough, 3 March 1782, in PRO SP 63/480, fo. 294.
[50] Carlisle to Hillsborough, 7 March 1782, *ibid.*, fo. 325.
[51] C.H. Wilson, *A Compleat Collection of the Resolutions of the Volunteers, Grand Juries, &c. of Ireland, which Followed the Celebrated Resolves of the First Dungannon Diet* (Dublin, 1782), pp. 5–32.

peace with America.'[52] It could no longer be doubted that recognition of American independence was only a matter of time. But the immediate importance of the motion lay in the evidence it provided that the administration's grip on the British House of Commons was slipping.[53] The signs of impending ministerial collapse were now evident to all sections of opinion in Ireland. Three further addresses from bodies unconnected with the Volunteers (the grand jury and freeholders of County Meath, the inhabitants of Belfast and the grand jury of County Waterford) either endorsed the Dungannon resolutions or asserted the legislative independence of the Irish parliament within a few days of 5 March, and a steady flow of similar resolutions continued during March as speculation about the demise of Lord North's administration mounted. A despatch from London dated 16 March which prematurely reported the prime minister's resignation was carried in the Irish press, but it was not until 27 March that the Marquis of Rockingham formed a new ministry.[54] By that date the freeholders of counties Cavan, Leitrim, Waterford, Tyrone and Mayo; the freeholders of Dublin city and Wexford borough; the inhabitants of the towns of Newtownards, Lurgan, Monaghan and Bangor; the grand juries of counties Wicklow, Fermanagh, Tipperary and Antrim; and a delegate meeting of the Volunteer corps of Connacht gathered at Ballinasloe, had all come out in support of legislative independence.[55]

Lord Carlisle, who had been optimistic that his administration could weather the approaching storm in the aftermath of the Dungannon meeting, was ready to admit defeat a month later. On 26 March he wrote to Lord Hillsborough, who would be out of office by the time his letter arrived in Whitehall, to report on the failure of efforts to block an opposition-inspired address in favour of legislative independence at the spring assizes in County Tipperary: 'the endeavors of the friends of government having been remarkably strenuous at those assizes, and having nevertheless failed of success, your lordship will from thence be able to judge with what degree of ferment the popular expectation has been raised upon the subject of a declaration of that right'.[56] Two days later, the lord lieutenant bluntly warned Hillsborough – by then the former holder of an abolished office – that the 'principle of independent legislation in this kingdom' would have to be conceded by government if a complete collapse of the administration's position were to be avoided:

[52] *DEP*, 5 March 1782.
[53] See I.R. Christie, *The End of North's Ministry 1780–1782* (London, 1958), pp. 327–8.
[54] For the premature report see *FLJ*, 23 March 1782.
[55] Wilson, *A Compleat Collection*, pp. 33–105. For the Tipperary grand jury, see *DEP*, 19 March 1782.
[56] Carlisle to Hillsborough, 26 March 1782, in PRO HO 100/1, fo. 3.

it is my serious opinion that if the first day of the next meeting of our parliament does not quiet the minds of the people on that point, hardly a friend of government will have any prospect of holding his seat for a county or popular corporation; and what is more immediately interesting they will also lose their present salutary influence over the armed associations.[57]

By late March the opposition bandwagon was rolling and nothing short of a dramatic reversal of the rapidly sinking fortunes of Lord North's ministry could have halted its progress. Instead, news of the formation of the Rockingham administration arrived to complete the rout of the 'friends of government'.

The likely implications of the change of ministry for Irish politics were immediately obvious to contemporary observers. An expatriate Irish peer wrote from London to advise the speaker that the duke of Portland, the new viceroy, and Richard Fitzpatrick, his chief secretary, expected that 'their time [in Ireland] will not be difficult, as everything we ask is to be granted'.[58] Publicly, the *Dublin Evening Post* provided its readers with a sketch of the next Irish administration which, however inaccurate it may have been in detail, correctly predicted the political complexion of Portland's government:

We hear that in conformity with the late ministerial revolution in Great Britain, one equally great and popular is immediately to take place in this kingdom; the following is said to be part of the arrangement:
Lord Charlemont, master general of ordnance.
Earl of Clanricarde, muster master general.
Henry Flood and George Ogle, esqrs. vice treasurers.
Henry Grattan, esqr; chancellor of the exchequer. And,
Hussey Burgh, esq, whatever he desires in the law department. Sir Edward Newenham, it is said, will be made a commissioner of the revenue.[59]

At the same time it was reported that a bill was about to be introduced in the British House of Commons to repeal the 1720 declaratory act (6 George I).[60] A record of patriotic opposition was about to become the key to high office. Along with a rapidly diffusing appreciation of the new balance of political power came the certainty of a patriotic majority in parliament. Volunteer corps, grand juries, county and town meetings, and even the electors of Trinity College, all hastened to place their support for a declaration of Ireland's legislative independence on record before the point was conceded. On 8 April Charles James Fox, the new foreign

---

[57] Carlisle to Hillsborough, 28 March 1782, *ibid.*, fo. 19.
[58] Lucan to Edmund Sexton Pery, 3 April 1782, in Emly Mss., HMC 14th report, appendix IX (1895), p. 164.
[59] *DEP*, 6 April 1782; reprinted in *FLJ*, 10 April 1782.   [60] *FLJ*, 10 April 1782.

secretary, in a speech on the floor of the British House of Commons described 'the names of Lord Charlemont, of Mr Yelverton, of Mr Grattan, of Mr Burgh, of Mr Flood' as those of 'the greatest, the ablest, and the honestest men in Ireland'.[61] When Grattan again moved a declaration of legislative independence on 16 April it was carried *nemine contradicente* as there was no longer a compelling reason for anyone to oppose it. This is not to say that all sections of political opinion were happy with the new dispensation. 'Paddy has got everything he has asked', wrote a peevish Thomas Conolly a day later, 'and more I am certain than is good for him.'[62]

The patriots in office

Anglo-Irish patriots greeted the formation of the Rockingham ministry and the arrival of the new viceroy, Portland, with something approaching euphoria. One author described the change of ministry as a 'change effected for the salvation of the British empire, for the general happiness of mankind, and to the overthrow of that hoary system of weakness, obstinacy and corruption, which had brought all his Majesty's dominions to the precipice of bankruptcy, slavery and destruction'.[63] Expectations of change were correspondingly high and Portland lost no time in advising the home secretary that the repeal of the 1720 declaratory act was now a political necessity:

it is no longer the parliament of Ireland that is to be managed or attended to. It is the whole of this country. It is the church, the law, the army, I fear, when I consider how it is composed, the merchant, the tradesman, the manufacturer, the farmer, the labourer, the Catholic, the Dissenter, the Protestant; all sects, all sorts and descriptions of men, who, I think, mistakenly upon some points, but still unanimously and most audibly call upon Great Britain for a full and unequivocal satisfaction.[64]

In the same letter, Portland identified the failure of British efforts to overcome American resistance as a factor emboldening all sections of Irish opinion to press their demands: 'having so recent an example of the fatal consequences of coercive measures before [them] . . . they are in no fears that Great Britain will attempt a second experiment of the same sort'.[65]

---

[61] *Ibid.*, 17 April 1782.

[62] Conolly to Buckinghamshire, 17 April 1783, in HMC Stopford-Sackville Mss., I (1904), p. 417.

[63] Robert Houlton, *A Selection of Political Letters, which Appeared during the Administration of the Earls of Buckinghamshire and Carlisle, under the Signatures of Junius-Brutus, Hampden, the Constitutional Watchman, and Lucius Hibernicus* (Dublin, 1782), p. 89.

[64] Portland to Shelburne, 24 April 1782, in PRO HO 100/1, fos. 135–6.

[65] *Ibid.*, fo. 136.

When news arrived of the debate in the British Commons on 17 May
in which Charles James Fox indicated the ministry's intention of repealing the 6 George I – news which arrived simultaneously with reports of
Admiral Rodney's decisive victory over the French fleet at the battle of
the Saints – Volunteer corps paraded and fired *feux de joie* and towns
were illuminated throughout the country in celebration of both events.[66]
The strongly patriotic *Dublin Evening Post* had no qualms about acknowl-
edging that 'nothing could exceed the brilliancy of the spectacle' in the
capital. At a stroke, the mood of the political nation was restored to something very similar to that which had prevailed in the early months of 1780
when the demand for free trade had been conceded and the prospect of
a British victory in America seemed bright. In 1782, Irish demands had
again been met and Britain, though humbled on land, had recovered her
former naval supremacy. On this occasion there was an additional factor
which heightened and seemed likely to perpetuate the prevailing sense
of political goodwill: in 1782, unlike 1780, the patriot leaders in parliament found themselves rewarded for the success of their opposition – or,
more accurately, for the success of their ideological counterparts in Great
Britain. Barry Yelverton became attorney-general; Walter Hussy Burgh
became prime serjeant; Henry Grattan was voted £50,000 by parliament,
a grant which was readily sanctioned by government; and John Forbes
was offered the post of solicitor-general.

With the notable exception of Henry Flood, who spurned the offer
of a place on the Privy Council as an inadequate recognition of his
talents, enthusiasm for the new administration and satisfaction at the
repeal of the 6 George I was general among leading patriots. On 28 May,
a joint meeting of the Volunteers' Ulster and Connacht provincial committees adopted an address which enthused that: 'The distinction between
Englishman and Irishman is no more – we are now one people – we have
but one interest, one cause, one enemy, one friend ... The late happy
change in his Majesty's measures and ministers in Ireland, as well as
Great Britain, seems the harbinger of prosperity and indissoluble union
to both kingdoms.'[67] The signatories to this address included both Francis
Dobbs, one of the principal promoters of the Dungannon meeting, and
Joseph Pollock. Pollock, who had once looked forward to the prospect of a
French invasion, now wrote an open letter to the First Newry
Volunteers in which he declared that 'England requires your aid: – and
England now deserves it!'[68] Relations between the Portland administra-
tion and the former opposition could scarcely have been more cordial. In

---

[66] See, for example, *DEP*, 23 May 1782; *FLJ*, 25 May 1782; *LJ*, 28 May 1782.
[67] *DEP*, 30 May 1782.   [68] *Ibid.*, 6 June 1782.

Dublin, where prominent Volunteer officers invited the newly appointed commander-in-chief – General Burgoyne of Saratoga fame – to dine with them, the general informed his hosts that he was sensible of the 'high honour' conferred on him by 'gentlemen of such distinguished worth; men, who so truly united the character of the experienced soldier, the faithful, the loyal citizen, and steady incorruptible patriot, the envy and admiration of Europe'.[69] A meeting of Ulster Volunteer delegates held at Dungannon on 21 June – which was much better attended than its predecessor in February – assured George III that 'Your Majesty's choice of those whom you have entrusted with the administration of public affairs gives us the most heart-felt satisfaction; public confidence is revived; and we doubt not but your Majesty's crown and empire will speedily be raised to the highest pinnacle of human glory.'[70] Less reassuring to the ears of government was the rider that 'should a more equal representation of the people be also adopted, our prosperity would be for ever secured'. Portland explained this jarring note in a covering letter to the home secretary as the work of 'a very active emissary who has come from England expressly for that purpose'.[71] A day later a meeting of Leinster Volunteer delegates in Dublin offered their 'grateful tribute' to the king for 'the late changes which your Majesty has been pleased to adopt in your councils and ministers',[72] and on 6 July the Volunteer delegates of Connacht meeting at Ballinasloe followed suit and presented their 'grateful acknowledgements' to George III for his 'having been graciously pleased to commit the administration of public affairs to men whose attachment to the principles of general liberty . . . have justly won them the confidence of the people'.[73] Like the Ulster delegates, those of Connacht also expressed the hope for 'a more equal representation of the people'. Dublin Castle was flooded with 'humble addresses' to the king. The freeholders of County Dublin, one of the first counties to present an address, expressed the hope and expectation that 'the restoration of the rights of Ireland will be speedily followed by the restoration of Britain's glory'.[74] Similar addresses followed in quick succession from county meetings in Wexford, Cavan, Meath, Longford and Tipperary, from the grand jury of County Wicklow, as well as from town meetings in Newry and Drogheda.[75]

The support offered to government by the political nation in general, and by the former opposition in particular, was practical as well as verbal.

---

[69] *Ibid.*   [70] Wilson, *A Compleat Collection*, p. 267.
[71] Portland to Shelburne, 25 June 1782, in PRO HO 100/2, fo. 158.
[72] *HM*, June 1782, 336.   [73] Address dated 6 July 1782 in PRO HO 100/2, fo. 250.
[74] Address dated 10 June 1782, *ibid.*, fo. 92.
[75] For the counties see *ibid.*, fos. 96, 110, 189, 217, 231 and 272; for the towns see *ibid.*, fos. 155 and 219.

On 27 May, the day on which the Duke of Portland announced in a speech from the throne that it was intended to amend Poynings' law by removing the power of the Irish Privy Council to suppress – and the power of both the Irish and British councils to amend – the heads of bills, and to limit the duration of the mutiny act to two years, a grateful House of Commons voted a grant of £100,000 towards the cost of raising 20,000 Irish volunteers for the Royal Navy on the proposal of Henry Grattan. A short time later, an act was passed to permit the withdrawal of up to 5,000 men from the Irish garrison in view of the threat of invasion then hanging over England. On 19 June a meeting of the 'nobility, gentry, and citizens' of Dublin under the chairmanship of the Volunteer commander, Lord Charlemont, was held in the Tholsel to discuss the best method of achieving the extremely ambitious target of 20,000 naval recruits. A plan was unanimously adopted which called on the Volunteer corps throughout the country to beat up for recruits in their own districts.[76] The Volunteers, in the words of the *Dublin Evening Post*, had previously 'brought an unkind sister kingdom to reason' and were now showing their readiness to 'generously stand forth to assist that sister in time of need, against her enemies'.[77] Sir Edward Newenham, ever the enthusiast, distributed a handbill which announced that he had 'entered two of his sons on board his Majesty's ship the *Belleisle*' and urged 'some of his beloved countrymen to serve on board the same ship with his sons'.[78] The plan to furnish an extravagant number of seamen for the British navy, and the Volunteers' eager participation in it, reflects the mood of ostentatious loyalty that gripped Protestant Ireland in the summer of 1782. It was a mood to which feelings of satisfaction at the realisation of the patriot political agenda and a renewed confidence in Britain's ability to repel the attacks of the Bourbon powers both contributed:

> Now let the sons of Ireland, who pant for lofty fame,
> behold the deeds of Rodney and Hood's exalted name,
> and pressing on at honour's call give all their heart cheers,
> to serve their country and their king, as Irish volunteers.

> Our laws are now amended, and all our griefs removed,
> our commerce now is opened; our sister's kindness proved,
> let us with heart and hand assist, and give her all our powers;
> huzzah! huzzah! huzzah! huzzah! Britannia's cause is ours.[79]

---

[76] *FLJ*, 19 June 1782.   [77] *DEP*, 6 July 1782.
[78] PRO ADM 1/2123; the handbill is an unnumbered insert in a volume of captains' letters.
[79] 'Britannia Triumphant', a song performed at the theatre in Smock Alley before the Duke and Duchess of Portland 'with great applause', in *DEP*, 27 June 1782 and *HM*, July 1782, 384.

But the seeds of fresh conflict between the Volunteer movement and the administration were being sown even as the above song appeared in print. On 22 June Portland outlined a scheme for raising a number of 'provincial corps' to replace the 5,000 regular troops that parliament had permitted to be withdrawn from Ireland. The measure, he believed, not only would serve a useful military purpose but also would 'give full scope to the general zeal which actually prevails'.[80] The proposal to raise 'provincial' or, as they soon came to be known, 'fencible' regiments was quickly approved but was to have consequences very different from those intended by its originator.

The patriots divided

The general satisfaction of the political nation with the Duke of Portland's administration lasted for little more than two months. Even before Lord North's fall, a habeas corpus bill was returned from England. The new administration quickly indicated its support for the repeal of the 1720 declaratory act, the amendment of Poynings' law, the limitation of the mutiny act to two years, and an act to provide for the independence of judges – measures that were enacted during June and July 1782. In the space of a few months the key constitutional demands that had occupied the attention of the patriot opposition for the previous generation had been conceded. It is not surprising that a period of near euphoria should have followed this sweeping success, or that a new set of demands was not immediately formulated.

There were some early indications that reform of parliament would be the next major constitutional issue to be agitated. As early as 20 May the Liberty Volunteers of Dublin, a corps commanded by Sir Edward Newenham, adopted a resolution calling for the abolition of 'useless employments and unmerited pensions' and the exclusion of all placemen 'except the great officers of the state' from the House of Commons – two residual demands from the traditional patriot agenda that had not been conceded. More original was the demand in the same resolution for a 'more equal representation of the people in the national assembly'.[81] On 11 June, Newenham gave notice of his intention to introduce a bill for the more equal representation of the people in parliament. Shortly afterwards he published a letter to the 'independent electors' of County Dublin giving details of his intended bill: it proposed to add two additional members

---

[80] Portland to Shelburne, 22 June 1782, in PRO HO 100/2, fo. 147a.
[81] *DEP*, 1 June 1782.

to Dublin city and one additional member to every county and city constituency and to Dublin University, while leaving the representation of the boroughs unaffected.[82] As was noted previously, both the Dungannon meeting of Volunteer delegates from Ulster held on 21 June and the corresponding meeting of Connacht delegates held at Ballinasloe on 6 July backed the call for a 'more equal representation of the people', a clear indication that appreciable support already existed for the cause of parliamentary reform.[83] One critic of proposals for reform was so alarmed by the outcome of the second Dungannon meeting that he published a pamphlet denouncing it as an attempt to 'diminish the influence which is naturally entailed on all men of landed property' and to exclude from parliament 'every member of the aristocratic body that is not in amenable submission to popular edicts'.[84]

Given the contemporary importance of the issue in Great Britain, the development of an agitation supported by sections of the Volunteers on the issue of parliamentary reform would have been a natural and predictable development. That such an agitation did not develop in 1782 was probably due to the emergence of a very different constitutional demand. On 11 and 14 June Henry Flood delivered two speeches in the House of Commons in which he argued that repeal of the declaratory act of 1720 offered inadequate security for the independence of the Irish parliament. Repeal of the act, he claimed, 'was only leaving the law as it was before [1720], a simple repeal of the declaration, but not the principle of that law'.[85] This was an exercise in pettifoggery that treated an *affaire d'état* settled by the votes of two parliaments as if it were a private contract that might be subject to future judicial review. Flood's legal hair-splitting was an unlikely line of argument to capture the attention of the political nation, the more so as it seemed to imply that the British parliament really had enjoyed the power to legislate for Ireland prior to 1720. But although the Ulster Volunteer delegates at Dungannon unanimously affirmed their satisfaction with repeal of the declaratory act on 21 June, by the time their Connacht counterparts met on 6 July Flood's position enjoyed the support of a substantial minority of delegates – more than one in five according to one report and fifteen out of forty according to a second.[86] In the interval between the two meetings, the First Belfast Company revived the old suggestion that the Irish

[82] *LJ*, 18 June 1782 and *DEP*, 27 June 1782.   [83] See p. 296 above.
[84] *Thoughts on the Present Situation of Ireland. In a Letter from the North, to a Friend in Dublin; in which the Late Extraordinary Meeting at Dungannon is Considered* (Dublin, 1782), pp. 17 and 18.
[85] *DEP*, 13 June 1782.   [86] *FLJ*, 13 July 1782 and *DEP*, 18 July 1782.

parliament should pass a law declarative of its legislative independence.[87] Clearly, Flood's expressions of concern struck a chord with some sections of the Volunteer movement which continued to distrust British intentions.

A number of circumstances now combined to give Flood's arguments more credibility than they had originally possessed. Rockingham's death in early July brought Lord Shelburne, Chatham's political heir, to the premiership. If the new prime minister was more populist than his predecessor, he also inherited Chatham's views on the importance of preserving the unity of the empire and was noticeably more reluctant than Rockingham had been to accept American independence as a *fait accompli*. Instead, he informed the British House of Commons that recognition of American independence would mean that 'the sun of England's glory is set for ever' – a speech which inspired a rejoinder from Thomas Paine which found a Dublin publisher.[88] Shelburne had also made injudicious comments about Irish affairs in the past and newspaper readers were reminded that 'the late Marquis of Rockingham always considered the Volunteers of Ireland as the soldiers of the constitution, while the present premier distinguished himself by giving them the appellation of an armed banditti'.[89] Inevitably, misgivings were voiced about the new administration's willingness to recognise Ireland's legislative independence. In Dublin, the Liberty Volunteers, a corps commanded by Sir Edward Newenham, announced that they would suspend their efforts to recruit seamen 'until they find that the new ministers are men in whom they can place a reliance equal to that which they did in the present [*sic*] administration'.[90] At the same time, the introduction by Lord Abingdon of a bill in the British House of Lords which declared 'the sole and exclusive right of the parliament of Great Britain, to regulate and control the external commerce of all the dominions of the English crown' was immediately identified as an event that would win many converts to 'Mr. Flood's doctrine of positive and unequivocal renunciation of any foreign right or power to bind us'.[91] As early as 18 July, John Beresford informed a correspondent that 'Flood's doctrine is, I think, pretty universally adopted . . . Mr Flood has published his two speeches on the repeal of the 6th Geo. I. in a pamphlet, and to do the more mischief has added Lord Abingdon's speech and bill at the end. This pamphlet is sent to all

---

[87] *DEP*, 27 June 1782.
[88] Thomas Paine, *A Letter to the Earl of Shelburne, on his Speech, July 10, 1782, respecting the Acknowledgement of American Independence* (Dublin, 1783).
[89] *LJ*, 22 October 1782.   [90] *Ibid.*, 16 July 1782 and *FLJ*, 17 July 1782.
[91] *LJ*, 16 July 1782.

parts of the kingdom, and will have its operation.'[92] The tide of opinion in the Volunteer movement was soon flowing strongly in Flood's favour. On 21 July the Galway Volunteers rejected 'simple repeal' and a short while later elected Flood to membership of their corps.[93] On 22 July Sir Edward Newenham's Liberty Volunteers unanimously pledged their support for 'every constitutional measure tending to secure upon the most permanent foundation, our inherent rights, not only of internal, but also of external legislation, in direct opposition to the bill proposed by the Earl of Abingdon'.[94] On the same day the Loyal Limerick Volunteers unanimously assured Flood that 'nothing short of your ideas will ever meet our unanimous and decided approbation'.[95]

Supporters of 'simple repeal' continued to defend their point of view in print, most notably in the *Hibernian Journal*, a newspaper which remained strongly supportive of Henry Grattan throughout the controversy. At a purely intellectual level, they had little difficulty in exposing the logical inconsistency inherent in Flood's position, as in the following parody of the resolution adopted by the Galway Volunteers:

Resolved, that (though Irishmen) we will deliberately give it under our hands, that an act of the British parliament can import an *authority* (not a *claim* of an authority, but an actual *authority*) over this kingdom which a repeal of the 6th of Geo. I cannot take away, therefore we confess such *authority* of the British legislature *now exists*, and we will insist upon it, that she does retain it whether she will or no.[96]

There were others who deplored the fact that a pedantic dispute about the implications of a British act of parliament – a legislative instrument which all sections of opinion now regarded as being of no force in Ireland – had distracted attention from the issue of parliamentary reform. When the freeholders of County Longford drafted a 'humble petition' requesting the House of Commons to shorten the duration of parliaments and to make 'the representation of the people more adequate and equal', the *Londonderry Journal* applauded their action and urged:

Instead of wrangling about 'repeal and renunciation', and becoming the dupes of certain selfish and disappointed individuals, who occasionally assume the cloak of patriotism merely to advance their own fortunes, let us unanimously join in the most likely means towards obtaining a more equal representation of the

[92] John Beresford to William Eden, 18 July 1782, in Beresford, *Correspondence of the Right Hon. John Beresford*, I, pp. 221–2.
[93] *DEP*, 6 August 1782. For an account of the contest between supporters of simple repeal and renunciation in the county, see Pádraig Ó Snodaigh, *Dílseoirí na Gaillimhe* (Dublin, n.d.), pp. 21–5.
[94] *DEP*, 30 July 1782.   [95] *Ibid.*   [96] *HJ*, 16 August 1782.

people, for on that great and necessary reformation hangs every other political good.[97]

None the less, it was soon evident that Flood – his case fortuitously strengthened by the controversy over the fencibles – was winning the argument at the political level. This reality was acknowledged even by the *Hibernian Journal*. In September, that newspaper lamented the fact that Grattan had become 'an object of indignation to an undiscerning populace. – He has sold us! (says one) – He never done us an atom of service! (cries another) – The new orator [Flood], the new opinion for ever, Huzzah! echoes from the mouth of every brawling porter house politician.'[98] A further legislative measure by either the Irish or British parliament to place the legislative and judicial independence of the former beyond doubt had become a political necessity by the final quarter of 1782. What was required, in the words of the Lawyers' corps of Volunteers, was a disclaimer of the British parliament's competence to bind Ireland 'in terms so explicit and unequivocal, as to exclude even the possibility of future doubt or cavil'.[99] The only question that remained by the end of the year was how such a measure could be introduced without appearing to acknowledge the correctness of Flood's objections to 'simple repeal'.

Recruitment after Yorktown

Parliament's offer to contribute towards the cost of recruiting 20,000 sailors for the British navy partly reflected the historic preference of patriots in both Ireland and Britain for war at sea rather then war on land, but it also reflected the military reality that naval recruitment had assumed a new importance with the cessation of operations in North America. The Admiralty responded to the offer with alacrity, despatching an Irish-born officer, Captain John McBride, to direct the campaign. Recruitment posters were issued showing the figures of Hibernia and Britannia embracing under the legend 'we are one', and bearing such martial slogans as '*lámh láidir in uachtar*' ('a strong arm uppermost') and '*dar Dia do gheobhadh muid orthu le maidí glasa*' ('by God we'd trounce them with green saplings'). More persuasively, perhaps, the prospect of prize money in the form of 'French Louidores!! Spanish Dolars!! Dutch Ducats!!' was held out to entice potential recruits.[100] Volunteer corps

---

[97] *LJ*, 17 September 1782.   [98] *HJ*, 18 September 1782.
[99] *FLJ*, 14 December 1782.
[100] PRO ADM 1/2123; the poster accompanies a letter dated 24 June 1782 from Captain McBride to the Admiralty.

throughout the country at first took part in the recruiting campaign with enthusiasm. The Dublin Independent Volunteers, of which Henry Grattan was colonel, was one of the first corps to beat up for recruits and it was reported that their efforts on the first day 'inspired upwards of twenty brave young fellows immediately to enlist'.[101] The large material inducements held out to naval volunteers must have been a factor in this success. One advertisement promised recruits that they would 'be treated like gentlemen, and live like princes, at the total expense of their sovereign'. In more concrete terms, landsmen who enlisted were offered an Irish bounty of £5-13-9, a British bounty of £1-12-6, and advance wages of £2-8-9 for two months, representing an immediate payment of £9-15-0.[102] None the less, reports of the results achieved were mixed and may reveal more about the political sympathies of their authors than about the reality on the ground. Thus a report from Limerick claimed that the 'spirit and desire of the Irish heroes to humble the pride and share the spoils of our perfidious enemies' was so great that 'upwards of 50 valiant young fellows have already entered'.[103] On the other hand, a more soberly worded report from Carlow stated that the efforts of the Volunteers there were meeting with only 'tolerable success'.[104]

The unanimous support of the Volunteer movement for the campaign to raise naval recruits was short-lived. With the sudden death of Lord Rockingham in July 1782 and the refusal of his party to serve in the new administration headed by Lord Shelburne, signs of dissent began to emerge in Volunteer ranks. On 18 July the Belfast Volunteer Company withdrew from recruiting because of 'the late very extraordinary bill introduced by the Earl of Abingdon into the British House of Lords' – the bill asserted the British parliament's right to legislate for Ireland in 'external' matters but failed to find a seconder.[105] A meeting of Munster Volunteer delegates resolved to continue recruiting seamen 'notwithstanding some reason has been given us by a late assertion in the British House of Lords, to apprehend a violation of the late compact between Great Britain and this country', but sixteen of the corps present dissented from this decision.[106] However the attitude of individual Volunteer corps may have had little influence on the relative success or failure of the campaign in their localities. In early August Captain McBride informed the Admiralty that the recruitment drive was meeting with much greater success in Ulster than in Munster: 'I propose being at Belfast at the end of the month at the Volunteer review where I have great hopes. I wish our business went on as well in the south.'[107] In a subsequent letter sent

---

[101] *DEP*, 25 June 1782.   [102] *LJ*, 23 July 1782.   [103] *FLJ*, 10 July 1782.
[104] *Ibid.*, 13 July 1782.   [105] Joy, *Historical Collections*, p. 214.   [106] *DEP*, 27 July 1782.
[107] McBride to the Admiralty, an undated letter in PRO ADM 1/2123.

from Waterford he confirmed that he had 'very good accounts from the north where all seems to go on well'.[108] Many of the less politicised corps continued to beat up for recruits despite the change in administration. In early September it was reported from Dublin that 'upwards of 200 brave fellows have been raised in this city and its neighbourhood within these ten days past'.[109] But by this time opposition to the principle of the campaign was being openly voiced and naval recruitment was being linked with the proposal to raise six fencible regiments:

> There is not a real friend to Ireland, and the liberties and constitution of his country, but should set his face against the present ruinous recruiting scheme, to drain this still oppressed kingdom of 20,000 men; to take away her standing army, and in time of peace to burden the poor with taxes for their support, now to adopt a wicked system of raising new mercenaries under the title of fencibles, is too gross as well as great an insult for the people to submit to.[110]

Opposition to the recruitment of seamen was closely associated with opposition to 'simple repeal' and those units which supported Grattan against Flood continued to recruit. In the capital, the Dublin Volunteers (commanded by the duke of Leinster), Grattan's own Independent Dublin Volunteers, and the Merchants' corps, were all beating up for naval recruits in October and their efforts were reported to be meeting with 'great success'.[111] None the less, the officer in charge of naval recruitment, Captain McBride, left Ireland in the same month.[112]

I have failed to find any official estimate of how many naval volunteers were actually raised during the 1782 recruitment drive. Unofficial estimates published in the press vary considerably but agree that less than half the projected figure of 20,000 men actually came forward. An estimate in mid-November put the number of naval volunteers raised up to that point at 'no more than 7800 men',[113] while a second contradictory report which appeared in January 1783 claimed that 'about four thousand' had been raised in all.[114] What is clear is that the flow of recruits increased dramatically in the same month for reasons which Lord Temple, Shelburne's nominee to replace Portland, explained to the home secretary: 'since the signing of the preliminaries of peace has been made public in this kingdom, great numbers of persons have offered themselves to enter into his Majesty's navy, solely with a view of getting the bounty, and in the

---

[108] McBride to the Admiralty, 14 August 1782, in PRO ADM 1/2123.
[109] *FLJ*, 7 September 1782.   [110] *Ibid.*, 11 September 1782.
[111] *Ibid.*, 9, 12 and 19 October 1782.
[112] His last communication with the Admiralty from Ireland was dated 8 October 1782, in PRO ADM 1/2123.
[113] *FLJ*, 23 November 1782.   [114] *DEP*, 21 January 1783 and *FLJ*, 25 January 1783.

fullest expectation of being almost immediately afterwards discharged'.[115] The lord lieutenant ordered an immediate halt to naval recruitment and requested instructions on what to do with 'upwards of eight hundred' last-minute recruits then on board tenders in Ireland.

As was mentioned in the previous chapter, the recruitment of a new infantry regiment in Ireland had been authorised in the autumn of 1781 and this decision was not rescinded when news arrived of the surrender at Yorktown. The new regiment was designated the King's Regiment of Irish Infantry and was commanded by a Scot, Colonel Ralph Abercromby. Advertisements in the press stated that the regiment's recruiting parties had 'the strictest orders not to trepan or kidnap any man' – a claim which suggests that recruiting parties from other regiments had not always been so scrupulous about observing the legal niceties.[116] The regiment was reported to be complete in April 1782 but by June it was necessary to announce a six-week period during which deserters who returned to the corps would be pardoned.[117] Indeed, later in the same month a general amnesty was announced for all deserters who returned to their units.[118] In September, the viceroy felt obliged to advise the home secretary that there was 'very little reason to imagine that any considerable exertion can be made to replace from Ireland those numbers which this very extensive war daily consumes'. He explained that the principal difficulty lay not so much in attracting recruits as in retaining them once they had enlisted, owing to the 'encouragement held out to daily deserters from the constant security given to them by the lower classes of people'. It was, he added, 'a matter of uncertainty, whether the column of recruits will in future balance that of the dead, discharged, and deserters. In the monthly return now before me, the first is only eighty eight: the amount of the three latter is two hundred and thirty four, of which one hundred and ninety eight are deserters.'[119] More severe penalties for desertion were introduced in November 1782.[120] In January 1783, one deserter was executed at Cork and three other men who had their death sentences commuted were given 500 lashes and sent to garrisons in Africa.[121]

The major recruitment effort in 1782 involved, not the regular army, but six new 'provincial' or 'fencible' regiments – of which two each were raised in Ulster and Munster and one each in Leinster and Connacht. Unlike normal regiments, the fencibles were recruited on the express

[115] Temple to Thomas Townshend, 29 January 1783, in PRO HO 100/6, fo. 34.
[116] *FLJ*, 19 January 1782.   [117] *Ibid.*, 6 April 1782 and *DEP*, 4 June 1782.
[118] Shelburne to Portland, 17 June 1762, in PRO HO 100/2, fo. 105.
[119] Temple to Thomas Townshend, 17 September 1782, in PRO HO 100/4, fo. 384.
[120] Temple to Townshend, 8 November 1782, *ibid.*, fo. 481.
[121] *DEP*, 11 January 1783.

condition that they would not be required to serve outside of Ireland and that men from their ranks could not be drafted into regular army units.[122] This scheme was, in part, an attempt to stimulate recruitment in order to facilitate the withdrawal of regular army units which were urgently needed in Britain, but it was also conceived as a useful means of bringing a section of the Volunteer movement under military discipline. In July 1782, Lord Portland spelt out this objective in a letter to the home secretary:

I can acquaint you that the disposition to raise provincial or fencible corps seems to be getting ground, and I am not without hopes that if it meets with support and encouragement from your side, it will not only tend to dissolve the present mode of Volunteering, but be the means of directing the spirit of it into its proper and natural channel.[123]

The political function of the fencible regiments was readily perceived by the Volunteers themselves. It was, as one newspaper article put it, 'one of the best digested and deepest strokes against the power and conse-quence of the Volunteer army of Ireland'.[124] Another writer predicted that 'unhappy animosities' were likely to arise between members of the two forces: 'The gibes of – "that's a fencible Volunteer – a mercenary Volunteer – a ministerial Volunteer", &c. will be uppermost on many occasions: the consequences may easily be foreseen.'[125]

Opposition to the scheme was a major factor in alienating large sec-tions of the Volunteer movement from the ministry. Many of those who opposed the fencibles also gravitated towards the opinion expounded by Henry Flood that 'simple repeal' of the 1720 declaratory act was insuf-ficient to secure the independence of the Irish parliament. It was not difficult to link the military and the constitutional questions. Thus the Kilkenny Rangers, in Flood's native county, resolved that the formation of fencible regiments was 'a measure tending to lay unnecessary burdens on the people, and to increase the influence of the crown'.[126] It may be noted that exactly the same words were used in a resolution adopted by the Independent Dublin Volunteers of which Henry Grattan was colonel – a strong indication of the direction in which rank-and-file Volunteer opinion was moving.[127] Opponents of the fencible scheme portrayed the Volunteers as exemplars of the disinterested and patriotic citizen-soldiers extolled by 'real Whig' ideology and, in contrast, represented those Volunteer officers who joined the new corps as mercenaries who had abandoned their principles and betrayed their country for a royal

---

[122] For details of the plan for raising fencible regiments, see PRO HO 100/4, fo. 360.
[123] Portland to Townshend, 23 July 1782, *ibid.*, fos. 282–3.
[124] *FLJ*, 28 August 1782.   [125] *DEP*, 29 August 1782.
[126] *FLJ*, 7 September 1782.   [127] *DEP*, 19 September 1782.

commission in a standing army. As the *Dublin Evening Post* put it:

> The turn of affairs in this kingdom, in favour of its commerce and constitution, may be justly termed the Irish revolution. That no door may be left open to tempt unnatural tyranny to enter again and afflict us, should be the especial care of our saviours. Not fencible regiments under government pay, but an impregnable fence against future oppression should be raised by our brave labourers in freedom's vineyard.[128]

In contrast, the other main organ of patriot opinion, the firmly pro-Grattan *Hibernian Journal*, argued that the decision to entrust the command of the fencible regiments to Volunteer officers was a clear indication of official goodwill and a development that ought to be welcomed by patriots: 'Can there, I ask, be a stronger proof given of the unbounded confidence of government in the Volunteers of Ireland, than to see men attached to the Volunteer cause, attached to the rights and liberties of their country, entrusted with the command of these regiments?'[129] Similarly, for Francis Dobbs, who himself accepted a commission in one of the Ulster fencible regiments, the matter at issue was simply 'whether we would rather have an army of English, Welsh, or Scots, than an army of Irishmen'.[130] It is clear, however, that the majority of Volunteers were deeply suspicious of the fencible regiments and correctly identified the scheme as an official attempt to undermine their own movement. When the Volunteer corps of Dublin city assembled in College Green for the annual commemoration of King William's birthday, the base of the king's statue was decorated with placards that associated opposition to the fencible regiments with the demand for a law declarative of the Irish parliament's independence:

> The VOLUNTEERS of IRELAND by persevering will
> Overthrow the FENCIBLE SCHEME;
> Procure an unequivocal BILL of RIGHTS; and
> Effectually establish the FREEDOM of their COUNTRY.[131]

Hostility to the new corps was widespread among the population but was not strong enough to prevent the required number of recruits being raised. The first of the six regiments to be completed, Colonel Talbot's Leinster regiment, was inspected and approved in late November when the inspecting officers pronounced it 'the finest new regiment they had ever seen'.[132] Similarly, when the first of the two Munster regiments, that commanded by Lord Inchiquin, was inspected in January 1783, it was

---

[128] *Ibid.*, 14 September 1782.   [129] *HJ*, 18 September 1782.
[130] Dobbs, *A History of Irish Affairs*, p. 146.   [131] *FLJ*, 9 November 1782.
[132] PRO HO 100/4, fo. 488 and *FLJ*, 27 November 1782.

reported in the press that no recruit was under 5'5" in height.[133] By the following month the four remaining regiments had also been inspected and approved.[134] But if the generous bounties on offer were sufficient to attract recruits it was more difficult to persuade them to remain in the service. In December a hostile observer in Dublin reported on the high rate of desertion from the fencible regiments with evident satisfaction:

The fatigue of drilling and other military duties, seems not to be relished by the privates of the new raised fencibles, as it is computed there are upwards of one hundred deserters already from these corps; to the great trouble and vexation of their officers, who are to be seen with anxious countenances in all parts of this city in pursuit of their run-away soldiers.[135]

This is not an unbiased account, but the extent of the problem is confirmed by official sources. State papers note that the 'illegal and dangerous opposition' of the Volunteers, along with the 'encouragement which all ranks of people held out to their [the fencible regiments'] deserters, obliged them to recruit in some instances near double their numbers'. Furthermore, the bounty offered to recruits, officially set at £3 per man, had in reality reached what was described as 'the enormous rate of £8 per man' – with the difference being furnished by the regiments' officers from their own pockets.[136] To complete this sorry tale, the new corps had no sooner been embodied than the peace preliminaries made it necessary to dissolve them in order to accommodate regular army regiments returning from overseas on the Irish establishment. A venture which had promised to be of political and military service to government ended as a political and financial fiasco.

Catholic opinion and the 'revolution of '82'

The early months of 1782 which witnessed the erosion of Lord North's majority in the British House of Commons also saw the progress through the Irish House of Commons of proposals for Catholic relief introduced by Luke Gardiner. The proposals met with a frosty reception in predictable quarters. Even before Gardiner had formally obtained leave to introduce a bill, Lord Charlemont, the Volunteer commander and *éminence grise* of the patriot party in parliament, deplored the fact that the Catholic question was again being agitated, and predicted that Gardiner's efforts would serve only to heighten sectarian tensions and might well be defeated in the House of Lords:

---

[133] *FLJ*, 22 January 1783.
[134] Temple to Townshend, 15 February 1783, in PRO HO 100/6, fo. 54.
[135] *FLJ*, 11 December 1782.
[136] Temple to Townshend, 2 February 1783, in PRO HO 100/6, fo. 36.

The House seems to be running mad on the subject of popery – Gardiner's bill, which, as castrated, may, for ought I know, be rendered innocent in its operation, is however, in my opinion extremely exceptionable in its mode...yet will this bill, I believe, be strongly opposed in the Commons, and possibly rejected by the Lords.[137]

Similar sentiments were expressed out of doors. The Loyal Sligo Volunteers addressed Owen Wynne, their colonel and a member of parliament, requesting him 'to oppose with your utmost exertion and influence, the repeal of any part of said [Penal] laws, that may in any wise endanger the constitution, as established on Revolution principles'.[138] Crucially, however, some prominent patriots had concluded from the success of the free-trade agitation in 1779 that the demand for legislative independence would be greatly strengthened if it enjoyed the enthusiastic support of the Catholic population. In February the delegates of the Ulster Volunteer corps meeting at Dungannon accepted a motion written and proposed by Joseph Pollock ('Owen Roe O'Nial') that rejoiced 'in the relaxation of the Penal laws against our Roman Catholic fellow subjects'.[139] Francis Dobbs explained the reasoning which inspired this *volte face* in the following terms:

Our enemies...were astonished and confounded with that noble benevolence and toleration, which must at once convince the Roman Catholics, that the supposed hatred of the Protestants of the north, existed only in the brains of shallow politicians – To divide and conquer was the policy of administration: – The policy of Dungannon, was to unite and be victorious.[140]

This was an unduly cynical view of the policy of Lord Carlisle's administration, which carefully refrained from casting its weight on either side of the scales when Gardiner's relief proposals were debated in parliament. The viceroy reported to Whitehall that his chief secretary, William Eden, left the chamber in the middle of the debate 'as it was not thought expedient that government should appear as taking a part on either side until the general sense of the nation was more fully opened by the first day's debate'.[141] In reality, the fault line separating the supporters and opponents of Catholic relief did not coincide with party divisions. Furthermore, it is clear that tensions on the question within the patriot party did not arise merely from differing pragmatic assessments of the extent to which Penal legislation might prudently be relaxed, but rather reflected a fundamental disagreement on a point of principle.

---

[137] Charlemont to Flood, 1 January 1782, in BL Add. Ms. 22,930, fo. 100v.
[138] *DEP*, 12 January 1782.
[139] For the entirely credible attribution of authorship to Joseph Pollock, see Dobbs, *A History of Irish Affairs*, p. 52.
[140] *Ibid.*, pp. 64–5.
[141] Carlisle to Hillsborough, 23 February 1782, in PRO SP 63/480, fo. 252.

Starkly different perspectives were articulated in the debate of 20 February by the two leading opposition orators in the House of Commons. Henry Grattan had entirely reversed his position on the question of Catholic relief since 1778 and now advocated the policy of reconciliation and unity that had won the backing of the Dungannon meeting. But he went much further than the position agreed at Dungannon, where it had been necessary to assure delegates that Catholics had left the 'bigoted and superstitious' ideas of their ancestors behind. Grattan, in contrast, praised those ancestors in a frank overture to Jacobite Ireland. He noted with satisfaction the prominent part played by Catholics in the agitation for free trade:

> When this country had resolved no longer to crouch beneath the burthen of op-pression that England had laid upon her – when she armed in defence of her rights, and a high spirited people demanded a *free trade*, did the Roman Catholics desert their countrymen? *no* – they were found amongst the foremost . . . I did carefully observe their actions, and did then determine to support their cause whenever it came before this house: and to bear a strong testimony of the consti-tutional principles of the Catholic body. Nor should it be mentioned as a reproach to them that they fought under the banner of King James, when we recollect that before they entered the field, they extorted from him a Magna Charta, a British constitution.[142]

This was ideological revision on a grand scale. The Catholic political na-tion of James II's reign, invariably represented by Anglo-Irish patriots as the compliant instrument of an arbitrary and tyrannical monarch, was now portrayed as the assertor of Ireland's constitutional rights; and the parliament of 1690, whose records had been burned in the aftermath of the Revolution, was held up as an example of resistance to royal authority worthy of emulation. Grattan did not seek to disguise the political mo-tives that inspired this exercise in historical reassessment. The question at issue was, in his view, nothing less than 'whether we shall be a Protes-tant settlement or an *Irish nation*?' The unity that would be essential for the latter project could, he believed, only be built on the foundation of Catholic relief:

> The question is not, whether we shall shew mercy to the Roman Catholics, but whether we shall mould the inhabitants of Ireland into a *people*; for so long as we exclude Catholics from natural liberty and the common rights of men, we are not a *people*; we may triumph over them, but other nations will triumph over us.[143]

The views expressed by Henry Flood in this debate stood in sharp contrast to Grattan's. Far from attempting to bridge the political chasm which

---

[142] Debate of 20 February 1782 in *FLJ*, 2 March 1782.   [143] *Ibid.*

divided Protestant patriots from the Catholic populace, Flood rehearsed a traditional Whig interpretation of the Revolution and stressed the critical need to ensure that the Protestant political nation would continue to enjoy a monopoly of political power:

Ninety years ago the question was, whether popery and arbitrary power should be established in the person of King James, or freedom and the Protestant religion in the person of King William – four fifths of the inhabitants of Ireland adhered to the cause of King James; they were defeated, and I rejoice in their defeat. The laws that followed this event were not laws of persecution, but of political necessity, and are you now prepared for a new government? Can you possibly suppose, though the Roman Catholics prefer you to every other people, that they will prefer you to themselves?[144]

Support for Flood's views came from both sides of the house. A contemporary press report linked the name of Alexander Montgomery, patriot member for County Donegal and brother of the American general killed at Quebec, with that of Guy Moore Coote, a government pensioner who sat for the pocket borough of Clonmel, as members who urged the house 'to consider of what they were doing, to take care of the Protestant interest, and not to do that in one hour which their posterity might be centuries in repenting'.[145] The opposition to Catholic relief was sufficient to defeat a bill that would have permitted intermarriage between Catholics and Protestants, but bills giving Catholics the right to purchase freehold property, repealing a series of provisions directed against the Catholic clergy and legalising Catholic schools made their way onto the statute book.

If it is true that there was no simple correlation between the members of the parliamentary opposition and the supporters of Catholic relief, it is equally clear that the former close linkage between patriotism and anti-Catholicism had been broken. It is likely that the bulk of the Catholic élite – the landed and mercantile strata from which the membership of the Catholic Committee was drawn – would have continued to look to administration for further relief irrespective of developments at Westminster, but the fall of Lord North and the sudden transformation of the leaders of the opposition into pillars of government meant that they were able to present the Duke of Portland on his arrival with an assurance of their 'unabating zeal for the success of his Majesty's arms' without fear of alienating the sympathy of either the executive or the erstwhile parliamentary opposition.[146] Equally, the Catholic clergy in Limerick were able to urge deserters to surrender themselves 'to his Majesty's most lenient government' under the terms of an amnesty, and to recommend

---

[144] *Ibid.*   [145] *Ibid.*, 6 March 1782.   [146] *Ibid.*, 8 May 1782.

enlistment to those who had no means of supporting themselves, without running the risk of being denounced as tools of arbitrary government.[147] In August, the leading Catholics of County Longford adopted a resolution which pledged their assistance to the local Volunteer corps in the task of raising naval recruits.[148]

If the loyalty of the Catholic élite and clergy to government was to be expected, the response of sections of the Catholic middle class to the changing political climate was less predictable. From the time of the Dungannon meeting onwards, middle-class Catholics increasingly gravitated towards the patriot-inclined milieu of the Volunteers.[149] As early as April 1782 it was reported from Limerick city that 'upwards of 50 of the principal Roman Catholic gentlemen' had been accepted into membership of a local corps, the Limerick Independents.[150] In the same county the poet Aindrias Mac Craith ('an Mangaire Súgach'), previously the author of militantly Jacobite verse, now eulogised Sir Richard Quin, the colonel of the Adare corps.[151] In Dublin, even more remarkably, a corps largely composed of Catholics was formed under the evocative title of the 'Irish Brigade' – a name which one outraged Protestant viewed as a provocation, referring as it did to 'that desperate set of renegadoes, who, deserting their country, have continued to fight against it, under the banners of the French king, for almost a century past'.[152] While the Jacobite allusion cannot have been accidental, it is most unlikely that the name was adopted as a deliberate provocation: the political orientation of the corps was patriotic and the 'Monks of the Screw' – a social club cum political society founded by Barry Yelverton which included many prominent patriots among its members – were granted honorary membership.[153] The name should therefore be seen as yet another attempt to appropriate elements of the popular Jacobite tradition for the use of the patriot cause. This was no longer impossible, at least at a superficial level. A song by a Munster author combined the stock Jacobite image of 'Carolus Rex mar Caesar calma' ('King Charles [III] like a valiant Caesar') with extravagant praise for the Volunteer delegates of Ulster and Connacht who attended provincial meetings at Dungannon and Ballinasloe in the months of February and March 1782:

---

147 *Ibid.*, 17 July 1782; quoted in Brady (ed.), *Catholics and Catholicism*, p. 220.
148 *DEP*, 17 September 1782.
149 Patrick Rogers, *The Irish Volunteers and Catholic Emancipation* (London, 1934), p. 66.
150 *FLJ*, 27 April 1782.
151 'Tá leoghan lannach lúfar leathan lúbach láidir' in Máire Comer Bruen and Dáithí Ó hÓgáin (eds.), *An Mangaire Súgach: Beatha agus Saothar* (Dublin, 1996), p. 155. For an example of this author's Jacobite verse, see p. 8 above.
152 [Patrick Duigenan], *The Alarm: or, an Address to the Nobility, Gentry, and Clergy of the Church of Ireland, as by Law Established* (Dublin, 1783), p. 23.
153 *FLJ*, 25 September 1782.

Ag Baile [sic] *na Slógh atá na slóite fearchoin*
  beoga calma óga groí,
is tuilleadh dá sórt atá ag pórt Dún Geanainn
  mórga, macánta, cróga i ngíomh.

(At Ballinasloe are hostings of heroes, vigorous, valiant, youthful, spirited, and more of their kind at the fort of Dungannon, noble, upright, brave in deed.)

But the same author's gleeful anticipation of a Bourbon descent on Ireland would have horrified the very delegates whom he applauded:

Ciodh fada atá Seoirse brónach feargach
  ag comhrac Washington, Jones is Lee,
is gur leagadh go leor dá chróntoirc leathana
  srónach cealgach glórach groí;
atá Laoiseach fós ag tabhairt gleo dó is anfa,
  Holónt á ghreadadh 's an Spáinneach buí,
is fé thosach an fhómhair atá Fódla dearfa
  a chomhachta leagtha go deo nó á gcloí.[154]

(While George [III] has long been dejected and furious, fighting Washington, [John Paul] Jones and [General Charles] Lee, and many of his bloated swarthy boars have been felled – big-nosed, treacherous, clamorous, stout; Louis [XVI] is still giving him tumult and terror, Holland is lashing him, and the swarthy Spaniard, and by the beginning of autumn Ireland is assured, his power will be overthrown forever or worn down.)

The constitutional concessions obtained by the patriot opposition were welcomed by the Catholic community. In May, for example, the inhabitants of the overwhelmingly Catholic town of Galway paraded behind an effigy of Lord Loughborough – a Scottish peer who was the only member of the British House of Lords to oppose the repeal of the 1720 declaratory act.[155] Similarly, Lord Abingdon's attempt to draw a distinction between the British parliament's powers of internal and external legislation over Ireland – the latter of which he hoped to preserve – attracted a rebuke from a Limerick-based author who signed his letter 'Ô H.' and was, in all likelihood, the antiquary Sylvester O'Halloran. The letter forcefully asserted a view of the country's constitutional position held by the native intelligentsia – the view that Ireland had 'ever been a distinct imperial kingdom, and the most ancient at this day in the world!'.[156] There were others whose sense of prudence was not entirely overcome by their satisfaction with the course of events: while Fr Arthur O'Leary readily acknowledged that the members of the Dungannon convention

---

[154] The author of this piece appears to have been named Ceallachán Mac Cárthaigh; I am grateful to Kevin Whelan for providing a transcript of the original manuscript in the Burns Library, Boston College.
[155] *Ibid.*, 5 June 1782.   [156] *DEP*, 25 July 1782.

'should be remembered with gratitude by the Catholics of this king-dom', he simultaneously doubted whether it would be 'expedient' for the Irish Brigade corps of Volunteers to express their gratitude in public lest they should thereby acquire 'the appearance of a Roman Catholic armed society'.[157]

It might be thought that the political contest between Grattan and Flood on the issue of the 'simple repeal' of the declaratory act of 1720 would have been viewed with indifference by lower-class Catholics or, if sides were taken, that Grattan, the advocate of Catholic relief and the defender of the Irish supporters of James II, would have commanded the support of the masses. The opposite was the case: Grattan's act in accept-ing a parliamentary gift of £50,000 and that of other prominent patriots in accepting office in the Portland administration effectively discredited them in the eyes of lower-class Catholics while Flood's stance of contin-ued opposition to the British ministry earned him applause in the same quarter. Maoileachlainn Ó Dúill – probably a County Clare author – fiercely denounced Grattan and other 'ministerial patriots':

> *Anois tuigim gur fíor nach díon is nach prapa*
> *don ríocht so Grattan do rinn í a dhalladh*
> *'s do stróic teora is an carthanas tríd;*
> *is cé damanta an ní gur cíocras airgid*
> *bíog ó bhreabanna is* fees *na* government
> *tóg fód is sealbh 'na chroí.*[158]

(Now I realise the truth that no shelter or support for this kingdom is Grattan who hoodwinked it, and who sundered restraint and friendship thereby; though it's a damnable thing that greed for money, the thrill of bribes and the *fees* of the *government*, took hold and possession of his heart.)

Ó Dúill likewise depicted Barry Yelverton as '*ag fiach na tairbhe*' ('hunting for advantage').[159] In contrast, Henry Flood, who travelled to England in August and remained there until October, was the hero of the hour. The poet prayed for his safe return:

> *Críost go leaga sé síos gach Galla-Whig*
> *do dhéanfas deacair ná díth do Harry*
> *gan ceo bróin go gcasa sé arís.*[160]

(May Christ strike down every foreign Whig who would cause Harry trouble or harm, without a cloud of sorrow may he return again.)

[157] Arthur O'Leary to – Kirwan, 4 October 1782, in W.J. Fitzpatrick, *Secret Service under Pitt* (London, 1892), p. 375.
[158] '*Anois tuigim gur fíor nach díon is nach prapa*' in Maynooth Ms. C 18, p. 48.
[159] *Ibid.*, p. 49.   [160] *Ibid.*, p. 48.

If popular hostility towards patriots-turned-courtiers is readily under-standable, the new enthusiasm for Flood requires some explanation. It is hardly conceivable that support for Flood reflected an intellectual con-viction in the inadequacy of 'simple repeal'. Rather, the key to under-standing it is provided in the note that a County Clare scribe, Labhrás Ó hÁinle, prefaced to his copy of the above work in 1786. Ó Dúill, he ex-plained, wrote the poem '*ag moladh Flood mar sheasamh go glan d'Éirinn agus ní mar rinn Grattan agus Yelverton do dhícheannaigh í tar éis mórán breibe*' ('praising Flood for standing forthrightly for Ireland and not like Grattan and Yelverton who beheaded her after a great deal of bribery').[161] Quite simply, the nationalist outlook of the Catholic community guaran-teed that the ideas of any outspoken opponent of the British ministry would be favourably received; conversely, cooperation with that ministry was inevitably interpreted as a betrayal of Ireland's interests.

Clashes between civilians and the military continued unabated after the granting of legislative independence. In July, a 'dreadful affray' took place at Ballyhack (probably the village of that name in County Wexford) between 'a considerable number of country people' and a party of sol-diers from an artillery unit in which persons on both sides sustained serious injuries.[162] In August a riot occurred at the fair of Beltra, County Sligo, when a group of locals numbering 'above one hundred' attacked a party of the Independent Tyreril Volunteers which was recruiting for the navy.[163] The same month saw a resumption of attacks on the mili-tary in Dublin when a soldier was houghed 'in a most inhuman manner' in Thomas Street; the attacker made good his escape 'notwithstanding there was a crowd of people passing'.[164] The chronic hostility between sections of the population and the military intensified after the start of the campaign to recruit the new fencible corps. When a captain in the Connacht regiment began to beat up for recruits in Galway city 'a large body of the inhabitants instantly assembled, silenced his drum, tore down the advertisement that had been pasted up, and commanded the printer of the Galway paper, at the peril of their utmost displeasure, not to insert any proposals for encouraging persons to enlist'. Similar opposition was reported from Eyrecourt and Loughrea in the same county.[165] A very serious clash took place in Drogheda when a party of men from Colonel Talbot's Leinster regiment of fencibles broke into a house in search of a deserter. A large crowd assembled and attacked the soldiers. A press report describes the sequel: 'two of them [the fencibles] were wounded in so desperate a manner with stones that they died yesterday. We are sorry

---

[161] *Ibid.*   [162] *FLJ*, 31 July 1782.   [163] *HM*, September 1782, 500.
[164] *FLJ*, 4 September 1782.   [165] *Ibid.*, 12 October 1782.

to hear, that this disturbance was renewed yesterday with great animosity on both sides; that another of the fencibles was killed on the bridge of that town, and that several of the inhabitants was [sic] severely wounded.'[166] The same report attributed the blame for the 'alarming affray' to the 'general odium and detestation in which the fencibles are held', an explanation consistent with the fact that order was restored on the arrival of the local Volunteer corps, the Drogheda Association, which 'mounted guard for three days on the barracks, to protect the men from receiving the smallest injury'.[167] A song by the County Clare poet Tomás Ó Míocháin attests to the geographically widespread nature of popular antipathy to the fencibles. When Lord Inchiquin accepted command of one of the Munster fencible regiments criticism from within the Ennis Volunteers obliged him to resign as commander of that corps.[168] Ó Míocháin lamented the fact that the head of the O'Briens of Thomond should have fallen so low as to exchange the honourable post of a Volunteer officer for the disgraceful one of a fencible officer:

> Nach daor an chúis i mbailtibh Thuamhan
> d'éarla, d'úrcheap eascair uais,
> de chaorthaibh cumhra Chais gan chuan
>   is de mhogall-bhua na Bóirmhe,
> go faon mar chúb ón mbrataigh mbuain
> is ón gcéim glan, glonnrach, gradaim fuair
> ina mhaor gan chlú, gan mheas, gan dúil,
>   ar scata trua pionsóirí?[169]

(Isn't it a grim affair in the townlands of Thomond, for an earl, the new head of a noble race, of the fragrant seed of unbowed Cas, and the familial virtue of [Brian] Bóirmhe, to have shrunk feebly from the steadfast banner, and from the honest, happy, esteemed rank he obtained, to be the commander without reputation, respect or expectation, of a wretched pack of fencibles?)

The hostility regularly expressed by Ó Míocháin towards the existing régime had not been lessened by recent political developments and this song was as militant in content as any of his earlier compositions:

> Séidtear dúinn an barra buabhaill,
> is téam i lúireach catha cruaidh,
> go ndéanfam brúscar bhealaigh mhóir
> den arm nua so Sheoirse.[170]

---

166 Ibid., 26 October 1782.   167 Ibid.   168 Ibid., 12 October 1782.
169 'Tá néalaibh cumha le seal dom bhuairt' in Maynooth Ms. C 13, p. 187; edited in Ó Muirithe (ed.), Tomás Ó Míocháin. Cas and Brian Bóirmhe were ancestors of the O'Briens.
170 Ibid.

(May the battle-trumpet be sounded for us, let us go with the cries of fierce battle, until we make highway refuse, of this new army of George's.)

Like so many other vernacular songs composed since 1691, this work concluded with the prediction of a Stuart restoration.

The end of the Irish privateers

The final phase of the war began as it was to continue for the Irish privateers – badly. In December 1781 Matthew Knight and James Sweetman, who had been captured while serving on board a French privateer, were executed in London for 'robberies and piracies committed by them on the high seas'.[171] Before long the same prospect confronted a much larger group of men when a British frigate captured a privateer – significantly named the *Anti-Briton* – commanded by the same Captain Kelly from Rush who had previously commanded the *Dreadnought*. The *Anti-Briton* was taken in the Irish Sea and its crew was landed at Dublin, a circumstance which caused legal difficulties for the prosecution and ultimately saved the ship's officers from sharing the fate of Knight and Sweetman. Thirty-six of the crew who were found on examination to be French were transferred to Kilkenny as prisoners of war but the remaining sixty were 'detained in Dublin to take their trials for high treason and piracy'.[172] Kelly was reported to be 'not in the least affected with his present situation' and to believe that his French commission would 'baffle the utmost efforts of the king's lawyers'.[173] Statements taken from witnesses with a view to prosecuting the officers of the *Anti-Briton* indicate that they were natives of either Rush, Skerries or Dublin city, and that their former occupations included those of fisherman, Jew's harp maker, carpenter and block maker.[174] Their case was aggravated by allegations that the *Anti-Briton* had continued to fire on one of its prizes, a British cutter named the *Hope*, after the latter had struck its colours, and the *Dublin Evening Post* demanded that Kelly be hanged on account of this incident.[175] The charge was indignantly rejected by the *Anti-Briton*'s lieutenant, a man named Kenna, who called on the crew of the *Hope* to acknowledge that they had left their colours flying on retreating to their quarters and that the British ensign was still flying when he boarded the ship.[176] This controversy provides further evidence of the privateers' perception of themselves as men engaged in regular warfare rather than piracy. Their discipline and *esprit de corps* were shown in late February when an attempt by Kelly and some of

---

[171] *DEP*, 13 December 1781.   [172] *FLJ*, 16 January 1782.   [173] *DEP*, 5 January 1782.
[174] PRO SP 63/480, fos. 111–16.   [175] *DEP*, 5 January 1782.
[176] *FLJ*, 19 January 1782.

his crew to escape from Newgate prison was foiled.[177] A second attempt was made within days, this time with the assistance of associates waiting outside the prison who 'had everything in readiness' but were noticed by guards who raised the alarm.[178] At the end of March two members of the crew finally succeeded in escaping before the guards were alerted and prevented others from following them.[179]

Further public attention was drawn to the activities of Irish privateers in April when reports appeared in the Irish press of the trials of Luke Ryan and Thomas Coppinger at the Old Bailey in London. The degree of public interest in the case can be gauged from the decision of the editor of the *Hibernian Magazine* to use a portrait of Ryan as the frontispiece of his April issue – a position occupied by portraits of Admiral Sir Samuel Hood and the Duke of Portland in the March and May issues respectively. While Coppinger was acquitted for lack of adequate identification, witnesses travelled from Ireland to testify to Ryan's Irish birth. He was duly sentenced to death but was reported to be 'little affected with his fate'.[180]

In April also a British privateer named the *Adventure* succeeded in capturing an American privateer, the *Independence*, after an action in which eleven crewmen were killed on the former and seventeen on the latter. While the *Independence* sailed under the American flag she was captained by John Roche, a native of Cork, and was reported to be 'chiefly manned with Irish, whom he brought from thence [Cork] at his own expense'.[181] In May a number of colliers sailing between Whitehaven and Dublin were taken and ransomed by what the Irish press termed 'Rush pirates'. The solidarity which prevailed among the Irish privateers was again demonstrated on the evening of 16 May when two ships commanded by Patrick Dowling and Locker Crosley anchored off Skerries and put parties ashore to burn the home of a revenue officer 'in revenge of his having been a material witness in the conviction of Luke Ryan'.[182] On the following day, however, one of the privateers involved, Crosley's *Reynard*, was captured off Lambay by a British frigate and brought into Dublin. Again, evidence was collected with a view to prosecuting the ship's officers. Crosley himself and Patrick Duff, the quartermaster, were certified to be natives of Skerries; and it was stated that Timothy Kelly, the *Reynard*'s

---

[177] *Ibid.*, 23 February 1782.   [178] *Ibid.*, 27 February 1782.
[179] *Ibid.*, 23 March 1782.
[180] *HM*, April 1782, 170. His subsequent pardon was attributed to American representations; see *FJ*, 10 April 1783. For an account of Ryan's career, see Eugene Coyle, 'An Irish buccaneer: the case of Captain Luke Ryan', *History Ireland*, summer 1999.
[181] *FLJ*, 27 April 1782.   [182] *Ibid.*, 22 May 1782.

master of arms and log-book keeper, had formerly been a schoolmaster at Rush.[183]

In June it was reported that the prosecution of the 'Hiberni-Galli confined in the several gaols of this kingdom, for being found in arms fighting against their country' was at last about to commence.[184] Later in the same month it was claimed that 'piratical captains and crews' had become so numerous in Irish prisons 'as to exceed all other criminals of whatever denomination'.[185] The threatened prosecution failed to materialise, however, and the crew of the *Anti-Briton* had still not been tried by October when twenty-eight of them were spotted on the roof of Newgate prison during another unsuccessful escape attempt.[186] The delay in bringing a prosecution against the crews of either the *Anti-Briton* or the *Reynard* was due not to lack of evidence but rather to the political impossibility of charging them in an Admiralty court constituted under the authority of a British act of parliament. Lord Temple bluntly advised the home secretary that it was 'beyond a doubt that no jury in this kingdom will find a verdict, nor will any punishment be awarded under a court so constituted'.[187] An Irish act (11 James I) that provided for a court of Admiralty 'appointed by the lord chancellor of Ireland under the great seal of Ireland' had fallen into disuse and the political will to revive it did not exist.[188] Faced with this legal difficulty, the administration offered a pardon to those among the privateers' crews who were willing to enlist in the Royal Navy, terms which were accepted by 'several' of them, but the remaining crew members rejected the offer and insisted on being tried 'from an expectation, to which they are strongly encouraged by their counsel, that under the circumstances of the constitution of the Admiralty court here they must be discharged'.[189] To circumvent this possibility, the viceroy proposed to send the prisoners to Plymouth in the expectation that the remaining crew members would prefer service in the Royal Navy to trial for a capital offence before a court whose jurisdiction was not in doubt once they found themselves in Great Britain. He recommended that they should then be despatched to 'the most distant part of his Majesty's dominions, that they may not speedily have an opportunity of returning to their old connections, and resuming their practices of piracy and treason' and proposed the East Indies as the safest destination.[190] In the event, both crews were still imprisoned in Dublin at the conclusion of peace.[191]

---

[183] PRO HO 100/8, fos. 26–32.   [184] *FLJ*, 12 June 1782.   [185] *Ibid.*, 29 June 1782.
[186] *Ibid.*, 23 October 1782.
[187] Temple to Thomas Townshend, 21 December 1782, in PRO HO 100/3, fo. 365.
[188] *Ibid.*, fo. 364.   [189] *Ibid.*   [190] *Ibid.*, fo. 365.   [191] *FLJ*, 8 February 1783.

Presbyterian opinion and the 'revolution of '82'

The Presbyterian community shared the sense of euphoria which gripped the political nation as a whole on the announcement that the Rockingham administration intended to repeal the declaratory act of 1720. In Derry, the city's Volunteer corps had paraded and fired a *feu de joie* to celebrate Rodney's victory at the battle of the Saints on the day before news arrived of the British parliament's resolution in favour of repeal but they turned out on a second successive day to fire another volley. That night 'the city was one blaze of light, [with] not a house, or even a cabin, unilluminated'.[192] The toasts drunk by the Belfast Volunteer corps when they marched to the Cave Hill on the occasion of the king's birthday a few days later illustrate the blend of loyal, imperial and Whiggish sentiments prevailing among the town's politically active citizens:

His Majesty, and long may he live the *patriot* king of a *free* people. Health and happiness to the queen and royal family. That friend of liberty and of mankind, the lord lieutenant of Ireland. General Lord Charlemont. The Volunteers of Ireland. Henry Grattan and the people of Ireland. The ministry, and the people of Great Britain. Lord Keppel, and the British flag. The brave Admiral Rodney, and his gallant and victorious fleet.[193]

Less reassuring for the ministry was a toast to 'Freedom of election, short parliaments, and an equal representation of the commons of Great Britain and Ireland' which was drunk on the same occasion. The mood of satisfaction with the Rockingham ministry is evident from the 'humble address' to George III adopted by the Synod of Ulster on 26 June. It was the first such address to be presented since 1763 – not even the 1780 repeal of the sacramental test excluding Protestant Dissenters from office had prompted the Synod to lay an expression of its gratitude before the throne. Likewise, the address made no mention of the legal recognition granted to Presbyterian marriages only a few months previously. While the address contained an assurance that 'no part of your dominions contains men more attached to those principles which seated your Majesty and your illustrious family on the throne of these kingdoms than the Protestant Dissenters of the north of Ireland', it is clear that its primary purpose was to express the Synod's satisfaction with the new political dispensation:

We behold, with veneration and gladness, the late change in your Majesty's counsels. We revere the magnanimity and goodness of your royal heart in adopting those maxims of government which have for their object the liberty and happiness of mankind. We rejoice in the pleasing prospect, now opened of having the

---

[192] *LJ*, 28 May 1782.   [193] Joy, *Historical Collections*, pp. 206–7.

sword sheathed and that brother will no more rise against brother. As Irishmen, we particularly rejoice in the justice and liberality of your Majesty's intentions towards this kingdom.[194]

The contrast between the enthusiasm of this address and the silence of the Synod on public questions during the previous nineteen years testifies to the misgivings that many ministers must have had about the policies pursued by Lord North's administration. But the prospect of peace with America had removed the impediment to whole-hearted support for the war effort and the Synod prayed that God might 'grant victory to your [George III's] fleets and armies over the antient enemies of freedom and these kingdoms'. Similar enthusiasm for the new British administration was evident at the annual meeting of freeholders held to celebrate the victory of 'freedom and independence' over 'servitude' in the County Antrim election of 1776. The toasts included the following:

The king, queen, and royal family, The Whig ministry and Whig interest, The lord lieutenant of Ireland, General Lord Charlemont and Volunteers of Ireland, Henry Grattan and the people of Ireland, Mr. Flood, and all those illustrious senators who have so strenuously and successfully supported the rights of Ireland. Perpetual union of affection, and of interest, to Great Britain and Ireland, Peace with America, and a hearty drubbing to the house of Bourbon ... annual parliaments, and an equal representation to the people of England and Ireland ...[195]

In Belfast, as in other parts of the country, the local Volunteer units participated in the campaign to raise 20,000 recruits for the Royal Navy and the *Belfast News-Letter* reported that '36 fine spirited young fellows' enlisted in a single day in early July.[196] But the rare mood of unanimity among the members of the political nation proved to be as ephemeral in Ulster as it was elsewhere.

As early as 27 June the First Belfast Company of Volunteers expressed doubts as to whether the repeal of the 1720 declaratory act provided sufficient assurance of Ireland's legislative independence and the company addressed Henry Grattan and Henry Flood with the suggestion that an act asserting the independence of the Irish parliament be enacted as an 'additional security'. While the Belfast Volunteers did not question the sincerity of Lord Rockingham's ministry, they argued that the good faith of all future administrations in Britain could not be taken for granted: 'Even the popularity of the present ministry, and our confidence in its justice, may lead to a neglect of those wise securities, the want of which might in a future administration, less attached to the rights of

[194] Address dated 26 June 1782, in PRO HO 100/2, fo. 233; the address has been published in *Records of the General Synod of Ulster*, III (Belfast, 1898), p. 46.
[195] *BNL*, 2 July 1782.   [196] *Ibid.*, 9 July 1782.

human nature, be ruinous to the freedom of this kingdom.'[197] It was soon clear that such concerns were not confined to Belfast. An address to Flood from the Volunteer corps of Raphoe, County Donegal, praised him for his opposition to 'simple repeal' and referred meaningfully to the 'premature generosity of the public' – a reference to the £50,000 voted to Grattan by parliament.[198] Lord Abingdon's attempt to introduce a bill in the British House of Lords that would have asserted the continuing right of the British parliament to regulate Irish trade helped to accentuate a trend which was already apparent. The Belfast Volunteer Company resolved on 18 July not to enlist men for the navy because of Abingdon's 'very extraordinary' bill and four days later the same corps resolved that 'an Irish law declaratory of the rights of Ireland, of the independency of our parliament, and of their exclusive right to external as well as internal legislation' was required.[199] These views were shared by the freeholders of Donegal who resolved at a county meeting held on 22 July that it was 'incompatible with the duty we owe our country, to assist in raising seamen for the navy of Great Britain, until that point [external legislation] is expressly and unequivocally relinquished'.[200] Supporters of Grattan temporarily stemmed the tide when a review of Volunteer corps from west Ulster held at Strabane on 18–19 July adopted a resolution expressing satisfaction with 'simple repeal'.[201] A more numerous review of corps from the east of the province was held at Belfast two weeks later and the rival patriot factions competed for the endorsement of the Volunteer rank and file. Francis Dobbs penned an evocative account of the highly politicised atmosphere he encountered there:

Anonymous papers in thousands were dispersed through the camp and garrison. Every private was taught, that he was competent to legislate, and consequently to express his sentiments on the most speculative points. – Declaration – Renunciation – Simple Repeal – Legal Security – Better Security, and Bill of Rights, were all before them – and they were to instruct their delegates on these important points.[202]

A proposal moved by Dobbs and supported by Joseph Pollock that would have endorsed 'simple repeal' was defeated by the narrow margin of thirty-one votes to twenty-nine, but when Flood's supporters moved a resolution calling for an Irish bill of rights a motion to adjourn was carried by 31 votes to 27. The Volunteer's had declined to endorse either of the contending parties, although both could take some comfort from the

---

[197] *Ibid.*, 16 July 1782.   [198] *DEP*, 18 July 1782.
[199] Joy, *Historical Collections*, pp. 214–15. The Belfast Volunteer Company is to be distinguished from the First Belfast Company.
[200] *DEP*, 27 July 1782.   [201] *LJ*, 30 July 1782.
[202] Dobbs, *A History of Irish Affairs*, p. 138.

defeat of their rivals. A supporter of 'simple repeal' hailed the outcome as a major setback for Flood: 'Thus the great orator's last anchor of hope was torn from him, and his bark left to founder on the sea of envious pride and disappointed ambition; and such was the result of his northern journey.'[203] This may have seemed a realistic assessment of the situation at the time but before long the fresh controversy over the formation of the fencible regiments further deepened the Volunteers' mistrust of administration and served to discredit several prominent supporters of 'simple repeal' who accepted commissions in the new corps.

On 9 September 1782 the Belfast Volunteer company resolved that 'the scheme of raising these fencible regiments is calculated to lessen the force of the Volunteer army'.[204] When a review of thirty Volunteer corps took place at Ballymoney, County Antrim, on 18 September a resolution was adopted which both demanded 'an Irish bill of rights' and condemned the fencibles proposal.[205] A Belfast town meeting followed the lead of the Ballymoney review on 5 October by resolving that the purpose of the fencible regiments was 'to disunite, to weaken, and, were it possible, even to annihilate the Volunteer army, those glorious independent defenders of their country, and to introduce in their place a *mercenary force*, which the experience of ages has proved *baneful to the liberties of mankind* – and to increase the influence of the crown, already much too great'.[206] On the same day effigies of Grattan and several Volunteer officers who had accepted commissions in the fencible regiments were carried through the streets of Belfast and 'afterwards hanged and burnt, amidst the acclamations of some thousands of spectators'.[207] A protest against the resolution of the town meeting was subsequently signed by forty-two prominent inhabitants of Belfast but by this stage opinion had hardened against both 'simple repeal' and the fencibles. In the following weeks reports appeared that fencible recruiting parties had been prevented from beating up for recruits in Lisburn, County Antrim, and Banbridge, County Down, while a recruiting party of 'offencibles' was unable to find billets in Derry city 'where their business is so extremely offensive to the inhabitants'.[208]

Peace

The impasse created by the demand for legislative confirmation of the Irish parliament's independence was finally broken in late November when judgement was given in a case that had been appealed from the court of king's bench in Ireland to the equivalent court in Britain. The

---

[203] *LJ*, 13 August 1782.   [204] Joy, *Historical Collections*, p. 216.
[205] *FLJ*, 25 September 1782.   [206] Joy, *Historical Collections*, p. 221.
[207] *FLJ*, 12 October 1782.   [208] *LJ*, 15 October 1782.

case had been referred before the repeal of the declaratory act and no such case could have arisen subsequently, but the fact that judgement was given appeared to undermine the claim of the 'simple repealers' that the House of Lords in Ireland was now the final court of appeal. While this fortuitous event naturally increased discontent in the short term, it also provided the supporters of repeal with a plausible reason for changing their position. The *Hibernian Journal*, in an article which characterised Henry Flood as 'the most corrupt and fallacious character which has ever appeared in the parliament of Ireland', nevertheless conceded that the British judgement was 'a breach of the late settlement – a breach which no Irishman can suffer, and which requires the whole spirit of the nation to have rectified'.[209] The lord lieutenant recognised that the government's position had become untenable: 'having struggled with infinite difficulty in resisting ideal grievances', as he put it in a letter to the home secretary, 'I have not the smallest reason to imagine that I could be successful in endeavouring to explain away this business'.[210] But Lord Temple also appreciated that government had been given an escape route from its predicament and he now proposed that the need to allay doubts created by the appeal should be cited as the reason for introducing a bill to confirm Ireland's legislative and judicial independence, 'a solution which will save the credit of both parliaments'.[211] William Grenville, the chief secretary, formally committed the ministry to such a course in a speech to the British House of Commons on 20 December. Disagreement about the scope and urgency of the proposed legislation persisted behind the scenes in a ministry preoccupied with the peace negotiations then taking place at Versailles.[212] Indeed, in mid-January the lord lieutenant threatened to resign unless satisfactory legislation was introduced quickly and even expressed the fear that his 'departure from Ireland upon such grounds, will throw the kingdom into revolt'.[213] But these strains remained hidden from public view and a general assumption prevailed in Ireland that a resolution of the 'renunciation' question was imminent. By year's end a factious and unproductive controversy that had virtually monopolised the attention of the political nation for six months was in the process of being resolved and the advocates of renunciation were content to enjoy their opponents' discomfiture: 'It is exceedingly diverting to remark with what assiduity the little expiring band of simple repealists

---

[209] *HJ*, 11 December 1782.
[210] Temple to Townshend, 30 November 1782, in PRO HO 100/3, fo. 301.
[211] *Ibid.*, fo. 303.
[212] For a full account of this episode, see Peter Jupp, 'Earl Temple's viceroyalty and the question of renunciation, 1782–3', *IHS* 17 (1971).
[213] Temple to William Grenville, 15 January 1783, in Fortescue Mss., HMC 13th report, appendix III (1892), p. 181.

are striving to gloss over the absurdity and weakness of their doctrine. Don't think say they, because the English parliament are about to give Ireland full satisfaction, therefore the repeal of the 6th of Geo. I. was not sufficient.'[214] As a consensus began to emerge on the renunciation question, the issue that it had driven from the political agenda, that of parliamentary reform, began to re-emerge – a development greatly assisted by William Pitt's efforts to steer a parliamentary reform measure through Westminster. Not for the first time, the concerns of the Irish political nation were seen to mirror those of its British parent. 'Perhaps it is a glorious work reserved for the son of the illustrious Lord Chatham, to give the people their due and efficient weight in the scale of the constitution', enthused the *Londonderry Journal* – a newspaper which had shown some prior interest in the question.[215] Even in the columns of the *Dublin Evening-Post*, the principal organ of pro-renunciation opinion, a columnist noted that Pitt was a 'near relation' (first cousin) of Lord Temple's and expressed the hope that the viceroy would 'as spiritedly forward a reformation and redress of this crying evil in Ireland, as his noble kinsman is striving to accomplish in the parliamentary representation of England'.[216]

On 26 January 1783 Lord Temple officially informed the lord mayor of Dublin, and through him the Irish public, that the home secretary had been granted leave to bring in a bill at Westminster 'for the removing and preventing all doubts, which have arisen or may arise, concerning the exclusive rights of the parliament and courts of Ireland, in matters of legislation and judicature'.[217] The news was received calmly and only a day later it was overshadowed by a further letter from the viceroy to apprise the lord mayor that preliminary articles of peace had been signed at Versailles on 20 January.[218] In a letter to the chief secretary, then in London, a relieved Temple commented that 'this fortunate pacification will have done more to quiet Ireland than all the hours which we have so studiously given to it'.[219] In Dublin on the afternoon of the 28 January 'the royal and Volunteer armies of this city, in conjunction, under the command of lieutenant-general Sir John Burgoyne, and general the right honourable Earl Charlemont, drew up on the North-quays, and made a grand *feu-de-joy* on the occasion of the signature of preliminaries for a general peace'.[220] It must have been an imposing spectacle, but the Volunteers were celebrating, not just the end of the war, but also the end of their own *raison d'être*.

---

[214] *DEP*, 14 January 1783.   [215] *LJ*, 31 December 1782.
[216] *DEP*, 2 January 1783.   [217] *Volunteer Journal*, 30 January 1783.   [218] *Ibid.*
[219] Temple to William Grenville, 27 January 1783, in HMC Fortescue Mss., p. 187.
[220] *FLJ*, 1 February 1783.

The end of hostilities was greeted with satisfaction by all sections of the Protestant community. At one end of the political spectrum the Hibernian Union, a recently formed Volunteer corps which had broken away from the Dublin Independent Volunteers when that unit re-elected Grattan as its colonel, resolved on 5 February that they would 'salute the first vessel which shall arrive in the harbour of Dublin under American colours, by firing three volleys'.[221] At the opposite pole of opinion, *Saunders' Newsletter*, a journal which had supported government throughout the course of the American conflict and catered for a commercial readership, was moved to entertain ambitious ideas concerning Ireland's future role as an entrepôt between Europe and America: 'from our present circumstances and local situation, we have it in our choice whether Ireland shall be considered as an obscure corner of the earth, or as the great medium of connecting the Old and New World'.[222] The *Belfast News-Letter*, likewise, described the appearance of the first advertisement for a ship sailing from Ireland to the United States as a 'matter of great exultation' and concluded that the resumption of commerce represented 'a glorious prospect of commercial prosperity to the people of Ireland'.[223] Peace was officially proclaimed in Dublin on 22 February. By the middle of March it was reported that:

The first fruits of our free trade has [*sic*] been experienced with America, four vessels having already sailed to that continent, viz. one from Cork, two from Dublin, and one from Belfast, laden with Irish manufactures. In consequence of our free constitution also, these vessels have got the start of the English, who are at present detained by an embargo.[224]

Less positively, Lord Temple informed the chief secretary that 170 emigrants had applied to sail on the first vessel to depart for Philadelphia, although he took some comfort from the fact that there was 'no property amongst them'.[225]

Elements of change and continuity were both in evidence on St Patrick's day, 1783. The attention of many members of the Irish political nation was focused on the ceremonial installation of the Knights of St Patrick (a newly instituted order of chivalry intended to reflect Ireland's enhanced constitutional status) which took place in St Patrick's cathedral, Dublin. The members of the nobility who accepted knighthoods in the order included the Duke of Leinster and Lord Charlemont, both prominent figures in the Volunteer movement. Lord Temple was pleased to report that: 'The parade of our Knights is over, much to my satisfaction; but

---

221 *LJ*, 11 February 1783.   222 *SNL*, 1 February 1783.
223 *BNL*, 31 January 1783.   224 *LJ*, 18 March 1783.
225 Temple to William Grenville, 9 February 1783, in HMC Fortescue Mss., p. 191.

very much, I believe, to the satisfaction of all Ireland, who seem to have
embarked eagerly in the idea. The Volunteers offered *me* their services,
which I accepted, to line a part of the streets, and the whole passed off very
well.'[226] The episode underlines the extent to which conventional sentiments of loyalty to crown, church and empire survived the American war,
notwithstanding the heavy blow dealt by American independence to all
three. It is unlikely that such an event would have attracted any public
criticism a decade previously but by 1783 an alternative viewpoint had
emerged. At the extreme margins of patriotism, among those who had
clamoured for 'renunciation' and were now turning their attention to
the more meaningful object of parliamentary reform, voices were raised
against the aristocratic mummery of the knights. An anonymous verse in
the *Dublin Evening Post* sounded a note of warning:

> Hibernia beware,
> this knighthood, I fear,
>   is naught but a trap to ensnare you.
> The old policy still
> of tyrannical will,
>   lords and knights with their vice to besmear you.[227]

More significantly perhaps, the editor of the non-partisan *Finn's Leinster
Journal* saw fit to carry a similar warning: 'The people should carefully
watch this accretion of new strength among the peerage, and counter-
act it by that vigour and efficacy which have rendered them respectable
in the eyes of Europe, and emancipated them from a state of Russian
vassalage.'[228]

If the installation of the Knights of St Patrick provides a useful illustration of the range of political opinions within the Protestant community,
other events that took place on St Patrick's day illustrate the growing com-
plexity of Irish society as a whole. In Cork, Arthur O'Leary, Capuchin
priest and 'Monk of the Screw', preached a sermon 'highly expressive of
the merits of our patron saint' to a congregation which included members of the local Volunteer corps. The preacher allowed his thoughts to
wander from the fifth century to the eighteenth:

The ingenious eulogist, with peculiar elegance of address, directed then his
encomiums to the sons of St Patrick, our honoured Volunteers – His happy
imagination failed not to discover the affinity between him who rescued our island
from the darkness of ignorance and idolatry, and those whose glorious exertions
liberated us from the chains of arrogance and shackles of despotism.[229]

[226] Temple to William Grenville, 20 March 1783, in Fortescue Mss., p. 202. Emphasis in
the original.
[227] *DEP*, 11 March 1783.   [228] *FLJ*, 1 March 1783.   [229] *LJ*, 1 April 1783.

The Catholic middle class had absorbed the lesson that the opposition of today could become the administration of tomorrow, that extra-
parliamentary agitation could wrest reforms from a reluctant government,
and that anti-Catholicism was no longer a necessary concomitant of
patriotism.

Cooperation between members of the Volunteers and more plebeian
Catholics was in evidence in Kilkenny city where one of the newly raised
fencible units, the Royal Leinster Regiment, arrived to take up garrison
duties on St Patrick's day. On the evening of the same day the regiment's
drummers were attacked, 'their drums were taken from them and broke;
and it is even said, the guard who accompanied them had their firelocks
wrested from them and destroyed'.[230] State papers identify those involved
in the initial attack as members of the Kilkenny Rangers, a local Volunteer
corps, but this initial attack proved to be only the opening incident in a
long series of disturbances. Assaults on the fencibles, said to have been
attended with 'circumstances of wanton cruelty, and open defiance of
the laws from the lower mob', continued into April and prompted the
despatch of regular troops from Dublin before order was restored.[231]

On St Patrick's day, as the Earl of Charlemont and his fellow knights
were being installed in Dublin, the Volunteers of Cork city were parading
to hear the homily of a Catholic regular, and the Volunteers and populace
of Kilkenny were expressing their detestation of the fencibles, a vicious
riot broke out in Castlebar, County Mayo, between the garrison and
the townspeople. The clash erupted when soldiers 'dressed two of their
companions in a ridiculous manner, in ridicule of St Patrick, and his wife
Sheela, as they called her' and hung 'potatoes in imitation of beads' about
their necks. Violence between the civilian population and the military
was a common occurrence but the outcome on this occasion would have
been inconceivable only a few years before: when the Killmain Volunteers
arrived on the scene they intervened on the side of the populace and were
variously reported to have killed either two or four of the military party –
telling evidence of the scale of the changes in Ireland during the course
of the American war.[232]

Conclusion

News of the surrender at Yorktown prompted renewed declarations of
loyalty to crown and empire from Protestant Ireland but this reaction sub-
sided as it became clear that the ministry had been dealt a mortal blow.

[230] *DEP*, 3 April 1783.
[231] Temple to Sydney, 4 April 1783, in PRO HO 100/8, fos. 271–2.
[232] *DEP*, 25 and 27 March 1783; *FLJ*, 29 March and 2 April 1783; *FJ*, 27 March 1783.

As Lord North's parliamentary majority melted away during the spring of 1782 the stock of the Irish opposition rose in tandem with that of their British counterparts and they were swept into office on the coat-tails of the Rockingham Whigs. With colonial independence now regarded as a *fait accompli* America ceased to be a political issue and the patriots in office voted lavish grants of men and money to support the war effort against France and Spain. This unaccustomed unanimity among the members of the political nation was disrupted as Lord Rockingham's death and the withdrawal of his followers from government, Henry Flood's legal quibbles, and the formation of fencible regiments, all combined to cast doubt on the durability of the new constitutional arrangements and the future of the Volunteer movement. The resulting dispute between supporters of 'renunciation' and 'repeal' overshadowed both the final stages of the war and the start of peace negotiations.

For the Catholic masses, Britain's military eclipse in North America was as welcome as it was unusual. Almost forty years had elapsed since Britain had suffered a comparable defeat at Fontenoy, and predictions of an imminent invasion and the overthrow of the existing constitutional order proliferated in political song. With the emergence of an influential body of patriot opinion sympathetic to Catholic relief, the Catholic élite was able to view the formation of a Whig ministry with equanimity. At the same time, the anti-British rhetoric employed during the 'renunciation' and 'fencible' agitations stoked the enthusiasm of the lower classes and produced a heightened sense of political tension which persisted after the end of hostilities.

Postscript

Various unproductive attempts have been made to trace the influence of the political ideas associated with the American revolution on Irish opinion. Raymond Barrett, author of the most sustained study of the kind, concluded that the Irish, despite their 'close contact with American thought... scarcely utilized the American material'.[1] This is what one would expect, given that Anglo-Irish constitutional theory was in advance of the American. The Irish House of Commons asserted its 'sole right' to initiate money bills (and consequently to levy taxation) as early as 1692, while Molyneux rejected the English parliament's authority to legislate for Ireland on the grounds of natural right eight years later. On the other hand, Westminster's power to legislate for – as distinct from its power to tax – the American colonies appears not to have been disputed before the 1760s, and its power to regulate imperial trade was acknowledged by American patriots until the outbreak of hostilities. Furthermore, while the members of the Irish political nation disagreed on the precise extent of the British parliament's authority over the colonies, they all, patriots and courtiers alike, assumed that the powers of the ancient parliament of the kingdom of Ireland were more extensive than those of the colonial assemblies. This assumption considerably diminished the relevance of colonial polemics and these, in any event, contained few novelties for the educated Irish reader: as Bernard Bailyn has noted, the ideas which inspired the American revolution derived largely from writings associated with the exclusion crisis of 1679–81 and the Williamite Revolution.[2] By 1775 even the students of Trinity College – once a Tory bastion and never a hotbed of patriotism – were being taught that 'the general consent of the people can alone supply a legitimate foundation

[1] Raymond J. Barrett, 'A comparative study of imperial constitutional theory in Ireland and America in the age of the American revolution' (PhD thesis, TCD, 1958), p. 23.
[2] Bernard Bailyn, *Faces of Revolution: Personalities and Themes in the Struggle for American Independence* (New York, 1990), p. 204.

330

in government', a view supported by reference to Locke's *Two Treatises of Government*.[3]

Yet it cannot be denied that the American revolution, and the international war resulting from it, accelerated the process of change in Ireland. Between 1775 and 1783 the glacier of Irish politics which had remained almost immobile since 1691 began to thaw with remarkable speed. The delight and astonishment of one contemporary at the 'wonderful alteration' produced in so short a time is vividly conveyed in a poem entitled 'Ireland's Glory' and subtitled 'a comparative view of Ireland, in the years 1776 and 1783' which was published at Newry, County Down. It deserves to be quoted in full:

> The king was a God, whom no subject dare squint at,
> a lord was a creature no poor man dare point at,
> and a member of parliament – wonderful wonder!
> to him, his constituents were forced to knock under.
>
> But great was the change in the year seventy-seven,
> we then were inspired by a spark sent from heaven,
> we shook off our sloth, took our muskets in hand,
> and in less than six years new-modelled our land.
>
> We could look at a king without much admiration,
> and a lord we considered the scruff of the nation;
> that each member of parliament was but our servant,
> and this was our creed most solemn and fervent.
>
> We made no distinction 'twixt Meeting or Mass
> and every God's creature was welcome to us;
> we wished freedom to mankind as well as ourselves,
> and judged all opponents mere priest-ridden elves.
>
> Our souls grew expanded, we banished distrust,
> and the knave, from example, grew honest and just,
> from a nation of slaves we've emerged into glory,
> and ages to come will record us in story.
> Alteration, alteration, Oh, 'twas a wonderful alteration.[4]

The changes were indeed real and substantial, but they were not inspired by American *thought*. They probably owed something to the force of American *example*, however, and it is indisputable that they were greatly

---

[3] Michael Kearney, *Lectures concerning History Read during the Year 1775*, in Trinity College, Dublin (Dublin, 1776), p. 12. The reference is to Locke, *Two Treatises of Government*, book II, § 102.

[4] *Ireland's Glory; or, a Comparative View of Ireland, in the Years 1776 and 1783* (Newry, n.d. – 1783?).

facilitated by an international conjuncture which restricted the ability of British government to oppose Irish demands. The American war was responsible for depleting the strength of the garrison in Ireland, thereby stimulating the emergence of the Volunteers as a national movement; for precipitating a severe economic crisis, thereby igniting the agitation for free trade; and, perhaps most importantly, for undermining Lord North's administration, thereby bringing the opposition into office in both Britain and Ireland. The patriots in office implemented the programme of reforms that had occupied their attention for a generation – an achievement which in turn brought the potentially revolutionary demand for parliamentary reform to the top of the political agenda.

The success of the opposition campaigns for free trade and legislative independence had profound effects on Irish politics and society. The backing which these campaigns received from the Catholic populace encouraged the emergence of a body of patriot opinion that was favourably disposed to further measures of Catholic relief and regarded Catholic support as an essential prerequisite for future political advance. 'When we are told by great authorities, that a union with Catholics is a dangerous expedient', declared William Todd Jones, member of parliament for Lisburn, County Antrim, at a Volunteer review in 1784, 'we ought anxiously to enquire by what mode they propose to accomplish a reform of parliament without their [the Catholics'] co-operation.'[5] It is impossible to conceive of such sentiments being uttered by the elected representative of an open constituency anywhere in Ireland – still less one in Ulster – in the period before the American war.

This sea change was mirrored on the other side of the politico-religious divide. The Catholic community at the start of the American war had been divided into an élite group which looked to the executive for relief, and the lower classes which continued to hope for a successful invasion by France or Spain and the overthrow of the Revolution settlement. By the end of the war the new willingness of patriots to countenance Catholic relief, together with the promotion of opposition leaders to positions of power in both Britain and Ireland, made the Catholic Committee's former policy of reliance on the grace and favour of administration increasingly untenable. Appreciable numbers of middle-class Catholics were illegally bearing arms as members of the Volunteer movement, in which capacity they also participated in the political debates and agitations of the day. At the same time the virtues of such Protestant republicans as Generals Washington, Lee, Wayne and Greene were being extolled in vernacular

---

[5] *Transactions of the General Committee of the Roman Catholics of Ireland, during the Year 1791; and some Fugitive Pieces on that Subject* (Dublin, 1792), p. 19.

song – as were the leading Anglo-Irish patriots. The Volunteers were likewise portrayed as an independent force defending Ireland's interests ('*saorarm gáirmhianach na Banban*') while their fencible rivals were vilified as mercenaries in the service of the British crown ('*arm nua so Sheoirse*').[6] If the American war was identified as the prophesied '*cogadh an dá Ghall*' at its outset, by the time it ended lower-class Catholics had developed a sympathetic view of certain elements among the *Gaill* both at home and abroad. Jacobite sentiment would persist until the death of Prince Charles Edward in 1788, but the American war prepared the ground for the new, republican, messianism that would characterise the 1790s:

> *A chlanna bocht' Gael tá i bpéin le fada*
> *éiridh feasta suas,*
> *is gabhaidh go géar ag gléas bhur n-arm*
> *is déanaidh treas gan trua;*
> *más Sasanach é ná* Quaker *cruaidh*
> *ná glacaidh féin leis éad ná fuath,*
> *ach preabaidh le chéile in éineacht suas*
> *ag turnamh Danar dóibh.*[7]

(O poor children of the Gaels who have long been tormented, rise up henceforth, set about preparing your arms quickly, and give battle without mercy; if he's an Anglican [literally 'Englishman'] or a sturdy *Quaker*, don't be jealous or hostile towards him, but both of you leap up together to overthrow the Danes.)

While demands for further constitutional reform were heard with increasing frequency in early 1783, many members of the political nation had already concluded that change had gone far enough and that the time had arrived to defend the status quo. The increasingly prominent role played by Dissenters and Catholics in extra-parliamentary politics was a source of particular concern to members of the established church and produced a backlash directed against the advocates of reform. For such conservatives, America was an object example of the perils to be avoided rather than an ideal to be emulated:

We have before our eyes a melancholy instance of the danger of altering an established form of government in the present lamentable state of America. The provincial assemblies heretofore respectable and important for their power, are now dwindling into bodies almost wholly insignificant. Congress endeavours to exert its delegated powers, the assemblies resist. What must be the end of these things?[8]

---

[6] See pp. 229 and 316 above respectively.
[7] '*I dtarngaireacht naomh is léir go bhfaca*' in Rónán Ó Donnchadha (ed.), *Mícheál Óg Ó Longáin, File* (Dublin, 1994), p. 80. The work dates from 1797.
[8] *A Reform of the Irish House of Commons, Considered* (Dublin, 1783), p. 18.

'Can we hesitate', asked the same author, 'between a constitution, the envy of the world...and one that Puritans and Catholics take upon them to frame for us?'[9] Patrick Duigenan, an outspoken advocate of what would shortly be termed 'Protestant ascendancy', condemned proposals for parliamentary reform as 'a scheme, purely calculated, for the ruin of the present establishment in church and state'.[10] It was, moreover, merely the visible outcrop of a deep-seated conspiracy hatched by Presbyterians and Catholics in concert: 'the real aim of these two factions, (however disguised under popular pretences) is to sever Ireland for ever from Great Britain; and to establish a republic here, under the protection of France'.[11] This contention could be amply supported by reference to the conduct of Irish Catholics during the American war:

a large body of Irish Catholics, in the service of France, fought, as well on the continent of America, as in the West-India Islands, against Great Britain; and their exploits against their country, at Savannah, at St. Lucia, at St. Kitts, and St. Eustatia, may be found in the journals of the times, and in the accounts of that war...All the French privateers which infested this channel during the late war, who plundered the British and Irish merchant ships, even in the bay of Dublin, were manned and commanded by Irish Catholics, – such as John Kelly, John Field, Luke Ryan, Patrick Dowling and others; and they were furnished with intelligence, with provisions, and even with powder, by Irish Catholics from several ports in the channel, in which the wives and families of many of them were then resident.[12]

While Duigenan's prescient fear of a coalition between Catholics and Presbyterians to establish an Irish republic with French support was still premature in 1783, it would be realised before the end of the century.

[9] *Ibid.*, p. 30.   [10] [Duigenan], *The Alarm*, p. 7.   [11] *Ibid.*, p. 25.
[12] Patrick Duigenan, *A Speech Spoken in the House of Commons of Ireland, on Monday, February the Fourth 1793* (Dublin, 1793), p. 8.

Bibliography

MANUSCRIPT SOURCES

BRITISH LIBRARY

Add. Ms. 22,930: correspondence of Henry Flood
Add. Ms. 33,118: papers of Thomas Pelham
Egerton Ms. 160: anonymous literary manuscript, 1781

GILBERT LIBRARY, DUBLIN

Mss. 93–94: Harcourt papers, 1772–77

NATIONAL ARCHIVES, DUBLIN

Ms. M. 600: correspondence of William Knox concerning recruitment in Ulster, 1776–77

NATIONAL LIBRARY OF IRELAND

Ms. 755: transcripts of letters to Lord Harcourt, 1772–76
Ms. 2,251: letters to Francis Dobbs
Mss. 13,034–60: Heron papers
Ms. 20,282: O'Hara papers
Microfilm positive 7,002–10: Sir Henry Cavendish's parliamentary diary, 1776–83
Microfilm positive 7,654: Passionists' archive

PUBLIC RECORD OFFICE, LONDON

ADM 1/1614–15, 1/2015, 1/2123–24, 1/2250: Admiralty, captains' letters, 1781–83
CO 42/35: papers on the Canadian campaign, 1776
SP 63/420: supplementary state papers, Ireland 1761–77
SP 63/445–80: state papers, Ireland, 1775–82
HO 28/1–3: Home Office correspondence with the Admiralty, 1782–83
HO 100/1–8: Home Office papers, Ireland, 1782–83

WO 1/610, 1/991-3, 1/997, 1/1007-9, 1/1014, 1/1018: War Office in-letters, 1774-83

ROYAL IRISH ACADEMY

Ms. 23 B 14: composite literary manuscript by Seán Ó Dálaigh, 1829 (p. 163) and Pádraig Cundún, 1825 (p. 244)
Ms. 23 C 5: literary manuscript by Seán Ó Conaill, 1767
Ms. 23 C 8: literary manuscript by Mícheál Óg Ó Longáin, c. 1835
Ms. 23 C 18: literary manuscript by Mícheál Óg Ó Longáin, c. 1830
Ms. 23 D 12: literary manuscript by Domhnall Ó Coileáin, 1818-19
Ms. 23 D 42: literary manuscript by Patrick O'Mahony, 1829-35
Ms. 23 E 12: literary manuscript by Nicholas O'Kearney, 1846
Ms. 23 H 39: literary manuscript by Tomás Ó Míocháin, c. 1780
Ms. 23 I 48: literary manuscript by Mícheál Óg Ó hAnnracháin, 1831
Ms. 23 K 10: literary manuscript by Maoilsheachlainn Ó Comhraí, c. 1815
Ms. 23 L 7: literary manuscript by Simon Macken, 1782-83
Ms. 23 L 35: literary manuscript by Peadar Ó Conaill, 1782
Ms. 23 M 4: anonymous literary manuscript, c. 1725
Ms. 23 M 14: anonymous literary manuscript, 1828-48
Ms. 23 O 26: literary manuscript by Pól Ó Longáin, c. 1839
Ms. 23 O 35: literary manuscript by Brian Ó Fearghail, 1777
Ms. 23 O 77: literary manuscript by Seán Ó Dálaigh, 1848
Ms. 24 C 26: literary manuscript by John Windele, c. 1847
Ms. 24 C 56: literary manuscript by Tomás Ó Conchubhair, no date – c. 1830?
Ms. 24 L 22: literary manuscript by Mártain Ó Gríofa, 1829-31
Ms. 24 P 20: literary manuscript by Dáibhí Ó Mathúna, 1816

RUSSELL LIBRARY, ST PATRICK'S COLLEGE, MAYNOOTH

Ms. C 13: literary manuscript by Maoilsheachlainn Ó Comhraí, c. 1812
Ms. C 15: literary manuscript by Maoilsheachlainn Ó Comhraí, 1816-17
Ms. C 18: literary manuscript by Labhrás Ó hÁinle, 1786

TRINITY COLLEGE, DUBLIN

Mun. Soc./Hist. 2-4: minute books of the Historical Society, 1773-84

UNIVERSITY COLLEGE DUBLIN

Ferriter Ms. 4: literary manuscript transcribed by P. Ferriter in 1895 from an original by Thomas O'Brien, 1831-35

PRINTED PRIMARY SOURCES

Agnew, Jean (ed.), *The Drennan–McTier Letters 1776–1793*, I (Dublin, 1998).
Bailyn, Bernard (ed.), *Pamphlets of the American Revolution, 1750–1776* (Cambridge, Mass., 1965).

Bartlett, Thomas (ed.), *Macartney in Ireland, 1768–72: A Calendar of the Chief Secretaryship Papers of Sir George Macartney* (Belfast, 1979).
Beckett, Colm, *Aodh Mac Domhnaill: Dánta* (n.p., 1987).
Beresford, William (ed.), *The Correspondence of the Right Hon. John Beresford*, 2 vols. (London, 1854).
Bodkin, M. (ed.), 'Notes on the Irish parliament in 1773', *Proc. RIA* 48 C (1942–43).
Brady, J. (ed.), *Catholics and Catholicism in the Eighteenth Century Press* (Maynooth, 1965).
Browning, A. (ed.), *English Historical Documents*, VIII (London, 1953).
Bruen, M.C. and Ó hÓgáin, D. (eds.), *An Mangaire Súgach: Beatha agus Saothar* (Dublin, 1996).
Clifford, Brendan (ed.), *Scripture Politics: Selections from the Writings of William Steel Dickson* (Belfast, 1991).
Davies, K.G. (ed.), *Documents of the American Revolution 1770–1783 (Colonial Office Series)*, I–XXI (Shannon and Dublin, 1972–81).
Dinneen, P.S. and O'Donoghue, Tadhg (eds.), *Dánta Aodhagáin Uí Rathaille* (London, 1911).
Edwards, R.D. (ed.), 'The minute book of the Catholic Committee, 1773–92', *Archiv. Hib.* 9 (1942).
Fortescue, John (ed.), *The Correspondence of King George the Third*, III (London, 1928).
Gilbert, R.M. (ed.), *Calendar of Ancient Records of Dublin*, XII (Dublin, 1905).
Harcourt, W.E. (ed.), *The Harcourt Papers*, IX and X (n.p., n.d.).
Hardy, Francis (ed.), *Memoirs of the Political and Private Life of James Caulfield, Earl of Charlemont*, second edition (London, 1812).
Historical Manuscripts Commission:
Carlisle Mss, 15th report, appendix VI (1897).
Charlemont Mss, 12th report, appendix X (1891) and 13th report, appendix VII (1894).
Dartmouth Mss, 14th report, appendix X; 15th report, appendix I (1896).
Donoughmore Mss, 12th report, appendix IX (1891).
Emly Mss, 8th report, appendix I (1881) and 14th report, appendix IX (1895).
Fortescue Mss, 13th report, appendix III (1892).
Knox Mss, Various Collections, VI (1909).
Lothian Mss (1905).
Stopford-Sackville Mss, I (1904) and II (1910).
Hunt, William (ed.), *The Irish Parliament in 1775* (Dublin, 1907).
Hutchinson, W.T. and Rachal, W.M.E. (eds.), *The Papers of James Madison*, II–V (Chicago, 1962–67).
Jensen, Merrill (ed.), *Tracts of the American Revolution 1763–1776* (Indianapolis, 1967).
Joy, Henry (ed.), *Historical Collections Relative to the Town of Belfast: from the Earliest Period to the Union with Great Britain* (Belfast, 1817).
Kiernan, T.J. (ed.), 'Forbes letters', *Anal. Hib.* 8 (1938).
Large, David (ed.), 'The Irish House of Commons in 1769' in *IHS* 11 (1958).
Lyons, J.B. (ed.), 'The letters of Sylvester O'Halloran', *North Munster Antiquarian Journal* 8 (1961) and 9 (1962–63).

MacErlean, J.C. (ed.), *Duanaire Dháibhidh Uí Bhruadair*, III (London, 1917).
McMinn, Joseph (ed.), *Swift's Irish Pamphlets* (Gerrard's Cross, 1991).
Mag Uidhir, Seosamh (ed.), *Pádraig Mac a Liondain: Dánta* (Dublin, 1977).
Ní Chinnéide, Síle (ed.), 'Dhá leabhar nótaí le Séarlas Ó Conchubhair', *Galvia* 1 (1954).
Nolan, J. Bennett (ed.), *Benjamin Franklin in Scotland and Ireland* (Philadelphia, 1938).
O'Brien, George (ed.), 'The Irish free trade agitation of 1779' in *English Historical Review* 38 and 39 (1923 and 1924).
Ó Buachalla, Breandán (ed.), *Cathal Buí: Amhráin* (Dublin, 1975).
Nua-Dhuanaire, II (Dublin, 1976).
Ó Coigligh, Ciarán (ed.), *Raiftearaí: Amhráin agus Dánta* (Dublin, 1987).
Ó Concheanainn, Tomás (ed.), *Nua-Dhuanaire*, III (Dublin, 1981).
Ó Donnchadha, Rónán (ed.), *Mícheál Óg Ó Longáin, File* (Dublin, 1994).
Ó Fiaich, Tomás (ed.), *Art Mac Cumhaigh: Dánta* (Dublin, 1973).
Ó Foghludha, Risteárd (ed.), *Amhráin Phiarais Mhic Gearailt* (Dublin, 1905).
Seán Clárach 1691–1754 (Dublin, 1932).
Cois na Bríde: Liam Inglis, O.S.A., 1709–1778 (Dublin, 1937).
Eoghan Ruadh Ó Súilleabháin 1748–1784 (Dublin, 1937).
Ar Bhruach na Coille Muaire (Dublin, 1939).
Éigse na Máighe (Dublin, 1952).
Ó hÓgáin, Dáithí (ed.), *Duanaire Osraíoch* (Dublin, 1980).
Ó Máille, Mícheál and Ó Máille, Tomás (eds.), *Amhráin Chlainne Gaedheal* (Dublin, 1905).
Ó Muirgheasa, Énrí (ed.), *Céad de Cheoltaibh Uladh* (Dublin, 1915).
Dhá Chéad de Cheoltaibh Uladh (Dublin, 1934).
Dánta Diadha Uladh (Dublin, 1936).
Ó Muirithe, Diarmuid (ed.), 'Amhráin i dtaobh Cogadh Saoirse Mheiriceá' in Seosamh Watson (ed.), *Féilscríbhinn Thomáis de Bhaldraithe* (Dublin, 1986).
Cois an Ghaorthaidh: Fílocht ó Mhúscraí 1700–1840 (Dublin, 1987).
Tomás Ó Míocháin: Filíocht (Dublin, 1988).
O'Rahilly, Cecile (ed.), *Five Seventeenth-Century Political Poems* (Dublin, 1952).
Public Record Office:
Calendar of Home Office Papers, 1760–1765 (London, 1878).
Calendar of Home Office Papers, 1766–1769 (London, 1879).
Calendar of Home Office Papers, 1770–1772 (London, 1881).
Calendar of Home Office Papers, 1773–1775 (London, 1899).
Records of the General Synod of Ulster, II and III (Belfast, 1897 and 1898).
Russell, John (ed.), *Correspondence of John, Fourth Duke of Bedford*, II (London, 1843).
Sayles, G.O. (ed.), 'Contemporary sketches of the members of the Irish parliament in 1782', *Proc. RIA* 56 C (1954).
Walton, James (ed.), *'The King's Business': Letters on the Administration of Ireland, 1740–1761, from the Papers of Sir Robert Wilmot* (New York, 1996).
Ward, C.C. and Ward, R.E. (eds.), *The Letters of Charles O'Conor of Belanagare* (Ann Arbor, 1980).

Ward, R.E., Wrynn, J.F. and Ward, C.C. (eds.), *Letters of Charles O'Conor of Belanagare* (Washington, 1988).
Willcox, W.B. (ed.), *The Papers of Benjamin Franklin*, XVI–XXXII (New Haven and London, 1972–96).
Witherow, Thomas (ed.), *Historical and Literary Memorials of Presbyterianism in Ireland (1731–1800)*, second series (Belfast, 1880).
Young, Arthur, *Tour in Ireland (1776–1779)* (London, 1892).

PERIODICALS

Annual Register, London
Belfast News-Letter
Cork Evening Post
Dublin Evening Journal, later *Dublin Evening Post*
Dublin Gazette
Dublin Mercury
Faulkner's Dublin Journal
Finn's Leinster Journal, Kilkenny
Freeman's Journal, Dublin
Hibernian Chronicle, Cork
Hibernian Journal, Dublin
Hibernian Magazine, Dublin
Londonderry Journal
Magee's Weekly Packet, Dublin
Saunders' News-Letter, Dublin
Universal Advertiser, Dublin
The Volunteer, Dublin
Volunteer Journal, Cork

BOOKS AND PAMPHLETS

[Abernethy, John], *The Nature and Consequences of the Sacramental Test Considered* (Dublin, 1731).
Abingdon, Bertie Willoughby earl of, *Thoughts on the Letter of Edmund Burke, Esq. to the Sheriffs of Bristol, on the Affairs of America* (Dublin, 1777).
Adams, Samuel, *An Oration Delivered at the State-House, in Philadelphia, to a Very Numerous Audience; on Thursday the 1st of August, 1776* (Dublin, 1776).
An Address from the Independent Freeholders of the Pr—v—ce of M—nst—r to Sir R—d C—x Baronet (London, 1754).
An Address to Hibernia, on the Late Most Happy Dissolution of that Dread Junto, the Legion Club (Dublin, 1761).
An Address to the Inhabitants of Pennsylvania, by those Freemen of the City of Philadelphia who are now Confined in the Masons Lodge (Dublin, 1777).
An Address to the People of Great-Britain, from the Delegates . . . in General Congress, at Philadelphia, September 5, 1774 (Dublin, 1775).
Advice to the Patriot Club of the County of Antrim on the Present State of Affairs in Ireland, and some Late Changes in the Administration of that Kingdom (Dublin, 1756).

The Alarm; or, the Irish Spy. In a Series of Letters on the Present State of Affairs in Ireland, to a High Lord in the Opposition. Written by an Ex-Jesuit, Employed by his Lordship for the Purpose (Dublin, 1779).

Alexander, Andrew, *The Advantage of a General Knowledge of the Use of Arms* (Strabane, 1779).

An Answer to a Pamphlet, Entitled, Observations on the Mutiny Bill by a Member of the House of Commons (Dublin, 1781).

An Answer to the Counter Address of a Pretended Free-Citizen (Dublin, 1766).

An Answer to the Late Proposal for Uniting the Kingdoms of Great Britain and Ireland (Dublin, 1751).

An Appeal to the Understanding of the Electors of Ireland (Dublin, 1776).

Archdall, Nicholas, *An Alarum to the People of Great-Britain, and Ireland: In Answer to a Late Proposal for Uniting these Kingdoms* (Dublin, 1751).

Baratariana: A Select Collection of Fugitive Political Pieces Published during the Administration of Lord Townshend in Ireland (Dublin, 1772).

Barber, Samuel, *A Sermon, Delivered in the Meeting-House of Rathfriland, October 24, 1779, to the Castlewellan Rangers, and Rathfriland Volunteers* (Newry, 1779).

[Bingham, Sir Charles], *An Essay on the Use and Necessity of Establishing a Militia in Ireland, and Some Hints towards a Plan for that Purpose* (Dublin, 1767).

[Boyd, Hugh], *Letters Addressed to the Freeholders of the County of Antrim* (Belfast, 1776).

[Brett, John], *To All the Serious, Honest, and Well-meaning People of Ireland* (Dublin, 1754).

[Brooke, Arthur], *An Inquiry into the Policy of the Laws, Affecting the Popish Inhabitants of Ireland* (Dublin, 1775).

[Bruce, William], *Some Facts and Observations Relative to the Fate of the Late Linen Bill, Last Session of Parliament in this Kingdom* (Dublin, 1753).

  Remarks on a Pamphlet Intitled Considerations on the Late Bill for Paying the National Debt (Dublin, 1754).

Burke, Edmund, *Thoughts on the Cause of the Present Discontents* (Dublin, 1770).

  The History of American Taxation from the Year 1763 (Dublin, 1775).

  The Speech of Edmund Burke, Esq., on Moving his Resolutions for Conciliation with the Colonies, March 22, 1775 (Dublin, 1775).

  A Letter from Edmund Burke, Esq. to John Farr and John Harris, Esqrs on the Affairs of America (Dublin, 1777).

[Bushe, Gervase Parker], *The Case of Great Britain and America, Addressed to the King, and Both Houses of Parliament* (Dublin, 1769).

Butler, Rev. Samuel, *A Sermon Preached in the Parish Church of St Michan, Dublin, on Sunday the 17th Day of October 1779*, third edition (Dublin, 1779).

[Caldwell, Sir James], *An Address to the House of Commons of Ireland* (Dublin, 1771).

Caldwell, James, *An Enquiry how far the Restrictions Laid upon the Trade of Ireland, by British Acts of Parliament, are a Benefit or a Disadvantage to the British Dominions in General, and to England in Particular* (Dublin, 1779).

[Campbell, Thomas], *A Philosophical Survey of the South of Ireland, in a Series of Letters to John Watkinson, M.D.* (Dublin, 1778).

A Candid Display, of the Reciprocal Conduct of Great Britain and her Colonies (Dublin, n.d. – 1780?).

The Case Fairly Stated, Relative to an Act Lately Passed in this Kingdom against the Exportation of Corn (Dublin, 1766).

The Case of Ireland in 1762 (title page missing; Dublin, 1762?).

Chatham, William Pitt earl of, *The Speech of the Right Honourable the Earl of Chatham, in the House of Lords, on Friday the 20th of January, 1775* (Dublin, n.d.).

A Collection of the Protests of the Lords of Ireland, from 1634 to 1771 (Dublin, 1772).

A Comparative View of the Public Burdens of Great Britain and Ireland. With a Proposal for Putting both Islands on an Equality, in Regard to the Freedom of Foreign Trade (London printed and Dublin reprinted, 1779).

Considerations on the Present State of the Military Establishment of this Kingdom, Addressed to the Knights, Citizens, Burgesses of Ireland in Parliament Assembled (Dublin, 1768).

Considerations upon the Augmentation of the Army. Address'd to the Publick (Dublin, 1768).

Coombe, Thomas, *A Sermon Preached before the Congregation of Christ Church and St Peter's Philadelphia, on Thursday, July 20, 1775* (Belfast, 1775).

[Cox, Sir Richard] 'Anthony Litten', *The Cork Surgeon's Antidote against the Dublin Apothecary's Poyson*, number II (Dublin, 1749).

Cox, Sir Richard, *Previous Promises Inconsistent with a Free Parliament: and an Ample Vindication of the Last Parliament* (Dublin, 1760).

Crawford, William, *The Connection betwixt Courage and the Moral Virtues Considered* (Strabane, 1779).

Creighton, James, *The Christian Soldier: A Sermon Addressed to the Volunteers of Ireland* (Dublin, 1780).

Crombie, James, *A Sermon on the Love of Country. Preached before the First Company of Belfast Volunteers, on Sunday, the 19th of July, 1778* (n.p., 1778).

The Expedience and Utility of Volunteer Associations for National Defence and Security in the Present Critical Situation of Public Affairs Considered (Belfast, 1779).

[Curry, John], *A Candid Enquiry into the Causes and Motives of the Late Riots in the Province of Munster* (London, 1766).

A Parallel between the Pretended Plot in 1762, and the Forgery of Titus Oates in 1679 (Cork, 1767).

An Historical and Critical Review of the Civil Wars in Ireland, from the Reign of Queen Elizabeth, to the Settlement under King William (Dublin, 1775).

Darcy, Patrick, *An Argument Delivered by Patricke Darcy, Esquire; by the Expresse Order of the House of Commons in the Parliament of Ireland, 9. Iunii, 1641* (Dublin, 1764).

Debates of the House of Commons of Ireland, on a Motion whether the Kings Most Excellent Majesty, and the Lords and Commons of Ireland, are the Only Power Competent to Bind or Enact Laws in this Kingdom (Dublin, 1780).

A Defence of Great Britain, against a Charge of Tyranny in the Government of Ireland, by an Irishman (Dublin, 1779).

Delap, Hugh, *A Sermon, Preached in the Old-Bridge Meeting-House near Omagh, the 14th, of November 1779: before the Omagh and Cappagh Volunteers* (Strabane, 1779).

A Dialogue between a Protestant and a Papist, Concerning Some Late Strange Reports about an Union and the Seditious Consequences of them (n.p., n.d. – 1759?).

A Dialogue between Jack Lane and Simon Curtin Freemen of Cork, concerning P—l—m—t Men (Cork, 1751).

[Dickinson, John], *Letters from a Farmer in Pennsylvania, to the Inhabitants of the British Colonies* (Dublin, 1768).

Dickson, William Steel, *A Sermon, on the Propriety and Advantages of Acquiring the Knowledge and Use of Arms, in Times of Public Danger* (Belfast, 1779).

Dobbs, Francis, *A Letter to the Right Honourable Lord North, on his Propositions in Favour of Ireland* (Dublin, 1780).

A History of Irish Affairs, from the 12th of October, 1779, to the 15th September, 1782, the Day of Lord Temple's Arrival (Dublin, 1782).

[Duigenan, Patrick], *The Alarm: or, an Address to the Nobility, Gentry, and Clergy of the Church of Ireland, as by Law Established* (Dublin, 1783).

Duigenan, Patrick, *A Speech Spoken in the House of Commons of Ireland, on Monday, February the Fourth 1793* (Dublin, 1793).

An Essay on the Act of Poynings, and the Present Mode of Appeal. Addressed to the Right Honourable William Eden, previous to his Becoming a Member of the Parliament of Ireland (Dublin, 1781), pp. 9–10.

[Ferguson, Adam], *Remarks on a Pamphlet Lately Published by Dr. Price* (Dublin, 1776).

[Fitzgibbon, John], *Commerce not a Fit Subject for an Embargo* (Dublin and Limerick, 1777).

The First Lines of Ireland's Interest in the Year One Thousand Seven Hundred and Eighty (Dublin, 1779).

Flood, Henry, *The Two Speeches of Henry Flood, Esq. on the Repeal of the Declaratory Act of the Sixth of George I* (Dublin, 1782).

Forman, Charles, *A Letter to the Rt. Hon. Sir Robert Sutton for Disbanding the Irish Regiments in the Service of France and Spain* (Dublin, 1728).

[French, Richard], *The Constitution of Ireland and Poynings' Laws Explained* (Dublin, 1770).

[Grattan, Henry], *Observations on the Mutiny Bill; with some Strictures on Lord Buckinghamshire's Administration in Ireland* (Dublin, 1781).

'A Grazier', *Thoughts on the Present Alarming Crisis of Affairs: Humbly Submitted to the Serious Consideration of the People of Ireland* (Dublin, 1779).

[Hely Hutchinson, John], *The Commercial Restraints of Ireland Considered* (Dublin, 1779).

[Henry, William], *An Appeal to the People of Ireland* (Dublin, 1749).

[Hill, Wills], *A Proposal for Uniting the Kingdoms of Great Britain and Ireland* (Dublin, 1751).

Historical Remarks on the Pope's Temporal and Deposing Power. With some Anecdotes of the Court of Rome, and Observations on the Oath of Allegiance (Dublin, 1778).

Houlton, Robert, *A Selection of Political Letters, which Appeared during the Administrations of the Earls of Buckinghamshire and Carlisle, under the Signatures of*

Junius-Brutus, Hampden, the Constitutional Watchman, and Lucius Hibernicus (Dublin, 1782).

[Howard, Gorges Edmond], *Some Questions upon the Legislative Constitution of Ireland* (Dublin, 1770).

A Humble Remonstrance, for the Repeal of the Laws against the Roman Catholics (Dublin, 1778).

Ireland's Glory; or, a Comparative View of Ireland in the Years 1776 and 1783 (Newry, n.d. – 1783?).

[Jebb, Frederick], *The Letters of Guatimozin, on the Affairs of Ireland* (Dublin, 1779).

[Jebb, Frederick and Johnson, Robert], *Thoughts on the Discontents of the People Last Year, respecting the Sugar Duties* (Dublin, 1781).

Kearney, Michael, *Lectures concerning History Read during the Year 1775, in Trinity College, Dublin* (Dublin, 1776).

Kennedy, Gilbert, *The Wicked Ruler: or, the Mischiefs of Absolute Arbitrary Power* (Belfast, 1745).

A Sermon Preach'd at Belfast, on Tuesday, April 25th, 1749 (Belfast, 1749).

[King, William], *The State of the Protestants under the late King James's Government* (London, 1691).

[Kirkpatrick, James], *An Historical Essay upon the Loyalty of Presbyterians in Great Britain and Ireland from the Reformation to this Present Year 1713* (Belfast, 1713).

[Langrishe, Sir Hercules], *Considerations on the Dependencies of Great Britain* (London, 1769).

[La Touche, James Digges], *A Short but True History of the Rise, Progress, and Happy Suppression, of Several Late Insurrections Commonly Called Rebellions in Ireland* (Dublin, 1760).

A Layman's Sermon, Preached at the Patriot Club of the County of Armagh, which Met at Armagh, the 3d of September, 1755 (Dublin, 1755).

Leland, Thomas, *A Sermon Preached in the Church of St Anne's, Dublin, on Wednesday the 10th of February, 1779* (Dublin, 1779).

A Letter from a Member of the House of Commons, to a Chief Magistrate of a Borough (Dublin, 1749).

A Letter from the Town of Boston, to C. Lucas, Esq. (Dublin, n.d. – 1770?).

A Letter to a Noble Lord, in Answer to his Address to the People of Ireland, with some Interesting Reflections on the Present State of Affairs, and a Short Address to Lord T—ns—d (Dublin, 1770).

A Letter to a Person of Distinction in Town, from a Gentleman in the Country (Dublin, 1753).

A Letter to Charles Lucas, M.D. Relative to the Annual Stipend of Three Hundred and Sixty-five Pounds, Proposed to be Paid him, during the City's Pleasure (Dublin, n.d. – 1766?).

A Letter to Sir L—s O—n, Bart. on the Late Prorogation; and in Answer to his Letter to Mr Faulkner, on the Subject of the Rejected Money-Bill (Dublin, 1770).

A Letter to the People of Ireland, on the Expediency and Necessity of the Present Associations in Ireland, in Favour of our own Manufacture (Dublin, 1779).

A Letter to the Right Honourable J—P—, S—r of the H—e of C—s in I—d, third edition (London, 1767).

A Letter to William Eden, Esq. Occasioned by a Pamphlet Commonly Attributed to Him (Dublin, 1781).

A List of the Absentees of Ireland and an Estimate of the Yearly Value of their Estates and Incomes Spent Abroad (Dublin, 1767).

Lord Taaffe's Observations upon the Affairs of Ireland Examined and Confuted (Dublin, 1767).

Lucas, Charles, *The Political Constitutions of Great-Britain and Ireland, Asserted and Vindicated* (London, 1751).

An Appeal to the Commons and Citizens of London (London, 1756).

To the Right Honourable, the Lord-Mayor, Aldermen, Sheriffs, Commons, Citizens, and Freeholders of Dublin (Dublin, 1765).

A Second Address to the Right Hon. the Lord Mayor, the Aldermen, Sheriffs, Commons, Citizens, and Freeholders of the City of Dublin (Dublin,1766).

A Third Address to the Right Hon. the Lord Mayor, the Board of Aldermen, and the Sheriffs, Commons, and Citizens, of Dublin (Dublin, 1766).

A Seasonable Advice to the Electors of Members of Parlement at the Ensuing General Election (Dublin, 1768).

To the Right Honourable the Lord Mayor . . . upon the Proposed Augmentation of the Military Establishment (Dublin, 1768).

The Rights and Privileges of Parlements Asserted upon Constitutional Principles (Dublin, 1770).

[Macartney, Sir George], *An Account of Ireland in 1773* (London, 1773).

[McAuley, Alexander], *Septennial Parliaments Vindicated: or, Freedom against Oligarchy* (Dublin, 1762).

McAuley, Alexander, *An Inquiry into the Legality of Pensions on the Irish Establishment* (London, 1763).

McBride, John, *A Vindication of Marriage as Solemnized by Presbyterians, in the North of Ireland* (n.p., 1702).

[McMahon, Thomas O'Brien], *Remarks on the English and Irish Nations* (Dublin, 1792; originally published at London, 1777).

[Macpherson, James], *The Rights of Great Britain Asserted against the Claims of America* (Dublin, 1776).

Madden, Samuel, *Reflections and Resolutions Proper for the Gentlemen of Ireland* (Dublin, 1738).

Moderation Unmasked; or, the Conduct of the Majority Impartially Considered (Dublin, 1780).

Molyneux, William, *The Case of Ireland's being Bound by Acts of Parliament in England, Stated* (Belfast, 1776).

[O'Conor, Charles], *A Counter-Appeal, to the People of Ireland* (Dublin, 1749).

The Case of the Roman-Catholics of Ireland, third edition (Dublin, 1756).

The Danger of Popery to the Present Government Examined (Dublin, 1761).

A Vindication of Lord Taaffe's Civil Principles (Dublin, 1768).

Observations on the Popery Laws (Dublin, 1771).

O'Leary, Arthur, *Loyalty Asserted, or, the New Test Oath, Vindicated* (Cork, 1776).

An Address to the Common People of the Roman Catholic Religion, concerning the Apprehended French Invasion (Cork, 1779).

Miscellaneous Tracts (Dublin, 1781).

Otis, James, *The Rights of the British Colonies Asserted and Proved* (London, 1765).

Paine, Thomas, *A Letter to the Earl of Shelburne, on his Speech, July 10, 1782, respecting the Acknowledgement of American Independence* (Dublin, 1783).

Paul, Rev. Thomas, *A Sermon, Preached at St. Thomas's Church, Dublin, on Wednesday the 10th of February, M DCC LXX IX; Being the Day Appointed by Proclamation for a General Fast and Humiliation &c.* (Dublin, n.d.).

[Pollock, Joseph], *Letters of Owen Roe O'Nial* (n.p., 1779).

[Preston, William], *A Congratulatory Poem on the Late Successes of the British Arms, Particularly the Triumphant Evacuation of Boston* (Dublin, 1776).

[Price, Richard], *Observations on the Nature of Civil Liberty, the Principles of Government and the Justice and Policy of the War with America* (Dublin, 1776).

The Principles of Modern Patriotism (Dublin, 1770? – title page missing).

Pulleine, James, *An Teagasg Criosdaidhe a nGoidhleig* (n.p., 1782).

Queries upon Liberty, the Freedom of the Press, Independency, &c. (Dublin, 1768).

Reasons for an Augmentation of the Army on the Irish Establishment, Offered to the Consideration of the Public (Dublin, 1768).

A Reform of the Irish House of Commons, Considered (Dublin, 1783).

Remarks on a Late Pamphlet, Entituled the Case of the Roman Catholicks of Ireland (Dublin, 1755).

Renovation without Violence Yet Possible (Dublin, 1779).

Robinson, Christopher and Tenison, Thomas, *The Respective Charges; Given to the Grand Jury of the County of Armagh, at the General Assizes Held there, July 23, 1763* (Dublin, 1763).

A Scheme for a Constitutional Association: with some Obvious Reasons for Adopting such a Measure (Dublin, 1780).

Seasonable Advice to the People of Ireland during the Present Recess of Parliament (Dublin, 1780).

A Second Letter to the Citizens of Dublin (Dublin, 1749)

A Serious and Affectionate Call to the Electors of Ireland (Dublin, 1761).

Sheridan, Charles Francis, *Observations on the Doctrine Laid Down by Sir William Blackstone, Respecting the Extent of the Power of the British Parliament, Particularly with Relation to Ireland*, second edition (London, 1779).

[Sheridan, Charles Francis], *A Review of the Three Great National Questions relative to a Declaration of Right, Poynings' Law, and the Mutiny Bill* (Dublin, 1781).

Smith, William, *A Sermon on the Present Situation of American Affairs, Preached in Christ Church* [Philadelphia], *June 23, 1775* (Dublin, 1775).

[Smith, William] 'Candidus', *Plain Truth: Addressed to the Inhabitants of America* (Dublin, 1776).

Some Authentic Minutes of the Proceedings of a Very Respectable Assembly, on the 20th of December, 1779 (Dublin, 1780).

Some Impartial Observations on the Proposed Augmentation (Dublin, 1768).

Some Reasons against Raising an Army of Roman Catholics in Ireland in a Letter to a Member of Parliament (Dublin, 1762).

The Speech of a Young Member of Parliament, on the Debate of the Septennial Bill (Dublin, 1761).

[Taaffe, Nicholas], *Observations on Affairs in Ireland from the Settlement in 1691, to the Present Time* (Dublin, 1766; third edition 1767).

Thoughts on News-Papers and a Free Trade (Dublin, 1780).

Thoughts on the Present Situation of Ireland. In a Letter from the North, to a Friend in Dublin; in which the Late Extraordinary Meeting at Dungannon is Considered (Dublin, 1782).

Transactions of the General Committee of the Roman Catholics of Ireland, during the Year 1791; and some Fugitive Pieces on that Subject (Dublin, 1792).

Truth against Craft: or, Sophistry and Falsehood Detected (Dublin, 1754).

The Tryal of Mr. Charles Lucas, on Certain Articles of Impeachment (Dublin, 1749).

A Vindication of the New Oath of Allegiance, Proposed to the Roman Catholics of Ireland, second edition (Dublin, 1775).

A Volunteer's Queries, in Spring, 1780 (Dublin, 1780).

Walsh, Rev. J., *A Sermon Preached at the Parish Church of Tawney, on Wednesday the 10th of February, M,DC,LXXIX* (Dublin, 1779).

[Wetenhall, Edward], *The Case of the Irish Protestants: in relation to Recognising, or Swearing Allegiance to, and Praying for King William and Queen Mary, Stated and Resolved* (London, 1691).

Wilson, C.H., *A Compleat Collection of the Resolutions of the Volunteers, Grand Juries, &c. of Ireland, which Followed the Celebrated Resolves of the First Dungannon Diet* (Dublin, 1782).

Witherspoon, John, *Dominion of Providence over the Passions of Men*, fourth edition (Belfast, 1777).

SECONDARY SOURCES

Bailyn, Bernard, *The Origins of American Politics* (New York, 1968).

Faces of Revolution: Personalities and Themes in the Struggle for American Independence (New York, 1990).

The Ideological Origins of the American Revolution, second edition (Cambridge, Mass. and London, 1992).

Barrett, Raymond J., 'A comparative study of imperial constitutional theory in Ireland and America in the age of the American revolution' (PhD thesis, TCD, 1958).

Bartlett, Thomas, 'The Townshend viceroyalty 1767–72' (PhD thesis, QUB, 1976).

'The Townshend viceroyalty, 1767–72' in Thomas Bartlett and D.W. Hayton (eds.), *Penal Era and Golden Age: Essays in Irish History, 1690–1800* (Belfast, 1979).

'Opposition in late eighteenth-century Ireland: the case of the Townshend viceroyalty', *IHS* 22 (1981).

The Fall and Rise of the Irish Nation: The Catholic Question 1690–1830 (Dublin, 1992).

Beckett, J.C., *Protestant Dissent in Ireland 1687–1780* (London, 1948).

The Making of Modern Ireland 1603–1923 (London and Boston, 1981).

Beresford, Marcus de la Poer, 'Ireland in French strategy during the American War of Independence 1776–83', *Irish Sword* 12 (1975–76).

Bigger, F.J., *The Ulster Land War of 1770* (Dublin, 1910).

Black, R.D. Collison, *A Catalogue of Pamphlets on Economic Subjects Published between 1750 and 1900 and now Housed in Irish Libraries* (New York, 1969).

Brewer, John, 'The misfortunes of Lord Bute: a case-study in eighteenth-century political argument and public opinion', *Hist. Jn.* 16 (1973).

Bric, Maurice J., 'Ireland, America and the reassessment of a special relationship, 1760–1783', *Eighteenth-Century Ireland* 11 (1996).

Burns, R.E., 'Ireland and British military preparations for war in America in 1775', *Cithara* 2 (1962–63).

Buttimer, C.G., '*Cogadh Sagsana Nuadh sonn*: reporting the American revolution', *Studia Hib.* 28 (1994).

Canny, Nicholas, *Kingdom and Colony: Ireland in the Atlantic World 1500–1800* (Baltimore, 1988).

Christie, I.R., *The End of North's Ministry 1780–1782* (London, 1958).

Clark, J.C.D., *English Society 1688–1832: Ideology, Social Structure and Political Practice during the Ancien Régime* (Cambridge, 1985).

Clark, William Bell, *Ben Franklin's Privateers* (Baton Rouge, 1956).

Clune, Eilish, 'The third parliament of George III, (1776–1783)' (MA thesis, UCD, 1943).

Connolly, S.J., *Religion, Law and Power: The Making of Protestant Ireland 1660–1760* (Oxford, 1992).

'Varieties of Britishness: Ireland, Scotland and Wales in the Hanoverian state' in Alexander Grant and Keith Stringer (eds.), *'Uniting the Kingdom?': The Making of British History* (London and New York, 1995).

Conway, Stephen, *The War of American Independence 1775–1783* (London, 1995).

Coyle, Eugene, 'Sir Edward Newenham – the 18th century Dublin radical', *Dublin Historical Record* 46 (1993).

'An Irish buccaneer: the case of Captain Luke Ryan', *History Ireland*, summer 1999.

Cummins, Séamus, 'Opposition and the Irish parliament 1759–1771' (MA thesis, Maynooth, 1978).

'Extra-parliamentary agitation in Dublin in the 1760s' in R.V. Comerford, Mary Cullen, Jacqueline Hill and Colm Lennon (eds.), *Religious Conflict and Coexistence in Ireland* (Dublin, 1990).

Curtin, Nancy J., *The United Irishmen: Popular Politics in Ulster and Dublin, 1791–1798* (Oxford, 1994).

Curtis, Edward E., *The Organization of the British Army in the American Revolution* (New Haven and London, 1926).

Day, John Patrick, 'The Catholic question in the Irish Parliament 1760–82' (MA thesis, UCD, 1978).

Dickson, David, *New Foundations: Ireland 1660–1800*, second edition (Dublin, 2000).

Dickson, R.J., *Ulster Emigration to Colonial America 1718–1775* (London, 1966).

Donnelly, J.S., 'The Whiteboy movement, 1761–5', *IHS* 21 (1978).

'Hearts of oak, hearts of steel', *Studia Hib.* 21 (1981).

'Irish agrarian rebellion: the Whiteboys of 1769–76', *Proc. RIA* 83 C (1983).

Donovan, R. Kent, 'The military origins of the Roman Catholic relief programme of 1778', *Hist. Jn.* 28 (1985).

Doyle, David, *Ireland, Irishmen and Revolutionary America, 1760–1820* (Dublin, 1981).

Draper, Theodore, *A Struggle for Power: The American Revolution* (London, 1996).

Eccleshall, Robert, 'Anglican political thought in the century after the Revolution of 1688' in D.G. Boyce, R. Eccleshall and V. Geoghegan (eds.), *Political Thought in Ireland* (London, 1993).

Edwards, Owen Dudley, 'The impact of the American Revolution on Ireland' in Library of Congress Symposia on the American Revolution, 4th symposium, *The Impact of the American Revolution Abroad* (Washington, 1976).

Elliott, Marianne, *Wolfe Tone: Prophet of Irish Independence* (New Haven and London, 1989).

Fagan, Patrick, *Divided Loyalties: The Question of the Oath for Irish Catholics in the Eighteenth Century* (Dublin, 1997).

Fagerstrom, Dalphy I., 'The American revolutionary movement in Scottish opinion, 1763 to 1783' (PhD thesis, Edinburgh, 1951).

Ferguson, K.P., 'The Volunteer movement and the government, 1778–1793', *Irish Sword* 13 (1977–79).

'The army in Ireland from the restoration to the act of union' (PhD thesis, TCD, 1980).

Fitzpatrick, W.J., *Secret Service under Pitt* (London, 1892).

Foster, R.F., *Modern Ireland 1600–1972* (London, 1988).

Froude, J.A., *The English in Ireland in the Eighteenth Century*, 3 vols. (London, 1872–74).

Hastings, Adrian, *The Construction of Nationhood: Ethnicity, Religion and Nationalism* (Cambridge, 1997).

Herlihy, Kevin (ed.), *The Politics of Irish Dissent 1650–1800* (Dublin, 1997).

Hill, Colin P., 'William Drennan and the radical movement for Irish reform, 1779–1794' (MLitt thesis, TCD, 1967).

Hill, Jacqueline, 'Religious toleration and the relaxation of the penal laws: an imperial perspective, 1763–1780', *Archiv. Hib.* 44 (1989).

From Patriots to Unionists: Dublin Civic Politics and Irish Protestant Patriotism, 1660–1840 (Oxford, 1997).

Hoffman, R.J.S., *Edmund Burke, New York Agent* (Philadelphia, 1956).

Hunt, W., *The Irish Parliament in 1775* (Dublin, 1907).

James, F.G., *Ireland in the Empire, 1688–1770* (Cambridge, Mass., 1973).

Jupp, Peter, 'Earl Temple's viceroyalty and the question of renunciation, 1782–3', *IHS* 17 (1971).

Kelly, James, 'The origins of the act of union: an examination of unionist opinion in Britain and Ireland, 1650–1800', *IHS* 25 (1987).

Henry Flood: Patriots and Politics in Eighteenth-Century Ireland (Dublin, 1998).

Kelly, Patrick, 'William Molyneux and the spirit of liberty in eighteenth-century Ireland', *Eighteenth-Century Ireland* 3 (1988).

'Perceptions of Locke in eighteenth-century Ireland', *Proc. RIA* 89 C (1989).

Kraus, Michael, 'America and the Irish revolutionary movement in the eighteenth century' in Richard B. Morris (ed.), *The Era of the American Revolution* (Gloucester, Mass., 1971; first published New York, 1939).

Lammey, David, 'A study of Anglo-Irish relations between 1772 and 1782 with particular reference to the "free trade" movement' (PhD thesis, QUB, 1984). 'The growth of the "patriot opposition" in Ireland during the 1770s', *Parliamentary History* 7 (1988). 'The free trade crisis: a reappraisal' in Gerard O'Brien (ed.), *Parliament, Politics and People: Essays in Eighteenth-Century Irish History* (Dublin, 1989).

Lecky, W.E.H., *A History of Ireland in the Eighteenth Century*, 5 vols. (London, 1892).

Leerssen, Joep Th., 'Anglo-Irish patriotism and its European context: notes towards a reassessment', *Eighteenth-Century Ireland* 3 (1988).

Lutnick, Solomon, *The American Revolution and the British Press 1775–1783* (Columbia, Missouri, 1987).

McBride, Ian, 'The school of virtue: Francis Hutcheson, Irish Presbyterians and the Scottish Enlightenment' in D.G. Boyce, R. Eccleshall and V. Geoghegan (eds.), *Political Thought in Ireland* (London, 1993). 'William Drennan and the dissenting tradition' in D. Dickson, D. Keogh and K. Whelan (eds.), *The United Irishmen: Republicanism, Radicalism and Rebellion* (Dublin, 1993). 'Presbyterians in the Penal era', *Bullán* 1 (1994). ' "When Ulster joined Ireland": anti-popery, Presbyterian radicalism and Irish republicanism in the 1790s', *Past and Present* 157 (1997). *Scripture Politics: Ulster Presbyterians and Irish Radicalism in the Late Eighteenth Century* (Oxford, 1998).

Mac Craith, Mícheál, 'Filíocht Sheacaibíteach na Gaeilge: ionar gan uaim?', *Eighteenth-Century Ireland* 9 (1994).

McDowell, R.B., *Irish Public Opinion 1750–1800* (London, 1944). *Ireland in the Age of Imperialism and Revolution 1760–1801* (Oxford, 1979).

McGeehin, Maureen, 'The activities and personnel of the General Committee of the Catholics of Ireland, 1767–84' (MA thesis, UCD, 1952).

McGuire, James, 'The Irish parliament of 1692' in Thomas Bartlett and D.W. Hayton (eds.), *Penal Era and Golden Age: Essays in Irish History, 1690–1800* (Belfast, 1979).

Mackesy, Piers, *The War for America 1775–1783* (London, 1964).

Malcomson, A.P.W., *John Foster: The Politics of Anglo-Irish Ascendancy* (Oxford, 1978).

Moody, T.W., Martin, F.X. and Byrne, F.J. (eds.), *A New History of Ireland*, VIII: *A Chronology of Irish History to 1976* (Oxford, 1982). *A New History of Ireland*, IX: *Maps, Genealogies, Lists* (Oxford, 1984).

Moody, T.W. and Vaughan W.E. (eds.), *A New History of Ireland*, IV: *Eighteenth-Century Ireland* (Oxford, 1986).

Morley, Vincent, 'Hugh MacCurtin: an Irish poet in the French army', *Eighteenth-Century Ireland* 8 (1993). *An Crann os Coill: Aodh Buí Mac Cruitín, c. 1680–1755* (Dublin, 1995). ' "Tá an cruatan ar Sheoirse" – folklore or politics?', *Eighteenth-Century Ireland* 13 (1998).

Murphy, N., 'Dr Troy, as bishop of Ossory, 1776–1786', *Irish Ecclesiastical Record*, 4th series, 2 (1897).

Murphy, Sean, 'Municipal politics and popular disturbances: 1660–1800' in Art Cosgrove (ed.), *Dublin through the Ages* (Dublin, 1988).

'The Dublin anti-union riot of 3 December 1759' in Gerard O'Brien (ed.), *Parliament, Politics and People: Essays in Eighteenth-Century Irish History* (Dublin, 1989).

O'Brien, Michael J., *A Hidden Phase of American History: Ireland's Part in America's Struggle for Liberty* (New York, 1921).

Ó Buachalla, Breandán, 'An mheisiasacht agus an aisling' in P. de Brún, S. Ó Coileáin and P. Ó Riain (eds.), *Folia Gadelica* (Cork, 1983).

'Irish Jacobite poetry', *Irish Review* 12 (1992).

'Seacaibíteachas Thaidhg Uí Neachtain', *Studia Hib.* 26 (1992).

Aisling Ghéar: Na Stíobhartaigh agus an tAos Léinn 1603–1788 (Dublin, 1996).

O'Callaghan, J.C., *History of the Irish Brigades in the Service of France* (Glasgow, 1870).

Ó Ciardha, Éamonn, 'A fatal attachment: Ireland and the house of Stuart, 1685–1766' (PhD thesis, Cambridge, 1998).

O'Connell, Maurice R., *Irish Politics and Social Conflict in the Age of the American Revolution* (Philadelphia, 1965).

'The American Revolution and Ireland', *Éire-Ireland* 11 (1976).

O'Connor, T.M., 'The more immediate effects of the American revolution in Ireland' (MA thesis, QUB, 1938).

'The embargo on the export of Irish provisions, 1776–9', *IHS* 2 (1940).

O'Flaherty, Eamon, 'The Catholic question in Ireland, 1774–93' (MA thesis, UCD, 1981).

'Ecclesiastical politics and the dismantling of the penal laws in Ireland, 1774–82', *IHS* 26 (1988).

Ó hAnnracháin, Peadar, 'Filidhe ó Chairbre', *Irisleabhar na Gaedhilge* 18 (1908).

O'Kearney, Nicholas, *The Prophecies of Saints Columbkille, Maeltamlacht, Ultan, Seadhna, Coireall, Bearcan, &c.* (Dublin, 1856).

Ó Snodaigh, Pádraig, 'Some police and military aspects of the Irish Volunteers', *Irish Sword* 13 (1977–79).

'The "Volunteers of '82": a citizen army or armed citizens – a bicentennial retrospect', *Irish Sword* 15 (1983).

'Class and the Irish Volunteers', *Irish Sword* 16 (1984–86).

Dílseoirí na Gaillimhe (Dublin, n.d.).

Refaussé, Raymond, 'The Irish economic crisis of the early 1780s' (PhD thesis, TCD, 1982).

Rogers, Patrick, *The Irish Volunteers and Catholic Emancipation* (London, 1934).

Sainsbury, John, *Dissaffected Patriots: London Supporters of Revolutionary America 1769–1782* (Montreal and Gloucester, 1987).

Sher, R.B. and Smitten, J.R. (eds.), *Scotland and America in the Age of the Enlightenment* (Edinburgh, 1990).

Simms, J.G., *Colonial Nationalism 1698–1776* (Cork, 1976).

Smyth, David, 'The Volunteer movement in Ulster: background and development 1745–85' (PhD thesis, QUB, 1974).

Smyth, Jim, *The Men of No Property: Irish Radicals and Popular Politics in the Late Eighteenth Century* (Dublin, 1992).

Smyth, P.D.H., 'The Volunteers and Parliament, 1779–84' in Thomas Bartlett and D.W. Hayton (eds.), *Penal Era and Golden Age: Essays in Irish History, 1690–1800* (Belfast, 1979).

Stewart, A.T.Q., ' "A stable unseen power": Dr William Drennan and the origins of the United Irishmen' in J. Bossy and P. Jupp (eds.), *Essays Presented to Michael Roberts* (Belfast, 1976).

A Deeper Silence: The Hidden Origins of the United Irishmen (London and Boston, 1993).

Tesch, Pieter, 'Presbyterian Radicalism' in D. Dickson, D. Keogh and K. Whelan (eds.), *The United Irishmen: Republicanism, Radicalism and Rebellion* (Dublin, 1993).

[Walsh, John Edward], *Sketches of Ireland Sixty Years Ago* (Dublin, 1847).

Wector, Dixon, 'Benjamin Franklin and an Irish "enthusiast" ', *Huntington Library Quarterly* 4 (1941).

York, Neil Longley, 'The impact of the American Revolution on Ireland' in H.T. Dickinson (ed.), *Britain and the American Revolution* (London and New York, 1998).

Index

Abercromby, Colonel Ralph, 305
Abernethy, Rev. John, 34, 35–6
Abingdon, Willoughby Bertie, 4th earl of, 145, 300, 301, 303, 313, 322
absentees, 43–4
Adams, John, 112, 153
Adams, Samuel, 114, 144, 146
Adare, Co. Limerick, Volunteers in, 312
Admiralty, 143–4, 302, 319
Alexander, Rev. Andrew, 214–15
Algiers, 110
America
Anglican views of, 18, 22, 23, 62, 71–81, 95–6, 98–106, 125–6, 144–8, 153, 161–3, 164, 168–9, 220, 222, 245–6, 249–54, 267, 269, 274–5, 277–9, 326
Articles of Confederation, 146
Catholic views of, 89, 106–15, 131, 133–7, 166–7, 169, 184–6, 228, 236–7, 256–8
Continental Congress, 73, 84, 87, 106, 114–15, 117, 123, 126, 127, 144, 146, 163, 172, 173, 185, 253, 333
emigration to, 31, 32–3, 82–3, 85, 116–17, 127
example of, 60, 95, 209–10, 218, 294, 330–4
French alliance, 170, 172, 173, 175, 184, 185, 189, 191, 198, 216, 241, 252, 269, 274, 275
independence, 106, 121–5, 146, 147, 148–50, 163–7, 172–3, 185, 219, 280, 292, 300, 327, 329
Irishmen in, 115, 117, 174, 251
non-importation agreements in, 53, 60, 210, 237
Presbyterian views of, 31–3, 81–5, 115–25, 127, 163–5, 169, 212, 214–16, 218, 249–51
quartering act (1765), 60
slavery in, 85, 114

stamp act (1765), 52–4, 58, 66, 95, 104, 151, 210, 246
stamp act congress, 57
Townshend duties (1767), 59, 68, 70, 95, 210
United States of, 167, 251, 273
see also individual colonies
André, Major John, 252
Anglicans
disaffection among, 294
historiography of, 14–16
loyalty of, 78–81, 198, 218–22, 240, 244, 249–55, 268–9, 275, 277–9, 285–7, 295–7, 327, 328, 333–4
opinion of, 16–27, 52–4, 77–8, 95–6, 98–106, 126, 150–3, 161–3, 168–9, 171–7, 231–3, 237–40
see also patriotism
Anne, queen, 5–6, 26, 34, 210
anticlericalism, 26
Antrim, county, 38, 83, 116, 159, 163, 189, 217, 244
election (1776), 119–21, 124, 190–1, 321
grand jury, 292
Volunteers in, 270
see also Ballymoney, Belfast, Carrickfergus, Cullybackey, Larne, Lisburn
Antrim, Randal MacDonnell, 6th earl of, 116, 140
Archdall, Nicholas, MP, 23
Armagh, city, 147, 164
Volunteers in, 233
Armagh, county, 3, 13, 38, 50–1, 63, 115, 120, 166, 217, 224, 238–9, 244
Volunteers in, 242, 280–1, 287–9
see also Armagh city, Lurgan, Moira
army, 14, 19, 43, 60, 61, 72, 101, 216, 247, 308
attacks on soldiers, 90–4, 127–9, 142, 181–3, 255–7, 271–2, 315